Take Back the Power

The New Craft of Intelligence by Robert David Steele is more than a book; it is the perfect weapon in our war against terror. I say our war because it is we who are dying and paying the consequences.

We fear what we do not know. Or in my terms the most dangerous thing in the world is *ignorance*. Steele's book gives you the basics to understand what threats we face, how to stay informed and how to change things.

This book will explode everything you held sacred about the dark, mysterious world of intelligence. In fact this book will make us wonder why our government has not adopted it as the *de facto* standard in teaching people how to understand and combat the dark forces among us.

Steele's concept is simple: Empower the citizen and private sector to gather and analyze intelligence so that we can make informed decisions in time to deter threats. This is a task that has been handed over to our government for far too long, at very great expense to the taxpayer and with little real success.

In the wake of the massive intelligence failure of 9/11/01 this book has a more urgent importance. It contains ideas and messages that our government doesn't want you to think about too hard. In a war where more citizens die than soldiers, where commercial airliners and rubber boats are now weapons of mass destruction, where journalists gather more information than intelligence agencies, where our government spends billions to fight shadows, it's time to take back the initiative and return it to the people.

Steele provides the background, methodology, contacts and resources to convincingly demonstrate that Open Source Intelligence gathering is faster, smarter, cheaper and more profound than relying on vast secretive government bureaucracies that work either in the dark or against each other. Understanding our world and its threats should not be a mystery left to bureaucrats, it should be the responsibility of every citizen.

Arm yourself with this book and push back the darkness.

Robert Young Pelton
Author, *The World's Most Dangerous Places*
Producer, *Come Back Alive* (Discovery TV)
Sponsor, www.comebackalive.com

Robert Steele's conceptions of intelligence, especially open source intelligence, are well known in France. I particularly remember one of his presentations in the French Senate, where I presided. Constantly committed to truth and honesty, this second book, like his first, demonstrates his ability to grasp the real issues and to take into account the views and concerns of men of good will from all nations and all cultures.

Pierre Lacoste
Admiral, French Navy (Retired)
Former Director of Foreign Intelligence (DGSE)

Robert David Steele, with this work, brings us his passion for reinventing intelligence in the wake of the September 11th tragedy. As always, he is at once a teacher, historian, critic, and guide to the future. His visionary insights allow us to form new perspectives on how best to protect the United States from foreign threats. This study goes beyond traditional boundaries to offer a wider frame of reference that both professionals and the attentive public alike will find valuable.

Loch K. Johnson, Ph.D.
Regent Professor
University of Georgia

Robert Steele is unusual for an American-born author because he is clearly internationalist in his orientation. His appreciation for the strategic pitfalls of the highly volatile geographical area where Turkey is located at the very center, and the critical challenges facing this region in terms of terrorism, water, energy, food, and natural disasters, merit careful attention. He has written a book that can bring us together in facing our greatest enemies: ignorance, poverty, and mistrust.

Hamit Gulemre Aybars
Rear Admiral, Turkish Navy (Retired)

No one is better at looking at intelligence issues "out of the box" than Robert Steele, the prophet of open-source intelligence. *The New Craft of Intelligence* presents valuable advice for finding and using intelligence and information in the 21st Century.

Bill Gertz, Author
The China Threat: How the People's Republic Targets America
National Security Reporter, *The Washington Times*

THE NEW CRAFT OF INTELLIGENCE

Personal, Public, & Political

Citizen's Action Handbook for Fighting
Terrorism, Genocide, Disease, Toxic Bombs, & Corruption

Foreword by Senator Pat Roberts (R-KS)

Robert David Steele
MA, MPA, NWC, USMC, CIA, OSS

OSS International Press
Oakton, Virginia

This book and others in the series are available at quantity discounts for group or class distribution. Please communicate with the publisher.

OSS International Press is the book-publishing arm of Open Source Solutions Inc., publisher of *OSS NOTICES* (occasional series) and *Proceedings of the Global Information Forum* (annual). Visit www.oss.net.

Published by OSS International Press (OSS)   April 2002
Post Office Box 369
Oakton, Virginia 22124-0369 USA
(703) 242-1700 Facsimile (703) 242-1711

Printed and bound in the United States of America.

Cover graphic: The view of Africa, Antarctica, the Indian and Atlantic Oceans from 23,000 miles out in space as the last Apollo flight coasted to the moon, December 1972. Original photo credit NASA 1989. Available in sticker form as item Apollo 17(E). Correspond with EarthSeals, Post Office Box 8000, Berkeley, CA 94707 USA.

9 8 7 6 5 4 3 2

LIBRARY OF CONGRESS CATALOGING-IN-PUBLICATION DATA

Steele, Robert D., 1952-

  THE NEW CRAFT OF INTELLIGENCE: Personal, Public, & Political— Citizen's Action Handbook for Fighting Terrorism, Genocide, Disease, Toxic Bombs, & Corruption/by Robert David Steele
      p.   cm.
  Includes bibliographical references and index.
  ISBN-13 978-0-9715661-1-8 (alk. paper)   ISBN-10 0-9715661-1-9 (alk. paper)
  1.   Intelligence service—United States.   2.   Intelligence service.   3.   Militai
    Intelligence. 4. Law enforcement intelligence. 5. Business intelligence. 6.
    Internet. 7. Organizational change. 8. Strategic planning. 9. Leadership. 10.
    Information Technology. 11. Economic forecasting. 12. Business forecasting.
    13. Knowledge, theory of. 14. Power (Social sciences). 15. Information
    science—social aspects. 16. Competition. 17. National security—management
    of. 18. Political planning.
I.   Title
JK468.I6S74 2002
327.1273—dc21   00-029284

PEACE

Our words go slowly out
and the sun burns
them before they
can speak. It is
as though the earth
were tired of our talk
and wanted peace, an end
to promises, perhaps an
end to us.

Philip Levine
7 Years from Somewhere
Athenium, 1979

This book is dedicated to the poets, for their sanity; to the mothers, for their suffering; and to the founders of the Internet, for providing us with a means to take back the power.

Robert David Steele (Vivas)

Foreword

Robert David Steele's first book, *ON INTELLIGENCE: Spies and Secrecy in an Open World* (AFCEA, 2001), became a valuable reference and primer on the challenges faced within our secret intelligence community and more importantly, provided a blueprint on what must be done to "reform ourselves."

Now, post-September 11, Robert has taken us further in describing and defining a road to a more secure future by defining his vision for the public side of national intelligence. His concept is intriguing: the "intelligence minuteman," based upon citizen-centered democracy and governance.

I believe this book will enable Americans to better understand the threats that pose challenges to our vital national interests and enable our citizens to play a greater and necessary role in the current national dialogue on homeland security and the need for new approaches at the state and local level.

The September 11 attacks caught everyone by surprise. Witness after witness had testified before the Emerging Threats Subcommittee of the Armed Service Committee and Commission after Commission warned such an attack was not a matter of "if," but "when." Yet, we were not prepared for the nature of the attack, its violence, its chosen civilian targets, or its suicidal means.

Having spent considerable time with regard to hearings and policy oversight and recommendations regarding the attack on the *USS Cole* and the investigation on Prisoner of War (POW) Captain Scott Speicher, USN, along with many other issues, my view is that our intelligence community faces serious systemic challenges. They include the full use of leap-ahead technology, coordination among all agencies within the community, the proper processing of all available information and most importantly, a re-evaluation of predictive analysis without risk aversion.

i

In both the Cole and Speicher cases, it is my opinion that available information was not properly processed nor analyzed and thus was not used to proper advantage. The bottom line: our intelligence community must improve.

In fairness, hindsight is 20-20 and there has been no single point of failure. As we have gone about the crucial task of structuring a homeland defense strategy, we have now seen virtually all parts of government, federal, state and local, have vital roles to play in safeguarding our national security. Our enemies today do not attack us in traditional ways. We must study these emerging threats and we must devise new nation-wide and government-wide means of detection, deterrence and crisis management both domestically and abroad in cooperation with our allies.

In this regard, secret intelligence alone cannot protect America. If ever there was a time for our citizens to take a pro-active interest in intelligence reform and the politics of intelligence reform, that time is now.

Obviously no one book or person has perfect vision regarding emerging threats and how to deal with them. However, whether or not readers will agree with all or some of the author's ideas, this book empowers the individual citizen attempting to better understand and deal with emerging threats to our nation. For that reason, this book is a "must read."

U.S. Senator Pat Roberts (Republican-Kansas)
Subcommittee on Emerging Threats
Senate Armed Services Committee

Table of Contents

List of Figures

Publications Review Board

CIA's Publications Review Board has reviewed the manuscript for this book to assist the author in eliminating classified information, and poses no security objection to its publication. This review, however, should not be construed as an official release of information, confirmation of accuracy, or an endorsement of the author's views.[1]

---

[1] The Publications Review Board completed its review in less than two weeks, and its recommended changes to the book were entirely reasonable and promptly accepted. The process works and I am very glad to have been able to avail myself of this professional means of ensuring that intelligence reform manuscripts are not inadvertently harmful to national security. *St.*

Acknowledgments

This book represents the intellectual experience I have had since publishing my first book in 2000, after twelve years of writing. Naturally this sequel builds on a lifetime in the national security community, but the bulk of the work reflects reading and thinking that occurred in 2000-2002.

Two individuals helped inspire this book: Alessandro Politi, Italy's best mind for these matters, who listened to me for an hour in 1992 and instantly coined the term "intelligence minuteman;" and Colonel Nick Pratt, USMC (Ret.), now Director of the Coalition Leadership Program at the George C. Marshall Center in Germany, who pushed me back into serious serial reading.

Mr. Don Gessaman, former Deputy Associate Director for National Security in the Office of Management and Budget (OMB), Executive Office of the President, and Mssrs. Arnie Donahue and John Eisenhour, now retired former OMB senior executives for all funds assigned to command, control, communications, computing, and intelligence (Donahue) and international security affairs (Eisenhour), have continued my education in the nuances of soft versus hard power, and the nuances of the politics and policies that shape the national budget. "It isn't policy until it's in the budget" is a great truth.

I salute Lieutenant Commander Andrew Chester, Canada; Captain David Swain, Royal Navy, United Kingdom; Brigadier General James Cox, Canada; Admiral Sir James Perowne, United Kingdom; and General William Kernan, United States; for their extraordinary commitment to the integration of Open Source Intelligence (OSINT) concepts and doctrine into the future intelligence architecture of the North Atlantic Treaty Organization as well as the Partnership for Peace and the Mediterranean Dialog nations.

The individual authors identified in the annotated bibliography are the real heroes of this age—the books they have written are the "virtual ammunition" for the Third World War, vital to empowering our citizens.

Lastly, to the United States Army, the long gray line, and especially to the Strategic Studies Institute and the Center for Strategic Leadership, thank you for helping me learn from other mid-career pioneers and practitioners. *St.*

Preface

My first book, *ON INTELLIGENCE: Spies and Secrecy in an Open World* (AFCEA, 2000 and OSS, 2001), is addressed primarily to intelligence professionals and the political appointees and elected politicians responsible for authorizing, appropriating, allocating, and obligating the $30 billion to $50 billion a year in tax-payer funds that go toward America's first line of defense, the U.S. intelligence and counterintelligence community. It also has a very strong internationalist thrust, for I have found in my dealings with intelligence leaders and professionals across over 40 countries that there is an urgent need for intelligence reform around the world. It is a professional reference work.

It, and other books by the intelligence reform authors whose books are recommended by the Council on Intelligence, and the efforts of many others both in and out of government who have sought constructive reform, have all failed to inspire adequate change at the federal level. While there have been a number of Commissions appointed by and reporting to either Congress or the President or both, and they have all produced really excellent findings and recommendations, I have found that all of them have been largely exercises in political theater. Neither Congress nor the Presidency has been willing to legislate a National Security Act that imposes mandated reform on the cluster of secret bureaucracies that today fail to provide the American tax-payer with their money's worth—or with real security. Funding first responders and hospitals is good, but if they are responding, we have failed and the war has come home again. Funding a military that can buy more of the same complex weapons systems and secret satellites that failed to prevent 9-11 and are largely irrelevant to the asymmetric forms of conflict characteristic of the 21st Century, also deprives the American public of the security that might come from a more balanced approach to national security—one that emphasizes, in equal measure, homefront counterintelligence and public health; global intelligence, and both *nuanced* soft power such as represented by diplomats, economic assistance and a Digital Marshall Plan; and *smart* hard power, a combination of conventional military and special operations capabilities spanning the spectrum of conflict.

I decided over the Summer of 2001 that Norman Cousins has it exactly right—only the people can perceive great truths, and the great truth the people must perceive and instruct their government in has to do with how "new means for meeting the largest problems on earth have to be created."[1] This book is written for the people of America as well as the people of all states and nations without states, so that they might reflect on matters of national security and perhaps rise up and instruct their governments.

The old paradigm of government, where the people are regarded as uneducated and unconnected, masses to be managed by government and other elites, is now the greatest threat to democracy, to security, and to prosperity. The new paradigm, made possible by the Internet, recognizes that citizen-centered governance at every level is both feasible and desirable. Citizens today are well-informed and capable of making choices and achieving consensus with or without a political party to guide them.[2]

We still lack campaign finance reform, and therefore the military-industrial-energy-legislative financial partnerships continue to dominate the largely secret discussions over how taxpayer funds will be spent. We need campaign finance reform, but even without campaign finance reform the Internet now makes it possible for citizens to oversee and hold accountable our elected representatives in a manner never before possible; and it makes it possible for citizens more effectively to use the one thing that counts more than money in a democratic Republic: their vote.

This book, dedicated to the citizens of the world who love their respective countries and care deeply about the future of their children, offers up both a prescription for intelligence reform that the citizens may impose on their government; and it offers up a guide to how citizens can use open source intelligence (OSINT)—legal and ethical sources and methods—to inform themselves on any issue, in this way girding themselves for the political battles that must be fought in every neighborhood, every county, every state, and every nation, if our taxpayer funds are to be spent wisely and our commonwealth is to be preserved and enriched for future generations.

May God Bless America, and the Whole Earth, and may each of you, acting as God shows you the light, be a vibrant part of the "world brain" that must now assume responsibility for global democratic governance. *St.*

---

[1] Norman Cousins, *The Pathology of Power* (Norton, 1987), pages 207-208.
[2] *Cf.* Ted Halstead and Michael Lind, *The Radical Center: The Future of American Politics* (Doubleday, 2001).

Overview of
Citizen-Centered Intelligence

A Nation's best defense is an educated citizenry.

Thomas Jefferson

The history of biology, of evolution, has demonstrated the value of intra-species communication as well as the value of "wildcards." To the extent that a community can simultaneously spawn and integrate diversity while also detecting and communicating changes in the external environment to which that community must adjust, or perish; to that extent will that community be strong, sustainable, and prosperous.

Western "scientific reasoning" has lost touch with two streams of consciousness vital to holistic behavior. On the one hand, the West has objectified nature and fallen prey to extremely prejudicial presumptions about how to value natural resources—this has led to enormous industrial endeavors that are liquidating the earth while imposing terrible public health consequences across both the Western world and the developing world. On the other hand, the West has chosen to secularize faith and diminish the role of faith-based values in personal and community life. The cost to a community of unfettered greed such as displayed by the energy industry (e.g. Enron), by the financial services industry (e.g. the Savings & Loans crisis and the Long Term Capital Management crisis), and by the insurance and medical industries, to name just three, has been enormous. We have sacrificed public health and financial health for short-term gains by a selfish few. The commonwealth has been looted by those who control both information and campaign contributions.

The Internet makes possible the resurrection of the collective will of the people. The Internet provides a virtually-free and here-to-fore uncensorable means for individuals to communicate, compute, and inform one another, and in so doing, carry out their responsibilities as citizens of the Republic.

There has, however, been one missing ingredient in the decade leading to the 21st Century: citizen-centered intelligence. However educated our citizens might be, and however well-intentioned, in the absence of a structured means of monitoring issues, of networking, and of wielding influence as a majority, our citizens have been abused and victimized by the tyranny of the well-funded minorities that Alexander Hamilton warned us against. This book, and the many books it discusses in the tutorially-oriented annotated bibliography, seeks nothing less than a change in the balance of power between citizens with the vote and corporations with the purse.

Consider the next three illustrations.

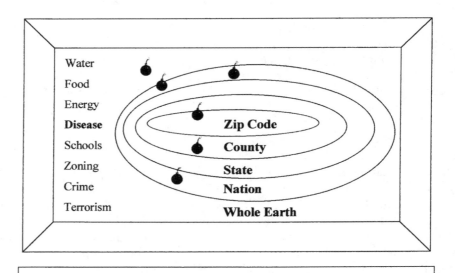

CITIZEN-CENTERED INTELLIGENCE

Figure A: Citizen-Centered Intelligence

As this book will make clear—providing at least a starting point—it is now possible for citizens to inform themselves about any issues they recognize as pertinent to the future of their children and their community.

What has been missing to date to empower the citizen, is the geospatial tagging of information so that citizens can pull what they need based on their zip code or geospatial position. As the previous figure illustrates, if all levels of government put all public information online, *with* geospatial and zip code tagging—this would allow citizens to monitor information directly pertinent to their geophysical location, yet spanning the full circumference of the globe.

Networking is actually well-underway and some of the cyber-advocacy organizations (many listed in Appendix 2) have both useful information and geographically-oriented forms of organization. They have not, however, created the standard "hooks" that would allow citizens to recognize their value based on specific events, issues, and causes directly related to the citizen's physical location. They are, in other words, issue-oriented rather than citizen-oriented. They do not provide for cross-fertilization (e.g. joining two different issue groups to send a single coherent message to the same Senator).

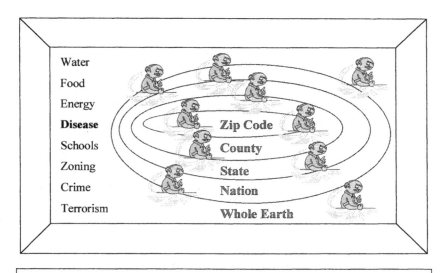

Water
Food
Energy
Disease
Schools
Zoning
Crime
Terrorism

Zip Code
County
State
Nation
Whole Earth

CITIZEN-CENTERED NETWORKING

Figure B: Citizen-Centered Networking

Individual cyber-advocacy organizations do provide for evaluating individual political figures, at least at the national level, but the leap has not been made toward holding individual political figures responsible for a cross-section of issues, nor for holding corporate executives responsible in every jurisdiction.

Issue Area: Disease & Public Health

Official	Score	Contact	Join
Iden A	24	boffo@	d.org
Iden B	57	flop@	s.org
Iden C	78	joe@	g.org
Iden D	39	raz@	cy.org
Iden E	86	wub@	go.org

CITIZEN-CENTERED INFLUENCE

Figure C: Citizen-Centered Influence

The above should be easily reconfigurable by a citizen to quickly identify the worst offenders (in the citizen's value schema) across both government and corporate lines, for both single issues and multiple issues. It should permit citizen's to rapidly join other like-minded citizens to influence specific individual politicians and corporate executives, and it should allow citizens to easily send both email and surface correspondence warning of their intent to recall or not reelect the individual. Finally, for every election at every level of governance, there should be a very public "scorecard" that the citizen can print out and take to the polls. We are approaching this condition—all that is lacking is a citizen-centered appreciation for the power that intelligence can add to networking and influence across the Internet.

This book does not advocate any particular position on any particular issue. Nor does this book concern itself with largely social issues such as abortion, privacy, the right to bear arms, and so on. This book is about the fundamentals of survival and sustainable prosperity, and how public intelligence can be achieved in support of more thoughtful national, state, and local policies. The book does suggest that citizens have largely abdicated their responsibility and power, in part because they have lacked the tools and in part because of the stress of modern life. Below are listed some issue areas where I believe that every citizen, every parent, every loved one, *must* take the time to understand and agitate.

Water	Is the per capita supply of clean drinking water going down? If so, what strategy should every level of government pursue to reverse that trend?
Food	Is the food we buy safe to eat? What changes are needed in inspection, processing regulation, and certification of imported food?
Energy	As the population, and the electrification of the world, grow, are changes needed in how we manage both demand and distribution and generation of energy?
Disease	Are our children truly protected from epidemics and plagues? From the return of smallpox? What public health investments must be made at the local, state, and national levels?
Schools	Are we teaching our children and our future leaders what they need to know about the real world? About how to reach decisions that are sustainable across cultural and geographic boundaries?
Zoning	Is the zoning process corrupt? How do we restore the concept of neighborhood in urban, suburban, and rural areas?
Crime	What needs to change to control white-collar crime and the increasingly corrupt corporations and their inept government oversight bodies?
Terrorism	What are the root conditions that spawn hundreds of thousands of potential terrorists, and what should we be doing about it? Is our foreign assistance program adequate and properly focused?
Defense	Are we spending the right amount of money on national defense? Are we buying the right mix of military and non-military national security capabilities?

This may sound simplistic, but it is my view that the public interest cannot be assured by any elite, however well-intentioned. Only the "swarm," only the "hive mind"[1] of the public at large, with its common sense and its intuitive grasp of what is best for the group, can be relied upon to be properly sensitive to its own interests.

Public intelligence + public voting = informed democracy.

---

[1] Kevin Kelly, *OUT OF CONTROL: The Rise of Neo-Biological Civilization* (Addison-Wesley, 1994) provides one of the best treatments of how the Internet makes possible a very agile public intelligence in support of the public interest.

Part I:
Why 9-11 Demands a
New Craft of Intelligence

Intelligence qua national collection, processing, and analysis of relevant foreign data is now too important to be limited to a handful of secret federal bureaucracies. It is imperative, in the aftermath of 9-11, that our citizens fully understand and demand government competency in covert technical and clandestine human intelligence, but we also must extend the proven process of intelligence to the entire federal government, to the state & local governments, and to the private sector. America must become a "Smart Nation" able to practice open source intelligence (OSINT) at every level and in every endeavor. National security and prosperity in the 21ˢᵗ Century require that we harness and apply the distributed intelligence of the entire Nation.

Part I is a citizen-centered orientation to:

what went wrong and why;

key concepts within the traditional craft of intelligence[1] that retain great value today;

key concepts in asymmetric threats (e.g. terrorist use of a civilian airline as a super-bomb or guided missile) that are not yet fully appreciated by the Pentagon or the Administration;

strategic perspectives on how the information environment has changed and in changing is cause for creating a new craft of intelligence; and finally,

past and present intelligence reform endeavors .

---

[1] *Cf.* Allen Dulles, *The Craft of Intelligence* (SIGNET New American Library, 1965).

1

Chapter 1, "What Went Wrong and Why?" itemizes five policy failures and six intelligence community[2] failures, with some explicit details, that allowed 9-11 to occur despite a year's worth of advance indications & warning.

Chapter 2, "Key Aspects of Intelligence as a Craft," is a citizen's orientation to the proven process of intelligence, a process that is much more complex and methodical than either scholarship or what passes for "business intelligence" in the private sector. The disciplines of intelligence and the levels of analysis briefly are discussed.

Chapter 3, "Core Ideas in Asymmetric War," is an introduction to one form of modern conflict, information warfare, where the complexity of our national electronic systems renders us vulnerable to anonymous attack by individuals and non-state actors, not only by other nations. In Part II several other chapters expand on the non-traditional global threat facing the Nation.

Chapter 4, "The Changing Environment for Intelligence," highlights several critical ideas upon which the new craft of intelligence is founded: the change from unilateral to multilateral and multi-cultural decision-making; the explosion of information sources that demand a shift in emphasis from finding secrets to making sense of non-secrets; the emerging virtual intelligence community; and the radical change in the speed of intelligence and decision.

Chapter 5, "Overview of Intelligence Reform," provides a very encapsulated summary of past official intelligence reform efforts, followed by a review of the key ideas in a number of recently published mainstream books on the urgent need for intelligence reform—a critical mass here-to-fore not existing.

---

[2] Intelligence includes counterintelligence, which is the most vital homefront aspect.

What Went Wrong and Why?

Sometimes not paying attention can be very costly.

9-11, the 11th day of September 2001, saw two hijacked civilian airliners loaded with gasoline achieve the complete destruction of the World Trade Center (two twin towers) and the death of over 3,000 civilians, including close to 300 fire-fighters and police officers; as well as a similar *kamikaze* attack against the Pentagon, destroying one side of the five-sided building and killing or wounding both military and civilian personnel. The attacks were well-planned, well-executed, and totally asymmetric. Our $400 billion a year national security community was caught flat-footed and was completely unable to defend the homeland.

What went wrong and why? Although this is the question that has been on every citizen's mind since that terrible day, the Administration has declined to address the failures of intelligence (including counterintelligence). Their newest budget, while throwing billions and billions of dollars at the military and at law enforcement, simply perpetuates the past emphasis on complex technical systems and high-end bio-chemical warfare solutions. Worse, the Administration is insisting that any Congressional inquiry into intelligence and counterintelligence failures be conducted in secrecy and kept from the public.

9-11 could have been much, much worse. A combination of accidents, including mechanical delays, appear to have prevented at least one and possibly two or three other aircraft from getting into the air where they could be hijacked and used as flying bombs against the Capitol or White House, against the Cable News Network (CNN) Headquarters in Atlanta, and against major "skyline" buildings in Chicago and San Francisco. Decisive action by the Federal Aviation Administration (FAA), grounding all 3,000 plus aircraft within 90 minutes, half within 30 minutes, eliminated any additional similar attacks that day.

9-11 was made possible by a series of policy and intelligence failures that are summarized in the table below.

Type of Failure	Professional Observation
Political Policy	In the aftermath of the 1st bombing of the World Trade Center, the threat was sidelined into law enforcement and judicial circles and no national-level commitment was made to take deep action at home or abroad.
Political Policy	In the aftermath of the various terrorist acts against the USA (including two Embassies, a barracks and a naval vessel), including an actual declaration of war by bin Laden, no determination was made to treat this threat as one meriting the full application of national resources.
Political Policy	After a lucky break in intercepting a terrorist arriving from Canada to do a millennium bombing, no actions were taken to improve Canadian or US procedures. Watch lists were not shared with state troopers.
Political Policy	Despite years of warning from terrorism experts, both the airline industry and the FAA declined to improve the security of the aircraft cockpits or the security of the check-in process.
Political Policy	Across America citizens seeing the terrorists in their day-to-day activities did not know how to interpret that nor whom to report it to—reports of terrorist flight training were the exception rather than the rule.
Intelligence Collection	Our very expensive technical satellites for collecting signals and images are no longer secret and no longer effective against terrorism; at the same time, our clandestine service has ceased to be fully operational.
Intelligence Data Entry	FBI field offices as well as CIA field and HQS offices, appear to have not entered or reported arrests and other leads into the system, either because they use pen and paper or because they did not wish to share.
Intelligence Translation	FBI has noted publicly that it has been unable to exploit all documents captured in the first WTC and other arrests, for lack of translators. Other experts have commented on CIA's reliance on Lebanese Muslims who constantly mis-translate terrorist documents and expressions.
Intelligence Processing	USG does not have a single all-source processing environment that automatically fuses and evaluates clandestine and law enforcement reporting, signals and open source intelligence, or operational traffic.
Intelligence Analysis	USG does not have a single global "plot" where all leads are monitored on a 24/7 basis and a skilled staff can detect emerging patterns or new threats in that context.
Intelligence Liaison	USG evidently did not press other nations for sustained efforts against terrorists, and permitted normal relations to go on between the US and nations known to be harboring terrorists.

Figure 1: Policy and Intelligence Failures Permitting 9-11 to Occur

In the aftermath of 9-11, there has been no strategic evaluation, no serious examination of what went wrong and why, and no change in the "mind-set" of both the political authorities and the leadership of the military and intelligence communities. We are throwing money at the problem, and that will only make it worse.[1]

The failures in Figure 1 are largely self-explanatory and will not be belabored here. My first book, *ON INTELLIGENCE: Spies and Secrecy in an Open World* (AFCEA International Press, 2000)[2], provides a 495-page critique of everything known to be wrong with the U.S. Intelligence Community *before* 9-11; all of those problems still need to be addressed, and they will not be addressed unless the voters make clear to the Administration and Congress that they will not allow the intelligence and counterintelligence failures to be covered up, and that a public debate on the future of national intelligence is required.

The remainder of this book will provide critical information that each citizen needs to know in order to hold their local, state, and federal authorities accountable for establishing an effective national security strategy and related capabilities, to include federally-funded but state-managed homeland security and counterintelligence capabilities.

During the Cold War, the intelligence "paradigm" called for highly secret efforts against a single main enemy capable of unleashing nuclear and conventional attacks against Europe and America. Today there is a new intelligence paradigm, one that recognizes that the most likely as well as the most dangerous threats are emerging from non-state actors using non-traditional weapons that include hijacked aircraft and virulent pandemic diseases. The new intelligence paradigm also recognizes that 90% of the casualties in today's conflicts are civilian, in their own homeland. Finally, the

---

[1] Michael Herman, the dean of authors with actual intelligence experience, concludes his latest book, *Intelligence Services in the Information Age* (Cass, 2002) with the observation that "The problems of counter-terrorist intelligence cannot be solved by just throwing money at them." (page 229). As my first book documented so clearly, old mind-sets will not change if they receive more money, only if they are forced to radically reduce their spending on very old and very expensive methods that do not work as advertised.

[2] The first edition is out of print; a second edition from OSS International Press is available at www.amazon.com.

new intelligence paradigm embraces the challenges and the opportunities represented by open sources of information in many languages—vast quantities of information that need not be stolen but do need to be "made sense of."

On this and the next two pages are three useful illustrations, all devised since my first book was published, each helping to explain why the taxpayer is not getting their money's worth from our $30 billion to $50 billion a year investment.

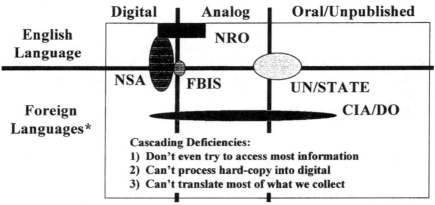

*29 predominant languages, over 3,000 distinct languages in all.

Figure 2: Intelligence Failures in Global Collection[3]

---

[3] NSA (National Security Agency); NRO (National Reconnaissance Office); FBIS (Foreign Broadcast Information Service); UN/State (United Nations/Department of State); CIA/DO (Central Intelligence Agency, Directorate of Operations).

The dirty little secret of U.S. national intelligence, apart from its deficiencies in what are supposed to be its core competencies (secret collection by technical and human means, all-source processing and analysis), is that it is not even close to serious about monitoring open sources of information in multiple foreign languages. The problem with spies is that they only know secrets—and they are out of touch with open sources.

Then we have the matter of processing. The truth is not pretty.

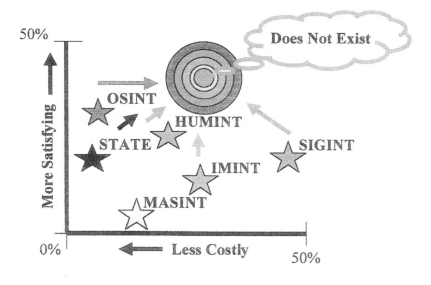

Figure 3: Intelligence Failures in All-Source Processing[4]

---

[4] This chart, less the all-source processing "bulls-eye" and comment, was created by the Collection Requirements and Evaluations Staff (CRES) of the Central Intelligence Agency (CIA) in the late 1990's when they conducted an evaluation of the relative cost of the various disciplines (discussed in the next chapter), and the degree to which each discipline was considered satisfactory in relation to its cost.

7

Despite the enormous expense of collecting information via technical means (signals is the most expensive, followed by imagery and then measurements), none of this technical information comes together in any one automated system. The all-source analysts are required to deal with these sources in piece-meal fashion. At the same time, the clandestine service refuses to allow its most sensitive reporting to be automated, and there is no serious portal or program for capturing and integrating open sources of information in many languages, with secret information. Hard as it might be to believe, we process less than 10% of our imagery, less than 6% of our Russian and Chinese signals, between 1 and 3% of our European and rest of world signals. We spend less that one-half of one percent of our $30 billion plus budget on acquiring relevant open sources of information. Between failures in collection and in processing, we can be said to be operating at 10% of capacity.

Finally, we have the matter of security and the mind-set that goes with an obsession about security.

OLD PARADIGM   NEWPARADIGM

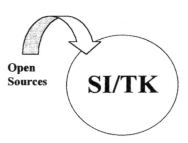
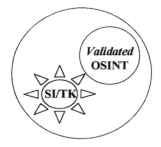

Open Sources

SI/TK

Validated OSINT

SI/TK

Selective Importation	**Just Enough, Just in Time**
System High/Firewall	**Default to Validated OSINT**

Open source information is more complex than secrets...

Figure 4: Security Keeps More Information Out Than It Allows In

The harsh truth is that the U.S. Intelligence Community is completely cut off from reality today. They only value and have access to extremely expensive secrets, and they are so obsessed with security that they are willing to shut themselves off from 90% of the relevant information needed for proper analysis of any threat. The old paradigm is still in effect.

The new paradigm, one that has already been adopted by the North Atlantic Treaty Organization (NATO) in anticipation of its need to share critical information with the Partners for Peace (PfP) and other coalition partners including non-governmental organizations, sharply limits secrecy, and places much greater emphasis on collecting and understanding open sources of information.[5]

Within this new paradigm, every citizen is an "intelligence minuteman."[6] Every citizen has a "need to know" what the global threat is, what we can do about it, and whether or not our government is managing our tax-payer funded intelligence and counterintelligence community effectively. With respect to this last question, right now, the answer is a resounding "NO."

Politicians are too often intimidated by intelligence leaders who claim, falsely, that national security will be undermined if any aspect of intelligence or counterintelligence is discussed publicly. The truth is that our opponents know very well what our total intelligence budget is, and they know most of our sources and methods. The Indian government, for example, easily was able to hide its preparations for a nuclear test because it knew *precisely* when our "secret" imagery satellites would be passing overhead, and it knew *precisely*

---

[5] Under the direction of General William Kernan, Commander-in-Chief of the Joint Forces Command (JFCOM), and also Supreme Allied Commander, Atlantic, responsible for the Atlantic half of NATO's operating forces and area, the Atlantic Command has produced the *NATO Open Source Intelligence Handbook* and the *NATO Open Source Intelligence Reader* as well as a volume on *Intelligence Exploitation of the Internet*. NATO is committed to fully integrating open sources of information into its future intelligence architecture, and all of the flag officers in charge of military intelligence for the 19 NATO member nations and the 43 partner for peace nations have been briefed on this initiative. Unfortunately, neither the other U.S. military Commanders-in-Chief, nor the U.S. Intelligence Community, are willing to take open sources of information seriously—an excellent example of their mind-set "blindspot."

[6] Dr. Alessandro Politi, one of Europe's foremost practitioners of open source intelligence (OSINT), coined this term in 1992, at the first open source conference.

what our "secret" signals satellites could and could not intercept. The same is true of terrorists. Unless the public is fully conscious of what kinds of trade-off decisions are being made on their behalf and with their hard-earned dollars, the government will not act in the wisest manner.

Certainly there are sources and methods that must be kept secret or they will lose their effectiveness. The identities of specific clandestine agents, the location and nature of specific tactical signals collection devices, the identities of our non-official cover case officers (those who handle secret agents without the protection afforded by official duties), all these should be kept secret.

However, to argue that the public does not have a right to know, in strategic terms already known to all other governments and non-state groups,

- whether we have language-qualified clandestine case officers and analysts, and enough of them (we do not);

- whether we have a means of collecting, digitizing and translating open sources of information in a comprehensive and timely fashion (we do not);

- whether we have an all-source processing capability that avoids the loss of key leads of forthcoming terrorist actions (we do not)

—this is the heart of the matter and most deserving of citizen attention.

Intelligence and counterintelligence are our first line of defense, and in an era when our financial, communications, transportation, and power infrastructures are extraordinarily vulnerable to asymmetric attack by non-state actors, it is the height of irresponsibility and political frivolity to deny our citizens a full role in an open political process for authorizing, appropriating, allocating, and obligating up to $50 billion a year in taxpayer funding of intelligence and counterintelligence.

With your help, and your vote, there is every reason to believe that we may yet achieve intelligence reform "of the people, by the people, for the people," and in this way harness the distributed intelligence of the world so that this Nation may neither suffer unnecessarily nor "perish from the earth."[7]

---

[7] The memorable concluding words from President Abraham Lincoln's Gettysburg Address are used here with deliberation.

Key Aspects of
Intelligence as a Craft

In foreign affairs and national security matters, there is no substitute for thorough, conscientious, and objective analysis, and of a weighing of the consequences—domestic as well as foreign—of all the options available.

George Allen[1]

Top managers' information is invariably either biased, subjective, filtered or late.

Ben Gilad[2]

"Intelligence" as it is used in this book refers to a generic process that produces tailored actionable knowledge. At one level, that of a sovereign state, it is a process that permits and indeed funds very expensive espionage measures that are intrusive and that freely violate the laws of other countries. At another level, that of the law-abiding business enterprise, intelligence, properly done, can offer extraordinary competitive advantages through the use an exacting process that monitors a broad array of legally-accessible sources in order to identify and make sense of relatively weak signals that are a portend of major changes and opportunities that lie in the future.

There is much that is good about the proven process of intelligence, and both statesmen and corporate chieftains will continue to suffer defeats when they denigrate or dismiss the profession of intelligence.

---

[1] George W. Allen, *None So Blind: A Personal Account of the Intelligence Failure in Vietnam* (Ivan R. Dee, 2001), page 282. Documents policy of shutting out intelligence.
[2] Benjamin Gilad, *Business Blindspots: replacing myths, beliefs and assumptions with market realities* (Infonortics UK, 1996), page 1.

In its largest generic sense, intelligence is both a process and a combination of specific disciplines, each meriting a lifetime of preparation and devotion. Intelligence is not a craft that can be lightly acquired nor easily retained. It is a complex combination of sources, softwares, and services that requires constant refreshment of both internal and external perspectives on what is available, what is achievable, what is affordable. Above all, intelligence is at root a mind-set that respects both the chaos of the global environment, and the possibilities for "making sense" out of a vast range of sources in many languages and many mediums.[3]

Before we begin, simply for the sake of perspective, let's take a look at what your taxpayer dollars fund in the way of a national intelligence program.

Agency or Program	Per Year
Central Intelligence Agency (CIA)—spies and all-source analysts	$3.2 billion
National Reconnaissance Office (NRO)—builds all satellites	$6.4 billion
National Security Agency (NSA)—collects and analyzes signals	$3.4 billion
General Defense Intelligence Program (GDIP)—theater centers	$2.0 billion
Defense Advanced Reconnaissance Program (DARO)—now hidden	$1.7 billion
Defense Intelligence Agency (DIA)—military spies and analysts	$0.6 billion
National Imagery & Mapping Agency (NIMA)—images into maps	$0.8 billion
USAF Tactical Intelligence—service-specific capabilities	$4.0 billion
US Army Tactical Intelligence—service-specific capabilities	$2.8 billion
US Navy Tactical Intelligence—service-specific capabilities	$1.8 billion
DoD Tactical Intelligence—odds and ends not controlled by services	$0.7 billion
Other stuff we really can't tell you about (might be stuff we lost)	$1.4 billion
Total Listed Here	**$28.8 billion**

Figure 5: Known Numbers for National Intelligence Budget[4]

---

[3] This chapter provides a very high-level overview. For details refer to my first book, *ON INTELLIGENCE: Spies and Secrecy in an Open World* (OSS, 2001) and to the 150 books discussed in the annotated bibliography for that book. I also recommend Lisa Krizan's *Intelligence Essentials for Everyone* (Joint Military Intelligence College, Occasional Paper Number Six, June 1999). The enterprising citizen can obtain a copy of this "limited edition" publication by writing to the Defense Intelligence Agency, Joint Military Intelligence College, Code MCE-2, Washington, D.C. 20340-5100.

[4] We are actually spending closer to $50 billion when we count increases since then and especially after 9-11, and defense personnel and facilities that are in support but not specifically dedicated to intelligence on a full-time basis. As my first book documents, at least one-third of this budget could be re-directed toward new initiatives.

From a rational taxpayer perspective, the following list identifies what is seriously wrong with our existing national intelligence budget:

1. 85% of the money is being spent on "secret" technical collection capabilities that are actually well-known to our opponents—neither the Indian nuclear test nor most of bin Laden's telephone calls have been captured because they know how to avoid being seen or heard.
2. We do not have a single all-source processing center where it can all come together, and except for our imagery and signals (which are processed by discipline specific centers using technology created in the 1970's), the rest of the intelligence is still in pen and paper and filing cabinet mode.
3. We spent almost nothing on advanced information technology for *processing*, and consequently process less than 10% of our images, less than 6% of our Russian and Chinese signals, less than 3% of our European signals, and less than 1% of our Rest of World (ROW) signals including terrorism and transnational crime targets.
4. We have a clandestine service that relies largely on official cover and young people who do not have adequate historical, cultural, or language skills to be effective. We have, in the past twenty year, largely eliminated secret agents around the world, and rely very heavily on what foreign intelligence services are willing to tell us....and those services are generally penetrated by their own opposition groups.
5. We have an all-source analysis service that is very young and generally does not have advanced degrees nor the historical, cultural, and language skills necessary to fully monitor and comprehend information only available in the original foreign language.
6. We invest almost nothing in collecting, digitizing, and translating open sources of information in foreign languages.
7. We invest almost nothing in creating bridges from our intelligence systems to our weapons systems, and our intelligence cannot be processed in near-real-time. The result is that we still cannot locate individuals and pieces of equipment on the ground in time for a weapons system to be brought to bear effectively, and we routinely kill some of our own people when fat-fingering target coordinates from one system to another because they were not designed to be digitally connected.

There are many specific reforms that must take place, and these are discussed in the first book—the new craft of intelligence focuses on your needs.

With that, let us consider some key aspects of the craft of intelligence. The elements to be discussed here are listed below

Process Elements	Disciplines	Levels of Analysis
Requirements Definition	Human Intelligence	Strategic
Collection Management	Signals Intelligence	Operational
Source Discovery	Imagery Intelligence	Tactical
Multi-Source Fusion	Measurements Intelligence	Technical
Compelling Presentation	Open Source Intelligence	
	Processing	
	Analysis	
	Counterintelligence	
	Covert Action	

Figure 6: Fundamental Aspects of Intelligence

The Process of Intelligence

The process of intelligence is straight-forward and includes the following elements:

Requirements Definition. This first step cannot be accomplished by the intelligence specialist alone, but demands an intimate discussion with the client—be they a politician or corporate executive—to determine the context of the decision being contemplated, as well as the specific factors that need to be investigated and analyzed so as to best support what could be a very costly financial commitment or re-direction. Politicians and corporate executives that are unwilling to take the time to engage in this essential first-step are inevitably going to be uninformed and often in error.[5]

---

[5] It is an unfortunate fact of life that ignorance is not necessarily painful or unprofitable for the government manager or corporate executive whose compensation is not tied to performance. The taxpayer and the stockholder often pay enormous costs for political and corporate stupidity, and these costs are concealed from the real bill-payers (taxpayers or stockholders). A major objective of this book is to set forth a means by which citizens can both hold their representatives accountable for "due diligence" with respect to making decisions informed by this proven process of intelligence; and can at once inform themselves so that citizens may hold their own in negotiations and confrontations with local and state governments (for instance, those seeking to build

Collection Management. Both government organizations and corporations have tended to be very insular as well as lazy when it comes to collecting and processing external information. Their executives tend to believe they know everything they need to know to make decisions, and it does not occur to them that world-class experts exist for every niche of knowledge, or that studies are constantly generating new findings relevant to pending decisions. The intelligence professional in any organization must be a master of four distinct competencies (today they master only the *last* one):

1) Can we <u>find</u> this in our existing knowledge bases? Among our existing employees, most of whose knowledge has not been codified or published; and our existing databases, most of which are "owned" by a specific division and not indexed for general access, does this information already exist so it can be acquired quickly and at no additional cost?

2) Can we <u>get</u> this information from someone we know, at no cost? From among our counterpart organizations, whether here at home or abroad, from media, academic, or other experts whom we help support, is this information available free and at a suitable level of detail and in time?

3) Can we <u>buy</u> this information from a private sector vendor, whether locally or internationally, at a reasonably inexpensive cost, in time, and without revealing our strategic intentions?

4) Lastly, if we cannot find, get, or buy this information, can we <u>task</u> an internal capability to create, locate, acquire, or otherwise devise the needed information, at whatever cost approved by management?

Collection management requires both special knowledge, and a budget. The greatest affliction of U.S. government intelligence is its reliance on multi-billion dollar secret capabilities funded by the U.S. taxpayer but utilized by the

---

high schools on top of super-fund toxic waste sites because the land is cheap) and corporations (for instance, those continuing to use chlorine in their chemical processes).

15

Department of Defense and other agencies of the federal government as if it were a "free" good. Government managers are not held accountable for funding their own capabilities to acquire open source information (OSIF), nor are they held accountable for making intelligent use of the very expensive classified capabilities.

Corporations, on the other hand, do not understand how valuable a well-managed business intelligence capability can be, with the result that they generally either do not fund such a capability, or treat it as a newspaper clipping service. In both cases, the Chief Information Officers (CIO) tend to be technicians, and devoid of appreciation for external open sources of information—and therefore also without a budget for acquiring value-added external information and intelligence support.

Source Discovery and Validation. It is a common misperception among both government and corporate officials that the Internet has made external information easily available. The reality is that the Internet, while growing rapidly, is in its infancy and has a fraction of the content, structure, reliability, and value of more conventional open sources such as Factiva or LEXIS-NEXIS or DIALOG. Internet sources tend to be self-published, unedited, unformatted, unpaginated, and often unsourced. They are also unstable, frequently moving as web sites are re-organized, often vanishing all together. Whether or not one is permitted to seek out sources willing to betray their employer or their country, the source discovery and validation process is a vital aspect of the proven process of intelligence. Intelligence specialists who limit themselves to sources that are in English, online, or locally available will find that they are operating with, at best, 2% of the available, relevant information. Only a global process of discovery, operating in at least English, German, French, Russian, Chinese, and Swedish, but ideally in 29 languages[6],

---

[6] Arabic, Catelan, Chinese, Danish, Dari, Dutch, English, Farsi, Finnish, French, German, Indonesian, Irish, Italian, Japanese, Korean, Kurdish, Kurmanji, Norwegian, Pashto, Polish, Portuguese, Russian, Serbian, Spanish, Swedish, Tamil, Turkish, Urdu. These were the languages relevant to a global identification and examination by OSS Sweden of 396 terrorist, insurgent, and opposition web sites. In terms of global risk and instability, if you do not have access to intelligence across this spectrum of languages, you are not going to be fully informed. This is not to say that you should be reading the raw materials, only that a trusted third party provider should be monitoring and mining this material on your behalf, in relation to your specific interests.

16

will yield a proper appreciation of current human knowledge in any given domain. Only a global process that can discover "gray literature"—limited edition hard-copy products that are not indexed nor listed by mainstream conventional publishers, will gain the kind of currency and depth that characterizes pioneering endeavors. Finally, only a global process capable of identifying the top human experts, both published and unpublished, will actually place the intelligence specialist within reach of the very edge of knowledge, the knowledge that is just emerging or known to be coming soon.

Multi-Source Fusion. Both government and corporate executives suffer from the delusion that they are their own best intelligence professionals, and that they simply need to have access to the raw information in order to render a complex judgment. At the other extreme are those executives who refuse to read, who are too busy "making decisions" to entertain relevant inputs. Aggravating the relative ignorance of senior managers are a coterie of well-meaning aides who either seek to protect the top people from the flood of information that is available, or to prevent negative information from reaching the boss. Senior executives who believe they do not need intelligence professionals should probably be sewing their own clothes and hunting rats for their dinner. Intelligence could be, should be, the "brain of the firm," rendering a unique contribution as a processor of multiple sources of information into a precisely tailored fused product—but it cannot do this unless the top managers understand that without intelligence, they will continue to be unintelligent.

Multi-source fusion is where a combination of information technologies, diverse analytical talents, and a superior understanding of the bottom line needs of the client come into play. The "information explosion" has made vast quantities of low-cost information, including commercial imagery and commercial foreign broadcast monitoring, easily available. However, most organizations, including the most expensive elements of the U.S. intelligence community, have failed completely in the areas of digitization, automated translation, massive multiple database visualization, and geospatially-founded presentation. All organizations, including the most well-known spy agencies as well as the most well-known global corporations, are stuck in the traditional and very labor-intensive "cut and paste" method of multi-source fusion.[7]

---

[7] The eighteen key functionalities, illustrated on page 136, include: conversion of paper to digital form; automated foreign language translation, image and signal

17

Compelling, Timely, Relevant Presentation. There is no quicker way for an intelligence professional to commit career suicide than to fail to provide the client decision-maker with a steady stream of compelling, timely, relevant presentations that are responsive and precisely tailored to the specific questions of greatest concern to the client. This is where most government intelligence organizations fail spectacularly, and where most business intelligence units do poorly. It is also where billions of dollars are being wasted by both governments and corporations all too eager to pay hundreds of millions of dollars for "consulting" that produces roomfuls of three-ring binders full of raw information collected and collated by junior MBAs with zero substantive knowledge. Given a relationship of trust and confidence, more often than not a one-page answer, done overnight and delivered as an attachment to email, is vastly more valuable than a binder full of paper delivered three weeks later.

The Disciplines of Intelligence

All of the disciplines of intelligence are relevant to the business world and a good understanding of them can improve both scholarship and investigative journalism.

Human Intelligence (HUMINT). Human intelligence can be illegal (bribery as well as treason) or legal. Human spies as well as military scouts and legal travelers existed before Christ. There is no substitute for boots on the ground and eyes on the target. If there is one major failing of U.S. Intelligence in the past 50 years, it is that it has substituted a reliance on satellite technology for everything else. [8] If there is one major failing within the business and

---

processing, automated extraction of data elements from text and images, standardization and conversion of data formats, clustering and linking of related data, statistical analysis to reveal anomalies, detection of changing trends, detection of alert situations, interactive search and retrieval across multiple databases, graphic and map-based visualization of data, modeling and simulation, collaborative work, notetaking and idea organization, structured argument analysis, desktop publishing, production of multi-media presentations including video, and finally, revision tracking and real-time group review and multi-track production from remote locations.

[8] The best, most detailed, and most pertinent treatment of how our clandestine service has collapsed in the past decade is that of Robert Baer, *SEE NO EVIL: The True Story of a Ground Soldier in the CIA's War on Terrorism* (Crown Publishers: New York, 2002),. He states bluntly that we have no substantive assets against terrorism, and especially in the Middle East and Afghanistan. Since the Director of Central

academic worlds, it is their reliance on incestuous inner circles of human experts, never reaching out to discover highly-cited experts from other domains and other countries who offer unique new insights. No one is doing well at tapping into the distributed intelligence of the Whole Earth.

Signals Intelligence (SIGINT). The experience fighting submarines in World War II, and our ineffectiveness at clandestine operations against the Soviets resulted in a decisive move toward remote technical collection. Ultimately America would become the 900-lb. Gorilla of Western intelligence because of its open-ended funding of what would become a uniquely comprehensive global grid of satellites and ground stations able to capture virtually any signal from anywhere. There are two aspects of SIGINT that are relevant to the future of a public international intelligence network:

1) Massive Computing. The National Security Agency (NSA) is uniquely qualified to establish the "mother of all databases" able to fully integrate all available foreign intelligence, law enforcement intelligence, and related private sector data (for instance, usage of credit cards by individuals approved for inclusion on the terrorist watch list). Although their culture is totally wrapped up in secret signals, firm leadership and directed funding could yet see NSA become the National Processing Agency (NPA) and the heart of an integrated Homeland Security Intelligence Program. [9]

Intelligence is reported to have told the President that we have a very "heavy asset base", each citizen should be concerned about which of these two officers is closest to the truth in their statements. Not having assets is bad enough—misleading the President into believing that we have assets where none exist is another matter entirely. For the latter statement, see *The Washington Post*, 31 January 2002, page A13, discussing what was said to the President at Camp David on 15 September 2001. Another excellent and reputable commentary on the decline of our clandestine service can be found in the article by Reuel Marc Gerecht, "The Counterterrorist Myth: A former CIA operative explains why the terrorist Usama bin Ladin has little to fear from American intelligence," *The Atlantic Monthly* (July/August 2001).

[9] The Report of the National Imagery and Mapping Agency Commission (December 2000) clearly articulated the view that we must redirect substantial funds toward Tasking, Processing, Exploitation, and Dissemination (TPED). Lacking a single focal point for all-source processing, your government fails to compute most of what it gets.

19

2) Operational Intelligence (OpIntel). This extraordinary competence, today resident only in the U.S. Navy and other advanced naval forces, consists of the ability to integrate, in near-real-time, a wide variety of SIGINT, to plot these on a geospatial map or chart, and to make reasonably reliable predictions as to where each of the pieces being plotted in going to be going. In today's threat environment, the ability to do this down to the individual terrorist level (rather than the more obvious Carrier Battle Group level) is going to become the heart of preventive policing and pro-active counterintelligence.[10]

Imagery Intelligence (IMINT). Imagery intelligence began with photography from tethered hot air balloons, then from low-flying propeller aircraft, and ultimately, in some extraordinary break-throughs, from the U-2 and secret satellites in space. Today we have seen another break-through—that which was Top Secret as late as 1990, is now commonplace in the private sector—commercial satellite imagery is offered at prices as low as $400, and can be purchased at resolutions as fine as 1–meter (meaning you can see something 1 meter wide from outer space). French 10-meter imagery is highly advanced, with two satellites and seventeen ground stations, and their 5-meter satellites promise to offer even faster and more detailed wide-area surveillance imagery. The business community appears to have been very slow to understand the amazing things that can be done with imagery at very low cost—precision farming that applies exactly the right amount of water and/or fertilizer; low-cost telecommunications surveys; rapid preliminary planning for road and pipeline routes; over-night evaluation of the status of all natural gas storage facilities in Russia—these are just a few of the uses for commercial satellite imagery.

Measurements and Signatures Intelligence (MASINT). This is the newest discipline, emerging in part because of the difficulty of studying nuclear, biological, and chemical (NBC) proliferation and contamination in denied areas. This discipline is extremely expensive and in my opinion has been seriously over-sold. "Signatures" refers to those unique patterns that can

---

[10] See my longer discussion in this book's annotated bibliography of Patrick Beesly, *Very Special Intelligence: The Story of the Admiralty's Operational Intelligence Centre 1939-1945* (Greenhill UK, 2000).

20

be detected, for instance trace elements in the air or in water or in soil, such that relatively firm conclusions can be drawn as to the presence of the target material or capability.[11] To the extent that it, like other technical disciplines, draws funding away from basics like HUMINT, OSINT, processing, and analysis, it is hindering rather than enhancing national intelligence progress.

Open Source Intelligence (OSINT). Open sources of information, while multi-disciplinary (including human, signals, and imagery) are treated as a discipline in their own right because OSINT is one area where all sectors of a Nation (government, business, media, academia, non-profits) can fruitfully collaborate. OSINT is also something that the classified disciplines have repeatedly demonstrated they do not understand, do not respect, and will not fund. OSINT must have its own champions. Appendix 1 provides a "Citizen's Guide to Open Sources & Methods," so no further detail will be provided here. In terms of return on investment within national intelligence, there is no better investment of the taxpayer dollar than OSINT. It provides the greatest value (40%) at the least cost (0.5%), and could easily meet 80-90% of our national intelligence needs if we invested 5-10% of our intelligence funds in OSINT.

Processing. In theory processing allows for the automated treatment of multiple sources of information in such a manner as to "make sense" of vast quantities of multi-lingual information. In fact, the U.S. Intelligence Community is still largely in the hard-copy filing and stove-pipe production era. We have spent hundreds of billions of dollars on single-discipline collection capabilities, and never invested the funds needed to either process all that we collect, or to bring multiple disciplines together in a single integrated and geospatially-organized master database. At the same time, we have deprived both the Department of State (which handles visa applications overseas) and the Federal Bureau of Investigation as well as the Drug Enforcement Administration the funds necessary for their communications and computing infrastructures. It gets worse—our state and local law enforcement—including the state troopers that made traffic stops on three of the terrorists prior to 911—are not connected at all to the national intelligence system, and have no way of knowing the names of the individuals that are on the counter-terrorism watchlists. Finally, we have made no progress since we first understood the possibilities in 1986, toward creating geospatial location

---

[11] By one account, the pharmaceutical factory in Sudan was bombed on the strength of a soil sample taken from outside the factory.

and time stamp attributes for all data, which would allow the mapping of all data in relation to specific locations (including changing locations) and times.

Analysis. Analysis is where everything is supposed to come together. All of the secret and open sources, all of the processing tools, all of the expert human knowledge that can be applied, all this is supposed to result in trenchant, timely, relevant "analysis" that a unique value can be associated with its delivered opinions and products. A well-managed analysis enterprise will strike an even balance between responding to critical inquires, assessing current developments, and forecasting future trends and other developments that merit policy-level attention. Above all, analysts must be able to *answer the question* irrespective of source or time constraints. Analysts provided informed judgments in their specific areas of expertise. This does not mean that the analyst is the final authority. In the age of distributed information (and expertise), the acme of skill for an analyst may be to serve as a matchmaker between a decision-maker with a complex question and exactly the right expert in the private sector—and to provide quality control, interpretation, and a second opinion   as the real-time interaction is producing intelligence.

Counterintelligence. In the months after 9-11, and in the years ahead, enormous investments are being made in physical security, personnel background checks, and other reactive and defense measures. The most important thing to understand about counterintelligence is that it dramatically lowers the cost of traditional defenses. Put another way, it is impossible to defend everything, especially when the attacker is an individual terrorist willing to commit suicide using unconventional means such as hijacked airlines (or chlorine tanker trucks). Offensive counterintelligence is the art and science of penetrating terrorist groups as well as the intelligence services of hostile nations (and to be fair, of allied nations that persist in spying on us despite our generosity toward them with military and other forms of assistance). Defensive counterintelligence includes measures to monitor your own personnel, to monitor known agents of foreign intelligence services or hostile non-state groups, and other measures such as computer auditing to flag unauthorized actions by individuals with access. It is safe to say that U.S. counterintelligence is in really terrible shape—as bad off as clandestine human intelligence. This is true both in the Federal Bureau of Investigation (FBI), where they believe their primary mission is crime-fighting; and it is also true of military counter-intelligence, where the functions are often set aside and the personnel assigned to various support duties instead of their primary mission area. If America is to be safe from further terrorist attacks, counterintelligence is going to have to be revived at the federal level and extended down to the state and local level. It is neither possible nor desirable to "federalize" state and local counterintelligence. Instead we must help each state and each city devise their own solutions, with all personnel under the authority of the respective Governor or Mayor.

Covert Action. Covert action refers to paramilitary operations where the support of the U.S. is ostensibly not attributable; to media placement and other psychological operations intended to influence foreign publics; and to "agent of influence" operations where individuals under our control take actions in their official capacities that are in our best interests. As a general comment, our paramilitary operations tend to cost a great deal of money, result in tens of thousands dead, and generally either do not yield the desired result, or do, and come back to haunt us in later years (e.g. we created bin Laden in Afghanistan). As we go further into this century and find that the Third World War is primarily between governments and gangs, I believe that covert action will require new forms of multi-lateral cooperation by mixed government groups against terrorists and translations criminal gangs, and be less and less justifiable between one government and another.

Levels of Analysis

The threat, and the metrics for evaluating what to buy and what to build in the way of national security capabilities, change depending on the level of analysis. This has not yet been understood by the defense managers responsible for our $400 billion a year defense budget.

At the strategic level, it is important to establish generalizations that will help optimize performance across a spectrum of possibilities. It is highly relevant, for example, that the average temperature in the world where we fight is 80° on average, and often humid....yet we persist in building aircraft to a standard aviation day that is 65° and not humid. What this means is that more often than not, our military aircraft can only carry half the advertised load, going half the advertised distance, and staying half the advertised time over the battlefield in support of our troops.

At the operational level (this is the regional or "theater" level), it is important to establish generalizations that will help frame what kinds of capabilities can be brought to bear. It is highly relevant, for example, to know that in Latin America the average bridge loading capability is under 30 tons (we have many tanks and trucks with artillery pieces that weigh more than that), the average line of sight distance for engaging the enemy is under 900 meters (we are optimized for 3000 meters and out), and there is no cross-country mobility—we must use the limited roadways that exist.

At the tactical level, details about specific individuals and vehicles and weapons and buildings become very important. This is especially true for unconventional forces that do not have fixed bases or common formations. Both in government and in business we have neglected this challenge, and we have not created capabilities suited to tracking (or fighting) anything below large "units."

Finally, at the technical level, where we have tended to focus, individual systems are studied. Our most common mistake, particularly in evaluating the Soviet threat during the Cold War (and now the North Korean, Iranian, and Iraqi threats) has been to assume that all technical capabilities are fully available and will work at their optimal level. This is known as "worst case" threat analysis. The reality is usually very different. Libyan tanks, for example, the best that Russian money can buy, are generally stored in the open, cannibalized for parts, and manned by untrained troops.

The Generic Craft of Intelligence

The generic craft of intelligence, briefly described above in terms of its process, the various disciplines, and the levels of analysis, is vastly superior to conventional academic scholarship or existing levels of business "intelligence" that are actually more related to clipping services or market research.

Properly done (bringing global multi-lingual collection, diverse human experts, simple and well as sophisticated automated tools, and a mind-set that is rigorously focused on both the internal question to be answered and the external possibilities or "wild cards" that conventional thinkers routinely dismiss), the generic craft of intelligence is the first line of defense as well as a unique form of asymmetric advantage against all forms of external threat, whether from individuals, organizations, or the general environment (natural, regulatory, or other).

How we spend taxpayer dollars on intelligence really matters.

Core Ideas in Asymmetric War

In the realm of military affairs and national security, asymmetry is acting, organizing, and thinking differently than opponents in order to maximize one's own advantages, exploit an opponent's weaknesses, attain the initiative, or gain greater freedom of action. It can be political-strategic, military-strategic, operational, or a combination of these. It can entail different methods, technologies, values, organizations, time perspectives, or some combination of these. It can be short-term or long-term. It can be deliberate or by default. It can be discrete or pursued in conjunction with symmetric approaches. It can have both psychological and physical dimensions.

Steven Metz and Douglas Johnson[1]

The attacks on the World Trade Center and the Pentagon were asymmetric warfare at its very best. Having previously failed in a relatively

---

[1] Steven Metz and Douglas V. Johnson II, *ASYMMETRY AND U.S. MILITARY STRATEGY: Definition, Background, and Strategic Concepts* (Strategic Studies Institute, Special Report, January 2001), pp. 5-6. Dr. Metz, who is also the director of the asymmetric studies program within the Strategic Studies Institute of the U.S. Army War College, is perhaps the most authoritative strategist as well as a specialist in asymmetry and non-traditional threats, now serving the U.S. government. This chapter as well as the book as a whole have been inspired by his efforts since the late 1990's to question the conventional wisdom seeking to fund a conventional military prepared for a two-front war. Others at the U.S. Army War College, notably Dr. Max G. Manwaring and including many resident scholars as well as funded speakers, have made substantial contributions to the emerging concepts and doctrine on homeland security and unconventional defenses against non-traditional and non-state enemies. For more information, visit <http://carlisle-www.army.mil/usassi/welcome.htm>.

conventional attack using explosives driven into the underground parking of one of the World Trade Center's two twin towers, the terrorists devised a new plan rich in conceptual simplicity.

They reconfirmed the American homeland, and the corporate materialist symbolism of the World Trade Center's twin towers, as ground zero.

They recognized that Americans would forget the first bombing after several years, and waited more years before striking again.

They identified commercial airlines loaded with fuel for a continental or trans-Atlantic crossing as the perfect combination of guided missile and aerial fuel explosive with the added advantage of "virtual stealth."

They sent at least 20 and possibly as many as 200 well-educated middle class faithful to enter the United States and live here for up to a year. Most of these individuals entered legally, with valid visas.

Several of the individuals paid for the flight training necessary to steer the commercial jets once hijacked.

They recognized that a combination of American doctrine on hijacking (be calm, see Cuba) and American laxity with respect to airport security, would allow them to get weapons on board and take control of airplanes with minimal resistance.

They went an extra step and limited their weapons to normally innocuous "box-cutters"—sheathed blades for cutting open cardboard boxes, yet capable of slicing a neck artery easily—as was done in one case.

At the end of the day of their own choosing, without detection on our part, on our home ground, for a price under $500,000, they turned New York into a death zone, destroyed a corner of the Pentagon, paralyzed the Nation for several days, gutted the economy for several months, and demonstrated to the entire world that a small group of individuals, with modest funding and suicidal motivation, could cause upwards of $20 billion in damages to any Western state.

Welcome to the world of asymmetric warfare.

The definition of asymmetry with which this chapter began warrants further elaboration. The original authors, Drs. Metz and Johnson, distinguish between dimensions of asymmetry and forms of asymmetry. These are outlined below and drawn directly from their seminal study.

Selected Dimensions of Asymmetry
1. Positive or Negative (Superior training is positive, inability to target weapons into jungle canopy, or lack of maps for Third World, are negative).
2. Short-Term or Long-Term (*blitzkrieg*, while extremely effective when first devised, was countered within a couple of years; willingness and ability to spend billions on defense is long-term)
3. Low-Risk or High-Risk (superior training low risk with moderate gains, suicidal hijackings high-risk with very high or zero gains)
4. Material or Psychological (equipment or character)

Selected Forms of Asymmetry
1. Method (something totally different—using civilian airlines as stealth bombs was brilliant—but it is also highly unlikely civilian passengers will ever again allow a hijacking)
2. Technology (such as precision munitions—until someone figures out how to use microwave ovens to lead them into empty fields)
3. Will (both individual suicidal will, and unit cohesion and willingness to take risks over time in the face of great odds)
4. Organization (phalanx, *levee en mass*, netwar, espionage)
5. Patience (tunnels of Chu Chi, acceptance of casualties)

The United States of America and its government, especially its military, has always had enormous difficulty with "unconventional warfare." Indeed, the opposition of the conventional military leadership to the very idea of having special operations forces was so strong that Congress had to legislatively-mandate a separate U.S. Special Operations Command and a completely separate budget for Special Operations and Unconventional Warfare. Had Congress not done so, the military-industrial complex and its traditional leaders would have neglected our special operations capabilities and they would not exist today.

Asymmetric warfare—and the unconventional thinking that must be used to achieve intelligence and counterintelligence successes against those who would practice asymmetric warfare against us, within our homeland as well as overseas—is a vital topic that is receiving lip service from the Pentagon.

Indeed, most informed observers, from Michael O'Hanlon[2] at the Brookings Institute to various Ambassadors and former senior officials writing on the Op-Ed pages of the major newspapers, have noted that the Pentagon does not need more money, it needs a new mind-set. The Administration, with the best of intentions, is making the problem worse. In giving the Pentagon as well as the U.S. Intelligence community tens of billions of additional taxpayer dollars to spend, the Administration has not only funded all of the *old* ideas that did not make earlier budget cuts, but they have encouraged the old mind-sets to propose even more *old* ideas for funding. The Secretary of Defense is widely perceived to have surrendered to the old mind-set and given up on his earlier and most urgently needed emphasis on transformation. The citizen taxpayer is being badly served by an Administration that seeks to solve problems with deficit spending in lieu of innovative thinking and the forced redirection of funding away from Cold War programs and toward Asymmetric War programs.

The remainder of this chapter will discuss some of the targets and tools that our enemy's might reasonably choose to attack here within our homeland. The targets are too numerous to discuss in detail, but they can be grouped into four large categories: physical, cybernetic, data, and mind-set. The tools are also too numerous to discuss in detail—tools as elementary as paperclips and pick-axes can inflict grave damage on very complex and inherently fragile systems. We remain our own worst enemy in our continuing refusal to recognize that in the age of digital information national security boils down to good code and observant neighbors.

This chapter was originally developed when our worst fears were directed toward anonymous attacks on our electronic infrastructures. We are still vulnerable there, but as will be seen in later chapters, we have both public health and conventional environmental vulnerabilities that are equally critical.

---

[2] O'Hanlon is one of a handful a really thoughtful commentators on conventional national security spending—two others are Daniel Goure and Andrew Krepinevich. The Center for Strategic and Budgetary Assessments, within which Krepinevich is the primary author, is a classic example of how one can be "best in class" in their chosen niche (conventional military expenditures) while missing the larger opportunity to evaluate the budget in broader terms—how we might better spend our taxpayer dollars across the *varied* instruments of national power.

TAKEDOWN: Targets and Tools for Asymmetric Attack

This is not a technical chapter—there are many of those, each delving into the minutia of taking down power, financial, transportation, or general communications systems.[3] Instead, I want to provide a general overview of target categories and potentially catastrophic outcomes; a review of the range of tools or means by which these targets can be taken down; and a brief discussion of the technocracy and its culture which perpetuates our vulnerability to cybernetic melt-down as well as attacks on our physical assets.

We need to explore a redefinition of national security and national power. Our information "order of battle", and in particular, our ability to protect and harness data in the private sector, and our ability to convert and continue to exploit data across human generations, must be recognized as the most critical factor contributing to national security and national competitiveness. The brittleness of our existing complex systems, with multiple embedded points of failure, is the lesser vulnerability. The larger vulnerability is at the data and knowledge level. Under these circumstances, "continuity of operations" takes on a whole new meaning, and indeed merits the scale of funding that once characterized the same term during the Cold War. This chapter reviews targets, tools, and technocracy in that larger context.

Redefining National Security

As we consider the targets and the tools that can be used to effect a "takedown" of America, we must do so in the context of a refreshed understanding of what constitutes "national security".

The bottom line, made crystal-clear by 9-11: the homefront is both absolutely vital and abysmally vulnerable. The center of gravity for national security as well as national prosperity is in the *private sector*. Our national

---

[3] Although other papers have been written since then, the three "originals" in the author's view are Major Gerald R. Hust, "Taking Down Telecommunications", School of Advanced Airpower Studies, 1993); Major Thomas E. Griffith, Jr., "Strategic Attack of National Electrical Systems", School of Advanced Airpower Studies, 1994; and H. D. Arnold, J. Hukill, and A. Cameron of the Department of the Air Force, "Targeting Financial Systems as Centers of Gravity: 'Low Intensity' to 'No Intensity' Conflict", in *Defense Analysis* (Volume 10 Number 2, pages 181-208), 1994. InfoWarCon and the related web site, www.infowar.com remain a useful point of current reference.

security spending is out of balance—we are spending $400 billion a year or more on preparing for major conventional wars "over there," and next to nothing on protecting ourselves here at home.

The "pyramid of vulnerability" for developed nations, and most especially for the United States of America—which owns, uses, and is severely dependent on the bulk of the communications and computing resources of the world—is illustrated below.

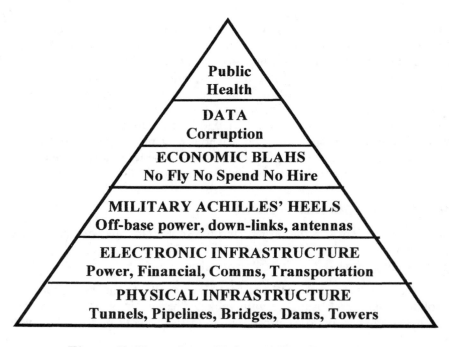

Figure 7: Homefront Vulnerability Pyramid

This pyramid of vulnerability seeks to distinguish between four distinct "kinds" of vulnerability:

1. The vulnerability of major physical infrastructure elements, such as:

- Bridges, Levees, and Dams—such as the 2800 readily mapped for the public of which 200 of so are of strategic consequence in isolation[4]
- Canals—such as the Panama Canal, with very vulnerable locks
- Pipelines—such as the Alaska Pipeline
- Critical railway switching points (e.g. Cincinnati)

2. The vulnerability of obvious military Achilles' heels, as well as obvious civilian infrastructure, such as:
   - AWACS and Aerial Tankers (anti-tank missiles, or plastique on landing gear—tend to be concentrated in one place)
   - Submarine communications antennas (e.g. Annapolis golf course)
   - Charleston channel (major sealift departure area)
   - Civilian power and communications nodes supporting command centers and key facilities (Falcon AFB, Kansas City payroll)
   - Major power grid nodes (both transfer and generation)
   - Major telecommunications nodes, including microwave towers

3. The vulnerability of core data streams vital to national security and national competitiveness, such as:
   - Historical environmental and other critical planning data
   - Civilian fuel stock data
   - Military logistics stock data
   - Transportation status data (induce rail crashes, cripple airports)
   - Financial accounts data (incapacitate procurement, induce panic, impose costs of alternative accounting)

---

[4] The Surface Water and Related Land Resources Development Map is designed to portray both the development and preservation aspects of Federal water resources activities, with the main theme being the spatial distribution of dams and reservoirs. Dams are shown that have normal storage capacity of at least 5,000 acre-feet, or a maximum storage capacity of at least 25,000 acre-feet. This includes about 800 dams owned by Federal agencies and about 2,000 dams owned by non-Federal organizations. *FGDC Manual of Federal Geographic Data Products - Surface Water Map* which used to be found at www.fgdc.gov/FGDP/Surface_Water_Map.html. Although since removed, I suspect a complete copy was made prior to 9-11 by various parties.

31

- Financial transfers data (corrupt transfers, place international and regional transfers into grid-lock, induce panic)

4. The vulnerability of our entire public health system which has been in severe decline for over twenty years:
   - Smallpox (50 suicidal volunteers glad-handing across each state until they expire)
   - Cholera
   - Ebola

At a more abstract level, we are also vulnerable when we fail to invest in foreign language and foreign area studies, and consequently fail to staff our diplomatic and intelligence organizations with individuals who are fully cognizant of global realities and fully qualified to interpret international and foreign "signals."

Prior to 9-11 when this was written, the above rough depiction sought to drive home the point that a "takedown" of America is not simply a matter of electronic attacks against electronic systems, but rather a much more comprehensive range and scale of vulnerability which encompasses everything from key geo-physical nodes to our intelligence mind-sets, and which can be attacked with a range of tools that includes: pick-axes and chain saws against selected cables; anti-tank missiles against AWACS and aerial refuelers and satellite dishes; eighteen-wheeler trucks with and without explosives against specific transformers or other key nodes; electrical attacks, and finally—the area least considered today, data and mind-set attacks and self-generated vulnerabilities, to include the collapse of our public health system as well as our ability to understand foreign realities. Now we know for certain that hijacked aircraft are potential weapons, and in the aftermath of 9-11 I would add private Lear jets loaded with radioactive materials or chemicals such as chlorine or nitroglycerin; as well as private cigarette boats (ocean-going racing boats also used by drug traffickers) similarly loaded.

"Top Ten" lists cannot possibly capture the full extent of the Nation's vulnerability, but they are a helpful means of highlighting the diversity and the imminence of our vulnerability. They can help accelerate constructive change.

We now know that non-state actors are capable of combining suicidal volunteers, unlimited funds, and bold innovative thinking to attack us in ways we are not expecting.

Takedown: Targets & Tools

John Perry Barlow, lyricist for the Grateful Dead and co-founder of the Electronic Frontier Foundation, once said that "the Internet interprets censorship as an outage, and routes around it."[5] Exactly the same can be said for any strategy that seeks to "harden" or protect specific nodes. It simply will not be effective. *It is impossible to lock-down or lock-out everything.*

We are at a point in time where, as Steward Brand has noted, the Year 2000 problem is but "a wholesome first sniff of the carnage to come". Our system of systems is internally vulnerable from the first line of code on up, and externally vulnerable at a very large number of physical as well as electronic nodes.

Let us take each of these in turn.

Representative Targets

1. Bridges, Levees & Dams. In the United States, the Mississippi and Missouri Rivers, natural wonders in their own right, are also natural obstacles of monumental proportions. There are exactly six mainstream railway bridges across these great rivers, across the vast majority of the grains must go from the plains to the East Coast cities, and the vast majority of the goods must in return from the Northeast and the South. As the natural flooding in 1993 demonstrated, [6] when these bridges are closed, whether by accident or intent, there are severe repercussions for trade, and

---

[5] He made this comment in his spontaneous remarks to an audience of 629 intelligence professionals attending the first open source intelligence conference, "National Security & National Competitiveness: Open Source Solutions", 2 December 1992, in Washington, D.C.

[6] During the major floods of 1993 four of the six bridges were closed. Major rail traffic delays and costs were incurred as traffic was routed to the northern and southern bridges still in operation. "Flooding Halts Railroad Traffic Through Major East-West Hub: Freight Lines, Amtrak Rush to Find Detours in North and South", *The Washington Post* (A4, Tuesday, 27 July 1993).

33

especially for the stockage of food and fuel. Recent breaks in levees in the south have demonstrated our vulnerability to the assumption that man can contain nature without regard to human attack. This bears emphasis: all insurance and risk calculations today assume natural causes of disaster. There are no calculations for risk and damage associated with deliberate human attack of any normal civil structure. Dams, in contrast, present computer controlled physical infrastructures which can be taken over to either release flood waters, or to avoid the release of flood waters with the intent of weakening if not destroying the dam.

2. Alaska Pipeline. This pipeline, going across vast stretches of unoccupied territory, carries ten per cent of the domestic oil for the U.S.[7]

3. Cincinnati Rail Yards. As of three years ago, and very likely still today, the entire East-West railway architecture depended on exactly one major turnstile for redirecting railcars. It is located in the Three Rivers area, and represents a significant vulnerability.[8]

4. Culpepper Switch. A popular target, this simply represents the kind of critical communications node (voice and data, especially financial and logistics data) which can be attacked in both physical and electronic ways. The Internet has various equivalent nodes, two of which merit special attention—MAYEAST and MAYWEST. Taking out MAYEAST disconnects the U.S. government from the rest of the Internet world, and not incidentally does terrible things to all of the Wall Street capitalists who are "tunneling" their Intranets across the larger Internet.

---

[7] The first "top ten" listing to be seen by the author was created by Peter Black. His article, "Soft Kill: Fighting infrastructure wars in the 21st century", *WIRED Magazine* (July/August 1993), listed the following targets:
1. Culpepper Switch, handling all electronic transfers of federal funds
2. Alaska Pipeline, carrying ten percent of the domestic oil
3. Electronic Switching System (ESS), managing all telephony
4. Internet, the communications backbone of science and industry
5. Time Distribution System, upon which all networked computers depend
6. Panama Canal, major choke point for U.S. trade
7. Worldwide Military Command & Control System (WWMCCS)
8. Big Blue Cube, Pacific clearinghouse for satellite reconnaissance
9. Malaccan Straits, the maritime link between Europe-Arabia and the Pacific
10. National Photographic Interpretation Center, processing center for imagery

[8] Winn Schwartau, personal communication, 17 March 1998.

5. Power Generators. Power generators and the grids they support can be browned out, burned out, and confused. Altering the computer readings can cause them to draw more power than they can handle, or less power than they need. Burning out the generators or melting core lines creates the interesting challenge of replacement in the absence of mainstream power. There are exactly eighteen main power transformers that tie together the entire U.S. grid, and we have only one—perhaps two—generators in storage. Interestingly, all of these come from Germany, where there is a six to eighteen month waiting period for filling orders—assuming the Germany generators have not been burned out at the same time by someone attacking the Western powers in a transatlantic cyber-war.[9]

6. Data Computers. Any computer holding large quantities of critical data, especially parts inventories and data associated with either the transfer of funds or the operational effectiveness of critical equipment, is vulnerable to data distortion—this is a far more insidious and dangerous problem than the more obvious denial or destruction attacks.

7. Fuel Stock Data. Fuel stock data is isolated because of its implications in terms of overloading large tanks, with the fire storm hazards of large spillage, or of failing to channel fuels because of false readings.

8. Federal Reserve. Until a couple of years ago there were twelve regional computing centers, one for each of the Federal Reserve regions. Now we have a single national system with a single hot back-up computing system, and an additional cold back-up alternative.

9. Downlinks. Past surveys have focused on buildings, but the more capable attackers will focus on downlinks. All of the main satellite downlinks—for both key other government departments as well as major corporations, are out in public sight and reachable with a hand-held anti-tank missile fired from outside the fence line.

10. Human Decisions. "We have met the enemy, and he is us." This often quoted line from Pogo is complemented by another observation, by Thomas Jefferson, to wit, "a Nation's best defense is an educated citizenry". This "target" is listed to bring out both a vulnerability and an opportunity for

---

[9] *Ibid.*

"hardening" our national defense. Just as "commander's intent" is used in planning for complex operations where communications may be lost, it is essential that there be a larger national decision-making architecture in which there are few secrets and the public is fully engaged. In this way, when disasters do happen and many communications channels do break down, the public will be less likely to panic and more likely to use common sense and good will to see the crisis through. A thorough public understanding of our vulnerabilities and our plans for dealing with those vulnerabilities is essential to our progress. This "target" is also intended to make the point that the weakest link in all systems is not the system itself, but the humans associated with the system.

Representative Tools

1. Pick-Axes & Back-Hoes. Paperclips have burned out strategic warning computers. Pick-axes can cut critical cables in strange places that are difficult to discover. Back-hoes easily take out cables—perhaps the most famous, popularized by Winn Schwartau, is the back-hoe which took out Newark Airport's primary communications and air traffic control and also—right there running alongside it, the "redundant" cable intended to serve as a back-up for the primary cable. Across America, at every cable crossing, we post large signs saying in essence "Cut Here".

2. Eighteen Wheelers. Eighteen wheelers, whether or not loaded with explosives, are a useful intellectual construct. Any critical node should be subject to the eighteen-wheeler test—what will happen if an eighteen-wheeler crashes through at full weight and speed at any one of various points; or alternatively, what will happen if an eighteen-wheeler "melts down" at a specific point and needs to be taken apart or lifted out piece by piece? [It never occurred to me, when I wrote this several years ago, to conceptualize aircraft loaded with fuel and flown by suicidal hijackers.]

3. Random Viruses. The recent spate of NT melt-downs are simply another step down the path started by the Robert Morris virus a decade ago. This situation needs to be taken very seriously because many of the viruses are encased in shrink-wrapped hardware and software coming directly from the

production facilities.[10] Until software is self-healing (and code is encrypted at levels above what is presently available), this will continue to be a serious vulnerability. All of the following problem tool areas will exacerbate this situation.

4. Info-Marauders. As has been noted by one prominent wag in this area, "hacker tools are now in the hands of idiots and criminals".[11] A single individual, empowered by hacking software freely available on the Internet, is now able to cause the kind of damage to corporate and national systems which was previously only in the province of Great Nations. Disgruntled, dishonest, crazy, and zealot individuals and gangs are now is a position to damage data, deny access, and extort funds from hapless system owners who did not realize that they were buying into a "naked Emperor" environment.

5. Angry Insiders. The losses to external penetrations and externally sourced viruses is much over-rated. As Dr. Mich Kabay, Director of Education for the International Computer Security Association (ICSA) has noted in his seminal work on computer losses,[12] the largest losses after fire & water/errors & omissions come from *insiders*—dishonest or paid insiders (roughly 10%) and angry insiders seeking revenge (roughly 10%). These are people with authorized access who are able to do unauthorized things that are not detected because the systems are all designed under the assumption that insiders can be controlled through a few simple (and often very poorly administered) control measures.

---

[10] In 1992 a major U.S. intelligence community entity, one extremely familiar with computers, briefed the Information Handling Committee with the results of its survey, over the course of one year, into viruses arriving at its loading docks in shrink-wrapped products. The total number found: 500.

[11] The author, keynote speaker at Hackers on Planet Earth (HOPE), an extraordinary event that drew over 1,200 hackers and phone phreakers to a dilapidated New York City hotel 13-14 August 1998. Hackers, as the author has noted with frequency, are *not* the problem, not even the symptom of the problem—they are a national resource in that they are demonstrating, without causing significant damage, just how vulnerable all of our systems are.

[12] Mich E. Kabay, *The NCSA Guide to Enterprise Security: Protecting Information Assets*, McGraw-Hill (New York, 1996). ISBN 0-07-033147-2. Chapter 1, Figure 1, page 11. The figure in his book is superceded by this text, provided by Dr. Kabay in personal communications, 12 March 1998.

6. Paid Insiders. Paid insiders can be simply dishonest employees who seek to exploit access for financial gain, or insiders who have been recruited by outsiders for a price. There are also former insiders who return to their place of employment (e.g. selected Wall Street firms with marginal physical access controls and worse computer access controls) to take internal actions which are not authorized and for which authorized access has expired administratively but not technically.

7. Calcutta Code. Also Moscow code....this refers to computer code written by the legions of off-shore coding houses. Computer code in the U.S. is notorious for its lack of documentation, with the result that older systems tend to have millions and millions of lines of code that are completely incomprehensible to the most skilled examiner, and replete with patches from a variety of sources, all also undocumented. When the Year 2000 problem was most urgent, many organizations were forced to provide intimate access to their code for legions of external programmers, generally without any assurance at all as to their criminal and psychological history, and also without any ability to audit their access or their code.[13]

8. Existing Electrical Engineering Skills. Our electrical engineering education is abysmal, despite the wealth of opportunity in the field and the shortage of skilled professionals. For reasons that escape the author, the electrical engineering discipline decided to completely ignore electronic security and counterintelligence issues after the demise of the mainframe (and even those standards were mediocre), and entire complex systems have been built from the ground up without any embedded security at all. In fact, some systems require or choose to turn off those rare security features provided in some software and hardware. Until national legislation establishes "due diligence" standards for managers responsible for the protection of intellectual property, and for communications and computing product and service providers, this severe and pervasive vulnerability will prevent any substantial success in hardening individual targets or constraining the utility of other attack tools.

---

[13] A typical assessment of this looming access problem is found in CIWARS Volume 10, Issue, Intelligence Report dated 2 November 1997. <www.iwar.org> contains this and many other interesting reports on electronic vulnerabilities around the world.

9. Existing Mind-Sets. Winn Schwartau, author of *INFORMATION WARFARE: Chaos on the Electronic Superhighway* deserves full credit for bringing this situation before the public. Without his efforts, including his many keynote speeches across the Nation, and his personal engagement in sponsoring a highly provocative series of InfoWarCon meetings, it is highly unlikely that the President's Commission on Critical Infrastructure Protection would have been created. Unfortunately, the U.S. government continues to drag its feet in assuming its proper role as a provider of "order & protection" services in cyberspace, and this has been cited by many in the private sector as the reason they continue to ignore computer security issues.[14]

Technocracy

Fully seventy percent of our existing and projected losses can be attributed to very poor design—poor data entry and data management programs that induce major errors & omissions (and cannot audit or flag possible errors & omissions in passing) and poor system design and system back-up practices which permit fire and water to wreak irreversible damage to important data. Only the last thirty percent have anything to do with humans. *Insiders* do roughly twenty percent of the damages. Roughly five percent of the remaining damages are done by outsiders, and a final five percent by viruses from various sources. Imagine, if we do this to ourselves, how much worse it would be if we were faced with a deliberate attack across various sectors, generally using anonymous tools!

In the immortal words of Robert Stratton, one of the most capable of international electronic engineers:

---

[14] In May 1997 an Information Security Industry Survey done by Delotte & Touche LLP, with 1225 organizations surveyed, reported that 40% blamed "unclear responsibilities" and 26-30% (sic) blamed "lack of central authority" as the reasons why they could not come to grips with computer and telecommunications security requirements. As noted in 11 February 1998 email from <Peerillo@DOCKMASTER.NCSC.MIL>.

> *If houses were built like computers, the first woodpecker to come along would bring down civilization.*[15]

The technocracy—the culture of technocracy—is the major impediment to change today, and we have to come to grips with the fact that all the money in the world is not going to heal our rapidly atrophying system of systems unless we first come to grips with the intellectual cancer that permeates this element of our society which is at once so very important, but also so very dangerous. *We have met the enemy, and he is us.*

Among the sins of the technocracy are the following:

1. Blind faith in technology
2. Not legally liable for failure (by permission of Congress)
3. No requirement for inherent security at the code and data level
4. No requirement for data integrity and survivability
5. Marginal adherence to existing back-up and access control standards
6. Elitist attitude about cryptography and privacy
7. History of ignoring detailed warnings
8. Recent record of lip service and tail chasing

The point of this chapter is that both the people and their government must accept responsibility for designing and protecting the future system of systems upon which every aspect of national security and national competitiveness must depend. It is we as individuals, willing to accept self-obsoleting technology with built-in hazards to our data, who have permitted this gross external diseconomy to persist, and it is we the people—not the profit-taking beltway-bandit creators of these systems—who will ultimately pay the final price for failure: individual poverty, scattered catastrophe, and national weakness.

---

[15] Statement made at OSS '96, where Mr. Stratton, a very highly regarded computer security engineer, was a speaker together with his partner, Mr. Chris Goggans, another brilliant security consultant. Today Mr. Stratton works for In-Q-Tel, the venture fund established by the Central Intelligence Agency to help it reconnect to innovation in the private sector.

There is another vital point that relates this chapter to the rest of this book: if it is not possible to defend everything against everyone, then how do we assure homeland security and national defense? A major part of the answer lies in the maturation of the "new craft of intelligence." If America adopts this new craft of intelligence and all that it recommends in terms of coming to grips with the flood of relevant information that we must master, in many languages, then it will also be buying in to a redirected and revitalized secret quadrant of intelligence. Within our traditional world of spies, satellites, and secrecy, no discipline has been more denigrated, more mistreated, than that of counterintelligence.

Counterintelligence and personnel security are going to be growth industries in the 21st Century. The ultimate asymmetric advantage that the United States of America can achieve, against any enemy, in any clime and place, is that of intelligence and counterintelligence. Only the new craft of intelligence, properly nurtured, can provide for sustainable national security in the face of asymmetric threats.

The Changing Environment for Intelligence

The problem with spies is they only know secrets.

Everything has changed. The political environment within which decisions are made has changed, making public intelligence not only more useful, but rather *essential.* Secret intelligence is losing its relative value.

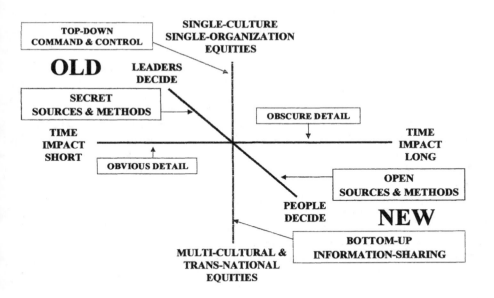

Figure 8: Changing Rules of the Game

The old political paradigm for national security was (some would stay still is) unabashedly unilateralist, reflecting a single culture adamant about having its way. Decisions were made by a small group of leaders relying heavily on secret sources. The new political paradigm, in contrast, is persistently multi-cultural and "bottom-up," demanding consensus and coordination across national and organizational boundaries. Open sources and methods acquire extraordinary value in this environment.

The information environment itself has changed, in essence "exploding" beyond anything we could have conceived of even as recently as 1994. Internet nodes—and the content that goes with them—is predicted by Dr. Vint Cerf, one of the two father's of the Internet, to be going from 400 million today to upwards of 3 billion by 2012.[1]

This means, among many other things, that we must shift our emphasis from collection to processing. Navigation becomes a vital skill. Knowing who knows,[2] and knowing how to filter masses of openly-available information—much of it free, the best of its available at modest cost to anyone—these become the core competencies of the information age.[3] Three areas of emphasis become vital: first the automation of first-order filtering, but with a

---

[1] Dr. Cerf and Robert Kahn are the two generally acknowledged founders of the Internet. His official web site, see especially his international slide shows, is http://www.worldcom.com/generation_d/cerfs_up/index.phtml?grph=1.

[2] Dr. Stevan Dedijer, the father of business intelligence, made this point when he led a delegation of 15 Swedes to the first open source intelligence conference sponsored by the author, in December 1992. The fact that 15 Swedes showed up for an open but not advertised event intended largely for the U.S. government, says a great deal about their global early warning network, and their inter-agency informal communications network.

[3] There are numerous books on how the information explosion is changing everything, and perhaps 20% of them actually have something interesting to say. Four that I have found useful (and have reviewed at www.amazon.com) include, in order of preference: Regis McKenna, *REAL TIME: Preparing for the Age of the Never Satisfied Customer* (Harvard, 1997); Thomas H. Davenport and John C. Beck, *THE ATTENTION ECONOMY: Understanding the New Currency of Business* (Harvard, 2001); Philip Evans and Thomas S. Wurster, *BLOWN TO BITS: How the New Economics of Information Transforms Strategy* (Harvard, 2000); and Don Tapscott, *DIGITAL ECONOMY: Promise and Peril in the Age of Networked Intelligence* (McGraw-Hill, 1996). This chapter a few original and derived ideas, not a summary of the literature.

44

very high degree of control and transparency; second, some form of permanent information tagging as to source, time, and location; and third, historical reach-back.[4]

At the same time, we have found that the existing "seams" between sectors are impediments to effective information sharing. Consider the following representation of the "virtual intelligence community."

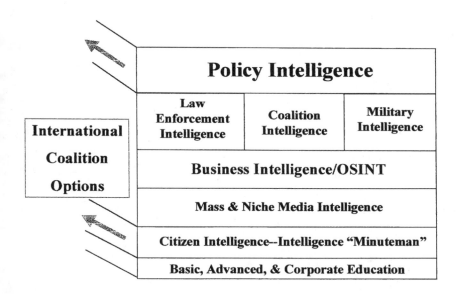

Figure 9: The Virtual Intelligence Community[5]

---

[4] The greatest evil of the digital era is found in its burial of all non-digital information including current and historical experience. Television only recognizes the last 40 years. Media analysts for the Foreign Broadcast Information Service sit at their cubicles in Reston, Virginia and read foreign articles completely out of context—they have no feel for what is actually going on around them. A really superior book that helped me understand these points is that of Bill McKibben, *The Age of Missing Information* (Plume, 1992).

The most important aspects of the new information reality are that first, it is not possible for any single individual or organization to get a grip on all the information that is available; and second, that there does exist a viable concept for a virtual intelligence community that can share the burden of creating an "information commons" useful to the larger group.

There is one last vital point to make about the information and warfighting environment within which the new craft of intelligence must be effective.

	Revolution	Civil War	WW II	Gulf War	Tomorrow
Orientation	Telescope	Telegraph	Radio/Wire	SATCOM (Nr Rl Time)	Wireless (Real-Time)
Observation	Weeks	Days	Hours	Minutes	Always
Decision	Months	Weeks	Days	Hours	Immediate
Action	Season	Month	Week	Day	Hour or less

Figure 10: Race to the Swift[6]

As we seek to orient, observe, decide, and act[7] in defense of our national security and to preserve and further our national prosperity, the speed with which we correct our intelligence deficiencies as well as the speed with which we execute the new craft of intelligence, will matter. Although this chart emphasizes "real-time" decision-making, it also applies to the longer-term strategic perspective—time matters more now.

---

[5] This figure emerged from a discussion between Alvin Toffler and the author as both were returning from a lunch with senior defense intelligence officials. We suddenly realized there were several boxes, all isolated from one another, that comprised the truly national intelligence community—but it is a community that does not have any leadership, concepts, doctrine, or architecture for fulfilling its desperately-needed potential to achieve "Global Coverage" and early warning on non-traditional threats—it is also a community whose self-imposed security barriers is restricting each block's access to real-world real-time information.

[6] This figure, slightly modified, is taken from Michael Brown, "The Revolution in Military Affairs: The Information Dimension", in Alan Campen, Douglas Dearth, and R. Thomas Goodden (eds.), *CYBERWAR: Security, Strategy and Conflict in the Information Age* (AFCEA, 1996, page 34. The classic modern book on this figure's theme is that of Brigadier Richard E. Simpkin, *Race to the Swift: Thoughts on Twenty-First Century Warfare* (Brassey's, 1985).

[7] Colonel John Boyd, USAF (Ret.) – the "OODA Loop".

Overview of Intelligence Reform

Criticism of our intelligence capabilities is not new. As far back as the late 1940's, there have been commissions to review our national intelligence capabilities.

YEAR	REVIEW
1949	**First Hoover Commission** • Adversarial relationships between CIA, State, and the military
1955	**Second Hoover Commission** • Counterintelligence & linguistic training deficiencies • CIA to replace State in procurement of foreign publications
1961	**Taylor Commission** • Failure in communication, coordination and overall planning • No single authority short of the President capable of coordinating the actions of CIA, State, Defense, and USIA
1971	**Schlesinger Report** • "rise in…size and cost [with the] apparent inability to achieve a commensurate improvement in the scope and overall quality…" • "unproductively duplicative" collection systems and a failure in forward planning to coordinate the allocation of resources
1976	**Church Committee** • DCI should have program authority and monies for national intelligence appropriated to the DCI rather than agencies • Recommended second DDCI for Community Management • State must improve overt collection of economic and political data • Raised issue of separating clandestine/covert ops from analysis
1992	**Boren-McCurdy** • National Security Act of 1992 (not adopted, Defense opposed) • DNI, two DDNIs, consolidate DIA and INR analysts with CIA

Figure 11: Historical Intelligence Reform Views[1]

---

[1] United States Information Agency (USIA), the cultural outreach element of the U.S. government that has been recently absorbed by the Department of State. DNI is Director of National Intelligence, DDNI is Deputy Director of National Intelligence,

Only the last review sought to modernize and reissue the original National Security Act. Today expert observers are suggesting that not only do we need a National Security Act of 2002, but that this would be a good vehicle within which to legislatively empower the Office of Homeland Security.

The National Security Act of 1992, a very promising effort at reform, was headed off by opponents of "right-sizing" any of the agencies.[2] A bi-partisan commission was appointed. The House Permanent Select Committee did its own review. Here are their major findings in an abbreviated side-by-side table.

Topical Area	Commission on Intelligence	IC21 Study (HPSCI)
Role of Intelligence	Support diplomacy, military operations, defense planning.	Too *ad hoc* today, lacks coherence, can be self-serving.
Policy/ Requirements Process	State and Defense dominate guidance, consumers group needed	Declining intelligence base and lost focus on future; system-driven
Global Crime, Law Enforcement	Need more coordination of operations overseas, more sharing of information	Need more information sharing and training, global operational coordination.
Organiz. and/ Comms.	DDCI/CIA and DDCI/CM, increases DCI authority	Authorized three ADDCIs for major functions of collection, production, infrastructure.
CIA Itself	Needs better management at all levels	Must move Centers to DCI level, improve quality of personnel
Budget	Substantial realignment needed to	Stove-pipes dominate resources,

and INR is the Bureau for Intelligence and Research of the U.S. Department of State. Figure created on the basis of an extraordinarily useful report by Richard A. Best, Jr. and Herbert Andrew Boerstling of the Congressional Research Service, "Proposals for Intelligence Reorganization, 1949-1996", dated 28 February 1996, and included as the final appendix to the *IC21: Intelligence Community in the 21st Century* report of the House Permanent Select Committee on Intelligence, 4 March 1996. This figure, and the next, were created for chapter 12 of *ON INTELLIGENCE: Spies and Secrecy in an Open World*.

[2] Given that "right-sizing" is often code for "down-sizing", the author believes that the U.S. Intelligence Community should be fenced at $30 billion a year and 100,000 total seats (uniformed, civilian, and on-site contractors), but that within those numbers, the Director of Central Intelligence should have the ability to redirect up to 10% of any element of the total intelligence community.

Structure and Process	aggregate functions, DCI does not have staff, tools, or procedures for performing budget management	rather than analysts or end-users; CMS should have withholding authority and evaluation ability
Intelligence Analysis	Must improve focus on consumers, on open sources	CIA's core function; assumes departmental capabilities okay
"Right-Size" and Rebuild	Consolidate senior executive service, liberal force reduction	Rationalize NFIP, JMIP, and TIARA[3], guide by function
Military Intelligence, Support DoD	DoD needs a single *staff* focal point for managing intel support	D/DIA to be Director Military Intelligence
Technical Collection	Endorses NIMA,[4] need more coordination of intel and DoD	Technical Collection Agency and Technical Development Office
Clandestine Service	Merge DoD HUMINT into CIA HUMINT[5]	Separate entity reporting directly to DCI, CIA feeds it
International Cooperation	Burden sharing in space operations	Not addressed, but notes need to buy more open source imagery
Cost of Intelligence	Cost reductions are possible but need better process to find; states 96% of USIP[6] is in DoD	States that DoD controls 86% of the resources; DCI lacks authority
Accountabili. & Oversight	Extend tenure of members of the oversight committees.	Ease or eliminate tenure limits.

Figure 12: Summary of 1993-1996 Reviews[7]

---

[3] National Foreign Intelligence Program (NFIP), Joint Military Intelligence Program (JMIP), Tactical Intelligence and Related Activities (TIARA).

[4] National Imagery and Mapping Agency (NIMA), created from the combination of the Defense Mapping Agency (DMA) and the National Photographic Interpretation Center (NPIC) that was previously dedicated to strategic analysis of imagery within the Central Intelligence Agency (CIA). There are many who believe this combination was ill-advised, and that the CIA should have restored to it offices for imagery, signals, and measurement analysis.

[5] One expert reviewer observes that those recommending the consolidation of CIA and DoD clandestine services do not understand the Defense Humint Service focus on fairly primitive forms of counterintelligence and a bureaucratic process of documentation and approvals.

[6] The USIP is my own term, intended to capture the totality of the U.S. intelligence budget including the National Foreign Intelligence Program (NFIP), the Joint Military Intelligence Program (JMIP) that replaced the General Defense Intelligence Program (GDIP), the Tactical Intelligence and Related Activities (TIARA) budget, and the odds and ends in the Department of Energy, the Federal Bureau of Investigation, and the Department of State.

Summary of Current Intelligence Reform Literature

The first book in this two-book set, *ON INTELLIGENCE: Spies and Secrecy in an Open World*, contains 495 pages of detailed examination of the existing status of the U.S. Intelligence Community, and that will not be repeated here. However, by way of setting the stage for the remainder of the book, below are summarized the six challenges identified by the author in 1990:

1. Intelligence for Public Programs[8]
2. Indications & Warning for Revolutionary Threats
3. Counterintelligence & Operational Security
4. Information Technology Strategy
5. Requirements System
6. Resource Alignments

In brief, eleven years ago, it was clear that intelligence was not meeting the needs of public programs; that we did not have adequate indications & warning methods for dealing with revolutionary surprise; that our counterintelligence and operational security cadres were well below par;[9] that we did not have an information technology strategy for integrating information across agencies and from different disciplines; that our requirements system was broken; and that our resources were out of alignment—too much money for technical collection and almost none for clandestine human collection, all-source analysis, processing, or counterintelligence. All this was known in

---

[7] Commission on the Roles and Capabilities of the United States Intelligence Community, *Preparing for the 21st Century: An Appraisal of U.S. Intelligence*, 1 March 1996. Also *IC21: Intelligence Community in the 21st Century*, a Staff Study of the Permanent Select Committee on Intelligence, House of Representatives, 104th Congress, 4 March 1996.

[8] Public Programs encompass both U.S. government operations that are not inherently associated with classified defense or intelligence activities, and include the other departments and agencies of the U.S. government (especially Treasury and Commerce but also Interior and others) as well as Public Diplomacy or outreach to foreign public.

[9] Among the best references pertinent to Army counterintelligence are those by Colonel Stuart Herrington, including "Reviving DoD Strategic Counterintelligence: An Appeal to the 'NCIX'," *American Intelligence Journal* (Winter 2000/2001), and his book, *Traitors Among Us: Inside the Spy Catcher's World* (Presidio Press, 1999).

1990.[10] None of it has been adequately addressed to date, and there are no signs that 9-11 is changing anything substantial about how we do business.

It was also clear, as set forth in the chapter on "Avoiding Strategic Intelligence Failures", first published in 1991, that we were paying cursory attention to both clandestine and open source collection; and that we suffered from severe mind-set inertia—a mind-set that discounted any threat from individual "ragheads."[11]

Finally, in the chapter, "A Critical Evaluation of U.S. National Intelligence Capabilities," we identified deficiencies at the strategic, operational, tactical and technical levels, with an average grade, in terms of emerging threats, of a "D."[12] Our unwillingness to shift from conventional threat analysis to unconventional threat analysis has cost us dearly.

Although this book was unusual for its level of detail, including a specification of $11.6 billion dollars a year in funding that is counterproductive and could be fruitfully redirected toward the new needs of the new craft of intelligence, it was not alone. In the years 1999-2001 there were no less than eleven other books apart from this one, focused specifically on intelligence reform.[13]

Never before in America's history have there been, in the space of only two years, so much attention to the urgency of repairing America's intelligence and counterintelligence capabilities. In the aggregate these books comprise a *critical mass* of public opinion about much-needed change. The best of them

---

[10] Spending too much money on technical collection has plagued the community since the 1970's. For an original statement on this and six other major deficiencies, see Loch Johnson, "Seven Sins of Strategic Intelligence", *World Affairs* (Fall 1983). Nothing has changed! This chapter was first published in the *American Intelligence Journal* (hereafter *AIJ*) in the Summer/Fall 1990 issue.

[11] *AIJ* (Autumn 1991).

[12] First published in the *International Journal of Intelligence and Counterintelligence* (Summer 1993).

[13] These books are all listed at www.council-on-intelligence.org, with direct clickable URLs to their respective pages at www.amazon.com.

books are summarized very succinctly here.[14]   Others are discussed in the annotated bibliography.

Intelligence Flaws Inherent in the Original Design

Dr. Amy Zegart[15] breaks new ground in understanding the bureaucratic and political realities that surrounded the emergence of the National Security Council, the Joint Chiefs of Staff, and the Central Intelligence Agency. The CIA was weak by design, strongly opposed by the military services from the beginning. Its covert activities emerged as a Presidential prerogative, unopposed by others in part because it kept CIA from being effective at coordinated analysis, for which it had neither the power nor the talent. [16]

Most usefully, she presents a new institutionalist theory of bureaucracy that gives full weight to the original design, the political players including the bureaucrats themselves, and external events. Unlike domestic agencies that have strong interest groups, open information, legislative domain, and unconnected bureaucracies, the author finds that national security agencies, being characterized by weak interest groups, secrecy, executive domain, and connected bureaucracies, evolve differently from other bureaucracies, and are much harder to reform.

On balance, Dr. Zegart finds that intelligence per se, in contrast to defense or domestic issues, is simply not worth the time and Presidential political capital needed to fix but that if reform is in the air, the President should either pound on the table and put the full weight of their office behind a substantive reform proposal, or walk away from any reform at all-the middle road will not successful.[17]

---

[14] Longer reviews by the author, for over 225 books relevant to the new craft of intelligence, are also readily available at www.amazon.com.

[15] Dr. Zegart studied under Dr. Condi Rice, today the National Security Advisor to the President, and developed this award-winning dissertation under the direction of Dr. Rice when both were at Stanford University.

[16] Amy Zegart, *Flawed by Design: the Evolution of the CIA, JCS, and NSC* (Stanford University Press, 2000), 342 pages.

[17] It could be said that the months following the 11 September 2001 attacks on America probably represent a sole and unique opportunity for introducing legislation to correct the long-standing deficiencies in U.S. intelligence.

Getting at "Best Truth" Within a Larger Information Environment

Dr. Bruce Berkowitz and Mr. Allan Goodman, speaking from the academic-practitioner perspective, place intelligence in the larger context of information, and draw a plethora of useful comparisons with emerging private sector capabilities and standards. They place strong emphasis on the emerging issues (not necessarily threats) related to ethnic, religious, and geopolitical confrontation, and are acutely sensitive to the new power of non-governmental organizations and non-state actors. "[18]

The heart of their book is captured in three guidelines for the new process: focus on understanding the consumer's priorities; minimize the investment in fixed hardware and personnel; and create a system that can draw freely on commercial capabilities where applicable (as they often will be).

Their chapter on the failure of the bureaucratic model for intelligence, and the need to adopt the virtual model—one that permits analysts to draw at will on diverse open sources—is well presented and compelling.

Non-Traditional Threats and Intelligence

Dr. Loch Johnson provides a tour d'horizon on both the deficiencies of today's highly fragmented and bureaucratized archipelago of independent fiefdoms, as well as the "new intelligence agenda" that places public health and the environment near the top of the list of topics to be covered by spies and satellites. [19]

Highlights of his excellent work, a new standard in terms of currency and breadth, include his informed judgment that most of what is in the "base" budget of the community should be resurrected for reexamination, and that at least 20% of the budget (roughly $6 billion per year) could be cut. [20]

---

[18] Bruce Berkowitz and Allen Goodman, *BEST TRUTH: Intelligence in the Information Age* (Yale, 2000), 224 pages.

[19] Loch Johnson, Bombs, Bugs, Drugs, and Thugs: Intelligence and America's Quest for Security (New York University Press, 2000), 288 pages.

[20] Dr. Johnson has on several occasions referred to a direct conversation in the early 1990's with then Director of Central Intelligence Jim Woolsey in which the DCI himself stated that fully a third of the intelligence community budget could be cut.

His overviews of the various cultures within the Central Intelligence Agency, of the myths of intelligence, and of the possibilities for burden sharing all merit close review.

The conclusion that one might drew from Dr. Johnson's latest work is that the U.S. Government as a whole has completely missed the dawn of the Information Age. We have simply have not adapted the cheap and responsive tools of the Internet to our needs, nor have we employed the Internet to share the financial as well as the intellectual and time burdens of achieving "Global Coverage."

Dr. Johnson has touched on what must be the core competency of government in the Information Age: how precisely do we go about collecting, analyzing, and disseminating information, and creating tailored intelligence, when we are all inter-dependent across national, legal bureaucratic, and cultural boundaries? This is not about secrecy versus openness, but rather about whether Government Operations as a whole are taking place with the sources, methods, and tools of this century, or the last.

Mind-Sets and Strategic Blunders

Mr. Willard Matthias, a former senior analysts with the Central Intelligence Agency, documents in great detail a number of extremely serious mistakes on the part of U.S. policy makers from World War II through to Reagan years, while also recounting the history of how the Pentagon helped destroy CIA's independent assessments capability. [21]

Time and time again throughout his work one sees references to "state of mind" and "mindset", and this is important. The author has a very fine grasp of how debilitating ingrained mindsets can be—the military mindset that focuses on buying more and more high technology even though it is demonstrably irrelevant to our most urgent strategic needs; the policy mindset that emphasizes the need for a tangible "main enemy" even as we destroy the environment and ignore catastrophic diseases and failed states; and the

---

[21] Willard C. Matthias, *America's Strategic Blunders: Intelligence Analysis and National Security Policy, 1936-1991* (Pennsylvania State University Press, 2001), 367 pages.

intelligence mindset that values secrecy and blind loyalty over public disclosure and public service.

Especially interesting is the account of the author's past responsibility for preparing the "Estimate of the World Situation", and how well he distinguishes between the great days when such estimates were both produced and consumed, and today's state of affairs, where only "hard targets" are the object of our obsession, and "rest of the world" is poorly addressed.

The integrity of intelligence, or lack thereof is a constant theme.

Warning as a Management Problem Not a Collection Problem

Maj Kristan Wheaton, a defense attaché still in service, has developed a thoughtful explanation on the conflict between the senior decision-maker's attention span (can only think about billion-dollar problems) and the early warning that *is* available but cannot break through to the always over-burdened, sometimes arrogant, and rarely strategic top boss. [22]

His work offers solutions on how to establish a scouting system that can be heard at the highest levels *in time*. It focuses on human understanding and human engagement with the world, and makes it clear that technology has almost nothing to do with how well we cope with the external environment that defines our future.

Additionally, Maj Wheaton excels at showing the deep importance of historical and cultural understanding as part of current political, operational, and all-source intelligence competency.

Signals Intelligence and Operations Security

Mr. James Bamford documents three vital areas of concern regarding signals intelligence (SIGINT). First, he shows how we consistently lack sufficient linguists and sufficient focus beyond Russia, China, and Europe. From North Korea to the Middle East to Somalia, Haiti, and Bosnia, the National Security Agency (NSA) is simply not up to the task of monitoring

---

[22] Kristan J. Wheaton, The Warning Solution: Intelligent Analysis in the Age of Information Overload (AFCEA International Press, 2001), 89 pages.

foreign language communications—not for a lack of money, but for a lack of linguists (i.e. a continuing lack of priority for other languages including Arabic and Hebrew).[23]

Secondly, Mr. Bamford provides an indictment of the U.S. military chain of command, from Viet-Nam to this day, for its failure to practice Operational Security (OPSEC). Especially troubling is his excellent look at how a North Vietnamese SIGINT cadre of 5,000 used everything from Soviet intercept equipment to tunnels dug right up under G-3 shops, to completely win the signals battle and with it, the war.

Finally, at the strategic level, it is important to note his observations on how SIGINT can be completely defeated when the enemy practices good OPSEC. Osama bin Laden needed a little help from an indiscreet politician to understand his vulnerabilities, but he went off the air when he finally got it. Imagery Intelligence (IMINT) is particularly essential when SIGINT blacks out [and, although Mr. Bamford does not address this, deep non-official cover clandestine intelligence is always needed in the most out of the way places where we generally do not target technical capabilities or where technical capabilities cannot reach—or where U.S. Embassies are suddenly expelled without prior notice.]

Reshaping Intelligence in the Information Age: The Bottom Line

Dr. Greg Treverton's is arguably the single best and most elegant presentation of why our $30 billion a year intelligence industry must be turned upside down and shift resources away from secret satellite technology and toward analysis, analytic tools, and access to open sources of information.[24]

He focuses on the fact that intelligence is about getting useful tailored information to the policy consumer, not about secrets per se. He is perhaps the best spokesperson for the view that the old paradigm—collecting secrets at great expense about a single enemy—must be replaced by the new paradigm—

---

[23] James Bamford, *Body of Secrets: Anatomy of the Ultra-Secret National Security Agency—From the Cold War Through the Dawn of a New Century* (Doubleday, 2001), 721 pages. See Chapter 2, note 6 on page 16 for a list of the 29 essential languages.

[24] Gregory D. Treverton, *Reshaping National Intelligence for an Age of Information* (Cambridge University Press, 2001), 282 pages.

making sense of vast quantities of information that is not secret and covers a diversity of constantly changing targets. He also focuses on the selection and intelligent analysis of information rather than the collection of isolated secrets—on making the most of open information.

Dr. Treverton's work is rich with anecdotal examples and makes a compelling case for dismantling the current intelligence stovepipes while simultaneously dismantling the culture of secrecy that prevents the sharing of useful information, not just within the Nation (e.g. with state and local law enforcement) but with coalition government and non-government allies of the moment.

He firmly believes that both the intelligence community budget and as much intelligence analysis as possible should be made public and be in the public service.

Just In and Highly Relevant

As this book was in its final editing and indexing phase, two books were brought to my attention , books whose real-world intelligence experiences with terrorism and insurgency are very relevant to how citizen-taxpayers should perceive the existing intelligence and policy situation in the aftermath of 9-11.

Mr. George Allen, the one person in American intelligence who followed Vietnamese matters almost from the inception of our involvement, for over seventeen years, has recently published a personal account that on the one hand celebrates the competency of American intelligence on this issue over time, and on the other documents the consistent manner in which policy-makers refused to listen to accurate intelligence estimates, while their Generals and Ambassadors stationed in Viet-Nam steadfastly "cooked the books."[25] As our policy-makers speak publicly about the "axis of evil" and clearly appear to have made up their minds with or without the benefit of intelligence, Mr. Allen's perspectives on just how chaotic and self-centered and uninformed national

---

[25] Others, notably Sam Adams in *War of Numbers* (South Royalton, 1994), and Bruce E. Jones in *War without Windows: A True Account of a Young Army Officer Trapped in an Intelligence Cover-Up in Vietnam* (Berkley, 1987) have documented the corruption of intelligence by military and diplomatic stake-holders, but Allen's book will stand as the most comprehensive, balanced account of the policy break-downs that occurred across several decades.

security policy can be, are of great value to citizen-voters looking ahead and seeking new means for both holding elected officials accountable, and for deciding which officials to elect in the future.

Mr. Robert Baer, a decorated veteran of two decades of clandestine operations against terrorists, has just published what may be the most damning book ever on the complete decline of America's spy service. He testifies, with gripping anecdotes and great credibility, to the gradual loss of virtually all our clandestine capabilities in the Middle East and with respect to terrorism. His book is all the more important to citizens because the President of the United States is being told by the Director of Central Intelligence that we have a "heavy asset base" and have everything we need to carry out a successful worldwide attack on terrorism.[26] The truth lies somewhere between these two positions, but as a former case officer who spent several years on the terrorist target, I believe that 75% of the weight is on Baer's side, and citizen-voters need to read his book and judge for themselves. How capable our clandestine service is against terrorism is very important. How accurately we communicate that capability, or lack thereof, to the President of the United States of America is something else again. Both are valid concerns for every citizen-voter.

A Critical Mass of Informed Public Opinion

Taken together with another five books[27] focused specifically on intelligence deficiencies and needed reform, and given the extraordinary purchases of these books by the public in the aftermath of 9-11, this matter of how effective our national intelligence and counterintelligence services are, appears to have achieved some standing in the public mind.

---

[26] As reported on page A13 in *The Washington Post* of 31 January 2002, documenting by the accounts of those present what was said at a special meeting of senior advisors with the President on 15 September 2001, at Camp David.

[27] The other intelligence reform books that merit attention but are not discussed here include: Craig Eisendrath (editor), *National Insecurity: U.S. Intelligence After the Cold War* (Temple University Press, 1999), 296 pages; Arthur Hulnick, *Fixing the Spy Machine: Preparing American Intelligence for the 21st Century* (Praeger Publishing, 2000), 248 pages; Mark Lowenthal, *Intelligence: From Secrets to Policy* (Congressional Quarterly Press, 1999), 276 pages; and David F. Rudgers, *Creating the Secret State: The Origins of the Central Intelligence Agency, 1943-1947* (University Press of Kansas, 2000), 246 pages.

Part II:
Global Threats and
Our Mis-Spent Tax Dollars

Neither our schools, nor the media, nor our intelligence community, are adequately informing our citizens or our elected and appointed officials, of the true threats to our homeland that are flourishing in every clime and place. There appears to be a vast plain of ignorance or complacency that has cast a pall over what should be a vibrant and concerned democracy. Few realize that there are 29 complex emergencies in this world; that 67 countries have hundreds of thousands of refugees each; that 59 countries are suffering plagues and epidemics of extraordinary proportions; that 27 countries are experiencing famine and starvation across their lands; and perhaps worst of all, that today, this minute, there are 18 active genocide campaigns going on, killings tens of thousands or more each year. Can our homeland long endure in the face of these global holocausts?

Part II strives to orient the citizen-voter as to the "ground truth"—the really fundamental realities of the external world that must inevitably threaten both our national security and our national prosperity. It is simply not true that we can maintain our quality of life and our domestic tranquillity in isolation from what is happening around the world. Billions of people perceive America to be a direct threat to their current and future security as well as prosperity. If we do not get a grip on this, and if we as citizens do not prevail on our government to pay greater heed to the urgent need for both increased non-military assistance to the rest of the world, and increased controls on corporate consumerism that enervates disadvantaged countries and further weakens their prospects for development, then we will not be able to assure our children and our grandchildren and their future generations the kind of security and prosperity that we ourselves have achieved, albeit unevenly across our social classes and ethnic groups. There are four distinct threat types that we must confront, but our government is only paying serious attention to one of the four.

Chapter 6, "Global Conditions Favoring Terrorism," provides an overview of trends and types of global conflict; introduces the concept of strategic generalizations relevant to how we train, equip, and organize our forces; and outlines several major contributors to global instability that ultimately reduce homeland security.

Chapter 7, "Plagues, Toxic Bombs, Resource Wars, & Water Shortages," briefly explores both the global condition with respect to major outbreaks of plagues and other epidemics overseas that can directly threaten our homeland, as well as how our chlorine-based industries are placing entire communities at risk to mass casualties. Additionally, around the world, fighting for the control of key resources, and for water, our most precious and vanishing resource, sets the stage for "endless conflict."

Chapter 8, "Overview of Global Genocide," is meant to shock and inform. Drawing on the work of two top experts on genocide, it lays out very precisely both the on-going and the historical genocide campaigns—eighteen active today, almost as many dormant, and a total of seventy campaigns over the course of history. We cannot be safe at home if we do not recognize and address the mass murders occurring around the globe.

Chapter 9, "Four Threat Types and Three Strategic Scenarios," provides an explanation of the four threat types we must confront, only one of which is being addressed properly. This chapter also simplifies the entire matter of the global threat in relation to homeland security with three simple scenarios: the break-out scenario (illegal immigrants flood America, Europe, and Australia); the black death scenario (continent-wide plagues in Near East and Africa migrate quickly to the West); and the barricade scenario, where the West uses either wealth to eradicate global problems, or force to contain them. It is highly unlikely that force will suffice. It may be that only citizen education and civic action can save the world—this is for you to decide.

Chapter 10, "A Command Sense National Security Strategy," is an introduction to some of the issues that are not being decided in our favor today. Trade-offs between hard (military) power and soft (diplomatic, economic, intelligence) power are not being made and the so-called Revolution in Military Affairs (RMA) is directing the bulk of our spending toward esoteric and very expensive systems that will not stand the test of sustained battle. A new core force, four types of forces, and a modern Navy are discussed.

60

Global Conditions Favoring Terrorism

You may not be interested in war,
but war is interested in you.

Trotsky

We can't be successful in fighting terrorism unless we
fight that other axis of evil—poverty, disease and ignorance.

George Soros

In the aftermath of 9-11, America began to read about terrorism, Islam, and global instability in a way never before evident. Not since SPUTNIK and the shock of that advance, which led to huge investments in teaching science & technology, have Americans been so surprised at their level of ignorance—in this case, about what is going on beyond the water's edge. This chapter does not explain terrorism, conflict, crime, or corruption. Nor does it seek to summarize or supplant the many superb books on these various topics that are readily available via Amazon or through conventional bookstores. Instead this chapter provides an overview of the actual situation around the world as depicted in the *World Conflict & Human Rights Map 2000*, a marvelous integrative efforts that brings together the deep knowledge of the following organizations: the World Group on the Causes of War (AKUF) at the University of Hamburg, Germany; the Heidelberg Institute for International Conflict Research (HIIK), Germany; the Department of Peace and Conflict Research (DPCR), University of Upsala, Sweden; Stockholm International Peace Research Institute (SIPRI), Sweden; and the Interdisciplinary Research Program on Root Causes of Human Rights Violations (PIOOM), University of Leiden, Netherlands.[1]

---

[1] This map, and the eight long (European length) pages of text and tables on the reverse, are in my judgment the world's finest example of open source information. Copies can

Below is a black & white depiction of the PIOOM map. In color, as a wall chart, it is a stunning graphic that powerfully communicates all that our schools, our media, and our traditional intelligence community have failed to grasp or explain to us or our elected representatives. The world is at war with itself. This Third World War is creating billions of dispossessed, and from within those billions emerge all manner of threats to the American, European, and Australian homelands: terrorism, crime, corruption, and plagues, to name just the top four.

With the exception of Greenland, Canada, the United States of America, Europe including the Nordic Countries, Australia, New Zealand, and just two countries in Africa, the world is torn by pervasive violent conflict.

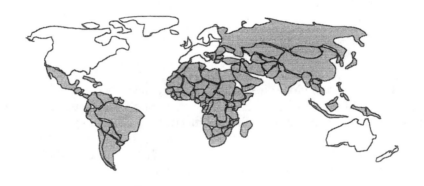

Source: PIOOM (NL), data with
permission © 2000 A. Jongman

Figure 13: World at War

be ordered for $15 retail, $5 in bulk (100+), from the Institute for International Mediation and Conflict Resolution (IIMCR) in Washington, D.C., (202) 347-2042; the Goals for Americans Foundation in St. Louis, MO, (314) 423-9777; or PIOOM itself in the Netherlands, ++(31 71) 527 3861. The 2001 map should be available by April 2002.

Each day, today, we have *on-going* 26 severe low-intensity conflicts that have killed over 300,000 people in 1999 alone, and have killed roughly 8 million over time. There are 78 less severe low-intensity conflicts, and over 178 violent political conflicts internal to specific nation-states, all going on today.

India, Nigeria, Indonesia, Pakistan, Colombia, China, Russia, Uganda, Ethiopia, and Sudan, all populous countries, are engaged, right this minute, in between 6 and 32 conflicts *each!*[2]

The trend lines are disturbing—although direct confrontations between states and their forces are generally leveling off, both unconventional conflicts and internal conflicts are on the rise.

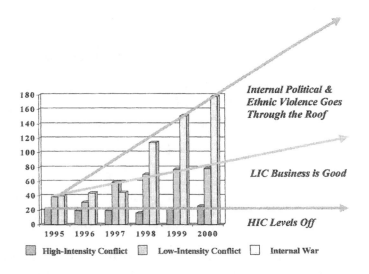

Figure 14: Trends in Global Conflict

---

[2] These numbers will change from year to year depending on who's counting and other circumstances. That does not matter—the breadth and complexity of these conflicts—most of them with severe ethnic and religious confrontations included, cannot be denied once recognized. America's problem has been it's willful ignorance and inattention.

In my view, the actual numbers of conflicts that are counted matter less than two facts: first, that the trend line is upwards for internal conflicts, and second, that in many cases the conflicts are so persistent that the societies actually lose any capability for stabilization in the absence of comprehensive external involvement and investment.[3]

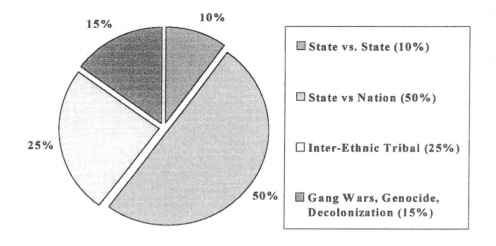

Figure 15: Types of Global Conflict

What should really strike the citizen-taxpayer here is the disconnect between the kinds of conflict that exist around the world, and how we spend our tax dollars on defense. The Pentagon that we have today, and the Pentagon that is being funded by the post 9-11 budget, remains totally focused on very expensive and very complex technical systems that are largely useless in the

---

[3] Monty Marshall, *Third World War: System, Process, and Conflict Dynamics* (Rowman & Littlefield, 1999) identifies six Protracted Conflict Regions (PCR): East Asia, Middle East, South(ern) Africa, Central America, South Asia, and Southeast Asia.

conduct of unconventional operations or the imposition of peace within a complex emergency situation, of which there are 29 declared by the United Nations. We have forces optimized for nuclear and conventional warfare, yet the Third World War is largely unconventional and at the sub-state level.

Worse yet, our conventional military forces have been created under the mantra of "bigger, faster, heavier" without ever stopping to consider what I term "strategic generalizations." The below table compares our existing force structure to real-world constraints of time and geography and climate.[4]

Real-World Condition	U.S. Force Structure	Comment
Need Embassy protection within 24 hours in crisis.	Ships 4-6 days away from anywhere because of emphasis on big decks.	Need 450 ship Navy with many small versatile platforms.[5]
Ports cannot be used in half the countries of concern.	Big ships need deep ports and larger turning radius.	Need 450 ship Navy with many small versatile platforms.
Most countries, even in the Third World, have airports suitable for landing forces.	Extremely limited air transports prevent deployment of substantive forces in <90 days.	Need major investments in strategic air lift for artillery, vehicles, rotor aircraft.
Aviation day hot (80°) and humid more often than not.	Both USAF and USN build aircraft to a warm (65°) day that is not humid.	Fly half as far, carry half as much, loiter time over battlefield is severely limited.
Bridges limited to 30 tons, sometimes 10-20	Main battle tank weighs 70 tons, heavy artillery and missiles 40 tons plus.	Biggest and most expensive assets stay home most of the time.
Line of sight distance in most countries is under 1000 meters.	Optimized for stand-off engagements at 3,000 meters and up.	We can't put it all together in close quarters.
1/4 mountains, 1/4 jungle, 1/4 urban	Optimized for plains and deserts.	Can't do mountains, intelligence helpless.

Figure 16: Real-World Strategic Generalizations

[4] These generalizations are drawn from *Overview of Programming and Planning Factors for Expeditionary Operations in the Third World* (Marine Corps Combat Development Command, March 1990). The author served as the study director for this endeavor, which has been institutionalized as the *Expeditionary Factors Study* and is now in its fourth generation.

[5] Cf. "Muddy Waters, Rusting Buckets: A Skeptical Assessment of U.S. Naval Effectiveness in the 21st Century", www.defensedaily.com/reports/gonavy.htm (17 November 1999).

Apart from our continued inattention to the realities of conflict and the conditions under which we must fight, there are many other aspects of real world instability that have a direct bearing on homeland security.

Complex Emergencies 29 Countries		**Peacekeeping Forces** 18 UN, 20 Other	
Refugees/Displaced 67 Countries		**Landmines** 62 Countries	
Food Security 27 Countries		**Torture Common** 94 Countries	
Modern Plagues* 59 Countries & Rising		**Corruption Common** 78 Countries	
Child Soldiers 42 Countries		**Censorship Very High** 63 Countries	

**State of the World Atlas* (1997),
all others from PIOOM Map

Figure 17: State of the Real World

The United Nations, active all over the world, as are other major non-governmental organizations such as the International Committee of the Red Cross (ICRC), has a term for ugly situations that confound even the combined resources of all of the governments whose resources the United Nations might bring to bear. They call these "complex emergencies." There are twenty-nine of them.[6] If we are to be safe and prosperous in this world, citizen-taxpayers, and their elected representatives, must understand these harsh realities.

---

[6] As of 2000, Croatia, Chechnya, Georgia in Russia, Azerbaijan, Armenia, Tajikistan, Bosnia-Herzegovina, Yugoslavia, Kosovo, Iraq, Afghanistan, Kenya, Congo-Brazzaville, Sudan, Congo-Zaire, Tanzania, Uganda, Eritea, Angola, Rwanda, Central

Below is a table of countries with displaced populations as of 1999.

1 Million Plus	500K – 1 Million	100K – 500K	100K or Less
Russia	Turkey	Cyprus	Slovenia
Bosnia-Herzegovina	Azerbaijan	Georgia	Macedonia
Palestinians	Yugoslavia	Armenia	Uzbekistan
Iraq	Kosovo		Tajikistan
Afghanistan	Sri Lanka	Israel	Iran
	India	Kuwait	Egypt
		Lebanon	Bangladesh
Sudan	Congo-Brazz.	Algeria	Namibia
Congo (Zaire)	Eritea	Syria	Botswana
Angola	Rwanda	Bhutan	Ghana
Burundi	Sierra Leone	Kenya	Togo
	Somalia	Uganda	Mauritania
		Ethiopia	Djibouti
		Liberia	Nigeria
			Senegal
			Mali
			Chad
			Guinea Bissau
Colombia		El Salvador	Mexico[7]
		Guatemala	Cuba
			Peru
			Nicaragua
			Haiti
Burma (Myanmar)		Philippines	Indonesia
		China (PRC)[8]	Cambodia
		Vietnam	Laos
			North Korea

Figure 18: Refugees and Internally Displaced Persons

African Republic, Guinea Bissau, Burundi, Ethiopia, Sierra Leone, Liberia, Somalia, Indonesia, North Korea.

[7] Mexico strikes me as severely under-represented given the degree to which the Mexican government actively encourages both legal and illegal emigration to the United States in order to reduce socio-economic pressures within its own borders.

[8] China also appears to be severely underrepresented given both earlier river floods, the displacements associated with its Three Gorges project, and its active strategy of exporting individuals into Russian territories.

Just glancing over this table, if one wishes to seek some form of correlation between terrorism and refugee status—or at least the potential for terrorism to be attractive—then it is worth noting which countries have the very highest number of refugees and displaced persons in 1999.

Food scarcity is a contributing condition leading to increased migration but only one such condition. There are twenty-seven countries listed as suffering from severe food scarcity in 1999; sometimes this is deliberate, as in the northern Sudan policy of starving two million southern Sudanese to death.

Modern plagues are covered in Chapter 7, along with toxic waste and related environmental threats to national security and national prosperity.

Child soldiers active in 42 countries, peacekeeping forces active in 38 countries, landmines scattered over 62 countries, torture common in 94 countries, corruption common in 72 countries, censorship very high in 63 countries—these are but indicators of the very dangerous state of the real world. If our citizens and our elected representatives are oblivious to these harsh truths, then we cannot expect to protect ourselves because we will not be voting for the right national security programs.

We do not have a national security strategy, and consequently a reasonable national security budget and acquisition plan, because we have lost touch with global realities. Both our national intelligence and our national defense capabilities are defined by what the military-industrial-congressional complex wants to build, rather than by what we need or by what represents the best value for the taxpayer. This book seeks to educate the citizen-taxpayer so that they can begin to hold their elected representatives, at all levels, accountable for making informed judgments that respect global realities, rather than selfish political judgments influenced primarily by cash contributions.[9]

---

[9] Our Senators and Representatives very properly concern themselves with funding programs that in turn create jobs within their States or Districts. However, in the absence of campaign finance reform we have an endless cycle in which the military-industrial complex is making the largest payments, in turn creating jobs that lead to even more waste of the taxpayer dollar. If citizens, and their elected officials, were to practice the "new craft of intelligence," they would be able to identify priorities and programs that would create the same amount of jobs, but be relevant to the real needs of the world as well as our own homeland security and prosperity.

Plagues, Toxic Bombs, Resource Wars & Water Shortages

Tens of millions are dying of new, untreatable forms of tuberculosis, malaria, strep, staph, and other organisms. Millions more are dying of AIDS. Measles and other vaccine-preventable diseases kill hundreds of thousands more children every year.

The idea that the health of every nation depends on the health of all others is not an empty piety but an epidemiological fact.

Laurie Garrett[1]

Disease and toxic bombs—including tanker cars full of chlorine—are a much greater threat to America than any conventional attack. Leaving aside the chaos that could be caused by a broad asymmetric attack against the homeland by several terrorist and extremist groups in concert, the reality is that a combination of extreme conditions in Africa, India, and other countries, combined with historically high levels of antibiotic administration, especially in Russia but also in Europe and the United States of America, have created severe biological threats to national security and national prosperity—at the same time that we are perpetuating a very dangerous reliance on chlorine as the foundation for our plastics industry, and neglecting the health of the oceans.

The other great threat, primarily to future generations, is that represented by the alarming downward spiral of water supplies—in one instance, the Aral Sea, once 28,000 square kilometers, simply vanishing to be replaced by a wicked wind-blown brew of toxic chemicals—and the equally alarming upward spiral of both energy consumption in the aggregate and its varied detrimental effects upon the Earth.

---

[1] Laurie Garrett, *BETRAYAL OF TRUST: The Collapse of Global Public Health* (Hyperion, 2000), cover and page 9.

69

Public Health—One World, Like It or Not

I seriously doubt whether anyone could improve on the in-depth look at global public health carried out by Laurie Garrett. Here are just a few snapshots from her 754-page book:

Bubonic plague and pneumonic plague erupted in India in 1994. Although the actual deaths were limited to fifty-six, with another 6,500 cases of treatable infection, 450,000 to 600,000 people—including most of the private physicians—fled the immediate area of the plague and caused a world-wide panic. The Bombay stock market crashed and many nations banned all travelers, goods, and transport from India. Now for the scary part: the U.S. Center for Disease Control had only one half-time scientist with expertise in the plague; none of the Western countries, including the United States, had quarantine programs at their ports of entry or anyone able to screen potential plague carriers. Laboratories around the world were not capable of screening for plague and the World Health Organization (WHO) was not capable of responding effectively. This plague is capable of lying dormant in soil for extended periods, over fifteen years, before emerging again in rats and fleas and then domesticated animals and humans.

Ebola virus flourished in the Congo (Zaire) in 1995 after a nineteen-year break. This incurable virus spread quickly because of the complete lack of a public health infrastructure—including laboratories capable of safely testing for this very hazardous disease. Even in the West, budget cuts and mandated down-sizing made it impossible to surge specialists and laboratories against this challenge. The available budget for Ebola for the WHO was less than $10,000. By 1995 WHO had only one individual monitoring tropical epidemics and no capabilities for emergency responses. Among the scary facts: while Ebola broke out in January of 1995, the world did not hear of it until May of the same year. As travelers got out, the disease was actually spread within hospitals unable to diagnose and then quarantine the victim. Hospitals became places of infection rather than healing.

In the early 1990's, coincident with the collapse of the Soviet Union, a series of epidemics spread across the twelve time zones—diphtheria, hepatitis, flue, typhoid, cholera, and dysentery infected hundreds of thousands. AIDs and sexual diseases exploded. Now for the troubling stuff: a history, during the good years, of over-prescribing antibiotics, creating resistant strains; a

70

command economy approach to water and sewage pipes put the sewage pipes above the water pipes, in the same trenches, ultimately infecting the drinking water when the sewage pipes cracked; a long history of ignoring pollution to the point that half the drinking supply is unsafe; tuberculosis runs out of control in Russian prisons; and finally, the piece de resistance, all this good stuff jumps out of Russia and former Soviet Union states, not only through their own travelers to the west, but through prosperous European businessmen who pop over for sexual vacations and then come to America looking for a similar good time.....making casual sex with new partners much more hazardous to your health than anyone might imagine.[2]

The bottom line, which Garrett arduously and excellently documents, is that America will never be safe from plagues and epidemics unless we support both a strong public health infrastructure at home, and an equally robust world-wide public health administration that is both international and embedded in every country down to the village level.

Environmental Responsibility at Home and Abroad

Toxic waste that we have dumped into the earth or disposed of improperly is the least of our problems. While serious, the cumulative negative effects of large deposits of waste are now understood, and the passing of the Superfund Law in 1980 is indicative of the gradual seriousness with which this threat is taken.[3]

---

[2] While books about germs and biological warfare are much in vogue these days, Garrett has written the definitive book as far as the health of America's public goes. It is a monster and these few examples drawn from her meticulous and carefully documented effort can only serve to point the reader toward the annotated bibliography. If the new craft of intelligence were in effect, a citizen would be able to enter their zip code at a public health web site, and immediately see the "state" of all public health investments relative to their location; a chart of all reported communicable diseases in relation to their location and spreading outwards with special emphasis on points having direct air and rail travel connections to the locality, and so on. Right now it is too hard for citizens to get a good sense of the actual state of affairs in this vital area.

[3] Al Gore, *Earth in the Balance: Ecology and the Human Spirit* (Houghton Mifflin, 1992), page 7. A number of other current books on the environment are featured in the annotated bibliography, including David Helvarg's *Blue Frontier: Saving America's Living Seas* (W. H. Freeman & Company, 2001); Brian Czech, *Shoveling Fuel for a Runaway Train: Errant Economists, Shameful Spenders, and a Plan to Stop Them All*

71

Much more pervasive, much more cumulative in its impact, and much deadlier in the long run, is chlorine, used either in direct applications, in intermediate applications to create plastics and other chemicals, or in the creation of organochlorine products.[4] All over America, outside major sewage plants and other locations, we have toxic bombs waiting to explode.

To comprehend the magnitude of this danger, it is helpful to recall the disaster in Bhopal, India.

> On the night of December 23, 1984, a dangerous chemical reaction occurred in the Union Carbide factory when a large amount of water got into the MIC storage tank # 610. The leak was first detected by workers about 11:30 p.m. when their eyes began to tear and burn. They informed their supervisor who failed to take action until it was too late. In that time, a large amount, about 40 tons of Methyl Isocyanate (MIC), poured out of the tank for nearly two hours and escaped into the air, spreading within eight kilometers downwind, over the city of nearly 900,000. Thousands of people were killed (estimates ranging as high as 4,000) in their sleep or as they fled in terror, and hundreds of thousands remain injured or affected (estimates range as high as 400,000) to this day.[5]

Had the airplane hijacked by terrorists and driven into the Pentagon been instead driven into the several train cars full of chlorine parked just outside the Washington, D.C. sewage treatment plant, it has been speculated that the combination of the chlorine and the burning airplane fuel would have produced a Bhopal-sized disaster in the National Capital Area.

9-11 has had a salutary effect on some cities that now realize that their tankers full of chlorine waiting to be used in waste water treatment plants as well as swimming pools are literally massive bombs waiting to be exploded and

---

(University of California, 2000); and Michael J. Novacek (ed.), *The Biodiversity Crisis: Losing What Counts* (American Museum of Natural History, 2001).
[4] Drawn from Joe Thornton, *Pandora's Poison: Chlorine, Health, and a New Environmental Strategy* (MIT Press, 2000).
[5] "TED Case Study" (American University, 1/11/97), at http://www.american.edu/TED/BHOPAL.HTM.

easily capable of recreating a Bhopal catastrophe within their jurisdictions. Unfortunately, industry has been less receptive. This is understandable—chlorine literally permeates the entire modern industrial and manufacturing base—but no longer acceptable. Citizens, as voters and stockholders, must act.

Resource Wars—The Hidden Agenda of Global Competition

There is no finer book on the topic of global resource wars than that written by Michael T. Klare, director of the Five College Program in Peace and World Security Studies based at Hampshire College in Amherst, Massachusetts.[6]

His survey of the global situation brings together an analysis of three intertwined conditions:

1) Rapidly increasing global demands for resources, stemming largely from population increases but also from advances in technical capabilities and new consumer-oriented ventures;

2) The consequent emergence of very significant shortages in resources, from water to energy to timber to raw minerals; and

3) The unusual degree to which major sources of key resources are located in areas claimed by more than one country or subject to the back-and-forth of international events—the collapse of the Soviet Union "freeing up" competition for the resources of the seven "stans"[7] as well as Armenia and Georgia on the one hand; the very unstable and murderous conditions in Africa and especially Central and Southern Africa on the other.

---

[6] Michael T. Klare, *RESOURCE WARS: The New Landscape of Global Conflict* (Henry Holt, 2001).
[7] Afghanistan, Azerbaijan, Kazakstan, Kyrgyzstan, Tajikistan, Turkmenistan, and Uzbekistan. The best book for understanding the geostrategic implications of both this resource arena and the related balance of power issues among Europe, Russia, China, Turkey, Iran and the United States on one side of the world, and the United States, China, Japan, India, Pakistan, the two Koreas, and the southern Muslim crescent on the other side of the world is that of Zbigniew Brzezinski, *The Grand Chessboard: American Primacy and Its Geostrategic Imperatives* (Harper Collins, 1997).

There is no substitute for buying and reading his book, as with most books cited in this citizen's guide. He concludes that only a robust international institution or series of institutions focused specifically on the challenges associated with managing scarce natural resources, could both avert major wars and develop means for allocating these resources.

He concludes with the observation that "The scientific and technical expertise of participating nations could be pooled in the search for new materials and production techniques." Later on in this book we will see that the "virtual intelligence community," a web-based and self-organizing transnational linking of the knowledge of both experts and citizens, is the fundamental pre-requisite for breaking out of the destructive spending and industrial patterns now common in the West.

He does not focus on demand reduction, so this merits a separate comment. As the next segment discusses, citizens rather than corporations waste most of the water (and by inference, most of the other resources). No matter how clever nations and experts might be, only citizens have the power to demand education, to establish new conventions and customs dedicated to the conservation of resources for future generations.[8]

WATER—the Most Precious Resource

If you read no other book in the near future than the extraordinary offering by Marq De Villers, *WATER: The Fate of Our Most Precious Resource*[9], this book of mine will have served you well. The author has

---

[8] It may sound idealistic, but at some point it would be helpful if a global international society, perhaps centered on a council of religious leaders with a larger outer ring of niche non-governmental advocacy organizations, were created with the specific purpose of serving as the representative of future generations. It is vital, if our children and grandchildren are to prosper, that much more care be given to making decisions that responsibly consider impacts on the "seventh generation" and that do not consume our seed corn because of the selfish coming together of corrupt politicians and equally corrupt corporate profiteers. Citizens have three things going for them: the vote, the power of the purse, and faith. Lacking here-to-fore, but now available, are the tools for no-cost networking at every level. If combined with the power of knowledge shared in a structured and responsible manner, there isn't a government or corporation in the world that can stand up to the power of the people united.

[9] (Houghton Mifflin, 2000).

74

combined both scholarly research and what I regard to be an extremely professional and comprehensive program of field research, from the Aral Sea

> *"the exposed seabed, now over 28,000 square kilometers, became a stew of salt, pesticide residues, and toxic chemicals; the strong winds in the region pick up more than 40 million tons of these poisonous sediments each year, and the contaminated dust storms that follow have caused the incidence of respiratory illnesses and cancers to explode."*

to the heart of China

> *"According to China's own figures, between 1983 and 1990 the number of cities short of water tripled to three hundred, almost half the cities in the country; those whose problem was described as 'serious' rose from forty to one hundred."*

Marq De Villers provides a thoughtful and well-structured look at every corner of the world, with special emphasis on the Middle East, the Tigris-Euphrates System, the Nile, the Americas, and China; and at the main human factors destroying our global water system:

• pollution,

• dams (that silt up and prevent nutrients from going downstream or flooding from rejuvenating the lower lands),

• irrigation (leading to salination such that hundreds of thousands of acres are now infertile and being taken out of production),

• over-engineering, and

• excessive water mining from aquifers, which are in serious danger of drying up in key areas in the US as well as overseas within the next twenty years.

His final chapter on solutions explores conservation, technical, and political options. Two of his assertions are especially pointed:

- first, that it is the average person, unaware of the fragility of our water system, that is doing the most damage, not the corporations or mega-farms; and

- second, that for the price of one military ship or equipped unit ($100 million), one can desalinate 100 million cubic meters of water.

The bottom line is clear: we are close to a tipping point toward catastrophe but solution are still within our grasp, and they require, not world government, but a virtual world system that permits the integrated management of all aspects of water demand as well supply. This book should be required reading for every citizen, student, and official.[10]

---

[10] The annotated bibliography to this book of mine is intended to stimulate the reader into at least considering the ideas of many other authors whose expertise in their chosen areas of interest cannot be replicated by either myself, or the average citizen. The whole point of the new craft of intelligence is to devise a web-based means whereby this kind of expertise can be routinely brought together, summarized, visualized, and made available to the average voter and buyer. Among the many books in the bibliography that I would especially recommend are those of Robert D. Kaplan, who combines historical and scholarly research with trenchant field observation (cf. *The Ends of the Earth: From Togo to Turkmenistan, from Iran to Cambodia—A Journey to the Frontiers of Anarchy* (Vintage, 1996)), and gloomy but compelling books by Robert S. McNamara and James G. Blight, *WILSON'S GHOST: Reducing the Risk of Conflict, Killing, and Catastrophe in the 21ˢᵗ Century* (Public Affairs, 2001) and by William Shawcross, *DELIVER US FROM EVIL: Peacekeepers, Warlords and a World of Endless Conflict* (Simon & Schuster, 2000). Let me be blunt: citizens cannot trust their elected officials—whether in the Administration or the Legislature—to read and understand these expert views. Given the physics of the 24-hour day and the competing demands of fund-raising and hand-holding, the typical elected official is forced to rely on pre-processed simplified and usually biased information, while also assigning value based on cash contributions rather than inherent wisdom. The new craft of intelligence gives the individual citizen, and citizens in the aggregate, the power to inform, to critique, and to engage. Many books that propose solutions are also included in the annotated bibliography and merit absorption by citizens, perhaps through citizen study groups and book clubs. Four in particular merit mention here: David L. Boren and Edward J. Perkins (contributing editors), *Preparing America's Foreign Policy for the 21ˢᵗ Century* (University of Oklahoma, 1999); Michael Howard, *The Invention of Peace* (Yale, 2000); Dalai Lama, *Ethics for a New Millenium* (Riverhead, 1999), and the rather practical but vital Michael O'Hanlon and Carol Graham, *A Half Penny on the Federal Dollar: The Future of Development Aid* (Brookings, 1997).

76

Overview of Global Genocide

> *Genocide—the deliberate destruction, usually through mass murder, of an ethnic, racial, or religious group—is the ultimate crime against humanity.*
>
> *John Heidenrich[1]*

> *We should not send our troops to stop ethnic cleansing and genocide in nations outside our strategic interest.*
>
> *George W. Bush[2]*

> *The "magnitude of human suffering" constitutes a threat to peace and security.*
>
> *United Nations[3]*

Nothing in this chapter is intended to suggest that the U.S. must become the world's policeman or somehow be responsible for "law and order" anywhere other than here at home. However, this chapter is intended to shock every reader with the depth of our ignorance—and consequently and concurrently, the ignorance of our politicians—with respect to genocide. There are, today, eighteen (18) active genocide campaigns going on around the world, killing upwards from 140,000 people in 2001; there are fifty-three (53) other genocide campaigns brewing, and a total of seventy-one (71) distinct campaigns of genocide or politicide (politically-inspired mass killings) that have killed at least 170 million in the past century, more than in all the wars

---

[1] John Heidenrich, *How to Prevent Genocide: A Guide for Policymakers, Scholars, and the Concerned Citizen* (Praeger, 2001). National genocide is also a category.

[2] Speaking to ABC News, 23 January 2000 and cited widely thereafter. Similar comments were made in the closing months of 1999, with the result that even prior to the election, funding was cut off for open source intelligence support to the monitoring and warning of gencocide.

[3] Security Council Resolution 751 of 24 April 1992, inspired by the Somalia situation.

combined.[4] This is a reality that impacts on homeland security—this is a reality that breeds and nurtures terrorists, disease, and war. The details are best studied by reading the books by experts, few that they are, as well as pressing for the availability of more information online.[5] This chapter will present original work by Dr. Greg Stanton that illustrates the breadth and depth of the genocide problem. First a map for general orientation.

21st Century Mass Atrocities & Ethnic Fault Lines
24 flashpoints and 12 faultlines--18 active campaigns

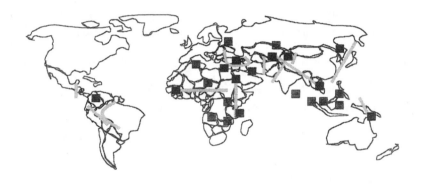

■ Flashpoints for Genocide & Politicide   Genocide & Politicide Faultlines

Copyright & Source: Dr.. Greg Stanton, International Campaign to End Genocide

Figure 19: 21ˢᵗ Century Genocide Flashpoints and Faultlines

---

[4] R. J. Rummel, *Statistics of Democide: Genocide and Mass Murder since 1900* (Transaction, 1999).
[5] Heidenrich's book is the best book on the marketplace and points to many other works. It does not, however, include the specifics provided here, which represent the unique efforts of Dr. Greg Stanton, one of America's foremost advocates for action on genocide. Stanton's book, *The Eight Stages of Genocide*, is currently being completed while he is a fellow at the Woodrow Wilson International Center for Scholars in Washington, D.C. Appendix 2 contains a table of useful public sites on genocide.

THE EIGHT STAGES OF GENOCIDE
By Gregory H. Stanton[6]

Classification
    Symbolization
        Dehumanization
            Organization
                Polarization
                    Identification
                        Extermination
                          Denial

Genocide is a process that develops in eight stages that are predictable but not inexorable. At each stage, preventive measures can stop it. The later stages must be preceded by the earlier stages, though earlier stages continue to operate throughout the process.

1. **CLASSIFICATION:** All cultures have categories to distinguish people into "us and them" by ethnicity, race, religion, or nationality: German and Jew, Hutu and Tutsi. Bipolar societies that lack mixed categories, such as Rwanda and Burundi, are the most likely to have genocide. The main preventive measure at this early stage is to develop universalistic institutions that transcend ethnic or racial divisions, that actively promote tolerance and understanding, and that promote classifications that transcend the divisions. The Catholic church could have played this role in Rwanda, had it not been driven by the same ethnic cleavages as Rwandan society. Promotion of a common language in countries like Tanzania or Côte d'Ivoire has also promoted transcendent national identity. This search for common ground is vital to early prevention of genocide.

2. **SYMBOLIZATION:** We give names or other symbols to the classifications. We name people "Jews" or "Gypsies", or distinguish them

---

[6] ©2002 Gregory H. Stanton. Reprinted by permission. Dr. Stanton can be reached via email at gstanton@genocidewatch.org His pioneering work on preventing genocide continues, and I regard him, together with John Heidenrich, as two of our foremost operationally-oriented experts in this area. This insert is also available as a self-contained paper at www.genocidewatch.org/8stages.htm.

by colors or dress; and apply them to members of groups. Classification and symbolization are universally human and do not necessarily result in genocide unless they lead to the next stage, dehumanization. When combined with hatred, symbols may be forced upon unwilling members of pariah groups: the yellow star for Jews under Nazi rule, the blue scarf for people from the Eastern Zone in Khmer Rouge Cambodia. To combat symbolization, hate symbols can be legally forbidden (swastikas) as can hate speech. Group marking like gang clothing or tribal scarring can be outlawed, as well. The problem is that legal limitations will fail if unsupported by popular cultural enforcement. Though Hutu and Tutsi were forbidden words in Burundi until the 1980's, code-words replaced them. If widely supported, however, denial of symbolization can be powerful, as it was in Bulgaria, when many non-Jews chose to wear the yellow star, depriving it of its significance as a Nazi symbol for Jews. In Denmark, legend has it that the reason the Nazis never imposed the yellow star is that the King, himself, said he would be the first to wear one.

3. **DEHUMANIZATION:** One group denies the humanity of the other group. Members of it are equated with animals, vermin, insects or diseases. Dehumanization overcomes the normal human revulsion against murder. At this stage, hate propaganda in print and on hate radios is used to vilify the victim group. In combating this dehumanization, incitement to genocide should not be confused with protected speech. Genocidal societies lack constitutional protection for countervailing speech, and should be treated differently than in democracies. Hate radio stations should be shut down, and hate propaganda banned. Hate crimes and atrocities should be promptly punished.

4. **ORGANIZATION:** Genocide is always organized, usually by the state, though sometimes informally (Hindu mobs led by local RSS militants) or by terrorist groups. Special army units or militias are often trained and armed. Plans are made for genocidal killings. To combat this stage, membership in these militias should be outlawed. Their leaders should be denied visas for foreign travel. The U.N. should impose arms embargoes on governments and citizens of countries involved in genocidal massacres, and create commissions to investigate violations, as was done in post-genocide Rwanda.

5. **POLARIZATION:** Extremists drive the groups apart. Hate groups broadcast polarizing propaganda. Laws may forbid intermarriage or social

80

interaction. Extremist terrorism targets moderates, intimidating and silencing the center. Prevention may mean security protection for moderate leaders or assistance to human rights groups. Assets of extremists may be seized, and visas for international travel denied to them. Coups d''etat by extremists should be opposed by international sanctions.

6. **PREPARATION:** Victims are identified and separated out because of their ethnic or religious identity. Death lists are drawn up. Members of victim groups are forced to wear identifying symbols. They are often segregated into ghettoes, forced into concentration camps, or confined to a famine-struck region and starved. At this stage, a Genocide Alert must be called. If the political will of the U.S. Government, NATO, and the U.N. Security Council can be mobilized, armed international intervention should be prepared, or heavy assistance to the victim group in preparing for its self-defense. Otherwise, at least humanitarian assistance should be organized by the U.N. and private relief groups for the inevitable tide of refugees to come.

7. **EXTERMINATION** begins, and quickly becomes the mass killing legally called "genocide." It is "extermination" to the killers because they do not believe their victims to be fully human. When it is sponsored by the state, the armed forces often work with militias to do the killing. Sometimes the genocide results in revenge killings by groups against each other, creating the downward whirlpool-like cycle of bilateral genocide (as in Burundi). At this stage, only rapid and overwhelming armed intervention can stop genocide. Real safe areas or refugee escape corridors should be established with heavily armed international protection. The U.N. Standing High Readiness Brigade -- 5500 heavy infantry -- should be mobilized by the U.N. Security Council if the genocide is small. For larger interventions, a multilateral force authorized by the U.N. led by NATO, should intervene. It is time for the NATO nations to recognize that they are the only force strong enough to intervene to stop genocide, and that the international law of humanitarian intervention has come to transcend the narrow interests of individual nation states. If NATO will not intervene directly, it should provide the airlift, equipment, and financial means necessary for regional states to intervene with U.N. authorization.

8. **DENIAL** is the eighth stage that always follows a genocide. It is among the surest indicators of further genocidal massacres. The perpetrators of genocide dig up the mass graves, burn the bodies, try to cover up the

81

evidence and intimidate the witnesses. They deny that they committed any crimes, and often blame what happened on the victims. They block investigations of the crimes, and continue to govern until driven from power by force, when they flee into exile. There they remain with impunity, like Pol Pot or Idi Amin, unless they are captured and a tribunal is established to try them. The response to denial is punishment by an international tribunal or national courts. There the evidence can be heard, and the perpetrators punished. Tribunals like the Yugoslav or Rwanda Tribunals, or an international tribunal to try the Khmer Rouge in Cambodia, or an International Criminal Court may not deter the worst genocidal killers; with the political will to arrest and prosecute them, some may be brought to justice. -- o --

I have taken the trouble to lay out the above stages in order to make two points: first, it really is possible now, because of the scholarship and field studies of experts like Dr. Stanton, to perceive and detect emerging genocidal campaigns early on; and second, our government does not do this.

Over the course of the past quarter-century, since completing my first graduate degree on the prediction of revolution,[7] I have been constantly alert to both Department of State and Central Intelligence Agency endeavors with respect to predicting instability and revolutionary conditions—as well as private sector political and economic risk management initiatives—and I have to say bluntly, we are not even close to institutionalizing this kind of intelligent analysis.

Genocide is perhaps the ugliest manifestation of global instability that can and inevitably will impact on homeland security. The sorry fact is that while we might study trends, we do not do a good job of either integrating varied in-depth studies, nor of sharing them with the taxpaying public.

And now, beginning on the next page, are the actual tables of the ongoing and historical genocidal campaigns for each region. Those at Stage 7 are currently at the mass killing stage and can be considered active genocide campaigns. They are erupting. The others are at various stages of dormancy, but could erupt again. The deaths in 2001 are separately identified, and the

---

[7] "Internal War" (MA Thesis, Lehigh University, May 1976)

countries where genocide is on-going today are identified with bold type (and also have the 2001 death toll identified).

NATION	EPISODES	AFRICA DEATH TOLL	DIVISIONS	STAGE in 2002
Burundi	1959 – 1962, 1972, 1988, 1993 – 1995, 1996 -- present	450,000 Hutus, 50,000 Tutsis **2001: 5,000**	Ethnic, political	7 – Genocidal massacres
Sudan	1956 – 1972, 1983 – present	2 million Nuer, Dinka, Christians, Nuba (Southern) **2001: 10,000**	Political, religious, racial, ethnic	7 – Politicide, Genocide
Democratic Republic of the Congo	1960 – 1965, 1977 – 1979, 1984, 1992 – 1996, 1997 – present	80,000 Tutsis, Hutus, 10,000's Hema, Lendu, 2 million (civil war) **2001: 80,000**	Political, ethnic	7 – Civil war, Genocidal massacres
Angola	1961 – 1962 1975 – present	40,000 Kongo, 500,000 Umbundu, Ovimbundu **2001: 5,000**	Political, ethnic	7 – Civil war
Algeria	1962 – 1963, 1991 -- present	60,000 OAS,Harkis Berbers **2001: 5,000**	Religious, political	7 – Massacres
Liberia	1990 – 2000, 2001 -- present	100,000 Krahn, Gio, Mano, etc. **2001: 1,000's**	Political, ethnic	7 – Civil war
Nigeria	1966 – 1970, 1972 – 2000 (sporadic) 2001 --present	1 million Ibos, Tiv, Hausa, Yoruba, Ogoni, others **2001: 1,000's**	Political, ethnic, religious	6 – Preparation
Zimbabwe	1982 – 84, 1998 – present	20,000 Ndebele, **2001: 100's**	Ethnic, political	6 – Preparation
Somalia	1988 – present	100,000 Somalis, Isaaq clan **2001: 100's**	Political, clan	6 – Preparation
Rwanda	1959 – 1963, 1994	800,000 Tutsi **2001: 100's**	Ethnic, political	5 – Polarization
Congo-Brazzaville	1997 – 2000	10,000's	Political, ethnic	5 – Polarization
Sierra Leone	1991 – present	100,000 (civil war)	Political, ethnic	5 – Polarization
Ethiopia – Eritrea	1976 – 1979, 1994 – 2000	100,000's Oromo, Muslims, Somali	National, religious, ethnic	5 – Polarization
Uganda	1972 – 1979, 1980 – 1986 1994 – present	500,000 Acholi, Lango, Karamoja 250,000 Baganda 1,000's LRA foes **2001: 100's**	Political, ethnic Lord's Resistance Army victims	5 – Polarization
Equatorial Guinea	1975 – 1979	200,000 Bubi, Macia Nguema foes	Political, ethnic	4 – Organization
Senegal – Casamance	1990 – 2001	1,000's Diola	Political, ethnic	4 – Organization

Kenya	1991 – 1993	1,000's Nilotics	Ethnic, political	4 – Organization
Côte d'Ivoire	1998 – 2001	100's Bambara, Senoufo, Bété, Burkinabe	Ethnic, national, Religious, political	4 – Organization
Chad	1965 – 1996	10,000's southern groups	Ethnic, racial, religious, political	4 – Organization
Morocco- Western Sahara	1976 – **present**	1,000's: Sahrawis	Political, ethnic	4 – Organization
Mali	1990 – 1993	1,000's Touareg	Ethnic, political	4 – Organization
Mozambique	1975 – 1994	1 million by MPLA, Renamo	Political, ethnic	4 – Organization
South Africa	1987 – 1996	1,000's Zulus, Xhosa, ANC	Racial, political, ethnic	4 – Organization
Botswana	1990 – **present**	100's Küng, Caprivi Namibians	Economic, political, ethnic	4 – Organization
Egypt	sporadic	100's: Copts	Religious, political	4 – Organization
		AMERICAS		
NATION	**EPISODES**	**DEATH TOLL**	**DIVISIONS**	**STAGE in 2002**
Colombia	1950's 1975 – **present**	100,000's 10,000's **2001: 1,000's**	Political Political, criminal	7 – Civil war, Narcotics wars
Venezuela	1900 – 1970's,	1,000's Yanomami	Racial, ethnic	5 – Polarization
Brazil	1964 – 1965, sporadic massacres	1,000's: Kayapo, Yanomami, etc.	Political, racial, ethnic	4 – Organization
Guatemala	1950's –1980's	200,000 Mayans	Racial, ethnic, political	4 – Organization
Cuba	1959 – 1964	10,000's "counter – revolutionaries"	Political	4 – Organization
Argentina	1900 – 1920's 1976 – 1980	10,000's Indians, 10,000's leftists	Racial, ethnic Political	4 – Organization
Chilé	1973 – 1976	10,000's leftists	Political	4 – Organization
Nicaragua	1980 – 1989	10,000's rightists	Political	4 – Organization
El Salvador	1980 – 1992	10,000's leftists	Political	4 – Organization
Paraguay	1900 – 1974	10,000's Indians, (Aché, others)	Racial, ethnic	4 – Organization
Mexico – Chiapas	1900 – 2001	10,000's: Mayans	Ethnic, political	4 – Organization
		ASIA		
NATION	**EPISODES**	**DEATH TOLL**	**DIVISIONS**	**STAGE in 2002**
North Korea	1949 – **present**	1,600,000 **2001: 10,000's**	Political, class	7 – Politicide
India Kashmir	1947, 1949 – **present**	100,000's Muslims, Hindus **2001: 1,000's**	National, religious, ethnic, political	7 – National, religious war, political terrorism
Peoples Republic of China	1937 – 1949 1949 – 1957 1971 – 1977	25,000,000 "class enemies", religious **2001: 1,000's**	Political, national, class, ethnic, religious,	7 – Police State executions
Sri Lanka	1983 – **present**	1000's: Tamil and Sinhalese civilians	Ethnic, nat'l, political,	7 – Ethnic civil war, terrorism

84

		2001: 100's	religious	
Myanmar (Burma)	1978 1949 -- present	10,000 Muslims 100,000 Shan, , Karen, Christians 2001: 100's	Ethnic, political, religious	7 – Politicide, ethnic, religious oppression
Indonesia	1965 – present	500,000 communist 10,000's: Aceh 1,000's: Irian Jaya 1,000's: Moluccas 1,000's: Sulewesi 2001: high 1000's	Political, ethnic Religious, political Political, religious, ethnic, national	7 – Sporadic massacres
Philippines	1972 – present	1,000's anti-,pro- communists, separatist Muslims (Moro,Abu Sayyef)	Political, religious	7 – Terrorism, sporadic massacres
Nepal	1996 – present	2,600 anti-Maoists 2001: 100's	Political	7 – Terrorist massacres
Afghanistan	1978 – 1992, 1993 – 2001	1,500,000, 50,000+ 2001: 10,000's	Political, national, religious, ethnic	6 – Preparation
Uzbekistan Fergana Valley	1991 – present	1,000's 2001: 100's	Political, religious	6 – Preparation
Pakistan	1947, 1971, 1973 – 1977 **present**	1,500,000 Bengalis & Hindus, Sindhis 2001: 100's	Political, national, ethnic, religious	6 – Preparation
Tibet	1959 – 1990's	1,600,000 Tibetan Buddhists 2001: 100's	National, political, religious, ethnic	5 – Polarization
Cambodia	1966 – 1975, 1975 – 1979	100,000's leftists, 1,700,000 Khmers, Cham Muslims, Viets, city people	Political, class, ethnic, religious, national	5 – Polarization
East Timor	1965 – 2000	200,000 Timorese	Political, ethnic, national,religious	5 – Polarization
Azerbaijan	1988 – 1994	10,000's Azeris & Armenians	Ethnic, political, religious, national	5 – Polarization
Vietnam	1930 – 1945, 1945 – 1975, 1975 – present	100,000's leftists, 2.5 million in war, 10,000's boat people, reeducated	Political, class, ethnic, national	4 – Organization
Laos	1950's – 1963, 1963 – present	10,000's leftists, Meo, Hmong, anti- communists	Political, ethnic	4 - Organization
		EUROPE		
NATION	**EPISODES**	**DEATH TOLL**	**DIVISIONS**	**STAGE in 2002**
Chechnya	1943 – 1957 1994 – present	50,000 Chechens, 1,000's Russians 2001: 1,000's	Ethnic, national, religious,political	7 – Ethnic war, Genocidal massacres
Serbia	1993 – 2001	1,000's minorities, dissidents	Political, ethnic, national,religious	8 – Denial 5 – Polarization
Kosovo	1998 – 2001	10,000 Albanian Kosovars, Serbs	Ethnic, religious, national, political	5 – Polarization

Macedonia	1999 - 2001	100's Albanians, Macedonians,	Political, ethnic	5 – Polarization
Bosnia	1992 – 1998	200,000 Muslims, Croats, Serbs	Ethnic, religious, national, political	5 – Polarization (partition)
Cyprus	1963 – 1967 1974	10,000's Turks, Greek Cypriots 100's (Partition)	Political, religious, ethnic, national	5 – Polarization (partition)
Russia: USSR Russia: Dagestan Ingushetia,	1917 – 1991 1943 – 1957 1996 – 2001	62 million class enemies,minorities 10,000's Ingushi, Karachai, Balkars 100's Ingushi	Ethnic, national, religious, political	5 – Polarization
Georgia: Abkhasia	1993 – **present**	100's Abkhasians	National, ethnic, political	5 – Polarization
Northern Ireland	1964 – **present**	1000's Catholics, Protestants	Religious, class, political, national	5 – Polarization
Croatia	1991 – 1995	50,000 Serbs, Bosnian Muslims	Ethnic, national, religious,political	4 - Organization
Ukraine	1933 – 1934, 1947—1950, 1944 – 1968	3 million Ukrainian Kulaks, nationalists, Crimean Tatars	National, ethnic, political	4 -- Organization
		MIDDLE EAST		
NATION	**EPISODES**	**DEATH TOLL**	**DIVISIONS**	**STAGE in 2002**
Israel – Palestine	1948 – 1955, 1956, 1967, 1973, 1990 – **present**	10,000's Israelis, Palestinians **2001: 100's**	National, religious, ethnic, political	7 – National, religious war terror
Iraq	1961 – **present**	100,000's Kurds, Shiites, Kuwaitis **2001: 1,000's**	Political, ethnic, national, religious	8 – Denial 7 – Genocide Politicide
Turkey	1914 – 1916, 1984 – **present**	1.5 mil. Armenians 100,000 Kurds	Ethnic, religious, national, political	8 – Denial 6 – Preparation
Syria	1981 – 1982	10,000's Kurds, Sunni Muslims	Political, religious,national	5 – Polarization
Iran	1978 – 1992	10,000's Kurds, monarchists, Bahai	Religious, ethnic, political, national	5 – Polarization
Lebanon	1965 – 1991	10,000's Christian, Muslims, Druze	Religious, political	5 – Polarization

Figure 20: Table of Mass Atrocities Both Current and Over Time

That's it. Genocide, all over the world, and it does not even appear in the news. Can we really shut this reality out of our everyday existence? Can we really believe that such mass atrocities can occur all over the world without affecting us, even if only indirectly? It is time for every citizen taxpayer to take responsibility for thinking independently while joining the "virtual intelligence community" of citizen taxpayers linked by the Internet and sharing their civic perspectives on the global threat to local security.

86

Four Threat Types,
Three Strategic Scenarios

The U.S. military has in modern times (during the Cold War) refused to recognize any enemy other than the traditional force-on-force enemy, the strategic nuclear-conventional threat represented by nation-states. It took an act of Congress, legislation, to create the Special Operations Command and the related Special Operations and Low Intensity Conflict (SOLIC) earmarked program.[1]

At that time, there was an emerging threat spectrum with just two primary threat types: strategic nuclear and conventional forces on the one side—for high intensity conflicts—and special operations forces on the other side—for low intensity conflicts.

General Alfred M. Gray, then Commandant of the Marine Corps, drew this distinction in an interesting manner. His original comparison of the two is shown on the next page.

---

[1] Cf. William G. Boykin (Col, USA). *Special Operations and Low-Intensity Conflict Legislation: Why Was It Passed and Have the Voids Been Filled?*. Carlisle Barracks, PA, Apr 1991. 66 p. (Army War College (U.S.) Study project) For a really excellent listing of core references to special operations, visit http://www.au.af.mil/au/aul/bibs/special/sofdoc.htm. See also Jane E. Gibish, *SPECIALOPERATIONS: A Selected Bibliography* (U.S. Army War College Library, Carlisle Barracks, PA, March 1995), at http://carlisle-www.army.mil/library/bibs/special.htm. However, it needs to be stressed that even with its own legislation the SOLIC community has struggled—Services are run by conventional flag officers with conventional mind-sets, and even the Assistant Secretary of Defense for SOLIC is largely helpless against the Comptroller or the Undersecretaries.

Conventional Threat	**Unconventional Threat**
Government	Non-Government
Nuclear/Conventional Forces	Unconventional Forces
Static Orders of Battle (OOB)	Dynamic OOB
Linear Capability Development	Random, Off-the-Shelf
Rule of Engagement Known	No Rules of Engagement
Doctrine Known	Doctrine Not Known
Known Intelligence Forces	Unknown Intelligence

Figure 21: Comparison of Two Major Threat Types

General Gray was also prescient in understanding that the non-traditional threat *environment* was part of the problem. In 1989 he said: "If threat is a factor in determining national investments in security assistance and foreign aid, then a more aggressive program of Third World intelligence analysis and forecasting is needed if we are to justify long overdue and underfunded *peaceful preventive measures* in this vital area of concern and potential.[2]

Although the fall of the Berlin Wall inspired many to speak and write of a "peace dividend", and to enthuse over how a Revolution in Military Affairs (RMA) could be funded by this peace dividend, the reality has been disappointing. In combination, the over-commitment of forces world-wide, with a very high tempo of operations, and the focus of such research and development as could be afforded, on exotic futuristic technologies, has prevented the U.S. military from seriously considering non-traditional threats and from developing asymmetric deterrence and engagement capabilities.[3] In retrospect, we can also see that we failed to inspire a revolution in intelligence, and have wasted ten years of precious time during which we might have

---

[2] General Alfred M. Gray, Commandant of the Marine Corps, "Global Intelligence Challenges in the 1990's", *American Intelligence Journal* (Winter 1989-1990). *Emphasis in original.*

[3] One expert reviewer of this paper suggested that the peace "dividend" was actually a peace "tax" and largely destroyed a pretty good Army that had finally rebuilt itself in the aftermath of Viet-Nam.

restructured and reformed the critical intelligence underpinnings of our national security community.[4]

In my own work as the senior civilian responsible for the development of the Marine Corps Intelligence Center (now Command), I helped General Gray devise the above comparisons, and then went on to refine the model. Below are discussed four distinct threat types. Each threat type represents a different challenge requiring a different "way of war" and consequently different concepts, doctrine, and force structure *as well as a different challenge to intelligence.*

High-Tech Brutes—the Violent State Threat[5]

This warrior class relies on strategic nuclear and conventional capabilities including uniformed troops and marked equipment. It applies high-technology to achieve some physical stealth, and relies heavily on precision targeting.

This is the *only* threat that we focused on during the Cold War, and this is the threat that we understand best. Russia, China, North Korea, Iraq, India, Pakistan and to a much lesser extent Cuba represent this kind of threat. The major countries in Europe, were they to become our enemy, represent this kind of threat.

This is the *easiest* threat to monitor and the easiest threat to plan against because it is so obvious, so large, and so complex that it cannot, by and large, surprise us. Most of our capabilities were designed for this threat, and are not especially effective against the other three threats—this is especially true of intelligence systems.

---

[4] The Intelligence Community suffered many declines in the closing years of the 20th Century, with a series of short-term Directors of Central Intelligence and substantial cut-backs in overseas presence, foreign language broadcast monitoring, and other areas vital to the craft of intelligence.

[5] These four paragraphs and Figure 1 are replicated from the author's "Presidential Leadership and National Security Policymaking", Chapter 12 in Douglas T. Stuart, Editor, *Organizing for National Security* (Strategic Studies Institute, November 2000), pages 249-251.

Low-Tech Brutes—the Violent Non-State Threat

The "low-tech brute" is violent but generally does not represent a state.[6] Terrorists and transnational criminal gangs present both defense and intelligence with the "low slow singleton threat" that is extremely difficult to detect in the absence of a pervasive human intelligence network. This threat is also very "random" in nature in that it does not have obvious military goals and can rely on an unlimited 5th column of either well-paid volunteers, or volunteers recruited for one-time *in extremis* support tasks.

The low-tech brute is the most common threat to the good order and prosperity of organized states and their peoples. Unlike "low-intensity conflict" (LIC) threats for which Congress wisely created the Special Operations Command and the new Special Operations and Low Intensity Conflict (SOLIC) Program, the low-tech brute is not necessarily "organized" into a revolutionary army but rather is an aggregation of violent individuals who come together in random or covert ways that are extraordinarily difficult for our intelligence and law enforcement communities to detect and counter. Terrorism, and especially faith-based terrorism, is the ultimate manifestation of this kind of threat, and also unusual because it prefers to fight within the U.S. homeland—where are defenses are weakest—rather than overseas.

Our national security structure—in policy-making terms, in acquisition terms, and in day-to-day operational capability terms—is not geared to challenge this threat class effectively.[7] As the 11 September 2001 attacks demonstrated so clearly, we do not have integrated national intelligence watchlists and communications; we do not have a national homeland defense analysis or counterintelligence capability in place; and we have not put in place the most basic security measures against internal attacks.[8]

---

[6] Low-tech brutes can of course have some form of state sponsorship or tolerance.

[7] It merits comment that the author emphasized transnational crime at the time these words were first written, in early 2000, because terrorism appeared to have been largely suppressed and in comparison to the costs of transnational crime, was at the time perceived to be "below the line" at the strategic level of net assessments.

[8] One expert reviewer has suggested that Army Regulation 381-10, *US Army Intelligence Activities*, has gone well beyond the bounds of DoD 5240.1-R and Executive Order 12333, with the result that Army intelligence has been seriously crippled to the point that Army intelligence has "one arm and two legs bound."

Low-Tech Seers—the Non-Violent Non-State Threat

This "threat" class is not inherently violent. This threat class should be viewed primarily as a challenge characterized by the unresolved and largely legitimate needs of large groups of people whose circumstances, culture and history force them into confrontations with either established states or other non-state groups. At root this threat class is about water, food, and freedom from fear. However, this threat class should also be viewed as the "sea" within which terrorists may swim undetected. Among the greatest home front challenges facing America is that of discerning between loyal immigrant citizens and disloyal dangerous immigrant terrorists who mean to do great harm. Our lack of trained law enforcement personnel from our diverse cultural base, and our lack of translators for all of the major languages for this threat group, including especially Dari, Farsi and Urdu, should be of great concern.[9]

Our intelligence community, with the tacit if not the active consent of our national security policy-makers, has neglected this threat because it has been perceived as one that does not require the collection of secrets and one that can be adequately understood through common academic, think tank, business, and other non-governmental study.[10] In fact, because this threat class numbers billions of human beings world-wide, it probably should be regarded as the most serious threat in the mid- and long-term.

---

[9] Lack of translators is a long-standing issue, not just within the intelligence community but throughout the U.S. government. The 300th Military Intelligence Brigade (Linguist), U.S. Army Reserve is a helpful step in the right direction but fails to meet day to day needs across the board. Nothing less than a major investment of funds will solve this problem, together with a deliberate decision to employ linguists as translators without requiring that they have clearances or be engaged in day to day intelligence mission area functions.

[10] More recently we have begun to realize the error of our ways. The (then) Associate Director of Central Intelligence for Analysis & Production, Dr. John Gannon, has spoken publicly several times about the challenges facing us in the 2015 timeframe, and he clearly appreciates the national security implications of population growth, migration and immigration, the environment including energy and water supplies, and disease. In May 2000 the Administration declared that AIDS is now a national security threat. This is all for the good, but just as it took us 50 years to evolve a national security structure; it will it take us at least a decade if not more to redirect our sources and methods so as to adequately address this threat.

91

High-Tech Seers—the Volatile Mixed Threat

In just the past few years a new threat has catapulted itself to the top position in our consciousness. Although terms such as cyberwar and information warfare are in vogue, this threat is much more complex. On the one hand we see in this threat class deliberate state-sponsored capabilities to wreak havoc with our domestic infrastructure (power, communications, transportation, and finance) as well as individual or gang capabilities to be very destructive while remaining anonymous. On the other we see more subtle uses of electronic access to conduct economic espionage at the state level, "political theft" at the terrorist gang level, and plain theft at the individual level. This threat class also includes information vandalism by our own disgruntled citizens as well as outsiders, and corporate irresponsibility in failing to provide properly developed communications and computing products that are "safe" on the information superhighway.[11] Finally, this threat class can combine with any other class, for instance, with the low-tech brutes, to create a hybrid threat.

We now know, in the aftermath of the 11 September 2001 attack on America, that we seriously underestimated the strategic brilliance, the financial self-sufficiency, and the obsession with confronting America, on its home ground, of one man: Osama Bin Laden. If nothing else, the success of bin Laden as a combination of high-tech seer and low-tech brute should help us understand that we need a new model for the analysis of threats to our Nation. It is time to revisit how we do intelligence, a function of government that some believe to be "flawed by design."[12]

---

[11] To the extent that the U.S. military was willing to think new thoughts, it was this threat—the threat of information warfare and information terrorism, which gripped everyone's imagination. Considerable funds have been spent on both critical infrastructure protection and on various service capabilities to achieve "information dominance." Information technology, rather than intelligence analysis, has been the major defining aspect of the newest fad within the U.S. military, that of Information Operations (IO).

[12] Amy Zegart, *Flawed by Design: the Evolution of the CIA, JCS, and NSC* (Stanford University Press, 2000), together with David F. Rudgers, *Creating the Secret State: The Origins of the Central Intelligence Agency, 1943-1947* (University Press of Kansas, 2000), fully describe the circumstances surrounding the birth of the CIA, such that it has never been fully effective. Other elements of the U.S. Intelligence Community, generally created to meet a military need, inside the Pentagon budget, and culturally

92

Below is an illustration of these four threat types, with some additional information on the different kinds of war they might engage in, as well as their sources of strength, their preferred mode of stealth, and their normal targeting practice.

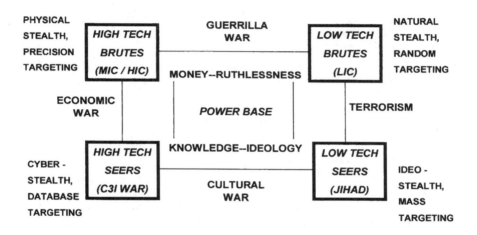

Figure 22: Four 21st Century Threat Types

This depiction is important because it helps the citizen taxpayer reflect on how our taxes are spent. In brief, we are spending $400 billion a year on just one of these four threat classes, the strategic nuclear-conventional high-tech brute, and we are spending a fraction of that amount on the other three classes—perhaps 5% of that amount on special operations and low intensity conflict (but almost nothing on transnational law enforcement and support to international police-driven peacekeeping missions); perhaps 1% on ideo-cultural outreach and foreign assistance for refugees; and roughly 5% on critical infrastructure protection. While the numbers have changed somewhat in the

oriented toward the Pentagon, are commensurately weak and unresponsive in relation to non-military intelligence requirements.

aftermath of 9-11, the harsh truth is that we have not related our budget to the threat because we don't understand the nuances among these four threat types.

Below is another way of looking at the four warrior classes in non-traditional threat terms.

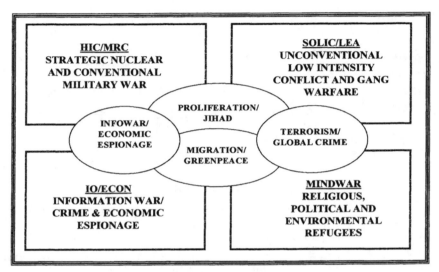

HIC/MRC: High Intensity Conflict/Major Regional Conflict
SOLIC/LEA: Special Operations Low Intensity Conflict/Law Enforcement Agencies
IO/ECON: Information Operations/Economic Espionage, Theft, and Vandalism

Figure 23: Non-Traditional Threat Challenges

We invest virtually nothing in dealing with major non-traditional threats including immigration and environmental threats.

The military would argue that the nuclear-conventional state-on-state and force-on-force scenario is the "worst-case" scenario for which we must be prepared at all times. They relegate the other threats to "minor" status and assume that we can deal with them using elements of our superior conventional power. They are not correct in this supposition. 9-11 demonstrates very clearly just what a really dedicated band of individuals can do when the combine money with a willingness to commit suicide and an extraordinary intellect.

94

At the same time, we have been slow to appreciate the dangers we face from non-traditional threats such as disease and massive non-violent migration.

Three Non-Traditional Scenarios

Reflecting on the confluence of factors that combine to destabilize the rest of the world to the point that a direct non-traditional threat might jump across the ocean and impact on America—and here we are thinking about non-violent but still deadly threats, consider the following representation.

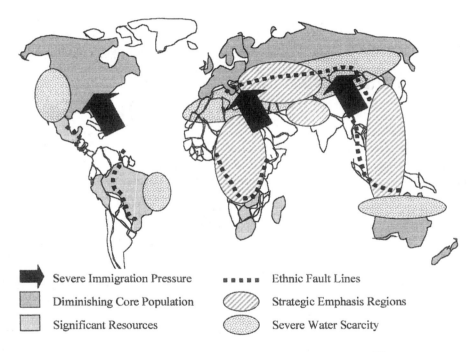

Figure 24: Non-Traditional Threat Overlay[13]

---

[13] Water scarcity is depicted in *The State of the World Atlas* (Simon & Schuster, 1981), on charts 53-54. Mineral Power is depicted on charts 13-14. Timber Power is depicted in the Penguin 1999 edition, on pages 100-101. Interestingly, population replenishment (or lack thereof) is the focus in the early edition, chart 3 while population control is the

North America, Russia, and Australia are not replenishing their populations. North America, Europe, and Russia are under severe immigration pressure. On the positive side, North America, Russia, and Australia are very rich in resources—head and shoulders above the rest of the world.

The non-traditional threat appears to be best understood as a race between sustainable development on the one hand, and a spasmodic and very destabilizing population explosion. North America, Europe, and Russia must either find a way to stabilize and contain that population explosion, or they face the real possibility of being "over-run" by dispossessed masses of humanity capable of bringing down any state. The new craft of intelligence is proposed as the primary means for achieving an asymmetric advantage[14] in dealing with the non-traditional threat over time.

This point merits further emphasis, for the new craft of intelligence must be capable of putting this race—this threat to our future—in a context that compels understanding and action among citizens, corporations, and governments.

Put simply, the existing Western approach to natural resources is liquidating the earth at the same time that it seeks to lower its costs of production by utilizing marginalized populations in the lesser developed countries.[15] In combination, our extraction of value from resources around the

---

focus of the later edition, pages 14-15. The genocide lines are from Dr. Gregory Stanton, whose work is featured in Chapter 8. Note that China is very much a wild-card—it lacks resources (over 300 Chinese *cities* are water-stressed), has a very large population living near the poverty level, and is pressuring Russia from the south with both planned and unplanned migrations.

[14] One is always inclined to question the liberal use of the word "asymmetric". In this book the word is used in the sense of unconventional or not symmetric. If those that seek to undermine our country can be said to have vast hoards of people to sacrifice, then our asymmetric response, lacking the ability to go man for man is going to have to revolve around being smart or being brutal. There is no other option and this global asymmetric challenge begs for action now. We can pay now on our terms or later on their terms. This is not a threat spectrum that can be left for our children to deal with.

[15] Brian Czech, *Shoveling Fuel for a Runaway Train: Errant Economists, Shameful Spenders, and a Plan to Stop Them All* (University of California, 2000) is a most serious and thoughtful presentation of this threat. Two books that address related issues are David Helvarg, *Blue Frontier: Saving America's Living Seas* (W. H. Freeman and Company, 2001), and Joe Thornton, *Pandora's Poison: Chlorine, Health, and a New*

globe, the increasing conditions of urbanization, deforestation, and water scarcity, and the global communications grid that is showing the dispossessed exactly how marginalized they are (and where they might migrate to), all appear to lead to one of the following two scenarios:

Break-Out Scenario: 5,000 mile marches, boat-lifts, and reverse blockades, in which Westerners are not allowed to leave, will stress the developed world and force the issue of humanitarian assistance while leading some developed states to collapse under the pressure of hundreds of thousands of refugees demanding food and water.[16]

Black Death Scenario. Millions die in plagues across Indonesia, Sudan, Nigeria, India, and Russia. Massive quarantine efforts fail, as the plagues cross borders and begin to infect the more developed countries including Australia,

---

Environmental Strategy (MIT Press, 2000). All three books focus on the fact that corporations are being permitted to both ravage the earth and poison everything including our food and water, without regard to the long-term effects (including a dangerous decline in sperm counts among American males) on future Americans.

[16] The U.S. borders, both land and sea, are simply not secure at this time. CIA mid-career class 101, of which I was a member, received a tour in 1986 of the Mexican border, at which time it was made clear that if the illegal immigrants ever massed and moved, ignoring the few Border Patrol individuals, there would be no keeping them back. For a recent story on this problem, see Shawn Zeller, "Nation's borders still aren't secure, agents say", *GovExec.com*, 4 October 2001, at http://www.govexec.com/dailyfed/1001/100401z1.htm. See also Stephanie Conner, "Border security needs improvement, INS, Customs tell panel", *GovExec.com*, 4 October 2001, in which Immigration and Naturalization Service Commissioner James Ziglar tells the Senate Treasury and General Government Appropriations Subcommittee that the border is not secure. "In addition to calling for an increase in INS Border Patrol agents and facilities, Ziglar encouraged expanding access to biometric identification systems, to data from the multi-agency Advance Passenger Information System and the National Crime Information Center Interstate Identification Index. He said these technologies would help prevent known terrorists and criminals from entering or fleeing the United States." He is *assuming* that individuals will come one at a time and agree to pass through established check-points. We are not ready for a boat-lift combined with a rush of desperate refugees across the border. Latter story is at http://www.govexec.com/dailyfed/1001/100401cdam2.htm.

Canada, and the U.S. Leaders are confronted with need to vaporize millions of dead.[17]

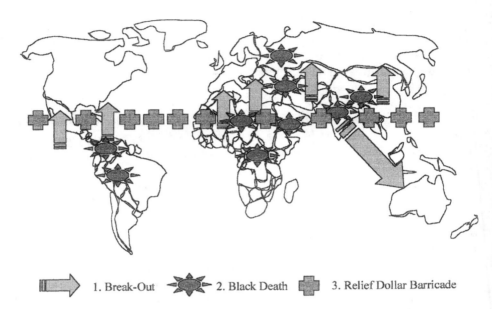

1. Break-Out   2. Black Death   3. Relief Dollar Barricade

Figure 25: Two Likely Scenarios, One Optional Scenario

---

[17] Laurie Garrett, *BETRAYAL OF TRUST: The Collapse of Global Public Health* (Hyperion, 2000) has written the definitive work on this non-traditional threat. 764 pages in length, it carefully documents both the frequency and depth of epidemics of pneumonic plague, Ebola virus, and tuberculosis as well as AIDS and other now common diseases, the complete collapse of normal public health measures, not only in threat countries, but in target countries like the U.S. On 4 October 2001, as these words were being written, there were two headlines of note: in Afghanistan and Pakistan, where we might be fighting shortly, from Tim Butcher in Quetta, "Ebola-Style Killer Virus Sweeps Afghan Border", *London Daily Telegraph,* October 4, 2001; here in the U.S., just one example, is from Susan Okie, "New E. Coli Strain Linked to Ailment", *The Washington Post,* 4 October 2001, page A3, in which this drug-resistant bacterium is said to have reached epidemic proportions.

It is not possible for a citizen to understand the porosity of our borders until they have actually witnessed the thousands of people lining up each night along the California, Arizona, and Texas borders with Mexico. In Europe, the looming migration issue is highlighted by the hundreds crossing from North Africa into France, and thence striving to run into the "Chunnel", the railroad tunnel now linking the Continent to England. In Australia, as genocide intensifies the pressures, boatlifts have increased toward Australia, and mothers are throwing their children into the water near Australian naval vessels, a last desperate attempt to give their children life by placing the onus for their death by drowning on an Australian.

To the extent that we, the citizen taxpayers, permit our government to ignore and underfund remedial measures and policies with respect to the viability of life on the rest of the planet, we are sentencing our own children to a much reduced, much threatened, quality of life from either of these first two "natural" scenarios.

There is, fortunately, a third optional scenario. It is not a scenario that the corporate world is ready to support, and therefore only the citizen taxpayers, the citizen voters, can elect and demand this scenario.

Sustainment Scenario. By demand of the American voters, the President convenes an emergency summit of the G-8 leaders, followed by an emergency session of the North Atlantic Treaty Organization (NATO) and then of the United Nations (UN). Among the G-8 nations, $250 billion dollars a year is committed for a ten-year period of emergency global stabilization and restoration of basic natural resources together with resettlements of entire tribes under quasi-subsidized conditions that include population control measures with a draconian emphasis on the urgent and thorough emancipation and education of women. [18] Simultaneously, the World Trade Organization adopts policies and regulations to be enforced by all nations, requiring corporations to dramatically revise their entire production processes to produce bio-degradable

---

[18] I have over time seen a number of references supporting the view that the single greatest return on foreign assistance investment, is in the education of women. Educating women appears to lead to ethical birth control, disease control, reduced crime, and a myriad of other societal improvements. Women in power and the education of women, would appear to be a vital underpining for any future strategy to create a sustainable stable world.

goods and to completely eschew chlorine chemistry.[19] NATO is given lead for the "New Marshall Plan". Included in the New Marshall Plan are a Digital Marshall Plan for extending Internet access to every village around the world; and a massive project to create an information commons in multiple languages where individuals can self-organize and utilize openly available information to join in the governance of their neighborhoods, states, and nations.

Terrorism will not disappear without *both* a focused strategy hunting down existing terrorists one by one, *and* a global campaign to bring prosperity to the rest of the world before its peoples become immigrants, refugees, or pensioners of the West.[20]

Time is the one element of strategy that can not be bought or confiscated.[21] The new craft of intelligence is time-sensitive.

---

[19] There is a growing body of responsible opinion—both in the streets and in the halls of power—that major changes are necessary to the World Trade Organization (WTO) and related bodies now dominated by Western and corporate interests. For an especially thoughtful and concise overview, see John Audley and Ann M. Florini, "Overhauling the WTO: Opportunity at Doha and Beyond", *Policy Brief* (Carnegie Endowment, Number 6, October 2001).

[20] I am indebted to Dr. Max Manwaring, of the U.S. Army War College and its Strategic Studies Institute, one of the top experts on instability and non-traditional threats, for a two-page overview of how terrorism, instability, failed states, and massive migration, disease, and other non-traditional threats all come together. Personal communication, 8 October 2001.

[21] Colin Gray, *Modern Strategy* (Oxford, 1999) is the finest guide to modern strategy available. His emphasis on time and strategic culture is relevant here.

A Common Sense
National Security Strategy

Trade-Offs

In very simple terms, the President and Congress make trade-offs, at the strategic level, among four different accounts: Entitlements and the Deficit; Domestic Spending; Military Spending; and Non-Military Spending for national security, meaning diplomacy, foreign assistance, and intelligence. I believe that the citizen taxpayer can no longer allow a combination of ideological mantras and corporate cash to influence the budget in ways that are very threatening to the future well-being of our children.

In my humble opinion, gratuitous tax refunds that empty the federal piggy-bank of rainy day cash reserves, and deficit spending, are terribly irresponsible and detrimental to the financial well-being of the commonwealth, of the Republic. It is not longer enough to vote for the candidate of your choice—you must now understand these issues, take a stand, and communicate your views to both candidates and elected officials.

I also believe that it is a terrible mistake to simultaneously reduce key domestic programs (especially education), increase the deficit, and throw billions of dollars at military programs that are not relevant to 21st Century threats. If anything, we should be moving more money into domestic education, water and energy conservation, universal health care, pension plan insurance, and programs that control illegal immigration while nurturing the screening and sustainment of new citizens.

This concluding section will focus only on national security trade-offs, my area of competency. Citizens themselves must organize to scrutinize and speak up on trade-offs being made with respect to deficit spending, additional tax cuts, and domestic programs.

101

Changing the Strategy[1]

Fundamental strategic thinking should include an appreciation for the fact that a national security strategy must be *holistic*—managing all sources of national power including diplomacy, economic assistance, cultural outreach, and information operations, not just the military—simultaneously. "War proper" is not just about military force, but rather about imposing one's will and assuring one's security in a complex world. Within this larger context, power without purpose is wasted, time is priceless, technology is not a substitute for strategy or thinking, asymmetric threats must receive co-equal attention with symmetric threats, and strategic culture *matters*.

Determining our national security strategy for the 21st Century must therefore be guided by two related principles: co-equal standing for asymmetric versus symmetric threats; and co-equal structure and funding, or at least some semblance of a rational balance, between *military* forces designed for the traditional symmetric threat, and largely *unconventional or non-military* forces designed to deal with the asymmetric threat.

On this basis, "forward engagement" and "shaping" of the theater environment make a great deal of sense, but with two caveats: there must be a force structure as well as funding for non-military investments, and we are probably better off talking about "nurturing" peaceful environments instead of the more imperial "shaping." At a minimum a strategy that is seriously committed to force protection through economic, cultural, and information peacekeeping must recognize the vital role played by the non-governmental organizations (NGO), the critical importance of being able to communicate and cooperate with indigenous organizations that are not part of a military force, and the overwhelming influence on any situation of environmental conditions including the availability of clean drinking water, sufficient food for the

---

[1] This material is excerpted from a longer article of 38 pages, 12 figures, and 51 notes. Those desiring to download and/or review the full document are directed to www.oss.net/Papers/white/AlternativeStrategy.rtf. An abbreviated version of the long article has appeared as Chapter 9, "Threats, Strategy, and Force Structure: An Alternative Paradigm for National Security in the 21st Century," in Steven Metz (contributing editor), *Revising the Two MTW Force Shaping Paradigm* (Strategic Studies Institute, April 2001).

children, and such medical provisions as might be needed to at least keep disease from spreading through epidemics.

Our new national security strategy must actually have five elements that are in complete harmony with one another: our *global intelligence strategy*, for ensuring that we can maintain global coverage and global warning; our *interoperability strategy*, for ensuring that what we build and buy is interoperable with both military and civilian coalition partners in a wide variety of "come as you are" circumstances; our *force structure strategy* for ensuring that we build to both the most likely as well as the worst case threats while balancing the relative roles of our military, the rest of the Federal government, the reserve force, the private sector, and external allies or coalition partners; our *preventive diplomacy strategy* for directly addressing conditions around the globe that spawn conflict and crises; and finally, our *home front strategy* for fully developing and integrating the defensive capabilities of our state & local governments and the private sector.

Elsewhere, in the longer original article, each of these five strategies is discussed in greater detail. For this abbreviated version, we need to grasp three core ideas: first, the Internet will be the backbone of 21st Century C4I and ISR, and we must therefore transfer our proven security technologies to the Internet at large, abandoning our fruitless pursuit of unilateral "Codeword high" electronic bunkers; second, the Revolution in Military Affairs (RMA) must be applied to all four threat classes and be about more than technology; and third, the RMA has created a strategic deficit—an interoperability gap—between the US and its allies, and between US commanders and the 98% of the Relevant Information they require to plan and execute any operation.

The old C4I paradigm, still in effect and very counterproductive to the needed strategic shift, assumes unilateral operations, top-down decision-making and command hierarchies based on secret sources, and relatively short-term time frames within which to both make and effect the decision. It also assumes complete interoperability by all parties with very expensive U.S. technology.

The new C4I paradigm, based on the new reality, demands a multi-cultural approach to information-sharing that supports bottom-up consensus and cooperation, relies largely on open sources, and focuses on relatively long time-frames that require both longer sustainment of the C4I system, and greater reliance on low-cost external sources of both information and processing.

103

The existing RMA flies in the face of common sense, and fails to leverage the natural development of critical technologies in the private sector, technologies that should be the basis for our Command and Control, Communications, Computing, and Intelligence (C4I) and related ISR investments.

RMA is a good concept, but it must be driven by real-world needs rather than domestic military-industrial complex wish lists. Consider Figure 26 below.

HIC/MRC **1/3 leap forward*** **1/3 anti-old technologies** **1/3 focus on people**	**SOLIC/LEA** **1/3 sensing technology*** **1/3 peace/civil technology** **1/3 focus on people**
CYBERWAR **1/3 electronic security*** **1/3 counterintelligence** **1/3 economic intelligence**	**PEACE** **1/3 historical thinking** **1/3 cultural thinking** **1/3 strategic thinking**

Figure 26: RMA in Context of Four Threat Classes

Asterisks in Figure 26 identify the three areas where the existing RMA does focus its attention. It is, however, neglectful of each of the other areas and therefore gets a "25%"—a failing grade—in the larger context of the real-world threat and the real-time needs of the United States of America.

Figure 27, on the next page, illustrates the trade-offs that we must make once we understand this larger perspective. Without spending too much time on these trade-offs, let us just note that there are three kinds of trade-offs

104

shown below: between the military and the rest of government; between the active force and the reserve force; and between the government as a whole and the private sector as a now vital part of the total security community. We will leave the issue of US versus allied or US versus NGO coalition levels of effort for another day.

"WAR" **80% Military – 20% Other** **75% Active – 25% Reserve** **75% USG – 25% Private**	**SOLIC/LEA** **50% Military – 50% Other** **50% Active – 50% Reserve** **50% USG – 50% Private**
HOME FRONT **20% Military – 80% Other** **50% Active – 50% Reserve** **25% USG – 75% Private**	**PEACE** **40% Military – 60% Other** **25% Active – 75% Reserve** **50% USG – 50% Private**

Figure 27: Transformative Force Structure Trade-Offs

"Real WAR" (HIC/MRC) forces must protect the core military and rely almost completely on active duty personnel "ready to go" without waiting for reservists; and will draw on private sector capabilities to the minimal extent possible.

SOLIC/LEA forces, by contrast, will see the U.S. Government (USG) fielding an even mix of military and diplomatic or justice or economic capabilities, while also drawing equally on active and reserve forces, and dividing the responsibility for dealing with terrorism and transnational crime equally between U.S. Government endeavors and private sector security and intelligence activities.

In PEACE, the military continues to provide a global logistics and communications infrastructure, but civilian elements of the U.S. government are in the majority role. Reservists skilled at foreign languages and with occupations vital to civil affairs and the restructuring of failed states come to the fore, while the overall effort is balanced between USG-funded and manned activities, and "overt action" by private sector elements including NGOs.

Finally, for IO/ECON (HOME), there remains a 20% commitment of military forces—largely in the National Security Agency (NSA) and related service Information Warfare centers—while the Justice, Treasury, and other Departments come to the fore; there is an even split between active duty forces carrying out Information Operations duties, and elements of the National Guard carefully positioned across all critical infrastructure nodes, with the funding—and the ultimate responsibility for day-to-day security—resting primarily with the private sector.

On the basis of this kind of approach, one can readily validate a need for four regional Commanders-in-Chief (Pacific, Southern, European, and Central) while conceptualizing four "threat-type" Commanders-in-Chief (WAR, SOLIC, PEACE, and HOME). It would be these eight CINCs that should comprise the working level of the new Joint Requirements Board under the direction of the Joint Chiefs of Staff.

Such a force structure strategy would at a minimum restructure the relationships between the Departments of Defense, Justice, and State; would establish minimal mandatory defense structure needs within the Departments of Commerce, Treasury, and Transportation as well as the Federal Reserve; and would create selective new relationships—including secure interoperable communications networks—with state and local agencies, the Immigration and Naturalization Service, the Federal Emergency Management Agency (FEMA), and such other civilian elements of government as must be better integrated into our "total force" strategy. The President's immediate staffs—the National Security Council and National Economic Council and other odds and ends, should also be restructured to conform to the need for matrixed management of integrated operations against each of the four threat classes. Such a force strategy would also establish, in clear terms suitable for a news media report as well as legislation, the minimal mandatory responsibilities of the private sector in support of our national security strategy, with a special emphasis on very high standards for electronic security.

106

An integrated national security strategy, then, must carefully develop, in tandem and with appropriate fiscal resources as well as force structure being assured for each element of this *holistic* strategy, each of the following: a global intelligence strategy; an interoperability strategy; a force structure strategy; a preventive diplomacy strategy (including economic assistance and cultural programs); and a home front strategy.

Those who would persist in limiting our national security strategy's emphasis to conventional military forces and "real war" are demeaning Clausewitz and undermining the security of the Nation.

Determining the Force Structure

A national security strategy that addresses all of these factors, with all of the legal, financial, and political implications that are associated with different kinds of "engagement", must inevitably find that we need *four* forces after next, not one.

While it is certainly possible to have one "core force" that includes the world-wide mobility, logistics, and communications capabilities that we are justly proud of, in fact our strategy must find that we need

1) a nuclear and conventional force that is smaller but very well equipped, fully modernized, and never committed to OOTW—the WAR force;

2) expanded and enhanced expeditionary, constabulary, and special operations forces able to put increasing force packages anywhere in the world within 24 to 48 to 72 hours—the SOLIC force including direct support to LEA;

3) a PEACE force, possibly combining substantial elements of the Civil Affairs, Army Engineers, and the Agency for International Development with new liaison elements specially trained to interact with civilian rescue units, as well as a new humanitarian assistance fleet within the U.S. Navy and also new Air Force lift capabilities relevant to peacekeeping; and finally,

4) a fully developed HOME Defense force that gives state and local authorities, not just federal authorities, everything they need to legally carry out their duties in preventing terrorism, economic espionage and electronic attack

107

against any of our critical infrastructures, while integrating the U.S. Coast Guard and appropriate other "continental" defense capabilities.

We cannot rely any longer on just the military, or on a "one size fits all" military where our people and equipment are assigned to all kinds of missions for which they have not been trained, equipped, and organized.

The "Core Force", as opposed to General Colin Powell's "Base Force" approach, draws a distinction between core functionalities and capabilities that are needed for a global presence—communications, logistics, mobility, manpower management—and those very distinct and carefully focused force structures and organizational arrangements that are self-sustaining and are very deliberately trained, equipped, and organized for optimal effectiveness in one of the eight "core competency" areas shown in Figure 28 below.

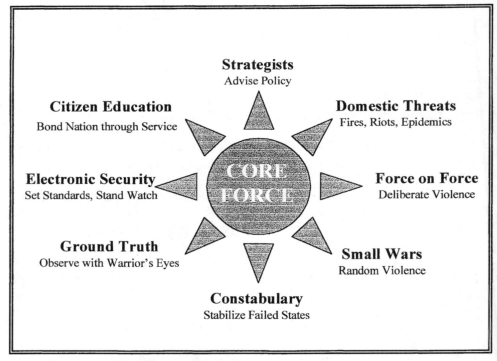

Figure 28: "Core Force" Visualization

Eight Functionalities, Four "Type" CINCS

Each of these eight functionalities should be actualized in corresponding force structure initiatives.

Strategists. Our national Net Assessment capability, and our national as well as our military strategic formulation processes, have broken down. They have become bureaucratic exercises of little value to long-term force structure planning. They are weak in part because no one has been willing to challenge the many false assumptions and premises that guide our current force structure decision-making process. We need, at a minimum, a dedicated National Security Strategic Center that has an even mix of representatives from each of the major slices of national power, as well as an even mix between long-term strategic thinkers specializing in each of the four threat classes, and "top 5%" personnel from the military, other elements of the civilian government, state & local law enforcement and public health, and the private sector, with special regard for selected non-governmental and non-profit sectors. This element should report directly to a new Presidential Council but be managed on a day-to-day basis by the Joint Chiefs of Staff.

Domestic Threat. The Federal Emergency Management Agency (FEMA) has improved incrementally in recent years, but needs a great deal more authority and financial support. We need to redirect a substantial portion of the National Guard toward national, state, and local emergency response duties, and to give them the training, equipment, and organization that they require to become extremely effective at dealing with fires, riots, and epidemics, in direct support of the constituted legal authorities being assisted. From communications to medical to civil engineering to public relations to food services, there are valid requirements that demand a "total make-over" for those elements of the National Guard fortunate enough to be selected for this very urgent and honorable aspect of national defense. This force, to include new investments in active duty personnel as a cadre and law enforcement specialists as well, should be under a "type" CINC for Home Front Defense who would also be responsible for Electronic Security and Citizen Education as discussed below, as well as for the national missile defense system as it develops over time.

Force on Force. This is the traditional military, responsible for creating the maximum amount of violence in the smallest possible space—responsible for being able to execute "scorched earth" missions that obliterate entire cities if

109

necessary, that can control significant areas of terrain in order to find and kill exactly the right key personnel threatening the United States with anything from transcontinental missiles to bio-chemical car bombs.. This force must receive all that the RMA can offer it, while also being protected from OOTW missions and other distractions. This force, under the leadership of a specific CINC responsible for the "total war" mission, should take over the bulk of the existing defense funding, and focus exclusively on maintaining its readiness while modernizing aggressively. This force must have air-ground task forces dedicated to specific regions of the world and at least one complete Corps specifically trained for each of the four major terrain types over which major wars might be fought: desert, jungle, mountain, and urban. Selected elements of all of the other forces (e.g. small wars, constabulary) would pre-plan and train for specific contingency missions in support of a Major Regional Conflict campaign, and in the event of an MRC, would be chopped at required over to the operational control of the regional CINC who would also receive operational control of force on force elements.

Small Wars. We keep forgetting our history. Both the British and the Americans have learned the same lesson more than once: forces designed for traditional conflicts do not do well in small wars until they have undergone such considerable adaptation as to render them unprepared and ineffective when required to return to traditional warfare. Small wars require a much higher standard of foreign area knowledge and language competency, to name just one significant difference, and are best fought by units trained, equipped, and organized specifically for small wars. The Special Operations Command (SOCOM) is ideally suited by both its strategic culture and its tactical excellence, to serve as the parent of a force of three division-wing teams optimized for expeditionary operations. This force would be especially skilled at joining international coalitions engaged in peace *enforcement* operations, and in executing violent complex forced entry missions.

Constabulary. The force that fights the small wars is *not* the force best able to maintain the peace, restore the functions of the failed state, and generally move as quickly as possible toward an exit that has been planned by the original engagement strategy. Constabulary forces require a combination of enormous numbers of civil affairs personnel, very high percentages of military police, engineering, medical, and food service personnel, and considerable communications, intelligence, and liaison personnel. This force must draw on and implement major civilian programs related to water purification and

110

desalination, food purity and distribution, and epidemic conditions. This force must excel at working with and sustaining long-term relations with NGOs—a major challenge where our traditional intelligence and operations leaders have failed completely. This force has to fully integrate indigenous personnel into every aspect of its reconstruction of society and the eventual turn-over of authority to indigenous leaders. This force has to provide considerable training in many skill areas including law enforcement, and at the same time needs to plan for a deliberate abandonment of most of its equipment, including communications equipment, as part of "the deal." This force would then return to the Continental United States to reconstitute itself. It should be under CINC SOLIC.

Ground Truth. The average Embassy officer is not trained, equipped, nor suited by nature to go in harm's way on a daily basis. Most of what we need to know in the Third World is not published at all, much less in digital form or in English. Our increasingly complex world requires that we have a force for establishing "ground truth" through direct personal observation, in every clime and place. Such a force, created in the defense attaché mode but with much greater freedom of movement and much deeper mobility and communications support, would integrate overtly assigned liaison officers; "circuit riders" assigned to entire countries or regions and told to stay out of the Embassy and off of the cocktail circuit; and very selective networks of clandestine and covert observers using third party passports or surreptitious entry to obtain their direct "ground truth" observations including sensitive measurements and signatures intelligence (MASINT). This force should be under CINC SOLIC, but in keeping with my recommendations for overall intelligence reform there should be a major Clandestine Services Agency (CSA) Station co-located with CINC SOLIC to ensure optimal coordination between these "early warning" observations by warriors focused on rural areas, and the more traditional civilian clandestine espionage activities focused on urban political and economic and military targets.

Electronic Security. We have a very long way to go before it is truly safe to live and work in cyberspace. Our financial, communications, power, and transportation infrastructures remain totally exposed and vulnerable for the simple reason that we will not be secure until there is a wholesale conversion of all existing electronic systems to a high level of security that must be embedded from the factories of the components on out. This will require three major national initiatives that are not yet being properly discussed in Washington: 1)

111

the definition of minimal mandatory standards for hardware, software, and personnel security in relation to electronic systems and their contents; 2) the imposition of these standards via "due diligence" legislation that requires all enterprises to be compliant within five years, with some systems to be secure within the year; and 3) the complete release of NSA-level encryption to the private sector so that the Internet can be as secure as Presidential communications. This level of security on the Internet is in fact a precursor to enabling the intelligence community as well as corporations to have access to *all* Relevant Information while still being able to process secrets. The minuscule effort being made today must be supplanted by a trained force responsive to CINC HOME, and electronic security brigades specializing respectively in financial, communications, power, and transportation systems, that are in turn integrated within a nationally distributed "virtual network" of private sector employees, National Guard specialists, and Home Front Force active duty cadre in new consolidated electronic operations centers focused on each of the major systems areas.

Citizen Education. "A Nation's best defense is an educated citizenry." As Senator Boren and David Gergen have noted publicly, we are in fairly desperate circumstances in relation to both policymaker and voter knowledge about the hard realities of the world we live in. A major investment must be made in the "internationalization of education", but even more so, we must find ways to better integrate our increasingly diversified population so as to create a minimal level of social cohesion over time. It is my view that we must restore the draft and require every U.S. citizen to serve for four years, in any combination of years (e.g. 2 + 2 or 1 x 4) between their 18th and 38th birthdays, with at least basic training and the first year being required before entering college. I must go further and in recognition of both the middle-aged immigration increases as well as the longevity increases in our population, and say that we must have an additional draft requiring 2 years of service (at once or in stints of 3-6 months) from all those who are citizens in their 38th to 58th years and have not served previously. At the same time, we must substantially increase private sector sabbaticals by our field grade officers and selected senior non-commissioned officers. This educational process does not require that every citizen bear arms—our *new* national defense force structure will offer many opportunities for those who do not wish to wear a uniform or learn how to kill. Only in this manner can be achieve the "total force" required by our new circumstances.

In summary, all but one of these eight functions would be integrated under one of four "type" CINCs that would in turn support the regional CINCs much as the services do today but with a vastly improved *focus of effort* that assures both air-ground-sea interoperability as well as joint training and doctrine suited to the specific "type" of warfare to be fought. Below, in very crude fashion, are some of the features of each of the ten force structure components of a new national security "total force."

CINCWAR	**Force on Force**
	Existing strategic nuclear forces, drawn down as appropriate, but modernized
	Four Army-Air Force Corps of 3 division-wing teams each (12 & 12)
	Strategic mobility (black and gray) to move one corps in four weeks
CINCSOC	**Small Wars**
	Complete absorption of the U.S. Marine Corps, without dilution of its
	Congressionally-mandated character or culture including uniforms
	Implementation of the 450-ship Navy (rapid response, littoral squadrons)
	Creation of two active/ four *Reserve* foreign area combat support brigades
	Constabulary
	Five active and five *Reserve* constabulary task forces
	Implementation of the 450-ship Navy (humanitarian assistance slice)
	Ground Truth
	Ten *Reserve* foreign area specialist companies
	Ten *Reserve* ground sensor /relay communications platoons (covert capable)
CINCPEACE	**State/USIA**
	1000 additional foreign service/foreign information officers
	100 new consular/open source information posts
	Peace Corps
	10,000 new Peace Corps volunteers per year
	Implementation of Peace Corps information assistance program
	Economic Aid
	10 new water, food, and medicine projects each year (2 within USA)
	Digital Marshall Plan for the Third World
CINCHOME	**Domestic Threat**
	50 National Guard Brigades, each with fire, riot, engineer, and medical
	battalions that train with state & local counterparts and also do international
	humanitarian assistance and disaster relief
	Individual State and City "Community Intelligence Centers"
	Absorption of the U.S. Coast Guard, without dilution of its character
	Electronic Security
	50 National Guard Electronic Security Centers
	50 National Guard Electronic Security Battalions, with specialist companies
	Citizen Education
	University of the Republic
	Universal Draft/National Defense Fellowship Program

Figure 29: Major Components of Four "Type" Commands

The above approach to managing how we train, equip, and organize our varying force structures to deal with four distinct threat challenges wipes out, in one grand "Goldwater-Nicols"-style revolution, all of the negatives of the existing Service "stovepipe" acquisition systems and the cultures that go with them. This kind of reform could be integrated into a National Security Act.

The U.S. Navy as an Example of Old versus New Thinking

U.S. Navy Ship Type	ACTUAL 1987 Navy	ACTUAL 1998 Navy	PLANNED 2010 Navy	DESIRED 2010 Navy	Notes
Ballistic Submarines	37	18	14	15	
Attack Submarines	102	65	50	50	
Troop/Attack Submarines	*0*	*0*	*0*	*15*	1
Aircraft Carriers (Blue Water)	14	12	12	8	
Aircraft Carriers (Littoral Ops)	*0*	*0*	*0*	*4*	2
Battleships	3	0	0	2	
Cruisers	36	29	27	36	
Destroyers	69	50	73	59	3
Expediters (Modified DDs)	**0**	**0**	**0**	**25**	4
Frigates	115	38	16	33	
Amphibious Warfare Ships	**63**	**40**	**36**	**36**	5
Patrol Craft/Brown Water Ops	*6*	*13*	*14*	*75*	6
Mine Warfare Ships	*22*	*16*	*26*	*20*	7
Combat Logistics Ships	56	39	18	18	
Mobile Logistics Ships	19	19	9	9	
Fleet Support Ships	24	11	7	7	
Strategic Auxiliaries	6	1	7	5	
Other (AGF-LCC)	14	11	9	9	
Assistance Ships (Large)	*0*	*0*	*0*	*8*	8
Assistance Ships (Small)	*0*	*0*	*0*	*8*	8
Hospital Ships (Large)	*2*	*2*	*2*	*3*	9
Hospital Ships (Small)	*0*	*0*	*0*	*5*	9
USMC Focus (%)	**11%**	**11%**	**11%**	**14%**	
Littoral Focus (%)	*5%*	*9%*	*13%*	*31%*	
TOTAL SHIPS	**588**	**364**	**320**	**450**	0

Figure 30: Old Navy, Proposed Navy, Needed Navy

The figure[2] above is instructive. It shows three navies: the Navy of 1980's (the "six hundred ship" Navy focused on the Soviets), the Navy of the 1990's (a down-sized Navy confused about its mission and its threat), and the Navy of the 21st Century, both planned (the third column) and as desired (my concept for a balanced naval force). The desired Navy is achievable from where we are today, and will provide three critical elements for success in future conflicts: sustainment of the amphibious fleet; expansion of the littoral fleet; and creation of a new peacekeeping fleet.

The thrust above is straight-forward. We strive to retain the global reach and striking power of the traditional Navy, while significantly spreading out our existing amphibious forces across more platforms widely distributed. At the same time we increase our ability to project a littoral force with dedicated carriers, shallow-water troop/attack submarines, reconfigured destroyers (leading toward a new class of ship, the *Expeditor*) and a combination of patrol craft and mine warfare ships. Finally, we add the Seaborne Peace Corps, actually an important part of force protection in the 21st Century—assistance and hospital ships for every clime and place.

These recommendations have been developed with the assistance of some of the best minds available to the Secretary of the Navy as well as to Members of Congress. A few specifics:

First, and there have been books on this topic, it makes sense to extend the utility of the attack submarine to the amphibious arena. There is no reason

---

[2] DOI: 2 April 1999. 1987 and 1998 data primarily from USN Battle Forces series with CRS, NHC input. 2010 planned data from Norman Polmar. Note 1: 15 *Los Angeles* SSNs refueled and modified pending new design. Note 2: 4 carriers with air wings dedicated to VSTOL/gunships, Marines and anti-mine work. Note 3: Keep every destroyer alive as gap-fillers. 84 vice 73-25 (Note 4) = 59. Note 4: 25 SPRUANCE DDs converted to DD963V/DDH (aviation aboard) pending new class. Note 5: Achieve better balance between large LHA/LPD and enhanced WHIDBEY-class LHDs. Note 6: Extend program, create 25 three-ship squadrons: 1 VSTOL, 1 Marines, 1 fire support. Note 7: Achieve savings and spread capability by focusing on distributed helicopter assets. Note 8: Create MPS Civic Action variant with integrated field hospital, engineers. Note 9: Get serious about continental-level diseases, configure for bio-chemical recovery. Note 0: Totals include Cat A NRF and Cat B Mine Warfare and Hospital Ships.

115

why 15 of the *Los Angeles* class submarines cannot be refueled and modified in order to carry 50-100 Marines and smaller vehicles. These SSN's have roughly fifteen years of service life remaining. With modifications, including improved sonar for shallow-water (<100 fathoms) operations and organic landing craft and related cranes for instream shallow-water offload, they would provide a stealthy and relatively invulnerable option for delivering reinforced platoons into urban and coastal areas where airfields servicing normal aerial delivery vehicles are not readily available.

Second, given the increased emphasis on littoral operations and especially the increased expectation of great turmoil in the rapidly growing urban areas of the Third World, it makes sense to earmark four of the Navy's twelve carriers for littoral/amphibious operations. These four carriers should have embarked, and be especially equipped to handle, air wings dedicated to a good mix of VSTOL/helicopter platforms for attack and close air support missions as well as very heavy lifting of large numbers of people and/or humanitarian assistance supplies. Each carrier should also have several anti-mine helicopters aboard, and be equipped to serve as a general repair facility for VSTOL and helicopter assets from the rest of the fleet. In those instances where a high level of air threat is anticipated, a companion "blue water" carrier with F/A-18 Hornets and (until 2010) F-14 Tomcats would be assigned combat air patrol duties. Air wing composition and embarked maintenance capabilities are the crux of the matter—*it is time the Navy gave amphibious aviation its due*.

Third, and many will say this is impractical, we should reexamine the symbolic as well as the military value of the battleship. Two are recommended, one for the Atlantic Command and one for the Pacific Command, each to serve as a Presidential summit site as well as a fire support capability when needed. Although battleships as a type are expensive, their ammunition is dirt-cheap when compared with the extraordinarily expensive not-so-precision munitions that we cannot rely upon for sustained barrages. In fact, the annual operations cost including salaries for one battleship is almost exactly equal to the cost of the 79 rounds of precision ammunition expended against the Saudi terrorist leader in Afghanistan in one 1998 attack that killed 26 and wounded 40.

Fourth, we must protect the destroyer fleet and use it to fill gaps in our fire support as well as our amphibious strike capability. It may come as a surprise to many (as it did to the author), but a series of modifications can be

116

made to the *SPRUANCE* (DD 963) that will permit it to carry as many as five Harrier-type aircraft or a couple of Harriers and a couple of heavy helicopters, while also embarking a reinforced platoon of up to fifty Marines. This same vessel can be fitted with a 64-cell VLS (vertical launch system) plus the enhanced 5-inch/62-caliber gun. Every destroyer should be kept alive, with 25 of them being refitted to carry Marines and amphibious aircraft, while the remaining 59 are upgraded in terms of fire support. In the 1970's Congress authorized funds for two DD 963 variants that could carry several VSTOL aircraft or helicopters, and designs were prepared. The Navy chose to ignore the will of Congress and built two normal *SPRUANCE* destroyers, leading to the termination of Congressional support for the variant. It is time to restore Congressional interest and make a serious commitment to this program as a means of refitting and retaining 25 of the existing *SPRUANCE* destroyers. A new class of ship can emerge from this initiative, one we have tentatively called the *Expediter*. The 2,000-ton *Streetfighter* described in a recent international publication does not exist, but it should—provided it is designed to carry Marines and VSTOL aircraft. At the same time, the planned DD-21, a $1 billion dollar a copy vessel, must be held to very high standards of over-the-horizon fire support *as well as embarked aviation* tailored to the needs of the Marine Corps.

Fifth, we must recognize the imbalance present in our plans for a limited number of very large LPH/LPD craft—each an enemy submarine skipper's dream target—and also take note of the fact that such large craft will tend to be four to six days away from crisis points at any given moment. Instead, if we accept the 24-48 hour response imperative and the implementing "pile-on" concept, we need to work toward a mix of the planned "big decks" and additional *WHIDBEY ISLAND*-class LHDs capable of carrying reinforced companies and VSTOL/helicopter gunships. In combination with the much faster modified *SPRUANCE*-class destroyers, this would give the Navy-Marine Corps team the ability to deliver *in extremis* platoons and companies anywhere in the world with only overnight notice.

Sixth, and here we take advantage of the newest class of vessel in the fleet, we need to dramatically expand acquisition of the *CYCLONE*-class patrol boat as well as the new deep-water patrol craft hull planned jointly by the U.S. Coast Guard with the U.S. Navy. The new craft, not a frigate but more like a corvette, is going to be in the 200-400 ton range, employing the SLICE technology (a modified SWATH design). Such a craft, at the mid-to higher

117

tonnage range, could carry up to fifty Marines for limited periods, and could also operate two H-60 helicopters or one H-53 helicopter and one Harrier. It could not, however, carry fire support missiles in adequate number at the same time. This suggests that a good out-of-the-box solution for 2010 brown water needs as well as high-seas drug interdiction and other coastal defense needs might be 25 three-ship squadrons, with one ship being primarily a troop carrier, one a helicopter/VSTOL platform, and the third a fire support ship with one VLS and a mix of heavy-caliber anti-air and surface-to-surface guns. In combination with the troop/attack submarines, the modified *SPRUANCE* destroyers, and a few additional *WHIDBEY ISLAND*-class LHDs, the Navy-Marine Corps team would now be able to lay claim to being a serious global presence able to put Marines on the beach anywhere within 24 hours.[3]

Seventh, we seem to have gone overboard on mine-laying ships, especially since the best element of anti-mine warfare is the helicopter. We can achieve savings and distribute the anti-mine capability more widely by reducing the planned number of ships from 26 to 20, while retaining the procurement program for the associated helicopters and their support packages and spreading these out as embarked organic assets across the fleet.

Eighth, somewhere in all the planning for the naval fleet of the 21st Century we seem to have over-looked operations other than war! The best force for the avoidance of conflict and the resolution of non-combat crisis is the force that can deliver food, water, medicine, engineering and other civil affairs relief *from the sea*, with a low logistics and ideological footprint. The seaborne peacekeeping force should be comprised of at least 16 roll-on/roll-off bulk carriers such as we use for the Maritime Prepositioning Ships (MPS) but modified to berth a few hundred engineering, police, and civil affairs personnel, to have a small field hospital capability combining onboard capabilities with MASH-type capabilities that can be established ashore, plus the right kind of supplies as well as a good mix of ground and air mobility assets. Half of these ships should be designed to operate in support of the half of the countries from which pier-side offload is not an option, i.e. they should be able to do a combination of instream and helicopter-borne offload.

---

[3] The U.S. Navy is not capable of defending itself, at this time, from cigarette boats (open ocean racing boats) loaded with explosives and driven by suicidal pilots.

118

Ninth and finally we come to hospital ships. Two exist in the reserve fleet and there are no plans for any more ships of this type. In the face of growing concerns about continental-level diseases and the risk of bio-chemical terrorism, and out of respect for the growing dangers of revolution and forced emigration related to starvation and disease, it would make sense to invest more heavily in medical assistance platforms, possibly with multi-national manning. A naval force properly cognizant of the four warrior classes and the deteriorating expeditionary environment should have three large hospital ships and five small hospital ships. In combination with the civil affairs platforms and a discreet mix of destroyers and patrol craft, these hospital ships (capable of cooking 7,500 meals daily while also distilling 75,000 gallons of fresh water daily) could be the centerpiece of a naval peacekeeping and humanitarian assistance force.

Yes, this will cost money. One rough estimate, outlined in the figure below, suggests that it will cost (very roughly) just under $20 billion dollars— or roughly 2% of the Department of Defense budget per year for just four years. Spread over four years, the cost is a number so small in the larger scheme of things that this becomes a no-brainer.

Rough Cost Calculations	Number of Ships	Acquisition Cost (M)	Conversion Cost (M)	Total (Billions)	Years To Do
Troop/Attack Submarine	15	0	200	3.000	2
Carrier Wing Realignment	4	0	50	0.200	1
Battleship Reactivation	2	0	125	0.250	2
Whidbey Island LHD Plus Up	9	0	75	0.675	2
SPRUANCE Conversions	25	0	200	5.000	2
Additional Patrol Craft	60	125	0	7.500	4
Reduction of Mine Ships	6	0	-125	-0.750	1
MPS Civil Affairs Conversions	16	50	100	2.400	2
Hospital Ship Conversions	6	50	200	1.500	3
TOTAL COST				19.775	

Figure 31: Rough Cost for Revitalizing the U.S. Navy[4]

[4] DOI: 2 April 1999. With appreciation to Ron O'Rourke, Congressional Research Service, for assistance in preparing very rough estimates. Costs are without refueling

119

At the same time, this entire cost is immediately convertible to jobs and new work for shipyards located in many different states. The practical effect of this expenditure must be carefully considered by those that authorized and appropriate our national security budget, for at one stroke we modernize the Navy, create a seaborne littoral and peacekeeping force, and dramatically increase our ability to protect Embassies and Americans overseas.

Adaptive engagement, understood in the context of the multi-faceted threat and the strategic generalizations that we have discussed above, provides a frame of reference for making deep and decisive changes in how we train, equip, and organize the Corps. Adaptive engagement will place a premium on foreign area and language skills; on civil affairs, military police, combat and non-combat engineering, public affairs, and intelligence skills. Adaptive engagement will place a premium on being able to "pile-on" anywhere in the world—a platoon with a Cobra overhead within 12-24 hours; a company with a couple of Harriers within 24-48 hours, a battalion landing team in full force within 72 hours, a regimental landing team within seven days, a full-up Marine Expeditionary Force within fourteen days. Adaptive engagement will also validate the need to reduce shooters and doers by ten percent so that intelligence and other forms of "engagement" can be doubled and tripled within the declining force structure.

Budgeting for National Security

Anyone can throw money at problems, especially if they are willing to abuse the unlimited borrowing power of the U.S. Government. It takes real thinking to make trade-offs within a budget. In order to implement this new strategy and effect these recommended force structure changes from within our existing budgets, we could make a straight-forward redirection of $20 billion a year from within the existing Program 50 budget, a budget now replete with an RMA that is both unaffordable and ineffective against the real-world threat.

---

of submarines. Battleship reactivation cost based on August 1995 Navy estimate to Senate Armed Services Committee (SASC) of $115-210M.

Program 50 Modifications		Program 150 Increases	
Kill 2+/JV 2010	-5.0	Digital Marshall Plan	+2.0
Kill Missile Defense	-3.0	Global Coverage Network	+2.0
Kill new attack sub	-2.0	Increase State Operations	+1.0
Kill fancy TacAir	-5.0	Double AID projects	+2.0
Kill CVN & DD21	-5.0	Peace Corps times five	+1.0
Build 450 Ship Navy	+5.0	USIA + Culture	+1.0
Home Front Force	+2.0	International Education	+1.0
Constabulary Force	+2.0		
Ground Truth Force	+0.1		
TOTAL Net Reduction	**-10.0**	**Total Net Increase**	**+10.0**
All dollar amounts in billions per year.			

Figure 32: Minimal Mandatory Budget Adjustments

Conclusion

We require a National Security Act, not only to repair the known deficiencies in our national intelligence and counterintelligence community, but to effect fundamental reform in how the taxpayer dollar in managed within the Department of Defense. This strategy, and the attendant force structure, are achievable within six years from where we are today, but will *not* be achievable as readily if we delay because the U.S. Navy is decommissioning ships as we speak—we must put a stop to their dismantling of our submarine, destroyer, and frigate capabilities because it is the U.S. Navy, as CINC PEACE, that will have the greatest burden to bear in support of CINC SOLIC (U.S. Marine Corps) and CINC WAR (U.S. Army). We must give CINC HOME (the U.S. Air Force) the financial resources—and culturally-powerful incentives—with which to rapidly reconfigure itself into an effective Home Front Defense that fully integrates and respects the needs and concerns of our state & local and private sector partners in our "total war" environment. If we adopt a 1+iii strategy and implement the recommendations of this review, America will enter the 21st Century with a national security architecture well suited to our needs and agile—able to fight and win in any clime or place.

Only citizen-soldiers and citizen-voters, willing to think about the threat and apply their common sense to their communications to our elected officials, can achieve this kind of reform and ensure passage of legislation.

121

Part III:
The New Craft of Intelligence

> *Those who won our independence believed that the final end of the state was to make men free to develop their faculties; and that in its government the deliberative forces should prevail over the arbitrary....They believed that...without free speech and assembly discussion would be futile;....that the greatest menace to freedom is an inert people; that public discussion is a political duty; and that this should be a fundamental principle of the American government.*[1]

Part III presents "the new craft of intelligence," a craft that combines the proven process of intelligence with the wealth of overtly available information in foreign languages, and utilizes the Internet, to create a new form of "information commons" such as was envisioned very early on by Pierre Tielhard de Chardin and later H.G. Wells.

The new craft of intelligence is personal, public, and political. It is personal because only a global grid of volunteer collectors and contributors can allow the necessary critical mass of localized data entry and distributed judgment to come together. It is public because the problems confronting mankind are well beyond the abilities of individual secret agencies or even entire governments to control—only a publicly devised and executed national security strategy, supported by a public intelligence process that issues public estimates and public warnings, can lead to the necessary consensus and the proper allocation of resources. Finally, it is political, because the new craft of intelligence is meaningless and ineffective unless the citizen voter, the citizen taxpayer, chooses to engage the issues confronting mankind, and chooses to take back the authority inherent in our Constitution and its belief in democratic governance. Public intelligence + public voting = informed democracy.

---

[1] Supreme Court Justice Louis Brandeis, *Whitney v. California*, 274 US 357, 372 (1927), as cited by Cass Sunstein, *republic.com* (Princeton, 2001), page 47.

Chapter 11, "The Lessons of History from All Cultural Perspectives," discusses both the need for and the means to collect, digitize, translate, and continually renew a very large database of historical perspectives as well as current opinions from all cultural perspectives. Such an endeavor could place special emphasis on Islamic and Chinese materials, and then expand rapidly to embrace Indian and Pakistani, Israeli and Arab, and varied African and Eurasian tribal heritages.

Chapter 12: "Web-Based Global Coverage in All Languages," discusses the obstacles to global coverage through multi-lingual media and gray literature monitoring, concluding that this endeavor, while essential to informed governance at all levels, is beyond the capabilities of any single government or nation. Only a multi-lateral application of the proven process of intelligence to open sources of information that are legally and ethically available, will succeed. The Internet, if reinforced by a Digital Marshall Plan funded by the United States of America, could become the "information commons" that is needed to study, understand, and deliberate upon the challenges facing mankind as a whole.

Chapter 13, "Creating a Truly National State-Based Intelligence Network," discusses the various elements of the distributed intellect of the Nation that are not now harnessed nor integrated, and proposes a state-based means of creating community intelligence networks within each state and city that in turn are part of a new national "virtual intelligence community."

Chapter 14, "Spies, Satellites, & Secrecy in Context and Narrowly Focused," provides an absolute defense and demand for the continuation of carefully focused clandestine and covert intelligence activities. There will always be great evil in the world, and there will always be very dangerous groups that must be penetrated if another 9-11 is to be avoided. While some unilateral spying will still be needed, by and large the spying of the future must be multi-lateral, bringing together civilized governments in common espionage ventures against uncivilized gangs.

Chapter 15, "New Rules for the New Craft of Intelligence," is the conclusion of the book and provides what the author hopes will be an inspiring and uplifting mission and vision statement for the smart citizens of all Nations.

124

The Lessons of History from All Cultural Perspectives

Diversify, or die. This is the core message of historical biology, and all the more important to our reflections on the future of intelligence and operations because this message is in stark contrast to the prevailing paradigm of incremental evolution.

The development of bureaucracy and of corporate cultures have further strengthened all forms of resistance to new ideas, and what passes for "revolutionary" in such environments is normally nothing more than a leap-frogging of one generation along the same evolutionary continuum.[1]

There are actually biological as well as sociological explanations for the die-hard resistance to new ideas. On the biological front, there are compelling studies that demonstrate that fully one-half of any adult brain has been "killed off" by that brain's being brought up in conformity with a specific language and culture. At the same time, other compelling studies have demonstrated that "reality" is a social construct, and that mass hallucinations as well as deeply-embedded "rules of the game" are the norm within any society.[2]

The attack of 11 September 2001 has brought to the fore the importance of *balance* or *diversification*. We must have balance between our

---

[1] As a general rule, bureaucracies are only open to diversity and new choices when there is a crisis and their existing structures and processes are clearly not working. However, if money is thrown at the problem to fund work-arounds, the bureaucracies will get over the crisis without having to do any fundamental restructuring. See Gifford and Elizabeth Pinchot, *The End of Bureaucracy & The Rise of the Intelligent Organization* (Berrett-Koehler, 1994), *passim*.

[2] Howard Bloom, *Global Brain: The Evolution of Mass Mind From the Big Bang to the 21st Century* (John Wiley and Sons, 2000), *passim*. See also the extraordinary book by Andrew Gordon, *The Rules of the Game: Jutland and British Naval Command* (Naval Institute Press, 2000). As a general note, for each book cited in these notes, there is a corresponding lengthy review in the annotated bibliography.

125

homeland defense and overseas defense capabilities; between domestic counterintelligence and foreign intelligence; and between symmetric and asymmetric concepts and doctrine and forces. This chapter introduces the new craft of intelligence—a craft that is comprehensive, reliable, swift, and *relevant* to both the traditional and non-traditional threats[3]—and discusses the first of the four quadrants, that dealing with the lessons of history.

The new craft of intelligence must be held accountable for explaining the threat in such compelling terms that political action cannot be denied—one means of doing so is by issuing public intelligence estimates and public intelligence warnings to the citizen-voters, at local, state, and national levels.

None of the traditional threats that our military understands have diminished—indeed, the attacks of 11 September 2001 demonstrate that our world is perhaps twice as dangerous as we might have imagined.

The stark reality is that only Australia, Canada, and the United Kingdom can be relied upon to be consistently favorable to our interests, and even then we cannot necessarily rely on them to make changes to their immigration and visa processes or to enhance their internal security measures against non-traditional threats.

America is very much "on its own" and whatever new craft of intelligence it may adopt, we must be able to achieve an asymmetric advantage over every threat to our national security and our national prosperity.

Intelligence is vital to our future security, not only overseas but also at home, where we need a new craft of *counter*-intelligence.[4]

---

[3] The predominant characteristic of non-traditional and asymmetric threats is their very character—*not* traditional, *not* symmetric. For this reason, as scholars like Dr. Steven Metz and Dr. Max Manwaring have pointed out, *conceptual flexibility* is the core competency of future leaders and the intelligence professionals that support them. The new craft of intelligence is thus the *fundamental* differentiator and factor in achieving asymmetric advantage against non-traditional threats. Dr. Max Manwaring, *Internal Wars: Rethinking Problem and Response* (Strategic Studies Institute, Studies in Asymmetry, September 2001), page 76; and Dr. Steven Metz, *The Future of Insurgency* (Strategic Studies Institute, 1993), *passim*.

[4] Counterintelligence (or, intelligence against enemy intelligence) is a major aspect of the craft of intelligence. When used together with intelligence, the term emphasizes the distinct responsibilities of the two sides of the intelligence coin. When the word

The new craft of intelligence must overcome both the political and the professional shortcomings that have plagued U.S. intelligence and counterintelligence for over a half century.

The new craft of intelligence is neither complex nor mysterious. It represents a thoughtful and balanced shift of emphasis from secrecy to openness; from traditional military concerns to concerns about non-traditional factors including water, energy, food, disease and general sustainability; from current monitoring to historical and cultural contextual analysis; and finally, from a fragmented community of secret government agencies, to a vibrant network that is able to harness the distributed intelligence of the Whole Earth. Above all, the new craft of intelligence is comprehensive, reliable, swift, and *relevant* to the challenges of all threat forms and especially non-traditional threat forms. The new craft of intelligence, properly effected, provides an *asymmetric advantage* in dealing with any challenges, be they violent or non-violent, state or non-state, immediate or long-term.

The new craft of intelligence will elevate the importance of spies and secrecy, but will do so by focusing this traditional element very narrowly.[5]

Most importantly, the new craft of intelligence makes deliberate investments in global history, a shared global open source network, and a homefront network.[6]

---

intelligence is used alone, it always includes and provides for counterintelligence as a substantive sub-set of intelligence.

[5] In no way should the new craft of intelligence be interpreted as suggesting a draconian cut in funding for secret satellites and spies. While there must be a better balance between what we spend on technical collection and technical processing (from 85% to 60%), funding for the human element—both clandestine spies and all-source analysts—must be at least doubled if not tripled.

[6] A Homefront Defense Analysis Center (HDAC), together with individual state-based Community Intelligence Centers under the sovereign authority of the respective Governors (i.e. *not* federalized) is an absolutely vital capability that should be mandated by Congress as part of any legislation dealing with homeland security.

Below is an illustration of the four quadrants of "the new craft of intelligence."

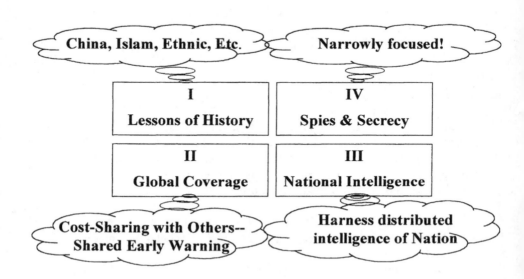

Figure 33: The New Craft of Intelligence

The Lessons of History

The first quadrant, the most fundamental, the most neglected, is that of the *lessons of history*. When entire volumes are written on anticipating ethnic conflict, and history is not mentioned at all, America has indeed become ignorant. We have failed to honor history, and we will pay the price. Despite the fact that most major government organizations have very talented historians who labor anonymously to keep that organization's past glories well burnished, very rarely does any political appointee or senior policymaker call for the historian to inquire: "what lessons have we learned in the past?" There is an easy fix to this—we must embrace the historian, empower the historian, demand that the historian be a member of the high table that advises the new leadership in each organization—a Presidential Board of Historians would be salutary, as would a national project to digitize, index, and make accessible to the public the major works of Chinese, Islamic, and foreign tribal histories, among others.

A Digital History Program, federally-funded, should identify, collect, digitize, and translate essential Chinese and Islamic historical materials including public pronouncements by leadership, and such other foreign language historical, political, economic, social, cultural, and related information, as needed to create a foundation for rapidly visualizing and modeling both historical patterns and relationships between current information and historical information. Included in this initiative should be an international network of eminent historians, organized into nodes of three experts for each area of interest (one U.S., one European, one non-European) to serve as a board of advisors and first echelon collection management cell for the acquisition and processing of new historical materials. All of this historical information should be made available via the Internet, in this way creating a genuine "information commons" for multi-cultural and multi-national analysis.

If a multi-lateral consortium of government and non-government organizations could come together in appreciation of the urgency of ensuring that deep historical and multi-cultural understanding be a requisite foundation for all national security decisions by any party, then a combination of a massive multi-lingual historical database, with a web-based means of accessing and displaying this information, could lead to a capability able to display, for any issue, a *side-by-side* view of differing cultural and historical perspectives.

The Spratley Islands, for example, could be brought up on the screen, and four points of view selected: Chinese, Vietnamese, Philippine, and U.S. Then, as the issues are reviewed, the viewer could see, in each of the four quadrants, the equivalent view with hot links to the original documents and their English-language translations. Using advanced visualization technology, changes over time within a cultural perspective, and changes between specific cultural perspectives, could be readily identified. If we commit ourselves to preserving multi-cultural and multi-lingual history digitally, we will be creating a store of knowledge of deep and lasting value to future peacemaking efforts.

Perhaps most importantly, by ensuring that the "commons" is open and robust, we can ensure that national security policy will respect multi-cultural history, and the common sense of the people.

129

Web-Based Global Coverage
In All Languages

The second quadrant is that of *global coverage*. Whether we agree or not with the former and present Directors of Central Intelligence who are on record as saying that our $30 billion a year can only cover the top tier targets (i.e. they do not permit us to focus on the lower tier issues and countries), the fact is that it is the lower tier countries where the future wars are being spawned, and it is the lower tier issues such as the collapse of global public health and the vanishing of major fresh water supplies, that will decide the fate of future generations.

Therefore, let us acknowledge that global coverage by spies and secret means is *unaffordable* and *unachievable* by any single nation. At the same time, let us acknowledge that the bulk of the information that is relevant to lower tier threats is both unclassified and in the private sector—in the hands of corporations and non-governmental organizations.

The Internet makes possible an alternative model for global intelligence that relies on distributed collection, distributed processing, distributed analysis, and *shared intelligence*. Perhaps more to the point, it permits *burden-sharing* and Global Information Management, an extension of the concept of Corporate Information Management—one-time data entry, global access.[1] A structured international project to establish shared current intelligence reports on every country and issue of mutual concern, together with related experts forums, Internet and private database link tables, and multi-lingual distance learning

---

[1] This term was characteristic of all that Paul Strassmann tried to do as Director of Defense Information in the 1990's. If redundant intelligence collection, analysis, and production could be eliminated among the strategic, operational, tactical, and technical intelligence organizations, an estimated savings of no less than 20% *per country* could be achieved in costs of personnel, equipment, and acquisition. The cumulative savings could easily fund the creation of the global virtual intelligence network, and its extension down to every neighborhood, county, and province or state, in the world.

packages, would go a long way toward *increasing* global consciousness and *reducing* the cost of *basic* intelligence.

There are six distinct initiatives that should be mandated by Congress as part of any revitalization of national intelligence.

Non-Governmental Organization Data Network

There is an urgent need to rapidly migrate all non-governmental organizations (NGO) toward digital information creation and processing. An NGO network and a massive federally-funded data exploitation center with advanced indexing, clustering, visualization, and other technologies, should be provided to all qualifying NGOs at no cost. NGO policy and other restricted materials need not be on this network, but normal NGO reporting, including especially reports from their field representatives regarding the actual conditions on the ground, and their formal published reports, would comprise an essential "bank" upon which governments, corporations, and citizens could draw to improve their understanding of the real world.

Global Virtual Task Forces

Every nation and every multi-national corporation has both a need to monitor global conditions across a wide variety of countries and topics, and expertise to contribute from their unique perspective. The time has come to create a "world brain" at varying levels of collaboration and openness.

For every country of the world a "Master Council" could be created, comprised of the top international experts for that topic, based on citation analysis,[2] together with various Working Groups corresponding to government and corporate needs.

---

[2] Citation analysis is surprising not well-known to most intelligence professionals or scholars. It utilizes the information created by the Institute of Scientific Information (ISI) and its publications, the *Science Citation Index* and the *Social Science Citation Index*, to identify individuals whose work is especially respected by others as shown their their citation of the work in their own original materials.

Below is a representation of the functionalities that could be made available, at varying levels of access and privilege corresponding to both proven expertise and government or corporate sponsorship.

Figure 34: Web-Based Virtual Intelligence Community[3]

One of the insights emerging from the author's decade of work in the open source intelligence arena has been the realization that not only are weekly reviews of the open literature (or in an all-source environment, both open and closed information) essential, but they are also terribly wasteful in that they are done countless times, each day, but different organizations. In addition, such reports are not the "end product" as the U.S. Intelligence Community and others have tended to assume, but rather they are the foundation for the true acme of skill among analysts and decision-makers, the near-real-time interactive

---

[3] Operational Planning Group (OPG) is a term of art within the U.S. military for virtually-distributed key personnel who are matrixed into a joint effort regardless of their location or other "fixed" responsibilities. Virtual Private Network (VPN) is any managed network that leverages Internet connectivity rather than dedicated circuits.

discussion that relates conditions to means and means to ends—the expert forums with multiple levels of both security and access.

Also required are distance learning modules to ensure both a shared foundation of knowledge as well as to provide individuals new to the topic with a place to go (rather than consuming precious time from experts who have better things to do than orient new people), a shared virtual library, and various shared features that are readily creatable with today's information technology, but have not been because of a failure of vision on the part of the existing leadership, as well as understandable but surmountable cultural obstacles from the various bureaucracies.

A shared "Rolodex" is fundamental.   There is no reason why individuals across various governmental and non-governmental organizations cannot have a web-based directory of key contacts that offers both a public service (contact information, expertise, background, current projects) as well as a private space for organizationally-specific information that is not in the public domain.

Similarly, a shared calendar, especially one that spanned various time zones and national interests, and then led to the formation of virtual interest groups able to access information from key events that they could not afford to attend personally (because of either funding or time limitations), would ensure that critical new knowledge was rapidly disseminated.

A shared virtual budget, a transparent consolidated spread sheet of all funds available for the procurement of sources, software, and services in relation to each OPG, would quickly reveal massive ignorance and waste. The bottom line is that if every organization's budget is actually visible to serious experts, they will quickly agree among themselves on how to spend that money in a much more collaborative and expert fashion. If the web-based OPG can access the information being funded by various disparate projects, there is every incentive for the experts to redirect funds from duplicative or badly focused endeavors, to new initiatives applauded by the experts in the group.

Finally, a 24/7 "virtual plot" is essential if we are to embed strategic as well as tactical warning into every issue area. There is no reason, with the existing capabilities represented by the commercial imagery and geospatial data and visualization industry, why every datum cannot have a time as well as a geospatial identity, and why every expert should not be able to access their information in a time and space continuum that quickly visualizes trends as well as patterns and anomalies.

Generic Intelligence Training Program

It has become clear to me in the past decade that even our most experienced intelligence analysts know almost nothing about what is available to them from the real world of open sources, softwares, and services. At the same time, our business and academic communities have failed to mature and urgently need training in the proven process of intelligence.

A web-based distance learning program in both these areas, supplemented by a multi-national mobile training team that can roam the world teaching government, non-government, corporate, and academic audiences how to move up to a new level of intellectual performance, appears to me to be a vital step in creating a true "world brain," and a web-based community of voluntarily collaborative efforts.[4a]

Each nation should have at least one center of excellence for each of these distinct but complementary domains of expertise, and we should over time ensure that both the process of intelligence as well as the specifics of open source information are embedded into every operational or functional training course offered by any university, corporation, or government.

Regional Open Source Information Networks

It is not possible for any single government to dominate global information in over twenty-nine languages[4b] relevant to national security planning and programming. It is, however, possible for the U.S. government to take the lead in establishing joint centers in each of the four regions where there is a U.S. military commander and a theater headquarters exists: the Pacific (with Australia); the Southern portion of the Western Hemisphere; Europe including the Turkish-Iranian axis; and the African-Eurasian collective.

[4a] Mr. Robert Heibel, FBI (Ret.), deserves great credit for having established the first undergraduate degree program specifically designed to train research and intelligence analysts, at Mercyhurst College in Erie, Pennsylvania, and also for conceptualizing the idea of a generic intelligence training program (GITI) for the U.S government.
[4b] See page 16 or page 187 for the complete list of these languages.

In partnership with at least one or more key nations (e.g. Australia, Chile, South Africa, Turkey, and Sweden), and including as interested parties Russia, China, and other countries, each of these centers would leverage the ally's indigenous language skills as well as regional direct access to both open and gray literature materials, while the U.S. provides the funding and the information technology to permit the daily harvesting of all relevant open source information.

Future Intelligence Collaborative Environment

The U.S. government routinely wastes hundreds of millions of dollars on information technology initiatives because it has no single focal point for coordinating generic requirements.

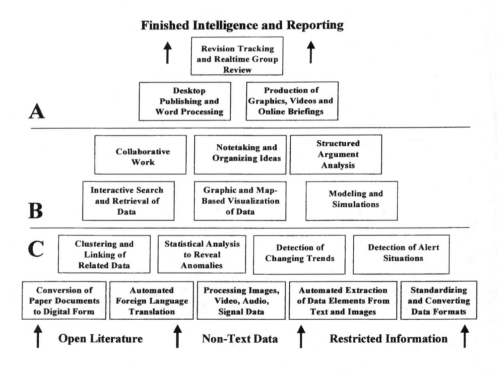

Figure 35: Generic All-Source Information Handling Functionalities

136

Billions of dollars are being earmarked for expenditure within the Defense Advanced Research Projects Agency (DARPA). Several worthwhile projects, meanwhile, including one focused on the Future Intelligence Collaborative Environment (FICE), are being sponsored by the Joint Forces Command, and by various elements of the U.S. Intelligence Community including the three technical agencies and the Central Intelligence Agency (CIA).[5] Further out, all of the "consumer" organizations in the U.S. government, the actual departments managing defense, foreign affairs, interior, justice, and so on, are all spending money on their own.

No one, anywhere, is actually beating heads together and communicating three fundamentals about the modern information environment:

1. Functionalities are generic, independent of the data type or sensitivity, and we should buy or build generic capabilities that can be migrated to state and local governments. Ideally we should encourage private sector standards, including transparent and stable Application Program Interfaces (API) that permit such functionalities to "plug and play" without having to pay tribute to a single predatory vendor.

2. Ninety percent of the expertise and information needed by government is in the private sector. Any funds being spent on secret private networks that are not fully integratable with the Internet (i.e. do not require separate hardware and software for access open versus secret information) are wasted funds, and are perpetuating the isolation of the government from its people and from private sector data.

3. The Internet is the backbone of 21st Century information sharing and knowledge development. Instead of being afraid to join the Internet, government must release the power of unencumbered encryption and raise the Internet's level of security to the point that the government is comfortable moving Top Secret and sensitive compartmented information across public Internet pathways.[6]

---

[5] The generic requirements on the previous page were developed by Diane Webb under the oversight of Gordon Oehler, in the Office of Scientific and Weapons Research (OSWR) at CIA. They remain the best requirements against which to coordinate efforts, not just within government, but in partnership with the private sector.
[6] A National Knowledge Strategy is long overdue for annual development & renewal.

Digital Marshall Plan

If there is one challenge that is truly beyond the ability of any government or combination of governments to address, it is the challenge of near-real-time open source information collection, digitization, and translation. The vast majority of the information relevant to national security decision-making, in so far as it is published or resident in the Third World, is simply not susceptible to technical collection because it is not yet digital.

A Digital Marshall Plan that extends the Internet down to every village eventually, but at least to every province, and that provides free Internet access and free web-publishing software and storage for indigenous publishers, including self-publishing academics and journalists, would break this log-jam and free the distributed indigenous knowledge from its current imprisonment by geography, poverty, and publishing industry conventions.

Administered by the Peace Corps, with diplomatic, military and law enforcement supplements managed by the Departments of State, Defense, and Justice, and perhaps also by the Departments of Agriculture and Commerce, such a program would literally change our worldview almost overnight. It would make available to every citizen "intelligence minuteman" a level of detailed knowledge here-to-fore reserved for very wealthy elites, and it would enable all the power of information technology to be brought to bear on those portions of the world that today reasonably can be described as being in the "Dark Ages."

Taken together, these six initiatives will put America back in touch with the real world, while also opening the door to a massive "information peacekeeping" campaign enabled by the creation of this information commons.

1. Non-Governmental Organization Data Network
2. Global Virtual Task Forces
3. Generic Intelligence Training Program
4. Regional Open Source Information Networks
5. Future Intelligence Collaboration Environment
6. Digital Marshall Plan

The future of intelligence lies here, not within a world of spies, satellites, and secrecy. The center of gravity is open, digital, and international.

138

Creating a State-Based Intelligence Community

National Intelligence Writ Large

The third quadrant requires that we construct a *virtual intelligence community* that brings together the elements of our *distributed* national intelligence (see Figure 9, page 45).

We must harness the full intellectual power of the nation, a distributed network of local and state government officials, corporate officials, military and police officials, non-governmental officials, journalists, academics, and individual students and citizens—the "intelligence minutemen" of the 21st Century."

The center of gravity for national security and national prosperity lie now in the private sector and its intellectual property as well as its accumulated knowledge.

As the 11 September 2001 attacks demonstrated so well, we really must take the asymmetric threats much more seriously, for they demand intelligence sharing between federal, state, and local levels of government and we must devise new means of addressing these needs. There are five critical characteristics of the new *national* intelligence community:

- First, it will use the Internet as the common communications and information-sharing medium;

- Second; it will default to unclassified intelligence the majority of the time—information can be sensitive or restricted without being classified;[1]

---

[1] Through appropriate senior consultations OSS has established that Secret information can be tunneled within the Internet now; that Top Secret tunneling could be approved

- Third; it will demand the rapid transfer of the proven process of intelligence—requirements definition, collection management, source discovery and validation, multi-source fusion, and compelling presentation—to each of these constituent elements of our Nation;

- Fourth, it will fully resource procurement of substantial information sources and services available from the private sector; and

- Fifth, it will create, state-by-state, integrated intelligence communities with a shared center.[2]

This is the quadrant where the U.S. Army could make an extraordinary contribution to national, state, and local intelligence. Acting upon its mandate as the lead DoD element responsible for home defense, the U.S. Army and its National Guard elements could establish, in short order both a Homeland Defense Analysis Center and—in each and every state—a Community Analysis Centers (CAC).

The National Guard, because of its unique status under the jurisdiction of each Governor, could offer up its intelligence specialists and some of its military police specialists for a new special program that would see them deputized as law enforcement officials. This is an elegant solution to the continuing challenge of being able to fully share and integrate national intelligence and law enforcement intelligence. Selected members of the regular and reserve Army intelligence corps could also be judiciously selected for federal deputization, at the same time that a cadre of top law enforcement

---

within the year; and that CODEWORD tunneling is expected to be approved within 3-4 years. The Internet is the new C4I backbone for *all* normal communications within the virtual (national) intelligence community, at *any* level of classification.

[2] Whether the states are regarded as the rear area for overseas war or the front line for defense against asymmetric warfare initiated by others, it is clear that a state-based Community Analysis Center (CAC) is needed, not only to interface with the national command authorities and intelligence networks, but to bring together within the state all of the relevant law enforcement, public health, emergency response, and other localized defense capabilities.

140

officers might be trained in national and military intelligence sources and methods.

State-Based National Intelligence Network

The spaghetti nightmare of federal elements that have varying responsibilities for aspects of homeland defense and security is such that no coordinator or director is going to be effective in the absence of three fundamental elements of authority: budget control, an oversight staff, and a fully operational intelligence center. Putting single representatives from each agency together in a room is insufficient.

A state-based national intelligence network must be comprised of four elements:

First, a national 24/7 homeland security intelligence center in which all relevant foreign intelligence, law enforcement intelligence, and corporate security intelligence can be received and plotted in near-real-time across a geospatial representation of the nation at one level, and the world at another. In the absence of such a center, with fully-qualified watchstanders around the clock, homeland security becomes just another program, and not a serious commitment.

Second, because homeland defense takes place at the state and local level, it is imperative that we avoid at all costs the federalization of any aspect of state and local security. State sovereignty is not a concept that is understood by most federal bureaucrats. State sovereignty, and the transfer of the proven process of intelligence to state employees, is an essential pre-requisite to *sustainable* state and local security. Individual state-managed Community Analysis Centers, each under the sovereignty of their respective Governor, and manned by trusted state employees, *not* by federal representatives, are essential not only to defeat terrorism, but to help states do a proper job of monitoring medical, public safety, and natural disaster indications & warning signals.

Third, some form of Chamber of Commerce network is needed to better integrate and encourage information sharing among state-based corporations and small businesses. Federal funding for an international chamber of commerce business information network, and the nurturing of business intelligence units within U.S. corporations, is recommended.

141

Ultimately the bulk of the funding will come from the corporations themselves, as they gradually realize that they have much to gain from joining a business-oriented global open source intelligence consortium.

Fourth, and finally, a University of the Republic, with state-based nodes, should be established to bring together and educate "cohorts" of mid-career subject-matter experts from state government, non-profit activities, businesses, local universities, and federal agencies. Over time this will create a vibrant network of professionals at both the state and the national levels who share a mutual respect for the importance of monitoring global activities relevant to state security and prosperity, and for sharing information across organizational and cultural lines.

A Note on Prosperity

It is absolutely vital that the funds being directed toward counter-terrorism not be spent in a manner that creates counter-terrorist specific capabilities that are useless against more generic challenges such as broad plague or epidemic or some form of natural disaster that cuts the state off from other states and the federal government. We cannot afford to build a special intelligence network for each distinct challenge. We must build a *generic* state-based intelligence network, one that uses the Internet rather than dedicated federal secret computers and communications lines, and this network must serve the state across all its needs, not just to counter terrorism.

Having said that, it should then be noteworthy that a state-based national intelligence network that relies predominantly on open sources of information could in fact be a major contributor to prosperity. As both state governments and state-based corporations and small businesses learn to apply the proven process of intelligence to their normal decision-making about what to build, what to buy, and so on, we can take state and local decision-making, both government and private, to a new level of sensibility. Informed decision-making will help cut costs, reduce taxes, enhance regulatory capabilities without onerous paperwork, and ultimately increase profits across the board.

We are a smart people, but a dumb Nation. A web-based global intelligence network, combined with a state-based national intelligence network, will create a Smart Nation with global reach on any topic.

Spies, Satellites & Secrecy
In Context

We still need spies, satellites and secrecy. The human condition has not changed, there is still great evil in the world, and it is all too easy for evil people to obtain weapons of mass destruction, to carry out electronic attacks on our financial systems, to engage in activities capable of killing hundreds if not tens of thousands. America and other nations will always need their spies and their secrets, and we honor that need.

The new craft of intelligence does not seek to diminish or alter the nature, structure, or funding of the classified intelligence community. It does recommend that no less than 5% of the classified intelligence budget be spent on open sources and services directly pertinent to the needs of the clandestine human collectors, the covert technical collectors, and the all-source intelligence analysts.[1]

The new craft of intelligence specifically concurs with and adopts the strong views of the Aspin-Brown Commission with respect to the following:

The Commission believes that intelligence agencies should not satisfy requests for analysis when such analysis

---

[1] The generally acknowledged figure for classified community spending on open sources is one-half of 1% of the budget or $150 million a year. Two-thirds of that is for the Foreign Broadcast Information Service (FBIS). At least $500 million a year should be spent in direct open source support endeavors for the all-source analysts, and another $500 million a year should be spent in commercial imagery procurement and post-processing to meet theater and service needs for military targeting and mapping applications. An additional $500 million a year would be reasonable to support a service of common concern for the rest of government. In short, nothing less than $1.5 billion a year, or 5 percent of the national intelligence budget, should be earmarked for a government-wide open source intelligence (OSINT) program.

143

could be readily accomplished using publicly available sources, unless for some reason the results of such analysis would require confidentiality or the specific expertise of the analyst would add significantly to the analysis of the open source material.[2]

In other words, the primary responsibility for the new craft of intelligence, for executing the three quadrants that are not secret, and for integrating the secret with the non-secret, is on the policymaker, the acquisition manager, and the commander—intelligence is an inherent responsibility of command.[3]

My first book, *ON INTELLIGENCE*, covers both the deficiencies and the recommended enhancements for the federal-level national intelligence community in great detail. Recently, however, I had an opportunity to develop a one-page summary of needed improvements, and wish to share that here.

21 November 2001

TALKING POINTS ON INTELLIGENCE REFORM

1. Special Committee. Retaining Senate Select Committee on Intelligence for day-to-day oversight of classified intelligence matters, each Committee of the Senate should establish majority and minority Member focal points for intelligence comprising a Special Committee as the steering group for strategic direction across all jurisdictions.
2. National Intelligence and Information Strategy. Engage all Senate jurisdictions.

---

[2] Aspin-Brown Commission, page 17. The general intent of the Commission as reflected throughout the report is for the bulk of "all-source" analysis to move back to the end-user, who is responsible for their own open source collection and exploitation. The U.S. Intelligence Community "all-source" analyst is expected to spend the bulk of their time on classified information, with such open sources as are needed for tip-off or context being provided as needed.

[3] I regret to having misplaced the reference, but must acknowledge that this observation comes from one of the students, a Marine major, at the Post Graduate Intelligence Program (PGIP) in the late 1990's.

144

3. <u>Consolidated NFIP</u>. Apart from moving NRO, NSA, and NIMA into the consolidated NFIP, there should also be established a separate Homeland Defense Intelligence Program and a National Security Education Program.

4. <u>Homeland Defense Intelligence Program</u>. Create a central homeland defense intelligence center with 24/7 watch teams, and single Community Intelligence Centers, also 24/7 in each state, each under the sovereign authority of the Governor. Enhance National Guard role.

5. <u>National Security Education Program</u>. "A Nation's best defense in an educated citizenry." Program will fund science, technology, foreign area, & foreign language experts.

6. <u>Director-General for National Intelligence</u>. Placement of new DGNI on President's Staff, with oversight over Director of Classified Intelligence (DCI), Chairman of the elevated NIC, and a new Global Knowledge Foundation.

7. <u>Director of Classified Intelligence</u>. Rename and separate DCI position from that of agency head positions for each element outlined below. Consolidate management of personnel, security, training, and general infrastructure functions under DDCI/Administration.

8. <u>National Intelligence Council</u>. Expand to 120, with 5 person teams dedicated to defense, foreign affairs, finance & commerce, law enforcement, environment & culture; elevate to EOP, 1 new NIO to every Governor, Senate to be involved.

9. <u>Global Knowledge Foundation</u>. $1.5B a year fund for open source intelligence (OSINT) needs of both IC and all government departments, includes $500M a year for procurement of commercial imagery source material for defense, OSINT procurement by Country Teams.

10. <u>Technical Collection Agency</u>. Upgrade NRO to manage all technical programs.

11. <u>Clandestine Service Agency</u>. Separate from existing CIA, relying exclusively on non-official cover and no longer responsible for routine declared liaison.

12. <u>National Analysis Agency</u>. Upgrade CIA to National Analysis Agency with restored imagery, signals, measurements, and open source offices and funds for analytic tools; 200 multi-lingual mid-career analyst hires, 1000 adjunct reserve analysts.

13. <u>National Processing Agency</u>. Upgrade NSA to National Processing Agency, both SIGINT & all-source processing including clandestine HUMINT and open source information, ensuring that all field station

145

reports from all agencies including FBI are readily exploitable with advanced software and languages where NSA excels.

14. <u>National Geospatial Agency</u>. Combine NIMA with USGS (Recommended by NAPA study).

15. <u>Coalition Intelligence Program</u>. Create a coalition intelligence center that combines the new initiatives of NATO/SACLANT with those of JFCOM, 24/7 watch, multi-lingual excellence.

16. <u>Covert Action Transfer</u>. CIA/SOG transferred to USSOCOM.

17. <u>Counterintelligence Program</u>. New FBI business and homeland defense divisions created.

18. <u>Regional Ground Truth Battalions</u>. Each regional CINC to have a FAO battalion with language-qualified companies for intelligence, civil affairs, PAO, JAG, MP, logistics.

19. <u>Information Peacekeeping Program</u>. Establish pegs between defense "hard power" spending and Program 150 "soft power" investments in information aid. *St.*

This is the best I can do as a single individual. Unfamiliar acronyms can be seen in the list of expanded abbreviations as the end of the book. As this book is being finished Congress has agreed to create a joint staff to hold hearings on the 9-11 attacks, not in the spirit of a witchhunt but rather to judiciously and expeditiously identify key failure points needing legislative attention for rapid correction.

I have confidence, that because of 9-11, the importance of national intelligence and counterintelligence as our first line of defense is now understood by the President and both parties. While I would be troubled if we simply threw more money at the existing mind-sets and methods, all of which failed to prevent 9-11, I am confident that for the first time since 1947 there is a reasonable prospect for the passage of a new National Security Act of 2002.[4]

Every citizen should be reflecting on these important matters, and especially on how a state-based network and a global web-based network might help protect their property and their children. Think, vote, and *communicate.*

---

[4] Chapter 14 of *ON INTELLIGENCE* provides the actual language for such an Act, modeled after the National Security of 1992 that was not passed. The list of initiatives in this chapter supersedes the first book, but the bulk of the history and thinking and detail on why these specific reforms should be undertaken are in the first book.

146

New Rules for the New Craft of Intelligence

The new craft of intelligence is the operational manifestation of the American way of "netwar," and can provide a decisive asymmetric advantage from the neighborhood level to the national level, against non-traditional threats.

New Rules for the New Craft of Intelligence

001 Decision-Support is the Raison D'être

The days of confusing secrets with intelligence are over. The new craft of intelligence carefully distinguishes between *data*, which is the raw text, image or signal; *information* which is collated data of generic interest and generally broadcast; and *intelligence*, which is information that has been deliberately discovered, discriminated, distilled, and delivered to meet a specific decision-making requirement. *Intelligence is defined by the end product not by the source mix.* If the commander needs an unclassified answer in fifteen minutes that is one page in length, that is the intelligence objective.

002 Value-Added Comes from Analysis, Not Secret Sources

The all-source analyst can no longer rest their conclusions and their reputation on the 2% of the information they deal with, most of it from secret sources. In an era when over 90%—some would say over 95%—of the relevant information is readily available to anyone in the private sector, and especially in the absence of processing and translation capabilities available to the mainstream profit-making institutions, it is analytic tradecraft—a truly superior ability to create value-added insights through superior analytical knowledge (including historical knowledge) and technique—that distinguishes and gives value to the new craft of analysis.[1]

003 Global Coverage Matters More

Whereas the traditional craft of intelligence has focused on hard targets, and this is natural for a conglomeration of bureaucracies established during the

---

[1] Jack Davis, founder of the precursor to the Harvard Executive Program on Intelligence and of the Intelligence Successes and Failures Course, author of the series on analytic tradecraft, is the absolute master in this arena. He and his teachings should be much more prominent as we transition to the new craft of intelligence, and he should be a full partner, together with Gordon Oehler and a few others who were a decade or more ahead of their time, in defining the analytic skunkworks of sources, tools, and techniques that is needed to catapult all-source analysis out of the basement and back into the running as a serious profession.

Cold War, the new craft of intelligence recognizes that *surprise* comes from unanticipated combinations and that the safest strategy for avoiding surprise, *especially* from non-traditional threats, is to cast a very wide net. The new craft of intelligence demands constant monitoring of all countries and topics, not necessarily in terms of collection, but in terms of "pulsing" and change detection.[2]

004 Non-Traditional Threats Are of Paramount Importance

Terrorism, genocide, proliferation, transnational crime, and toxic bombs, to name just five, are non-traditional threats of the first order. Disease, water shortages, and energy as well as resource conflicts are also of vital importance. The new craft of intelligence divides its emphasis roughly equally among state, non-state, and environmental threats.

005 Intelligence without Translation is Ignorant

This requires very strong emphasis. The failure of our government to translate all of the Arabic documents captured after the first World Trade Center bombing will stand in history as the single dumbest counterintelligence decision ever made. Conceptually, doctrinally, and financially, we have disparaged and blocked out the reality that the really important intelligence information is more often than not going to be in a foreign language. We must have an army of translators and a capability to rapidly scan in foreign language materials, route them to the right person, and get back accurate translations within 24 hours—for long documents, this may require a combination of 20-30 people, all working through the Internet. America is too great a nation to be "out of touch" with the realities and perceptions of the rest of the world. This is an easily established capability; it simply needs funding and attention.[3]

---

[2] A commercial example may be helpful here. In the early 1990's the French steel industry funded a very strong competitive intelligence campaign against other steel industries. In focusing only on steel, they completely overlooked the plastics industry that was busy creating a vast array of substitutes for automobile parts and other traditional steel elements.

[3] Apart from funding, which is easily obtained now that we understand the depths of our ignorance and past incapacity, we must still overcome security mind-sets that

006 Source Balance Matters More

The traditional craft of intelligence has focused almost exclusively on secret sources, and within secret sources, very heavily on sources amenable to technical as opposed to human collection. The new craft of intelligence strives to restore the balance between technical and human collection (whether secret or not), between collection and processing, between production and reflection, and between data base stuffing and directed inquires.[4]

007 "Two Levels Down"

Instead of focusing on nation-states or specific organizations, the new craft of intelligence focuses on sub-state actors and organizations at the branch level. "Two levels down" raises the standard for acceptable intelligence very high—it requires that sub-state actors be understood at the provincial and county or township level, and that organizations be understood in terms of the personalities and resource constraints characteristic of the branch level. This degree of granularity can only be accomplished through the new craft of intelligence and its simultaneous emphasis on the optimization of open source collection (previous rule), on processing (next rule), and on burden-sharing (last rule).

It merits comment that this rule also makes intelligence much more useful to the military and to law enforcement—military forces fight individual

---

persist in thinking that only people with security clearances can be allowed to translate captured materials. This is simply absurd and we need to get over it. The nation needs a global network of translators, some with clearances, most without, who can be surged up for any challenge.

[4] If applied to the classified community, the new craft of intelligence, as a very rough rule of thumb, would limit collection costs to 60% of the total intelligence budget (with one sixth of those costs, or 10% of the total, for clandestine collection), with the other half *evenly* divided between Tasking, Processing, Exploitation, and Dissemination (TPED) and analysis. The increased investment in processing (including the use of the Internet for global collaborative work) would help reduce standing armies of intelligence specialists while enhancing the professional qualifications of the remaining analysts and considerably expanding the range of experts from other governments and the private sector that be tasked on an "as needed" basis.

people and individual mobility platforms, the police go after gangs and members of gangs. Intelligence has *not* been organized to this level of detail.

008 Processing Matters More, Becomes Core Competency

Regardless of whether or not secret information is part of the mix, processing matters much more within the new craft of intelligence and must become a core competency. There are three reasons for this: first, casting a wide net that is inherently multi-lingual will increase the amount of material that must be translated and indexed; second, human productivity in the information age depends more and more on computer-aided tools; and third, only by establishing a digital network for collection, processing, exploitation, and dissemination can the full resources of various governments, corporations, and non-governmental organizations be brought to bear on topics of common concern such as terrorism and crime.

009 Cultural Intelligence is Fundamental

Americans have never understood cultural intelligence, in part because we have never been willing to believe that an analyst must be a native speaker of the language and have an in-depth understanding of history and religion, to be effective in studying a specific country or topic. The new craft of intelligence elevates cultural intelligence to the highest table, above orders of battle and political or economic intelligence. It is fundamental and all else follows from getting this bit right.

010 Geospatial and Time Tagging is Vital

It is no longer possible for even the best analysts with the best human filtering services to "make sense" of the vast volume of information that is available in English, much less in foreign languages. It is now essential that all data have geospatial and time tags so that automated pattern analysis can impose a degree of order as well as a degree of automated change detection and anomaly detection. International standards are needed that can be promulgated

151

and nurtured by the cooperating national governments, with shared information benefits to those that cooperate.[5]

011 Global Open Source Benchmarking

Before pattern analysis can be useful, a global open source benchmarking endeavor is needed across all countries and topics. Essentially, the art and science of pattern analysis from signals intelligence must now be brought over to the open source world, both in print and broadcast media monitoring.

012 Counterintelligence Matters More

In additional to automating the benchmarking process, both operational counter-intelligence and analytic specialization in denial & deception (D&D) require greater emphasis under the new craft of intelligence. In the face of the information explosion, immigration, and other aspects of globalization, the "needle in the haystack" problem in terms of anticipating non-traditional unconventional threat attacks becomes even more difficult. Counterintelligence is one of four core competencies needed to protect ourselves from being mis-led—the other three are cultural intelligence specialization, denial & deception specialization, and the combination of global open source benchmarking (as well as classified benchmarking) with vastly improved processing to detect anomalies and patterns.

---

[5] In 1988 or 1989, at a General Defense Intelligence Program (GDIP) conference, Keith Hall, then the head of Budget staff for the Senate Select Committee on Intelligence, and I, had this conversation. We both agreed that all-source fusion was impossible until every datum from every discipline carried with it time and geospatial location tags—and implicitly—was available within an all-source processing system. Despite the best of intentions, all of our intelligence community leaders in the past decade have failed to focus on fundamental such as this one.

152

013 Cross-Fertilization Matters More

The "chain of command" characteristic of the traditional craft of intelligence, the old paradigm, has a requirement go from the consumer to the analyst, from the analyst to the collector, from the collector to the source, and then back up the chain. This is the *linear* approach, an approach that is both too slow, and too structured for fluid situations where nuances matter. The new approach is the *diamond* approach, such that the acme of skill for an all-source analyst may be the ability to place a consumer with a very complex question in direct touch with a private sector expert that can create new knowledge— nuanced tailored knowledge—that is "just enough, just in time."[6]

014 Decentralized Intelligence Matters More

In the age of distributed information, when 80% or more of the relevant information is *distributed*, the concept of "central intelligence" loses its meaning. Instead of the maintaining the archival files, "knowing who knows" and being able to orchestrate a combination of "just enough, just in time" collection, specialized processing, and just the right mix of analytical talents (online and offline) becomes the core competency. Above all, having the distributed network in place, with trusted relationships and pre-approved access, becomes more important than any sort of *central* intelligence organization.....we still need a *national* intelligence agency, but it should be the center of a *distributed* network.

015 Collaborative Work and Informal Communications Rise

The bureaucratic office with analysts physically co-located with one another must give way to virtual task forces comprised of the top individuals

---

[6] The new craft of intelligence will create risks and uncertainties of its own as it develops. For example, when the analyst places a consumer in direct touch with a source, there needs to be some means for the analyst to monitor and evaluate what the source is telling the consumer, and to provide the consumer with editorial/analytical input on possible gaps in the source's understanding.

from different bureaucracies, each having a personal reputation that is more important "(in terms of the analyst's day-to-day work) than their parent organization's reputation. Personal "brand names" and informal peer-to-peer networks will be subsidized and nurtured by organizations that understand that only a vibrant self-directed network with global reach will attract the bulk of the relevant information—analysts and nodes will be magnets for relevant information from private sector peers.

016 New Value is in Content + Context + Speed

The traditional craft of intelligence has tended to fragment content from its context, and be largely oblivious to timing. This is true both in the collection cycle and in the production cycle. The new craft of intelligence recognizes that the value of any given information, apart from its relevance to the decision at hand, stems from a combination of the content in context, and the content in time. Both collectors and producers of intelligence must be acutely sensitive to the day-to-day needs of their consumers.

017 Collection Based on Gaps versus Priorities

The new craft of intelligence respects priorities on the first pass but then shifts to gaps all the way down the line. One pass of Global Coverage (encompassing all lower tier countries and topics) is better than one hundred passes on five hard targets and nothing at all on the rest of the world.

018 Collection Doctrine Grows in Sophistication

The new craft of intelligence trains all collection managers, and provides the tools necessary to, first, *find* the data if it has already been collected; second, *get* the data from a friendly party if it can be gotten (requires a meta-database of possible sources); third, *buy* the data from the private sector (requires a meta-database of best sources and prices); and fourth, last, only if the first three are not available options, *task* the classified or proprietary/internal capabilities.[7]

019 Citizen "Intelligence Minutemen" are Vital

In the age of constant surprise and impossible-to-anticipate mutations of the threat, no bureaucracy can be effective. Only a global network of citizens who know what to look for and who to tell, a "hive mind", is capable of rapidly spotting, assessing, and reporting real-time intelligence. The new craft of intelligence respects and educates the citizen as a "virtual minuteman", and provides a web-based means for citizen inputs to be rapidly received, evaluated, and collated with other sources of information.[8]

020 Production Based on Needs versus Capabilities

The new craft of intelligence produces what the consumer needs, when they need it, tailored to the context of their need, and by definition created for the individual rather than the organization. The new craft of intelligence does not burn up its analysts with routine production—all production is hand-crafted to support a specific decision, and when not doing tailored production the analyst should be reflecting, training, traveling, or working in the consumer's spaces to better understand the consumer's intelligence needs in context.

---

[7] This is an order of magnitude improvement in the craft of intelligence. Combined with the other new rules and especially the empowerment of analysts, the new craft of intelligence can be said to be a double order of magnitude better than the traditional craft.

[8] Alessandro Politi, one of Europe's foremost commentators and practitioners on the new craft of intelligence as it applies to the future needs of the European community, devised the term "intelligence minuteman" during his participation in the first international open source intelligence conference in December 1992.

021 Strategic Intelligence Matters More

The new craft of intelligence restores the original emphasis on strategic (estimative) intelligence, and adds strategic cost-benefits analysis to demonstrate conclusively the value of preventive investments over punitive or reactive investments.

022 Budget Intelligence Is Mandatory

The new craft of intelligence recognizes that the budget *is* the policy, and allocates a portion of its resources to the analysis of the budget and the identification of discrepancies between the budget and the threat. "*The budget is where the trade-offs are real—priorities are set and conflicts among agencies and programs are resolved. The budget is where government, private sector, and international realities collide.*" [9] The new craft of intelligence is not bashful about highlighting for the policymaker, commander, and acquisition manager—and for the public—significant discrepancies between how the national security budget is spent and how the national security threats are actually perceived by the objective all-source intelligence professionals.

023 Public Intelligence Drives Public Policy

The new craft of intelligence recognizes that in a democracy it is the educated public that must be addressed and kept informed—the issuance of annual strategic threat assessments and quarterly operational threat assessments *to the public* underlie all other classified endeavors. Presidents and Congress will not make hard decisions on the appropriation of funds for what the Commandant of the Marine Corps has called *peaceful preventive measures* until the need for those investments is crystal clear to the public.

---

[9] Mr. Don Gessaman, former Deputy Associate Director for National Security at the Office of Management and Budget until his retirement in 1995, has taught me what little I know of the federal budgeting process. Budgeting matters, not just as a source of funds, but as a source of insight for where intelligence is failing to make its case with sufficient urgency. "It isn't policy until it's in the budget."

024 Analysts are Managers

The new craft of intelligence elevates the all-source intelligence analyst to oversight status as a manager. Unlike the traditional craft of intelligence where analysts are hired right out of school and "grown" over time, the new craft of intelligence hires analysts at mid-career, after they have achieved a personal standing and complete fluency at the expense of the private sector. To handle secrets the analyst must be one of America's top ten cited authorities in their given area of expertise. In this context, all analysts become individual branch chiefs, responsible for managing relations with a senior set of consumers; for managing a network of external counterpart authorities; for managing a substantial open source support fund; and for managing the tasking and evaluation of classified assets.[10]

025 New Measures of Merit

All elements of the U.S. Intelligence Community will no longer be evaluated in terms of gross results (messages intercepted, images taken, agents recruited, reports produced). Instead each collection or production individual will be evaluated in relation to how well they are contributing to the larger community. Technical managers will be expected to destroy old systems in order to create newer ones; case officers will be expected to focus on multiple-source reporting instead of single-source reports—in essence becoming operational analysts; analysts will be evaluated based on their achieving a balance between consumer relations, travel, training, reflection, and production to include *ad hoc* answers orchestrated among various experts with no formal product actually created.[11]

---

[10] Intelligence analysis is a craft in itself, and well-beyond routine scholarship. However, the new craft of intelligence recognizes that it is easier to teach the new craft of intelligence to a mid-career expert in the subject matter under consideration, that it is to make an intelligence analyst deeply expert in a subject matter. The new craft of intelligence shifts to bulk of the opportunity cost to the private sector and uses the marketplace to pre-screen mid-career hires.

[11] I have recently confirmed, with very great dismay, that the training and level of expertise among both our clandestine case officers and our all-source analysts has sunk to new lows, in part because of exceptionally poor management over the past decade. Case officers are incapable of recruiting (and often denied permission to recruit), while

026 Multi-Lateral Burden-Sharing is Vital

Finally, and this is the last and the most important rule for the new craft of intelligence, it is imperative that multi-lateral burden-sharing be the foundation for all intelligence concepts, doctrine, organization, and funding. This does not preclude unilateral compartmented operations, but it forces the entire system to respect the fact that more often than not there is a cheaper, faster, better solution to be had through multi-lateral burden-sharing. This is especially true for non-traditional threats from cultural traditions that we do not understand very well—such as terrorism rooted in extremist Islamic groups.[12] Most multi-lateral sharing will revolve around web-based exchanges of *unclassified* information with successively smaller amounts of secret, top secret, and codeword information being shared, over the web, with varying numbers of multi-lateral partners, both in and out of government. The age of the "virtual intelligence community" has arrived.

---

analysts are doing even more cutting and pasting of information and generally unable to "connect the dots." I understand that in the aftermath of 9-11 an outside survey found all the information necessary to predict and prevent 9-11 in the archives—but it was so scattered, and the individual analysts so diverse focused, that it simply never came together, not even in the Counterterrorism Center created for this precise purpose.

[12] The new craft of intelligence will create new complexities that will have to be dealt with over time. For example, as increased reliance is placed on collectors and analysts outside the traditional bureaucracies, much more emphasis will have to be placed on achieving a common training baseline (in effect, bringing others up to the level of the best of the all-source professionals) while also carrying out constant validation exercises and quality-control evaluations (as well as denial & deception counter-analysis). Ultimately, all-source analysts will again be the high priests of knowledge.

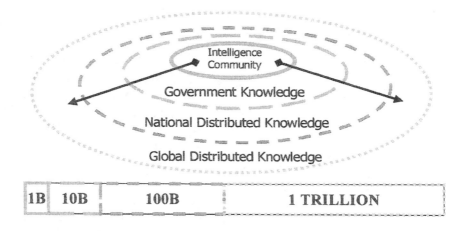

Figure 36: The New Global Integrated Intelligence Community

The "what" of intelligence must inevitably change once the new craft of intelligence is adopted. The days of planned production are largely over. Instead the intelligence analyst, whether in government or in the private sector, must focus on four distinct levels of support to their decision-making clients.

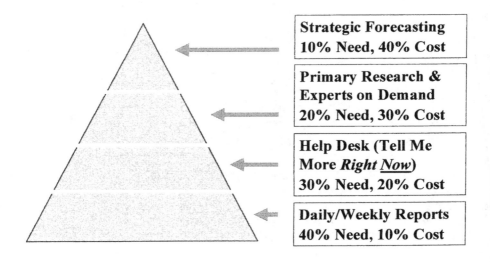

Figure 37: Four Levels or Forms of Intelligence Support[13]

Each of these levels or forms of support requires a different kind of source mix, different processing capabilities, and different personalities. Hybrid intelligence units, for instance, help desks, may be found necessary to properly mix and match government and private sector skill sets. It will be especially important to devise new means for mixing personnel with varying degrees of "clearance" for restricted information. Translators and open source specialists should not be held to the same arcane background requirements as those handling our most sensitive secrets.

In essence, the next generation of intelligence community leadership is going to have to come to grips with the reality that most of the experts are going to be in the private sector and only available "by the task" rather than as

---

[13] This figure was devised by Mr. Jan Herring, former National Intelligence Officer for Science & Technology who went on in retirement to become the father of U.S. business intelligence and be a co-founder of the Academy of Competitive Intelligence.

full-time employees. Our personnel systems, including our benefits system, are going to have to change. Money is going to have to be redirected away from secret technical collection systems toward clandestine human and all-source analysis capabilities, while also funding a global grid of open source information collection, digitization, and translation. Lastly, the intelligence managers of the future must understand that it is the citizen taxpayer that funds national intelligence, and it is the citizen taxpayer that must be informed as to the threats facing our Nation.

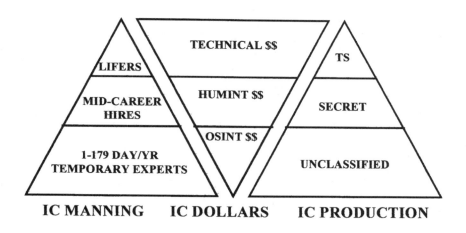

Figure 38: New Balance for the New Craft of Intelligence

The new craft of intelligence is personal, public, and political. I would not have it any other way, and hope that the citizen taxpayer will join me in demanding that our government revitalize and enhance our intelligence community along the lines suggested here. We *can* become a Smart Nation.

Appendix 1:
Citizen's Guide to
Open Sources & Methods

The material which follows has been developed by myself over the past five years, first in support of the first *Open Source Intelligence Handbook* published by the Joint Military Intelligence Training Center in October 1996, and more recently for the publication of the *NATO Open Source Intelligence Handbook* in November 2001 under the signature of General William F. Kernan, U.S. Army, who is both Supreme Allied Commander, Atlantic, and also the Commander-in-Chief, Joint Forces Command. While there is much here that is useful for the individual citizen or corporate researcher, the original thrust in favor of the all-source government intelligence professional has been retained to permit this volume to be helpful to governments around the world.[1]

---

[1] This appendix does not include sections on software services, imagery, and analysis as they appear in the *NATO Open Source Intelligence Handbook*.

Scope & Purpose

This publication provides preliminary joint and coalition training information on the subject of Open Source Intelligence (OSINT). It discusses the fundamentals of OSINT support to both the all-source intelligence process, and to the unclassified intelligence requirements of operators, logisticians, and civilian organizations participating in joint and coalition operations. The focus is on relevant information that can be obtained legally and ethically from the private sector, and that is not classified in its origin or processing. The information may become classified in relation to the commander's intent or its association with classified information when it is included in an all-source intelligence report.

Executive Summary

Open Source Intelligence, or OSINT, is unclassified information that has been deliberately discovered, discriminated, distilled and disseminated to a select audience in order to address a specific question. It provides a very robust foundation for other intelligence disciplines. When applied in a systematic fashion, OSINT products can reduce the demands on classified intelligence collection resources by limiting requests for information only to those questions that cannot be answered by open sources.

Open information sources are not the exclusive domain of intelligence staffs. Intelligence should never seek to limit access to open sources. Rather, intelligence should facilitate the use of open sources by all staff elements that require access to relevant, reliable information. Intelligence staffs should concentrate on the application of proven intelligence processes to the exploitation of open sources to improve its all-source intelligence products. Familiarity with available open sources will place intelligence staffs in the position of guiding and advising other staff elements in their own exploitation of open sources.

OSINT is a vital component of any future vision for collaborative efforts with other organizations, and especially for endeavors that cross national and cultural boundaries. Through a concentration upon unclassified open sources of information, OSINT provides the means with which to develop valid and reliable intelligence products that can be shared with external parties in a joint international endeavor.

The Internet is now the default C4I[2] architecture for virtually the entire world. The principle exceptions are most militaries and intelligence organizations. The Internet facilitates commerce, provides entertainment and supports ever increasing amounts of human interaction. To exclude the information flow carried by the Internet is to exclude the greatest emerging data sources available. By the same token, while the Internet will be a source of much knowledge, all information gleaned from it must be assessed for its source, bias, and reliability. The Internet *requires* that the proven process of here-to-fore classified intelligence (especially source discrimination) be applied to it. As a source of reliable information, the Internet must be approached with great caution. As a means with which to gain access to quality commercial sources (fee for service) of validated information, the Internet is unbeatable.

A vision of open source exploitation must not be limited exclusively to electronic sources. Traditional print, hard-copy images, and other analog sources continue to provide a wealth of data relevant to most international endeavors. Russian military maps and very high-resolution commercial imagery are two examples of poorly understood open sources.

As the "information explosion" creates more and more sources of information, the focus of effort for the intelligence professional must change. Instead of attempting to collect everything and store it in structured form, the emphasis must be placed on "knowing who knows," or on source discovery and discrimination, such that when a question is asked in the future, the specialist can rapidly tap into a variety of external sources, and pull back "just enough, just in time."

OSINT is an essential building block for any serious endeavor. While it cannot replace the unique knowledge and insights that stem from either classified access or management knowledge, OSINT is able to complement any information and intelligence production process with essential support including tip-offs, context, and validation of other sources.

---

[2] Command, Control, Communications, Computing, and Intelligence.

Introduction

> *Open source intelligence (OSINT) is not a substitute for satellites, spies, or existing organic military and civilian intelligence capabilities.*

> *It is, however, a foundation—a very strong foundation—for planning and executing coalition operations across the spectrum from humanitarian assistance to total war. OSINT provides strategic historical and cultural insights; it provides operationally-helpful information about infrastructure and current conditions; and it provides tactically-vital commercial geospatial information that is not available from national capabilities.*

> *In coalition operations, OSINT is both the foundation for civil-military cooperation, and the framework for classified bilateral intelligence-sharing.*

Open Source Intelligence (OSINT) is distinct from academic, business or journalistic research in that it represents the application of the proven process of national intelligence to a global diversity of sources, with the intent of producing *tailored* intelligence for the commander.

OSINT is also unique, within a coalition operations context, in that it simultaneously provides a multi-lateral foundation for establishing a common view of the shared Area of Operations (AO), while also providing a context within which a wide-variety of bi-lateral classified intelligence sharing arrangements can be exploited.

Figure 1 illustrates these concepts.

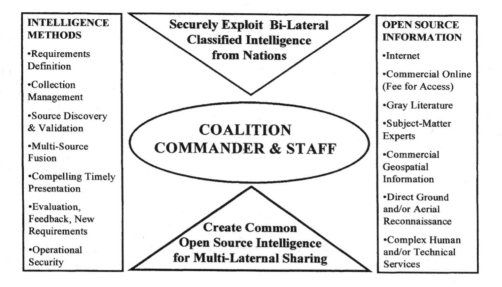

Figure 1: Relationship Between Open Source and Sensitive Information

       OSINT is valuable to nations, and to individuals, in that it can be used to provide a common understanding of the AO across all elements of its forces and its civilian and non-governmental organization (NGO) counterparts. Elements of the forces that are not authorized access to the full range of classified information, often including such vital components as military police, logistics elements, engineers, and the public affairs staff, can be made more effective through the utilization of tailored OSINT. At the same time, external parties with whom coordination is critical, but who are also not authorized access to classified information, can received tailored OSINT that is helpful to a shared understanding of the AO and the challenges facing the coalition and all its elements. The next figure illustrates this concept.

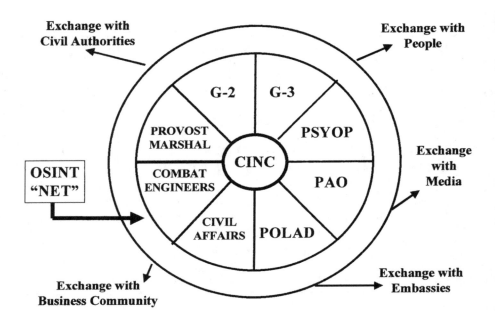

Figure 2: Utility of OSINT Next for Internal and External Exchanges

OSINT consists of four distinct categories of information and intelligence.

Open Source Data (OSD). Data is the raw print, broadcast, oral debriefing, or other form of information from a primary source. It can be a photograph, a tape recording, a commercial satellite image, or a personal letter from an individual.

Open Source Information (OSIF). OSIF is comprised of data that can been put together, generally by an editorial process that provides some filtering and validation as well as presentation management. OSIF is *generic* information that is usually *widely disseminated*. Newspapers, books, broadcasts, and general daily reports are part of the OSIF world.

Open Source Intelligence (OSINT). OSINT is information that has been deliberately discovered, discriminated, distilled, and disseminated to a *select* audience, generally the commander and their immediate staff, in order to address a *specific* question. OSINT, in other words, applies the proven process of intelligence to the broad diversity of open sources of information, and *creates intelligence.*

Validated OSINT (OSINT-V). OSINT-V can only be produced by an all-source intelligence professional, whether working for a Nation or for the coalition staff, with access to classified intelligence sources. Validated OSINT is that OSINT for which it can be said that there are either confirming classified sources, or there are no available classified sources disputing the OSINT. Only a government (or client corporate) employee with full access to classified information can produce Validated OSINT.[3]

OSINT and Information Operations

OSINT is an essential contextual and foundation element for classified intelligence operations. Overt human sources can help target and validate clandestine human intelligence (HUMINT) sources. Overt broadcast information can be used to better understand covertly collected signals intelligence (SIGINT). Commercial geospatial information, especially wide-area surveillance imagery, can be used to significantly enhance the value of the more narrowly focused covert imagery intelligence (IMINT) capabilities. OSINT can also make contributions to the emerging discipline of Measurements and Signatures Intelligence (MASINT), to Counterintelligence (CI), and to Operations Security (OPSEC).

OSINT is the major new "force" in 21st Century Information Operations (IO). OSINT is not "new" in that Nations and organizations have always understood the value of legal travelers, direct observation, structured reading, and legal purchases of information services. What *is* new about OSINT is the confluence of three distinct trends: first, the proliferation of the Internet as a tool for disseminating and sharing overt information; second, the consequent and related "information explosion" in which published knowledge in growing exponentially; and third, the collapse of many formerly denied areas.

---

[3] Dr. Joseph Markowitz, the only Director of the Community Open Source Program Office (COSPO) before it was relegated to branch status deep within CIA, devised this concept. His views on the need for an aggressive open source investment strategy running no less than 3% and no more than 5% of the total intelligence budget, are consistent with my own. Neither of us has been able to persuade the right leaders.

OSINT is important to coalition commanders and their staffs for another reason: emerging threats, and the lower end of the spectrum of conflict, increasingly demand out-of-area operations and engagement in operations for which classified intelligence support is not readily available. Humanitarian assistance and disaster relief operations in the countries of Africa, and perhaps in the future in the countries along the border of Russia, all are characterized by complex information needs related to infrastructure, demographics, health, and other matters not traditionally addressed by classified intelligence collection operations.

OSINT is vital to government operations, and especially to coalition operations, for one additional reason: the changing nature of command & control in the 21st Century. In the past, Nations and even coalitions relied heavily on a top-down "chain of command" that relied on closed sources to direct generally unilateral actions with short-term time frames. Today, as non-governmental organizations come to the fore and are often the predominant actors in many of the operations that the military must support, the dynamics of both command & control and information have changed.

Within coalitions, operations must be planned and executed in a multi-cultural fashion, with bottom-up consensus often being the most effective means of arriving at sustainable decisions. This is particularly true with the vital role played by non-coalition troop contributing nations. Under these circumstances, a common view of the operating area, formed with the help of validated OSINT is often the most effective means of delivering decision-support.

There are, however, challenges in the exploitation of OSINT in support of coalition operations. The remainder of this manual will discuss private sector information offerings and the open source intelligence cycle. OSINT should be a core element of the any Future Intelligence Architecture.

Special Note on Operational Security

The most common objection to the use of open sources of information, apart from the general lack of knowledge and funding with which to exploit open sources, relates to Operational Security (OPSEC). The Open Source Intelligence Cycle makes full provision for OPSEC at every stage, and ample methods exist to conceal the commander's intent, the source of the inquiry, and other sensitive aspects of the open source collection requirement.

Private Sector Information Offerings

The four pillars to an OSINT strategy are sources, software, services, and analysis. The private sector can address all four to some degree. Analysis is the key enabling skill that is essential to the successful integration of OSINT into an all-source intelligence capability. While some analysis of open sources can and should be acquired from private sources, those analytical skills necessary to integrate open source derived intelligence must be grown and nurtured within intelligence staffs. This section is intended to expose the wider audience to the range of OSINT related products that the private sector are optimized to provide.[4]

Sources

Traditional Media. To many, media sources were the only open sources that they were familiar with prior to the onset of the Internet. These include traditional foreign print and broadcast media, radio and TV as well as the current array of electronically available products from these traditional information sources. For current intelligence purposes, media sources remain the core capability necessary for an OSINT effort.

Media sources are available from a variety of providers. Direct wire service feeds are available. Commercial online premium sources discussed below all provide an array of media sources on a fee for service basis.

While not private sector information providers, the U.S. Foreign Broadcast Information Service (FBIS) and the British Broadcast Corporation (BBC) Monitoring Service each provide excellent near real time translation of foreign media sources. In addition, an array of media analysis products

---

[4] Both private sector software and private sector analysis sections have been deleted. Neither of those sectors is efficient enough to be recommended to the public.

supplement the direct gisting of foreign broadcasts and provide useful insight into the general character of foreign media reporting on particular issues.

Internet. The Internet has, since 1994, literally exploded on to the world scene and changed forever the manner in which individuals might carry out global research. The Internet remains in its infancy. According to Dr. Vinton Cerf, acknowledged by many to be one of the founders of the Internet, it will grow from 400 million users in November 2000, to over 3.5 billion users by the year 2015.

Apart from this exponential increase in the number of human beings using the Internet, other experts project a double or triple order of magnitude increase in the use of the Internet to connect devices, from geospatial locators in vehicles to temperature detectors in soda machines to usage monitors in doorways. The Internet is at the very beginning of its development as a global grid of enormous value to coalition operators, logisticians, and intelligence professionals.

The Internet is also over-sold. A study by the Community Open Source Program Office (COSPO) within the U.S. Intelligence Community concluded in 1994 that the Internet only contained roughly 450 useful substantive sites, and that 99% of the Internet was not content of intelligence value, but rather pornography, opinion, and advertising. While the Internet has grown substantially in value since 1994, the intelligence professional must be very cautious about both over-reliance on the Internet, and about the source bias of materials found on the Internet. In general, Internet sources are not dated, formatted, paginated, edited, filtered, or stable, even when addressing substantive topics.

The Internet is an "easy out" for operators and other consumers of intelligence. It is an attractive option for commanders and staff in a hurry. If intelligence professionals do not demonstrate that they monitor and exploit the Internet, and/or if intelligence professionals make it too difficult for consumers to obtain usable all-source intelligence, the Internet represents a "threat" to the existing intelligence process. Increasingly, intelligence professionals must act to place information that is widely available on the Internet into its proper context—either confirming its validity or disputing the information based on classified collateral reporting.

172

In general the Internet today provides two benefits to the coalition professional: first, as a means of rapidly communicating with counterparts around the world, primarily to exchange unclassified information and professional insights; and second, as a means of rapidly accessing both free and premium (fee paid for access) information sources. However, the Internet also has its dangers. Electronic mail and attached documents comprise a permanent record in cyber-space, and the sender has little control over subsequent dissemination and exploitation.

OSINT Professional Note: Anyone with access to the Internet should download two programs. The first, available free or in an advanced version, is a meta-search engine that combines the best features of multiple search engines, while also permitting subsequent searches for new information (remembering what has already been seen). Download this program from www.copernic.com. The second is a "cookie manager", an essential means of managing the security of one's personal computer. With a credit card, go to www.kburra.com and pay $15 to download this basic tool for blocking unwanted intrusions to your computer.

Commercial Online or "Premium" Services. There are numerous commercial online premium sources, that is, sources that charge either a subscription fee or a usage fee for access to their information. It is essential that every professional understand the availability and the value of commercial online premium sources. They represent decades worth of editorial selection, authentication, formatting, indexing, abstracting, and presentation management. In general, source material obtained through a commercial online premium service has been created by a reputable commercial enterprise subject to scrutiny and the judgment of the marketplace. Below we discuss the three best known to governments and corporations. There are many others, some unique to Europe or Asia or Russia. Each professional is urged to consult their librarian or their OSINT collection manager to gain a better understanding of what their options are for high-quality commercial information relevant to their action responsibilities.

FACTIVA	LEXIS-NEXIS	DIALOG
www.factiva.com	www.lexis-nexis.com	www.dialog.com
Best web-based user interface, easiest means of searching all available publications. Limited to	Two separate channels, one focused on legal sources including public records	A very large collection of various commercial offerings that can be searched "by the file". Especially

current and past calendar year, primarily focused on sources of current information. Includes Jane's Information Group material as well as British Broadcast Corporation (BBC) transcripts. Does not include Foreign Broadcast Information Service (FBIS) information.	(primarily in the United States but very helpful in tracing real estate, aircraft, and water craft including international ships), the other focused on news sources but offering archival access, i.e. ability to reach back several years or more on any topic.	valuable for access to conference proceedings, academic and policy journals, dissertations, book reviews, and the Social Science Citation Index (SSCI). The latter is ideal for finding and ranking individual experts, to include discovery of their official address.
Flat fee or actual cost pricing.	Flat fee, actual cost, or pay as you go credit card pricing.	Flat fee, actual cost, or pay as you go credit card pricing.

In general, and in part because of the high cost of mistakes or unnecessary retrievals, all commercial online premium services should be searched by those staff with sufficient training on the database and a thorough understanding of its pricing structure. Even commands with flat-fee pricing should be aware that their next contract will be increased in price based on actual usage during the current flat-fee period. Alternately, an option is to gain access to commercial sources via the services of a professional librarian or commercial information broker. Most professional information brokers, such as those belonging to the Association of Independent Information Brokers (AIIP), specialize in either LEXIS-NEXIS or DIALOG. In the case of Factiva this is less vital but can still make a big difference in both the success of the searchers, and the cost of the searches. Factiva has the best and most user-friendly interface and is suitable for use by anyone, in part because it does not have the complexity of distinct databases offered by the other two services.

OSINT Professional Note: Always ask for search results in electronic form. Copy the results into a Word document. Add pagination. Add a title page and a blank table of contents page. Sort the items into larger categories (e.g. Political, Military, Economic) and label the categories as "Heading 1". Then go through the document label each individual headline as "Heading 2". These headings are choices in the bar at the upper left that generally says "Normal". Finally, go to the Table of Contents and use the Insert, Index and Tables, Table of Contents choices to insert a table of contents. If desired, use the Replace function to find and make bold all of the original search terms.

Other Commercial Services. There are a vast range of commercial sources available through direct subscription, both on the Internet and in the form of hard-copy or CD-ROM publications. The table below identifies just a few sources of common interest to military commanders and their staff. There are many more than those listed here.[5]. OSS and its clients continue to progress on a concept of operations for establishing broad access to such sources at the most competitive prices possible.

Source Type or Function	Source Name and URL
Broadcast Monitoring	BBC Online http://www.bbc.co.uk/
Broadcast Monitoring	FBIS/NTIS World News Connection http://wnc.fedworld.gov/ntis/home.html
Commercial Imagery	Autometric http://www.autometric.com/AUTO/SERVICES/GIS
Current Awareness (Conferences)	British Library Proceedings http://www.bl.uk/services/bsds/dsc/infoserv.html#inside_conf
Current Awareness (Journals)	ISI Current Contents http://www.isinet.com/
Current Awareness (Regional)	Oxford Analytica http://www.oxan.com/
Defense Monitoring	Janes Information Group http://www.janes.com/geopol/geoset.html
Defense Monitoring	Periscope http://www.periscope1.com
Defense Monitoring (NATO)	Orders of Battle Inc. http://orbat.com
Directories of Experts	Gale Research http://www.gale.com/
Foreign Affairs Discussions	Columbia U. Int'l Affairs Online www.ciaonet.org
Foreign Affairs Monitoring	Country Watch.com www.countrywatch.com
Global Risk Monitoring	Political Risk Service (Country Studies) www.prsgroup.com
Maps & Charts	East View Cartographic http://www.cartographic.com

Gray Literature. Grey literature is that information that is legally and ethically available, but only from specialized channels or through direct local access. It is generally understood as that information whose distribution is not controlled by commercial publishers, and/or that information that is not published, distributed, catalogued or acquired through commercial booksellers and

---

[5] SACLANT has undertaken to develop and maintain a common NATO inventory of open sources and access points to which RFIs can be directed. The U.S. Government, ten years after the formation of the Open Source Council (of which the author was a founding member), continues to fail in this regard, having chosen to shut out rather than engage open sources.

subscription agencies. Grey literature includes working papers, pre-prints, technical reports and technical standards documents, dissertations, data sets, and commercial imagery. Producers of gray literature include non-profit and educational organizations; government agencies and commercial enterprises creating documents for internal use as well as for clients and suppliers; and a wide variety of informal and formal associations, societies, and clubs. University yearbooks, boat club registries, corporate trip reports, and personal notes from public events that are posted to a public bulletin board are examples.

Overt Human Experts and Observers. The ultimate open source is a human expert or human observer with direct experience. In many places of the world, Africa, for example, it is not possible to obtain published information on specific locations or conditions. For many topics, even those with great quantities of published information, it is not possible to find exactly what is needed even when the time and money is available to collect, process, and analyze all available published information. The human expert—someone who has spent a lifetime at someone else's expense mastering the sources and methods of a particular topic—is often the most efficient and the most inexpensive means of creating new open source intelligence that is responsive to a specific requirement from the commander or their staff. The identification and interviewing of those with direct on-the-ground experience is also a valuable means of ascertaining "ground truth."

OSINT Professional Note: There are essentially four ways to get to expert humans. The most effective means is through citation analysis using the *Social Science Citation Index* (SSCI) or the *Science Citation Index* (SCI). This generally requires a specialist searcher with access to DIALOG for the SSCI or to the Scientific and Technical Network (STN) for the SCI. The second means is through professional associations such as listed in the *International Directory of Associations* published by Gale Research, or as found through a copernic.com search of the Internet. The third means is by doing a Factiva.com search and identifying experts or "talking heads" that have been quoted in the media on that topic. Last, and often the least efficient, is through a labor-intensive series of telephone calls to various known government agencies or official points of contact. As a general rule, it is best to do a comprehensive professional search for international experts with the most current knowledge, rather than relying on the in-house focal points or whomever might be casually known to in-house points of contact.

It merits comment that official communications from organizations, and most media reporting, tend to rely on second-hand reports. Unless the information is meticulously sourced and from a very trusted source, more often than not it will be less reliable than direct human expert judgment or observation.

Commercial Imagery. The commercial imagery industry continues to mature with the launching in recent years of a number of satellites that offer militarily significant capabilities. Extraordinary 1-meter resolution electro-optical imagery available to the private sector is not only possible now but also likely to be de regure in the future. By 2003, at least eleven private companies expect to have high resolution commercial remote sensing satellites in orbit. Their products will be available to whoever has a credit card.

While this will bring new capabilities to friend and foe alike, commercial imagery provides unique opportunities for friendly organizations as well. Unbridled by security constraints, which limit the use of imagery derived from military satellites, commercial imagery acquired by the sponsor can be freely distributed within the constraints of copyright agreements with the original provider. This provides a host of options regarding cooperation with broader coalition partners who do not have access to classified information.

Managing Source Access. It is a relatively easy endeavor to identify private information sources that can support the information needs of an OSINT Program. With the proliferation of restricted and open access Intranets, there is great pressure to place all information acquired onto web-based dissemination systems.

While single copy licenses to information sources are typically attractively priced, multiple user licenses increase in price. License costs are generally a factor of the number of users that have access to the information. To place information directly onto servers without the knowledge and consent of the information provider is a violation of copyright laws.

An option to reduce costs is to determine the information needs of the organization based on communities of interests. Some information is required by all staff and merits a general site license. Other information is of interest to a more restricted audience. Lloyd's shipping data for example may be of

177

general interest to a wider audience but of job specific interest to a select group of analysts. The purchase of a limited site license and the use of restricted access within the Intranet will greatly reduce license costs yet still provide the information in the most effective manner. Finally, *ad hoc* information requirements may be addressed with the acquisition of single copies of key information sources.

As a general rule, there are few information sources that are required by all members of a staff. Restricting access to some sources will increase the range of open sources that are available for purchase within an organization's OSINT budget. Careful planning and the identification of the logical communities of interest for individual open sources is a reasonable approach to manage scarce resources.

Services

Collection. Collection services include online collection (searchers that specialize in Internet, deep web, and premium commercial online source exploitation); offline gray literature or document acquisition; telephone surveys and electoral or other forms of polling; private investigation and human intervention services ("boots on the ground"); and aerial surveillance or reconnaissance services.

Processing. Processing services include data conversion from hard-copy or analog to digital, indexing and abstracting of hard-copy or soft-copy textual data or images, interpretation and annotation of imagery or signals, database construction and stuffing, and complex modeling & simulation projects with the best ones including geospatial and time-based visualizations.

When integrated with well-planned open source collection and the right analytical expertise, complex processing services can yield substantial dividends by compressing large amounts of data into manageable tailored products that address specific intelligence requirements.

Analysis. A wide variety of commercial and academic organizations offer diverse analysis and production services. As a general rule, the best value is found through the hiring of single individual experts with no overhead, rather than through broad contracts with organizations that then add a substantial fee for their considerable overhead expenses. The very best value results when niche collection, niche processing, and niche analysis services can be "mixed and matched" to obtain precisely the desired results. The very worst value comes when an organization is hired because of a convenient contract, they do not have a niche expert, and they repurpose an underemployed employee with no subject matter expertise who then "makes do" with what they can find at the local library on their own (very expensive) time.

Industry leaders can best be identified with reference to citation analysis and familiarity with their product set. This is best accomplished through the identification of other organizations with similar intelligence problems and exchanging information concerning those validated information vendors that they employ. Web-site analysis is another tool that can be applied to vet the capabilities of a potential information vendor.

Data Conversion	ACS Defense www.acsdefense.com
Database Construction & Stuffing	ORACLE www.oracle.com
Document Acquisition	British Library Document Centre http://www.bl.uk/services/bsds/dsc/
Human Intervention	The Arkin Group www.thearkingroup.com
Imagery Interpretation & Annotation	Boeing Autometric www.autometric.com
Indexing & Abstracting	Access International http://www.accessinn.com/
International Studies Analysis	Monterey Institute of International Studies www.miis.edu
Modeling & Simulation	Boeing Autometric www.autometric.com
Online Collection	Association of Independent Information Professionals www.aiip.org
Open Source Advisory Service	Open Source Solutions Inc. www.oss.net
Private Investigation	Intelynx (Geneva) www.intelynx.ch
Scientific & Technical Analysis	CENTRA www.centratechnology.com
Signals Processing	Zeta Associates Incorporated www.zai.com
Telephone Surveys (Primary Research)	Risa Sacks & Associates www.rsacksinfo.com

As a general rule, there are no "portal" companies that serve as honest brokers for helping governments "mix and match" best in class niche providers at the most economical cost.

Open Source Intelligence Cycle

Planning and Direction

Overview. Whether one is going after open source data, information, or intelligence, there is a proven process of intelligence, the intelligence cycle, which will yield good value when applied. The open source intelligence process is about discovery, discrimination, distillation, and dissemination—the 4 D's. A good understanding of the open source intelligence cycle makes possible the harnessing of private sector knowledge and access using only legal and ethical means, and generally at a very low cost in comparison to covert technical or clandestine human collection. Since many requirements that are urgent for the commander and their staff may not qualify for nor be appropriate for secret collection methods, the open source intelligence cycle is in fact *vital* to any organization's planning and operations. As will be seen in the following discussion, OSINT is an emerging discipline and the emphasis will often be on informal coordination rather than formal tasking.

The OSINT PROCESS

Discovery – Know Who Knows

Discrimination – Know What's What

Distillation – Know What's Hot

Dissemination – Know Who's Who

Organization and Responsibility. Intelligence is an inherent responsibility of command and cannot be delegated. The commander is ultimately responsible for establishing the essential elements of information (EEI) and for applying the resources necessary to satisfy them, to include the funding of commercial acquisition. Open source intelligence is *not* necessarily the responsibility of, nor available from, national-level intelligence organizations.   While the intelligence staff typically act as the staff principal for OSINT activities, other staffs are frequently well placed to both collect open sources and to facilitate the further development of sources on behalf of the Command. The subordinate commanders for Civil Affairs, Public Relations, Military Police, and Combat Engineering may often be the best channels for seeking out OSINT, and can comprise an informal advisory council to the commander.

> **a. National-Level Intelligence Organizations**. Although they are not responsible for satisfying the commander's needs for OSINT, national-level intelligence organizations may have relevant open source information that can be provided. Some countries, such as The Netherlands, United Kingdom, Denmark and Norway, are exceptionally competent in this area and have fully integrated OSINT into their all-source collection and production environments. Others may have selected units that can be called upon, but have not yet mastered this discipline.

> **b. Diplomatic Missions**. The established diplomatic missions of the various member nations are often the best source of OSINT, at no cost, if they are approached by one of their nationals acting in an official capacity on behalf of the commander. Such missions are under no direct obligation to respond, but informal coordination may yield good results.

> **c.   Chambers of Commerce**. Many of the member nations have Chambers of Commerce and these often have established small communities that bring the general managers and key business executives from their national firms in any given country together. On an informal basis, with clear disclosure of the commander's interest, useful OSINT may be acquired. The is particularly true in deployed areas.

> **d.   Non-Governmental Organizations**. The International Committee of the Red Cross (ICRC), Doctors Without Borders, and the many elements of the United Nations as well as the many international relief and charity organizations, have deep

direct knowledge that can be drawn upon through informal coordination.

e. Religious Organizations. Many Coalition Operations have very substantial human mass migration and ethnic conflict aspects as witnessed during Operation Allied Force. These issues are often best understood by religious organizations. The Papal Nuncio and the local Opus Dei, the B'nai Brith, the Islamic World Foundation, and other equivalent religious organizations are an essential source of overt information and expert perceptions.

Requirements Definition. The greatest challenge for the commander will be the establishment and maintenance of a rigorous and disciplined process for defining the requirements to be addressed through open sources of information. The common attitudes of "tell me everything about everything" or "if I have to tell you what I need to know you are not doing your job" represent unworkable direction.

Commanders and their staff must carefully evaluate the specific information needs in the context of their concerns and their plans and intentions, and they must articulate, in the narrowest possible way, precisely what they want to know and why. The commander's intent is as vital to the intelligence professional as it is to the operations professional. Only by understanding the context and direction of the commander's requirements, can a truly focused and flexible collection effort be undertaken.

OSINT is the most fundamental and fastest means of satisfying basic informational needs, including needs for historical background, current context, and general geospatial information. Each commander should distinguish between their tailored intelligence requirements in support of their future planning, and the basic information requirements that will permit operational and logistics and other special staff planning (e.g. Civil Affairs) to go forward. OSINT is highly relevant to both kinds of intelligence support.

Evaluation and Feedback. Planning and direction is a continuous process. The commander and their staff must digest, evaluate, *and provide feedback on* all received intelligence, whether open or secret. Intelligence is an inherent responsibility of command and cannot be delegated. As open source intelligence is received and reviewed, it must be shared with staff principals and subordinate commanders, evaluated, and the results of the evaluation passed directly to the staff element responsible for coordinating OSINT support to the commander.

Collection.

Overview. The heart of intelligence collection is research – it is the matching of validated intelligence requirements to available sources with the aim of producing an *answer* responding to a valid need. Once an intelligence need has been identified, open sources should be reviewed by intelligence staffs to determine if that intelligence need can be addressed through those resources organic to the intelligence staffs, those resources that the staff can access, if an RFI to nations is required, or if a combination of these approaches is required.

Collection requires the translation of an intelligence need into an intelligence requirement—an action plan to answer that need. A collection strategy is developed to tap available sources. Those sources optimized to the problem are selected and the information is collected. This generic collection approach is equally applicable to classified sources as it is to open sources.

In the coalition context, OSINT is a contributing source to an all-source intelligence effort. Open sources are used to compliment the classified intelligence that exists and can be collected on a specific area. OSINT-derived products are created to answer a specific intelligence need to which open sources are best optimized.

Knowing Who Knows. During periods of stability as well as crisis, it is incumbent upon intelligence staffs to establish and nurture sources that will help satisfy information requirements. It is vital that the OSINT professional, known in some governments as Open Source Officers (OSO), focus initially on "knowing who knows" – the ability to rapidly identify subject matter experts on topics of direct relevance to the commander's mission and to seek information from them.

An approach favored by some is the concept of collected sources rather than information. While the array of available open sources is staggering, the ability to focus collection quickly on an emerging issue of intelligence interest

183

is the key capability. Rather than having a stale open source product to draw upon, the ability to rapidly direct collection on an issue, identify the leading experts on the field and either draw upon their most recent work or contact them directly is the most effective use of an OSINT capability.

Therefore, a standing collection priority should include a preliminary inventory of subject-matter experts (SME) within the parent commands and its subordinate, adjacent, and higher commands, but should then extend further, throughout the parent government and into the national private sector. The business community with its international chambers of commerce, the academic community with its various professional associations, and the non-governmental organizations including the peace institutes resident in many countries, are all vital points of reference.

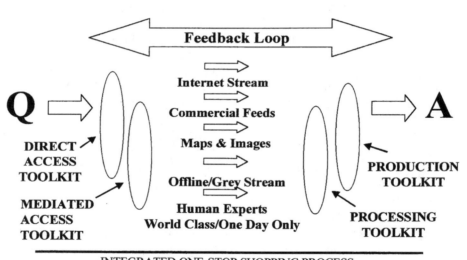

Figure 3: OSINT Collection and Production Process

Discipline. There is no faster way for an OSO to lose his commander's respect than to try to do too much, and end up taking too long to produce simple

184

answers. Time management, and a very disciplined approach to the art and science of OSINT collection, is at the heart of every success.

The ever-increasing array of open sources provides a rich environment for thoughtful research. OSINT managers must ensure that their staffs are aware of the degree of detail required for each OSINT product being prepared. The Internet and commercial premium online sources are seductive to the analyst.

Within any OSINT effort, time spent in collection is always at the expense of analysis. The desire to continue with the collection and acquisition of open sources at the expense of their evaluation and presentation as an analytical product reduces the effectiveness of the OSINT contribution to the all source effort. In few other fields is the mantra that "perfection is the enemy of good enough" more appropriate than it is for open source collection.

OSINT Professional Note: A recommended time-table for a standard OSINT collection and analysis task is provided below:

15 Minutes	Requirements Definition. Ensure an understanding of intent.
30 Minutes	Internet Collection. Rapidly identify top sites and review.
15 Minutes	Internet Table. Create Internet Table as reference document.
60 Minutes	Commercial Collection. Identify top 20 items for exploitation.
60 Minutes	Analysis. Read, understand, evaluate, and structure information.
60 Minutes	Production. Create analytical summary, contents, and slides.
4 Hours	Total time required to create any OSINT report.

Collection efforts can be reduced if time spent in the evaluation of the reliability and objectivity of specific open sources does not have to be replicated each time an analyst begins a project. OSINT managers should ensure that their staff maintains a dynamic compilation of the open sources that they exploit for specific issues. This reference aid will serve as the starting point for subsequent analytical tasks.

Issues. There are several collection issues that always surface whenever commanders and staff first consider OSINT as a structured area of emphasis. These include Operations Security (OPSEC), Copyright Compliance, Foreign Language Shortfalls, and External Networking.

Operations Security (OPSEC). OPSEC is easily achievable in the OSINT environment through two measures: first, the concealment of the origin of the search through the use of trusted intermediaries; and second, the utilization of normal commercial Non-Disclosure Agreements (NDA) when necessary to protect direct discussions of a commander's concerns and intentions.

In general, most OSINT inquiries will be amply protected by existing processes, but when appropriate, a trusted local national with information broker skills can be hired (or a Reservist utilized) to distance the inquiry from the command. It is a misconception to believe that any discussion with OSINT providers must be itself open.

The private sector is accustomed to protecting proprietary and corporate confidential discussions. A standard private sector NDA is just as a good as a government secrecy agreement, with the added advantage that the private sector partner has a financial motivation for honoring the NDA—they want more business and discretion is part of what they are selling.

Copyright Compliance. In the past, many governments have felt that copyright compliance did not apply to their official needs, and some governments have resorted to the classification of open source information as a means of concealing their routine violation of private sector intellectual property rights. It is now essential for all governments to learn how to properly comply with all applicable copyright provisions. This is important for two reasons: first, to maintain the highest standards of legal and ethical behavior; and second, because more often than not, OSINT must be shared with external private sector parties (e.g. humanitarian assistance organizations) or used as a means of exchange (pooling information on Sudan, for example), and thus copyright compliance is a vital means of maintain *future flexibility* in the exploitation of the OSINT available to any command.

Foreign Language Shortfalls. Despite the multi-cultural and multi-lingual nature of any alliance, many out-of-area contingencies require foreign language skills that are not readily available with the home force, and especially not within the home force that has security clearances.

Over time it is vital that each commander identify foreign language shortfalls and that these be consolidated and evaluated as part of their larger Future Intelligence Architecture plan.

Understanding international terrorism, insurgency, and violent internal political opposition movements, to take one example, requires competency in a minimum of 29 foreign languages: Arabic, Catelan, Chinese, Danish, Dari, Dutch, English, Farsi, Finnish, French, German, Indonesian, Irish, Italian, Japanese, Korean, Kurdish, Kurmanji, Norwegian, Pashto, Polish, Portuguese, Russian, Serbian, Spanish, Swedish, Tamil, Turkish, Urdu.

External Networking. There are four obstacles to external networking relevant to any organizations competency in OSINT.

First, there is a lack of knowledge about who the real experts are on various regional and topical issues.

Second, there is a fear of revealing the question as an official inquiry—in some countries, there are even prohibitions against direct contacts between intelligence personnel and private sector experts.

Third, there is the lack of funding for compensating subject-matter-experts—everything must be done on a barter or exchange of favors or information basis.

Fourth and finally, the existing command & control, communications, computing, and intelligence (C3I) architectures tend to prohibit routine access to the Internet, and often make it difficult if not impossible to migrate unclassified information from the Internet into classified databases.

All of these obstacles can be overcome. A major outcome of any OSINT initiative must be the definition and resolution of each of these obstacles.

Nuances. The Internet, although it will never be a completely trustworthy source for information, has become the *de facto* C4I backbone for everyone other than the military. It is essential that our intelligence, operations and logistics staffs develop new doctrine and new methods for fully exploiting the data sources and the human experts that are easily accessible through this medium.

As one deals with more and more non-traditional threats and more and more out-of-area as well as civil stability scenarios, OSINT will become a much more important element of the all-source solution. It is vital that every commander and staff principal begin now to understand and plan for their OSINT needs.

Training in open source exploitation is relevant not only to the intelligence professionals, but to all staff elements. OSINT is not the exclusive purview of the intelligence profession. The intelligence professionals should be available to reinforce the commander and their staff, but as a general rule, if a staff principal can answer their own information requirement exclusively through those open sources available to him, then that staff principal should manage their own collection effort.

Intelligence staffs should enable all staff elements to access open sources as directly as possible. Intelligence staffs should serve to facilitate the flow of OSINT and open source material and should serve to provide source evaluation and guidance. Applying this process will enable many potential RFIs to be self-satisfied and thus not submitted. A robust OSINT program can reduce the number of unnecessary RFIs that bog-down the all-source intelligence staff with information requests that can otherwise be addressed.

While each commander will have their preferred means of managing OSINT, what is required is that they have a formal point of contact for OSINT matters, an established process, and that they ensure that OSINT is fully integrated into every aspect of their command & staff operations.

The Internet, despite its current and projected growth, is primarily a vehicle for open collaboration, rather than a repository of knowledge. Commercial online sources such as Factiva, DIALOG, LEXIS-NEXIS, STN and Questel-Orbit have huge repositories of information that have been professionally selected, evaluated, indexed, abstracted, structured, and made available in a very stable format with authoritative sourcing, formatting, and dating.

In many cases, the information provided through these services have been "peer reviewed"—an exhaustive evaluation process by established leaders in the field of study to ensure the accuracy of the information and the rigor of the research. The Internet is not a substitute for premium (fee-for-service) commercial online databases, and it is vital that no professional fall prey to this illusion.

Each commercial service, has its own strengths and weaknesses. A robust OSINT capability should include the understanding of and the means to exploit each service accordingly. Some are best for current news, others for legal records, and others for access to conference proceedings and dissertations.

According to some OSINT experts, only a fraction of known knowledge is available online, either through the Internet or through the commercial online databases. Grey literature, the limited edition publications that are not available through normal commercial channels, comprises a vital "middle ground" between online knowledge and human expertise capable of creating new knowledge in real time. Therefore the OSINT process includes the inventory and evaluation of gray literature sources, and the development of a strategy, a budget, and a process for assuring that gray literature sources are fully integrated into the SPONSOR Future Intelligence Architecture.

Finally, there is the human element. As OSINT doctrine is developed, it would be helpful to think of three distinct forms of overt human intelligence (Overt HUMINT) support. First and foremost are internal subject-matter-experts. These are scattered across commands and within various elements of the member nation governments. Second are the private sector experts who have achieved a favorable reputation based on their proven record of accomplishments and publications. Thirdly, there are "local knowledge" experts, including legal travelers and local residents, that are rarely exploited by resident defense attaches for lack of time or funding with which to reimburse individuals for their time and expense.

New means must be found for defining what local knowledge and local observation is needed, and for combining direct observation by qualified personnel, with out-sourced overt collection and production.

Processing and Exploitation

Overview. After the vital role played during the collection portion of the intelligence cycle, when "knowing who knows" and being able to "mix and match" niche providers of varying pieces of the OSINT solution is essential, it

189

is in the processing and exploitation portion of the cycle that the OSO really makes a mark.

Open sources, just like clandestine or covert sources, require the application of human judgment in order to sort out the important from the unimportant, the timely from the dated, the relevant from the irrelevant, the trusted from the untrusted. As so much of OSINT is *not* in digital form, hands-on human translation and evaluation is the most important part of processing and exploitation.

In the absence of a common technology tool-kit for processing OSINT, OSINT processing and exploitation emphasizes human methods and a deliberate approach.

Analysis. When working from open sources, there is considerable danger for the analyst to be susceptible to unwanted biases and deception from open source authors. While it is never wise nor acceptable practice to attribute as fact intelligence solely because it was received from a national intelligence agency, in those cases, the analyst is able to make certain judgments regarding how that agency managed its information prior to releasing its report. This is not always true for open sources. It is essential that the analyst remain mindful of the origin of the information that has been gathered and the degree of trust that can be assigned to it.

In the production of OSINT reports, it is critical that the reader be aware of what is know and what is being speculated about. The analyst should always be careful to distinguish between information and fact. If the original source material is not provided in full text, it is important to make reference to it and provide an assessment of the source's credibility.

If at all possible, the original sourcing information should never be separated from the open source reporting. A complete description of where the open source information was acquired, the identification of the source, the timing of both the production of the open source information and the timing of its acquisition—these all comprise fully half the value of an OSINT product. Without the sourcing pedigree, the open source substance must be considered suspect and of minimal value to the all-source intelligence analysts or the operations or policy consumers being supported.

It is also helpful when processing open source (or classified) information manually to have in mind a clear model of analysis that distinguishes between military, civil, and geographic information, and also between the levels of analysis—strategic, operational, tactical, and technical—for the threat *changes* depending on the level of analysis. This also helps the analyst to recognize gaps in their collected information, and the relationship between different types of information.

Web Site Authentication and Evaluation.[6] Content on the Internet continues to grow at geometric rates. The Internet has become an essential enabling element for commerce. It is also enabling other forms of human interaction across borders which two decades ago were unimaginable. The intelligence value of information found on the Internet is variable. The dangers of creating misleading analysis through the bleeding of unevaluated biased information into the all-source intelligence picture are ever present. Therefore, the OSINT analyst must take steps with each open source to evaluate its reliability. The standard criteria for the evaluation of web-sites are as follows:

> **Accuracy.** Is the information that is provided consistently accurate based on other sources? The OSINT analyst is able to compare information provided from the web-site with validated all-source intelligence. Benchmarking open sources against validated all-source intelligence assists in assessing the likely accuracy of other information contained on the web-site to be used to address intelligence gaps.

> **Credibility & Authority.** Does the web-site clearly identify itself? Is there merely an E-mail address or a full name, address and telephone number. *Sam Spade* (www.samspade.org) is a web service that provides various online tools to validate a web-site. These include diggers that trace routes used by the web-site.

> Does the web-site demonstrate a degree of influence? Do other media cite that web-site in their reporting? Has the web-site been attacked electronically or in official government statements?

---

[6] This portion is taken with permission from military staff contributing to the development of the *NATO Open Source Intelligence Handbook*.

The use of free web-hosts such as Geocites.com or Cybercafe.com often suggest limited financial support for the web-site and a lack of authority in its message.

Hit-meters/Counters that note the number of times the web-site has been visited can also provide some indication as to the influence of the web-site. These can be misleading and should only be used as an element of an assessment of a site's authority.

Currency. Does the web-site provide information that is timely or are its pages dated? Some dated information can still be relevant for less dynamic topics (e.g. trade statistics) but may be misleading in tracking current events (e.g. presence of insurgent activity).

Objectivity. Does the web-site correspond to a known advocacy group? Does the site represent individuals or an organization? Does that site claim to speak for the organization? Is that site the main web-site or a satellite web-site that represents only a sub-element of the organization.

To whom does the web-site link? Many sites provide a list of relevant links. These attempt to direct visitors to a community of interests that share similar interests or views. An evaluation of those links can further illuminate the views of the web-site authors.

Relevancy. Is the information contained on the web-site relevant to the question at hand? Many web-sites provide information related to a particular topic but do little to add to the understanding of the issue. Information provided can often be interesting but not relevant to the OSINT analyst.

Production

Overview. There are four main elements of OSINT production. These are illustrated on the next page. Another distinction of OSINT is its reliance upon outward engagement beyond the institutional confines of the intelligence staffs.

Engagement is essential to the successful exploitation of open sources. This requires knowledge and understanding of information outside of intelligence channels in order to locate and exploit the best sources of information relevant to an intelligence problem and engage them in a meaningful exchange.

OSINT's four production elements will be explained within this section. While the degree of complexity will vary depending upon the intelligence requirement, those four elements will all remain applicable. A major difference between the OSINT process and the traditional all-source intelligence process exists in how "reports" are treated. In the traditional classified intelligence process, reports are the end of the process—in the OSINT process, they are the beginning, one of four key elements in the *interactive* and *consumer-oriented* process of OSINT support. The four elements of an integrated OSINT support system are Reports, Link Tables, Distance Learning, and Expert Forums.

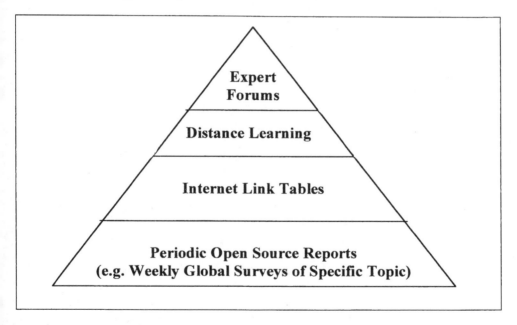

Figure 4: Four Elements of an Integrated Open Source Program

Reports. Open Source Information (OSIF) is data that has been collated together and is of generic interest, and usually broadcast or widely

193

disseminated. Open Source Intelligence (OSINT) is information that has been deliberated discovered, discriminated, distilled, and disseminated to a specific consumer in order to answer a specific intelligence need.

OSINT specialists will have occasion to do both kinds of reports, but must be very clear in their own mind, when doing a report, as to whether it is an information report for general broadcast, or an intelligence report for a specific operational or logistics purpose.

A report should have an analytical summary. This is value-added expertise from a trained professional who has first screened and integrated multiple stories into an underlying framework, and then devised an executive summary that can stand on its own.

Generally a Report, e.g. a report on Macedonia, will have more than one section, for instance, sections on political, military, insurgents, health, police, and external assistance. Each section should in turn have a short summary, no more than a paragraph in length. The section summaries can be used to create the over-all report summary, but should be further distilled and not simply strung together.

Within each section (or linked to each section summary if done in a web-based format) should be between one and five key items of raw information—whether a transcript from a news conference, or a wire service release, or a commercial image, or an extract from a foreign military map.

A major difference between OSINT and other clandestine or covert sources is that OSINT strives to provide concurrently both analytical value and direct access to raw materials. OSINT sources rarely require protection. Text-based products can be stored and disseminated easily by electronic means.

By providing the consumer (the commander, the operator, the logistician, or the all-source intelligence analyst) with direct convenient access to the best of the raw materials used to create the OSINT report, the OSINT analyst is enabling the consumer to dig deeper if they chose to while satisfying the initial RFI.

Reports should always show, on the first page, the date and hour at which collection (not production) was cut off, and the time period in days and/or hours that the report covers. Reports can be organized by source (Internet, Commercial Online, Grey Literature, Experts) or by topic. They should always identify the author and if appropriate the reviewer of the Report, and provide complete contact information so that readers may quickly ask follow-up questions of the originator.

Link Tables. Internet search engines, even the recommended meta-search engine, have severe limitations. By some accounts, any one search engine will cover only 10-15% of the visible web, and even all the search engines working together will overlook what is known as the "deep web." The deep web consists of complex sites with many levels, many free and some by subscription, where search engines are simply ineffective. While some tools such as the affordable software program *Lexibot* are available to assist in collection from the "deep web", considerable time is spent in the identification and analysis of open sources relevant to the information requirement. For this reason, a major aspect of the OSINT support process is the skilled creation of Internet Link Tables that serve as a ready reference for the commander or staff officer who desires to rapidly scan external information sources without necessarily requesting a report. This browsing endeavor can often help the commander or staff principal reflect on their requirements and better articulate their next demands for finished OSINT. An Internet Link Table should generally be in the form of a Table with three columns, such as is illustrated below. By using the Word Table feature, this allows the sorting of the information based on either the Rank or Weight assigned to the site, the URL or title of the site, or the description category of the site. Over time, as various components cooperate and share Link Tables with other allied forces such as the various regional Joint Intelligence Centers, a very comprehensive directory of web resources, one that is tailored to one's needs, should emerge. An extract from a sample link table is shown below.

10	http://allafrica.com/libya/	**All Africa News – Libya** – Up-to-date news on Libya, in English and in French.
10	http://memory.loc.gov/frd/cs/lytoc.html	**Library of Congress Libya Country Study** – Excellent, in-depth country study
10	http://members.aol.com/LibyaPage/	**Libya Resources on the Internet** – Excellent, comprehensive site, includes news, Qadhafi info, maps and satellite photos, military and intel, etc.
10	http://www.un.int/libya/	**The Permanent Mission of Libya to the UN** Website – Includes press releases & statements, ambassador's remarks and links.
10	http://www.nfsl-libya.com/	**The National Front for the Salvation of Libya** - The NFSL is an opposition movement against the

		dictatorial regime of Gaddafi in Libya, and was formed in October, 1981.
8	http://www.libyamazigh.org/	**Libyan Amazigh** site. Contains info on Libya's Amazigh (Berber) culture, language and history.
8	http://www.libyaonline.com/index.html	**Libya Online** Website – Contains basic facts about Libya, tourism, business, arts, literature and sports.

Distance Learning. The Internet, while rendering a major service to those who would like to share information efficiently and also interact inexpensively with diverse people all over the world, has also reduced the productivity of the most experienced personnel in those instances when it allows very inexperienced personnel to constantly interrupt or insert questions that would be better answered through individual study. For this reason, there is an urgent need for Distance Learning modules on all countries and topics that are of interest to the sponsor. The objective is to ensure that all new personnel, and especially new action officers, have an online resource that can serve as a sophisticated turn-over file and reference point. This is also a place where unclassified biographic information can be made available, and where annual reviews of each country or topic can be placed.

The U.S. Pacific command initiative known as the Virtual Information Center is an excellent example of this process. It can be accessed at www.vic-info.org.

Expert Forums. A number of software programs exist with which to manage a variety of Expert Forums, including private teams with their own newsletters, calendars, and automated email alerts whenever new information is posted. One of the most popular is the Alta Vista Forum. The newest, with powerful security features, is offered by Groove Inc. (www.groove.net) and represents the emerging shift in communications and computing power away from centralized server farms toward what are known as "peer to peer" edge units.

Expert Forums can be internal, external, or some combination of the two. Once experts have been identified, they may be invited to join the Expert Forum sponsored by any sponsor element, with the understanding that they will contribute their time and insights on an occasional basis, in return for being granted access to the OSINT being produced by the element sponsoring the Expert Forum. Such a forum can also be a place where individual experts "audition" for short-term consulting contracts, and where the biographies of

196

available efforts can be made available for anonymous review by potential sponsor employers.

Expert Forums should consist of several parts, all of them of potentially great value to the sponsor OSINT process. First, while it is possible to register anonymously for a forum, the greatest value comes from an open registration that includes a photo, biographic note, and complete contact information. Second, the forum will quickly self-organize, with a variety of topics to which individuals can not only contribute observations, but to which they can upload documents, images, even video. The flexibility and scalability of these forums cannot be overstated—but they do have one major flaw: at this time, it is not possible to apply visualization or other technologies to the varied contents of a forum—each item must be copied down to a master database first. Soon the technology will be available to index and abstract all information contributed to a forum, at which time the best of all worlds will be available: distributed experts able to cast a wide net, and a centralized "banking" function for information freely contributed by various parties. Third, the forum permits the rapid organization of private working groups, and offers calendar, newsletter, and other coordination features. Fourth and last, the forums can provide an automatic email alert to any member whenever new information is posted to a topic of interest to them, relieving them of the need to constantly check the forum site.

Dissemination & Evaluation

Overview. There is a major difference between OSINT and the other intelligence disciplines that are inherently classified: OSINT can be shared with *anybody* that the commander deems appropriate, without having to request security or political clearances.

This makes it extraordinarily valuable in humanitarian operations as well as in dealing with civil sector coalition partners—including the Non-Government Organizations (NGO) that traditionally distrust intelligence professionals specifically and the military in general. OSINT has become even more valuable in the 21st Century, as there has been a major change in the over-all C3I paradigm.

OSINT appears to offer a very substantial advantage as the default intelligence source and method with which to achieve consensus and a common understanding of the shared area of operations

Methods.[7] Once open source information had been developed into OSINT, it can be disseminated via the Internet in a "push" mode, or it can be "pulled" off the Internet on demand. Whether via email, or video-teleconferencing or recorded messages, or open web sites, OSINT has unlimited and inexpensive dissemination alternatives open to any party.

The limitations placed on its dissemination are based on the security policies of the organization producing it. While some OSINT products may be shared openly, others may provide details of capabilities or intentions and should therefore be restricted in their dissemination. The dissemination policy should be driven by the mission requirements. The approach should nonetheless be flexible to fully leverage the ability that the production of OSINT products provides for the engagement of non-sponsor elements in security discussions or the development and dissemination of a common view of the operating area.

Within the protected architectures, options exist for the dissemination of OSINT products via the classified wide-area network (WAN) or directly through the Internet. The advantages of the WAN are the direct access afforded to the operations and policy staffs at all levels including deployed units as well as the security afforded by the use of a classified system of dissemination. The principal disadvantage of the WAN for OSINT dissemination is the necessary separation of the products from their source material. Without a direct linkage between an OSINT product and the sources of information, the recipient is less able to drill deeper for additional information or further evaluate the original sources of the information.

Another option is the use of a virtual private network (VPN). A VPN is a restricted community of interest that communicates on the Internet but use security safeguards to limit the access from others who are not members. By using a VPN, OSINT products can be accessed safely and with working links directly to the original source material. Link tables can also be maintained that enable the rapid collection of information. A VPN provides the means with

---

[7] This section is also drawn from military staff.

which to exchange OSINT products with other OSINT centers across a coalition. Finally, the use of a VPN provides the means with which to disseminate OSINT products with NGOs and other international organizations as mission requirements demand. For these reasons, the development of a VPN to support OSINT endeavors is recommended.

General Reference Link Table

Academic/Educational Information	http://www.academicinfo.net/index.html
Car Rentals	http://www.bnm.com/rcar.htm
Country Background Notes	http://www.state.gov/r/pa/bgn
Currencies	http://cnnfn.cnn.com/markets/currencies
Defense Link	http://www.defenselink.mil
Dictionaries, International	http://www.facstaff.bucknell.edu/rbeard/diction.html
Dictionary, English	http://www.m-w.com/netdict.htm
DoD Dictionary	http://www.dtic.mil/doctrine/jel/doddict
Electronic Lists and News Groups	http://encarta.msn.com/encyclopedia/weblinks/default.asp?ty=more&ca=XXX
Encyclopedia (Encarta) Web Links	http://encarta.msn.com/encyclopedia/weblinks/default.asp?ty=more&ca=XXX
Hotels	http://www.all-hotels.com
Jane's Defence	http://www.janes.com/defence
Jane's Defence Glossary	http://www.janes.com/defence/resources/defres_gloss.html
Map (Street) with Directions	http://www.maps.com
Maps, General	http://www.lib.utexas.edu/maps/index.html
Media—*The New York Times*	http://www.nyt.com
Military Doctrine (fas.org)	http://www.fas.org/man/doctrine.htm
National Defense University	http://www.ndu.edu
NDU Strategic Forum	http://www.ndu.edu/inss/strforum/h6.html
Per Diem Rates	http://www.state.gov/www/perdiems/index.html
Politicians of the World	http://www.trytel.com/~aberdeen/v.html
Postal Information	http://dir.yahoo.com/Reference/Postal_Information
Travel Warnings	http://travel.state.gov/travel_warnings.html
Virtual Reference Desk	http://thorplus.lib.purdue.edu/reference/index.html
Weather	http://www.cnn.com/WEATHER/index.html
World Time	http://www.timeanddate.com/worldclock
Worldwide Web Virtual Library Index	http://vlib.org/Overview.html
Reminder Service	http://www.internetreminder.com
Emergency Numbers, International	http://ambulance.ie.eu.org/Numbers/Index.htm
First Aid Guide	http://expage.com/page/lacieking
Medical Care, Global	http://www.internationalsos.com
Embassies in USA (All Countries)	http://www.state.gov/s/cpr/rls/dpl
Embassies of the USA (All Countries)	http://usembassy.state.gov
Financial Times	http://news.ft.com/home/rw
Der Spiegel	http://www.spiegel.de
Le Monde	http://www.lemonde.fr
Jerusalem Post	http://www.jpost.com
Canadian Forces College News Review	http://www.cfc.dnd.ca/spotlight.en.html
Oxford Analytica Early Warnings	http://www.oxan.com/earlyw1.html
The Economist	http://www.economist.com
British Broadcasting Corporation	http://www.bbc.co.uk

Training Table

The Open Source Intelligence Proceedings include over 5,000 pages from over 500 international authorities including the (then) Director General of the International Red Cross and many other European and Asian experts, and comprise the "information commons" on the state of the art for open source intelligence.

OSINT Presentation to SHAPE/PfP Flags	http://www.oss.net/Papers/white/SHAPE.ppt
New Craft of Intelligence	http://www.oss.net/Papers/white/TheNewCraftofIntelligence.doc
Information & Intelligence Bibliography	http://www.oss.net/Papers/white/23-BibliographyAnnotated.rtf
Core Information Concepts for the Future	http://www.oss.net/Papers/white/INFORMATIONCONCEPTS.html
OSINT HANDBOOK (Original, 1996)	http://www.oss.net/DispFrame.html?Proceedings/96Vol1/index.html
OSINT READER (Original, 1996)	http://www.oss.net/DispFrame.html?Proceedings/95Vol1/index.html
Eight Self-Paced OSINT Lesson Plans	http://www.oss.net/DispFrame.html?Papers/training/index.html
Creating an OSINT Cell (DIA Report)	http://www.oss.net/DispFrame.html?Papers/white/DIAReport.html
Business Intelligence Primer (1994)	http://www.oss.net/DispFrame.html?Papers/white/THETHEORYANDPRACTICEOFCOMPETITORINTELLIGENCE.html
Information Peacekeeping Concepts	http://www.oss.net/DispFrame.html?Peacekeeping.html
Virtual Intelligence Paper	http://www.oss.net/Papers/articles/VirtualIntelligence.html
Open Source Intelligence Proceedings	http://www.oss.net/Proceed.html
Index to OSINT Proceedings	http://www.oss.net/Papers/white/index.rtf
Open Source Intelligence White Papers	http://www.oss.net/White.html
OSINT and the Military	http://www.oss.net/Proceedings/95Vol1/aab0aw.html
Non-Traditional Threats (Powerpoint)	http://www.oss.net/Papers/white/Strategy.ppt
Modern Conflict: The Reality (Powerpoint)	http://www.oss.net/Papers/white/ModernConflict.ppt
Threat, Strategy, and Force Structure (Alternative Paradigm for 21st Century)	http://www.oss.net/Papers/white/AlternativeStrategy.rtf
Law Enforcement OSINT Review	http://www.oss.net/Papers/white/LEAReview.rtf
OSINT Notices (Historical Interest)	http://www.oss.net/Notice.html
Canadian Intelligence Studies	http://www.sfu.ca/igs/CASIS/
Come Back Alive "Ground Truth"	www.comebackalive.com/df/index.htm
Future of Intelligence	www.future-intel.it
History of Intelligence	http://intelligence-history.wiso.uni-erlangen.de
Intelligence Resource Program	http://www.fas.org/irp/index.html
Links to International Media	http://www.esperanto.se/kiosk/index.html
Literature of Intelligence	http://intellit.muskingum.edu
Open Directory Project	http://dmoz.org/
Strategic Intelligence	http://www.loyola.edu/dept/politics/intel.html

REMINDER: www.oss.net contains, in the Open Archives, close to 5,000 pages from over 500 authorities speaking to the annual international open source intelligence forum. Attending the conference, with its full day of open source intelligence training, the advanced Internet course, and the three day conference (a federal day, an exhibits and deep skill workshop day, and an international day) is the best means of joining the network of forward-thinking intelligence professionals. See the conference home page icon at www.oss.net.

Appendix 2:
Citizen's Guide to
Useful Internet Sources

I personally favor and recommend Copernic as the best tool for finding useful Internet sources. It is especially nice for remembering what you have seen before and showing you only new material. However, no matter how good the Internet search tools are that you might use, generally they will not penetrate the "deep web" that is unindexed. Creating your own Internet table is always the best way to manage your sources. In this appendix I provide a number of Internet tables put together by Ms. Jenny Zullo, the Senior Analyst and Trainer for OSS Inc. (panther@oss.net). This chapter can be downloaded from www.oss.net/Papers/white/Appendix2.doc, should you wish to have "clickable" URLs right at hand.

Corruption

Anti-Corruption Gateway for Europe & Eurasia
The Gateway "serves as an easily accessible repository of anti-corruption project documentation, legislation, regional and international agreements, news, survey results, reports, and research." Includes country info, current events, reference center, and discussion groups. USAID-sponsored.
http://www.nobribes.org/
Center for Responsive Politics
CRP is a non-partisan, non-profit research group based in Washington, D.C. that tracks money in politics, and its effect on elections and public policy. The site looks at paybacks, money in politics – including campaign finance law – and statistics on individual donors.
http://www.opensecrets.org/
Common Cause
The website for this well-known group focuses on soft money, election reform and reducing PAC influence.
http://www.commoncause.org/
Conspiracy Plant
Site developed & designed by Doug Trocino. Claims to be the "alternative news & history network – your antidote to media cartel propaganda." As name implies, believe there is corruption and/or conspiracy in every U.S. government agency and policy.
http://www.conspiracyplanet.com
Corruption on the Border
Site produced by John Carman, a former U.S. Customs agent and whistleblower. The newsletter claims to uncover corruption within the Customs Service. Also includes recommended readings of other whistleblower publications.
http://www.customscorruption.com/
Global Exchange
The USA page looks at democracy in the U.S., including campaign reform and human rights. Also views labor issues and prison reform among other topics. Good links to other sites.
http://www.globalexchange.org/campaigns/usa/
OECD Anti-Corruption Division
Serves as the focal point within the OECD Secretariat to support the work of the OECD in the fight against bribery and corruption in international business transactions.
http://www.oecd.org/EN/home/0,,EN-home-86-3-no-no-no,FF.html
Transparency International
Based in Berlin, TI "the only international non-governmental organisation devoted to combating corruption, brings civil society, business, and governments together in a powerful global coalition." Site includes newsroom, knowledge center, links and activities pages.
http://www.transparency.org/

U.S. AID Anti-Corruption Resources	

U.S. AID Anti-Corruption Resources
Site includes anti-corruption info, news, AID programs to fight corruption and links.
http://www.usaid.gov/democracy/anticorruption/

U.S. Dept. of Commerce
Transparency and anti-bribery initiatives site. Includes legislation, documents, links to US and international anti-corruption initiatives.
http://www.ita.doc.gov/legal/tabi.html

UNDCP Corruption Site
Very extensive site defining and promulgating the UN's role in the fight against international corruption. Includes publications and an anti-corruption "toolkit."
http://www.undcp.org/corruption.html

World Bank Anti-Corruption Site
Four main goals of this program as espoused on the site include: preventing corruption in Bank projects; helping countries reduce corruption; mainstreaming anti-corruption in Bank projects and; supporting international efforts. Includes info about upcoming events, new reports and projects, and the anticorruption investigations unit.
http://www1.worldbank.org/publicsector/anticorrupt/

York University's Nathanson Centre for the Study of Organized Crime and Corruption
Canadian-based site, includes research results and publications, a bibliographic database, and links to other organized crime websites.
http://www.yorku.ca/nathanson/

Cyber-Advocacy[1]

Action Network	www.actionnetwork.org
AFL-CIO	www.aflcio.org
American Civil Liberties Union	www.aclu.org
American Conservative Union	www.conservative.org
Americans for Democratic Action	www.adaction.org
Benton Foundation Best Practices	www.benton.org
Center for Democracy & Technology	www.cdt.org
Center for Responsive Politics	www.opensecrets.org
Christian Coalition	www.cc.org
Coalition to Protect Americans Now	www.prtectamericansnow.com
Congressional & Presidential Studies (AU)	www.american.edu

---

[1] All sites are as listed in two really great publications, both by the Foundation for Public Affairs at www.pac.org: *Creating A Digital Democracy: The Impact of the Internet on Public Policy-Making* (1999); and *Cyber-Activism: Advocacy Groups and the Internet* (2000). Call them at (202) 872-1750 or visit their web site.

Corporate Watch	www.corpwatch.org
Defend Your Privacy	www.defendyourprivacy.com
Democracy Online (GWU)	www.democracyonline.org
Earth to Kids (Environmental Network)	www.Earth2Kids.org
Electronic Policy Network (Ideological)	www.epn.org
Environmental Defense Scorecard	www.scorecard.org
E-the People	www.e-thepeople.com
Free-Market.net	www.free-market.net
Human Rights Campaign	www.hrc.org
Kennedy School Vision for Governance	www.ksg.harvard.edu/visions
Million Mom March	www.millionmommarch.com
National Rifle Association	www.nra.org
Political Information	www.politicalinformation.com
Project Vote Smart	www.vote-smart.org
Rainforest Action Network (Fax Blasts)	www.ran.org
Satellite Reform (Thinking Small)	www.SatelliteReform.org
Save Our Environment Action Center	www.saveourenvironment.org
Second Amendment Sisters	www.sas-aim.org
Smart Voter	www.smartvoter.org
TechRocks	www.techrocks.org
Town Hall (Ideological)	www.townhall.com
Virtual Activist	www.netaction.org
World Wildlife Fund	www.worldwildlife.org

Disease & Public Health

Centers for Disease Control and Prevention– Travelers' Health
Site includes latest information on health threats worldwide, including details on diseases ranging from African sleeping sickness to yellow fever. Also has traveler information on vaccines, safe food and water, outbreaks, etc.
http://www.cdc.gov/travel/

GlobalHealth – Office of International and Refugee Health
A division of the U.S. Dept of Health & Human Services. This site addresses global health, and the link between domestic and international health issues. Site includes info on what's new, data resources, international travel, and links & dialogue.
http://www.globalhealth.gov/

International Public Health Watch
An advocacy group of public health professionals, based in Australia, providing organized access to current resources on public health. "We believe that WHO and all national governments need support to their activities by an independent watchdog organization focusing on: reviewing public health programs and projects and their

206

impact on public health on national and international level; making evaluation reports on those programs and projects available on this web-site."
http://www.ldb.org/iphw/index.htm

Life and Death in the 21st Century: Future Plagues
"The shocking thing about life in the 21st century is that the dream of wiping out infectious diseases may never be realised. In fact, despite all the progress of modern medicine, we face the future knowing that science will never defeat viruses and bacteria. They are the dominant species on the planet. New and deadly viruses will continue to emerge in the 21st century, and killer diseases we thought we had defeated will return." From a BBC program which aired 5 Jan 2000. Site includes the program transcript, biographies, a glossary and links to further information.
http://www.bbc.co.uk/science/horizon/future_plagues.shtml

Population Resource Center
The Population Resource Center, a non-profit organization based in Washington, DC and Princeton, NJ aims to further the development of public policy by bringing the latest demographic data to policymakers through policy briefings and small-group discussions. The programs help inform the debate and serve as a bridge between the social science community and the world of public policy. The goal of PRC is to enable policymakers to incorporate the latest research findings in population change into the development of public policy. Site includes info on morbidity and mortality, women and children issues, diseases, and food and agriculture.
http://www.prcdc.org/home.html

ProMED Mail
The global electronic reporting system for outbreaks of emerging infectious diseases & toxins. It is a program of the International Society for Infectious Diseases. Includes announcements, how to report or comment on outbreaks, links to articles, references & related sites and maps of current outbreaks.
http://www.promedmail.org/pls/promed/promed.home

Third World Network – Health Page
Includes most recent articles on Third World health policies, structural adjustment and health, new and emerging diseases, traditional medicine, and drugs.
http://www.twnside.org.sg/heal.htm

University of Michigan Healthweb
Excellent site with links to information on general public health & epidemiology issues, cancer, emerging diseases, HIV/AIDS, other diseases, prevention, and journals and newsletters.
http://www.lib.umich.edu/hw/public.health/epidemiology.html

World Health Organization
Disease outbreaks, emergency and humanitarian actions, travelers' health, and a press media section make this the premier website for world health issues. Recent articles include "First Shipment of Vital Tuberculosis Drugs Arrives in Moldova" and "Responding to the deliberate use of biological agents and chemicals as weapons."

---

http://www.who.int/home-page/
World Wide Web Virtual Library for Epidemiology
Includes links to government agencies and international organizations, university sites, professional societies and organizations, infectious diseases and AIDS, data sources, publications, and meetings & courses.
http://www.epibiostat.ucsf.edu/epidem/epidem.html

Education

Canadian Education on the Web
The purpose of Canadian Education on the Web is to bring together everything relating to Canada and education that has a presence on the World Wide Web. The page is developed and maintained by the University of Toronto.
http://www.oise.utoronto.ca/~mpress/eduweb/eduweb.html

Educating.net
Education portal for all quality educational services on the Internet, including distance education, homeschooling, K-12, college & university, professional re-training, continuing education, fun learning and more.
http://www.educating.net/

Education Index
The Education Index is an annotated guide to the best education-related sites on the Web. They're sorted by subject and lifestage, so you can find what you're looking for quickly and easily.
http://www.educationindex.com/

EducationNews.org
"The world's leading source of education news 7 days a week."
http://www.educationnews.org/

Global Learning On-line
Based in the UK and supported by the EC, this is an educational site for teachers on global and development education.
http://atschool.eduweb.co.uk/rmext05/glo/

Homeschool Zone
A comprehensive site of homeschooling resources. Events, FAQ, recipes, crafts, and support pages included.
http://www.homeschoolzone.com/main.htm

Measuring Up 2000
Site is the first state-by-state report card of higher education with grades on performance in five categories: preparation, participation, affordability, completion, and economic and civic benefits.
http://www.refdesk.com/educate.html

U.S. Dept. of State Geographic Learning Site
This site provides info about the U.S. Department of State: the interesting countries

where U.S. Diplomats work; places where the Secretary of State travels; geographic
Hot Spots and Cool Sites; international affairs and important international issues; and
more!
http://geography.state.gov/htmls/plugin.html

**WWW Virtual Library: International Affairs Resources – International and
Comparative Education**
Site lists links to over thirty education-related sites from all around the globe.
http://www.etown.edu/vl/intleduc.html

Environment including Water

Center for Sustainable Systems – University of Michigan
CSS develops life cycle based models and sustainability metrics to evaluate the
performance and to guide the continuous improvement of industrial systems for
meeting societal needs. They promote sustainability by developing these tools and
knowledge in collaboration with diverse stakeholders so that better informed decisions
are made. The site includes information on sustainability research and development,
education, and sustainability indicators.
http://css.snre.umich.edu/index.html

Environmental Background Information Center
EBIC provides grassroots groups facing threats to their health and environment with
three basic services, at no charge: Track records of corporate polluters; environmental
justice mapping; and strategic assistance.
http://www.ebic.org/

Environmental Resources Trust
ERT (The Environmental Resources Trust, Inc.) is a Washington, DC-based, non-profit
organization that pioneers the use of market forces to protect and improve the global
environment. Founded in 1996, with the assistance of the Environmental Defense Fund,
ERT is harnessing the power of markets to address the challenges of tempering climate
change, securing clean and reliable power, and encouraging environmentally beneficial
land use.
http://www.ert.net/index.html

Greenpeace Toxics Site
The Greenpeace Toxics Campaign seeks an end to the manufacture, use and disposal of
hazardous, synthetic substances - particularly persistent organic pollutants. Greenpeace
also seeks an end to the migration of dirty technologies to regions of the world least
equipped to deal with inevitable, industrial disasters. Our activists raise public
awareness about the dangers of industrial pollution, and encourage governments and
industries to convert to clean modes of production.
http://www.greenpeace.org/~toxics/index.html

Oregon Statue University Transboundary Freshwater Dispute Database
The site includes: A searchable database of summaries and full text of 150 water-

related treaties. A similar database of 39 interstate compacts within the United States; Negotiating notes and other primary and secondary sources for 14 case studies of the processes of international water conflict resolution; Descriptions of indigenous/traditional methods for the resolution of water disputes; News files and bibliographic entries of acute water conflicts; A digitized inventory of international watersheds; An annotated bibliography of the state of the art of Transboundary Freshwater Dispute Resolution.
http://terra.geo.orst.edu/users/tfdd/

Sierra Club Environmental Update Page
Site addresses energy issues, toxic waste, clean water, global warming, global population and environment, etc.
http://www.sierraclub.org/environment/

Sustainable Business
This site includes four major sections : Sustainable Business Insider - news, articles, and columns from over 35 leading sustainable business trade publications and individuals; Business Opportunities; Green Dream Jobs; and SustainableBusiness.com Library, which compiles the most useful web sites, databases, reports, books, and other resources for sustainable business.
http://www.sustainablebusiness.com/

U.S. EPA Environmental Issues
EPA's Clean Air Market Programs address several environmental issues using emissions caps and allowance trading. This section of the site provides information about each, especially scientific details. Issues include acid rain, smog/ozone transport and regional haze.
http://www.epa.gov/airmarkets/envissues/index.html

U.S.G.S. Water Resources of the U.S.
Site includes real time water data, GIS, water quality, water use, and "water watch" – maps and graphs of current water conditions in the U.S.
http://water.usgs.gov/

WaterWeb
"The WaterWeb consortium has been created to promote the sharing of information concerning water and the earth's environment. Our organization seeks to create a global community, bringing together educational, governmental, nonprofit, & commercial entities interested in water research, conservation, and management. WaterWeb's goals are to advance water related issues, promote the use of quality information, and share information with water use stakeholders and decision makers."
http://www.waterweb.org/

Genocide

Armenian Genocide Institute – Museum
Located in Yerevan, Armenia. Principal activities include scholarly exposition of

historical-documentary materials, archival documents, photos on the Armenian Genocide in 1915-1923. Also obtains historical and documentary materials from State Archives of different countries of the world. Eye-witness accounts of massacres have been and are being collected for eventual publication. Many archival documents have been translated.
http://www.armenocide.am/

Cambodian Genocide Project
Based at Yale University. Features tribunal news, includes biographic, bibliographic, geographic and photographic pages, as well as links.
http://www.yale.edu/cgp/

Gendercide Watch
"GENDERCIDE WATCH seeks to confront acts of gender-selective mass killing around the world. We believe that such atrocities against ordinary men and women constitute one of humanity's worst blights, and one of its greatest challenges in the new millennium."
http://www.gendercide.org/

Genocide Research Project
A joint project of the University of Memphis and Penn State University. Site includes info about the project, a bibliography, news and events and links.
http://www.people.memphis.edu/~genocide/

Genocide Watch
Group is the coordinator for the international campaign to end genocide. Site includes information on the eight stages of genocide, links to members of the international campaign to end genocide, and a monthly news monitor.
www.genocidewatch.org

Holocaust and Genocide Studies
Based at Webster University's Center for the Study of the Holocaust, Genocide and Human rights, headed by Dr. Linda Woolf. Site includes recommended readings, chronology of the holocaust, and an extensive links listing to information on regional genocidal issues.
http://www.webster.edu/~woolflm/holocaust.html

Institute for the Study of Genocide/International Assoc. of Genocide Scholars
Features genocide definitions, info on conferences, book reviews, issues and alerts, links to other sites and current and archived newsletters.
http://www.isg-ags.org/

International Criminal Tribunal for Rwanda
"The Tribunal was established by a United Nations Security Council Resolution in 1994 to prosecute the organizers and leaders of the genocide in Rwanda in 1994. This web site is designed to help you find all the information you may need about the organization and work of the Tribunal, whatever your degree of interest."
http://www.ictr.org/

Society of Threatened Peoples

The Society has consultative status as NGO at the United Nations (ECOSOC). In documents and statements the Society publishes their research on cases of human rights violations committed against religious and/or ethnic minorities, among them the Indigenous Peoples and genocide.
http://www.gfbv.de/gfbv_e/index2.htm

Web Genocide Documentation Centre
Comprehensive site for resources on genocide, war crimes, and mass killing. Compiled by Dr. J.S. Stine, University of the West of England.
http://www.ess.uwe.ac.uk/genocide.htm

Homeland Defense

Anser Institute for Homeland Security
This is a very new site responsive to the recent interest in homeland security; it includes a budding *Journal for Homeland Defense,* a weekly newsletter, links, current news, upcoming events, etc.
http://www.homelandsecurity.org/

Center for Civilian Biodefense Studies at John Hopkins University
The goal of the center is to increase national and international awareness of the medical and public health threats posed by biological weapons, thereby augmenting the potential legal, political and moral prohibitions against their use. Site provides facts on bio agents, as well as news, a cyber library, and upcoming events info.
http://www.hopkins-biodefense.org/

CSIS Homeland Defense Site
Center for Strategic and International Studies (CSIS) has initiated an 18-month study to improve our understanding of Homeland Defense and chart a course for improving policy in this area. [This project was established prior to the 11 September terrorist attacks on America and contains information from both prior and subsequent to the attacks.]
http://www.csis.org/burke/hd/index.htm

Critical Infrastructure Assurance Office
Official website. The Critical Infrastructure Assurance Office (CIAO) was created in May 1998 as a mechanism to assist in the coordination of the Federal Government's initiatives on critical infrastructure protection. Site includes statements, articles and executive orders. Also features. Apart from this site see also www.fedcirc.gov, www.cybercrime.gov, and www.cert.org.
www.nipc.gov

FirstGov.gov - U.S.G. Response to Terrorism Site
Comprehensive site, includes info on how to protect yourself and your country, precautions regarding bioterrorism, what you can do for victims and their families, victims benefits and assistance programs, and travel information.
http://www.firstgov.gov/featured/usgresponse.html

212

Information Security Wire Magazine Comprehensive site involving information security, infosec news, editorials, events, issue archives, and *Information Security Wire Digest.* http://www.infosecuritymag.com/current_daily.shtml
NationalSecurity.org A project of the Heritage Foundation. The website is devoted to disseminating information and policy analyses regarding U.S. national security issues. This site is meant to function as a clearinghouse for reporters, researchers, and concerned Americans interested in gaining access to publications and links on a wide spectrum of national security issues. http://www.nationalsecurity.org/
State Guard Association of the U.S. Official website. The SGAUS is the national association for the organized state militia, often known as State Defense Force, State Guard, or State Military Reserve. These state military forces are the official "well regulated" Militia of their respective states. The SGAUS does **not** support private groups who may call themselves "militia," but who are not officially recognized, unless the group is bona fide and seeking such official state recognition. http://www.sgaus.org/
Texas Homeland Security Task Force - Homepage Governor Rick Perry has created a Governor's Task Force on Homeland Security to advise him on matters relating to homeland security. The goal of the task force is to reassure Texans that the state is doing all it can to ensure their safety by identifying threats before they are carried out and by being able to respond effectively if a threat is carried out. http://www.governor.state.tx.us/homelandsecurity/
U.S. Office of Homeland Security Official website. "The Office of Homeland Security is coordinating national strategy to strengthen protections against terrorist threats or attacks in the United States." Site includes latest news, speeches, photos and links to useful sites. http://www.whitehouse.gov/homeland/

Instability

Center for Strategic and International Studies "For four decades, the Center for Strategic and International Studies (CSIS) has been dedicated to providing world leaders with strategic insights on—and policy solutions to—current and emerging global issues." Site includes numerous articles on instability and insurgency issues. http://www.csis.org/index.htm
Freedom House Through a vast array of international programs and publications, Freedom House is

working to advance the remarkable worldwide expansion of political and economic freedom. Includes annual "Nations in Transit Report," the only comprehensive, comparative, multidimensional study focusing on 27 former Communist states.
http://www.freedomhouse.org/

Insurgency Online Project
Insurgency On-Line is a theoretically-based and broadly cross-national comparison of Internet use by anti-government political movements. The project focuses on how selected groups use the Internet as an information provision tool in campaigns against particular governments. Based at York University, Toronto.
http://www.yorku.ca/research/ionline/insuron.htm

International Crisis Group – Crisis Web
Headquartered in Brussels, the International Crisis Group (ICG) is a private, multinational organisation committed to strengthening the capacity of the international community to anticipate, understand and act to prevent and contain conflict.
http://www.intl-crisis-group.org/

Freedom Fighters, Dissidents and Insurgents
Provides an extensive list of separatists, para-military, military, intelligence and aid organizations that have web sites.
http://www.cromwell-intl.com/security/netusers.html

Georgetown University's Guide to Terrorism and Insurgency Research
This is a guide to sources for doing research on terrorism and insurgency. The focus of most materials is terrorism, but many of them also cover insurgency.
http://gulib.lausun.georgetown.edu/guides/terrorism/

POINTS
Project on Insurgency, Terrorism and Security. POINTS is a privately-funded public resource on terrorism, insurgency, violence, and individual security. The pages and links are designed to serve those people with a need to know--including academicians, security personnel, risk managers, researchers, and media reporters.
http://www.paladin-san-francisco.com/

PovertyNet
The World Bank's poverty site, resources and support for people working to understand and alleviate poverty. Includes information on political, economic and social inequality.
http://www.worldbank.org/poverty/index.htm

WorldWatch
The internet source for cross-disciplinary, global environmental information. Includes information on how environment, environmental changes, technological developments, natural disasters, etc. affect the human condition.
http://www.worldwatch.org/

Intelligence

Canadian Association for Security & Intelligence Studies
The Canadian Association for Security and Intelligence Studies (CASIS) is a nonpartisan, voluntary association established in 1985. Its principal purpose is to provide informed debate in Canada on security and intelligence issues. Membership is open and currently includes academics, concerned citizens, government officials, journalists, lawyers, students, as well as former intelligence officers.
http://www.sfu.ca/igs/CASIS/

Council on Intelligence
An informal coalition of international citizens concerned about the future of intelligence as the first line of defense against terrorism and other threats. Offers a list of recommended books, other seminal papers, and various discussion forums and email alert lists. Supported by OSS Inc.
www.council-on-intelligence.org.

CIA Maps & Publications
This site includes purchasing information for publicly available maps (listed by country) and publications.
http://www.cia.gov/cia/publications/mapspub/

European Intelligence and Security Studies Forum
Site includes cryptography, terrorism, organized crime, proliferation and geopolitical issues information. Also contains papers from the Priverno Conference On Intelligence in the 21st Century, held in February 2001.
http://www.future-intel.it/

Federation of American Scientists Intelligence Resource Program
This site provides a selection of official and unofficial resources on intelligence policy, structure, function, organization and operations.
http://www.fas.org/irp/index.html

International Intelligence History Association
Founded in 1993, the International Intelligence History Association was established to promote scholarly research on intelligence organizations and their impact on historical development and international relations.
http://intelligence-history.wiso.uni-erlangen.de/

Literature of Intelligence
An in-depth bibliography, compiled by a former career intelligence officer turned college dean, of a great variety of intelligence-related issues.
http://intellit.muskingum.edu/

Loyola Homepage on Strategic Intelligence
Strategic, military and economic intelligence are the focus of this site, which includes links and information on the intel community, history, reorganization, specific organizations, etc.
http://www.loyola.edu/dept/politics/intel.html

National Counterintelligence Center
The website of the CIA's CI center. A comprehensive site, including news, publications, including a CI bibliography, links, and seminar info.
http://www.ncix.gov/index2.html

National Institute for Computer-Assisted Reporting
NICAR is a program of Investigative Reporters and Editors, Inc. and the Missouri School of Journalism. Founded in 1989, NICAR has trained thousands of journalists in the practical skills of finding, prying loose and analyzing electronic information.
http://www.nicar.org/

Open Directory Project
The Open Directory Project is the largest, most comprehensive human-edited directory of the Web. It is constructed and maintained by a vast, global community of volunteer editors. The ODP covers a vast variety of topics, including intelligence and intelligence-related issues.
http://dmoz.org/about.html

Open Source Solutions – OSS, Inc.
Site includes information on OSINT education, open source marketplace, information arbitrage, information merchant banking. Also includes access, by subscription, to up-to-the-minute OSINT reporting on a variety of issues.
http://www.oss.net/

Private Investigation Resources
Claims to be the largest resource site on private investigation on the web.
http://www.pimall.com/nais/home.html

Robert Young Pelton's Most Dangerous Places
The author and adventurer's website. Lists the world's most dangerous places, includes warning and adventure guide.
http://www.comebackalive.com/df/index.htm

Worldnews
Website presents the most recent news items, as well as search capabilities for over 20 languages, by headline, Boolean, any/all words, date, source, word frequency.
http://www.worldnews.com/

Proliferation

Carnegie Endowment – Proliferation News & Resources
Site includes today's news, analysis, country resources, weapons information, online resources, nuclear numbers & tracking.
http://www.ceip.org/files/nonprolif/default.asp?Action=default&projectID=

Center for Defense Information
The "issues" section allows the visitor to view info on CBW and nuclear proliferation issues.

http://www.cdi.org/issues/
Center for Nonproliferation Studies Monterey Institute for International Studies – includes info on NBC proliferation, current events, terrorism, publications, and is also broken out by region. http://cns.miis.edu/index.htm
Federation of American Scientists Weapons of Mass Destruction – Intelligence Threat Assessments – site lists states with WMD, links to official documents, and other sources on the topic. http://www.fas.org/irp/threat/wmd.htm
Global Beat – NYU Nuclear Weapons & Proliferation site –Contains expert analyses and commentary on nuclear weapons, proliferation and weapons of mass destruction. http://www.nyu.edu/globalbeat/nukes.html
Henry L. Stimson Center This organization performs research on a variety of national security topics, including NBC proliferation. http://www.stimson.org/?SN=TI200110174
InfoManage International Nonproliferation of WMD – very extensive site includes basics on proliferation in all areas and links to many useful sites. http://infomanage.com/nonproliferation/
Nuclear Control Institute NCI is an independent research and advocacy center specializing in problems of nuclear proliferation. NCI monitors nuclear activities worldwide and pursue strategies to halt the spread and reverse the growth of nuclear arms. http://www.nci.org/index.htm
Nuclearfiles.org Proliferation section includes NPT issues, country portals, issue research portals, international laws & international regimes. http://www.nuclearfiles.org/prolif/
SIPRI Projects Stockholm International Peace Research Initiative – Site includes several ongoing projects, including disarmament, arms transfers and NBC issues. http://projects.sipri.se/

Slavery & Human Trafficking

Andrew Vachss Human Trafficking Resources Site Site is hosted by internationally known juvenile rights attorney. Includes articles on international child abuse (to include sexual, slavery and trafficking) cases, as well as extensive resources on the topic. http://www.vachss.com/help_text/human_trafficking.html

Anti-Slavery
"Anti-Slavery International is the world's oldest international human rights organisation, founded in 1839. It is the only charity in the United Kingdom to work exclusively against slavery and related abuses. We work at local, national and international levels to eliminate the system of slavery around the world." Site includes info on campaigns, news, and resources.
http://www.antislavery.org/index.htm

Australian Institute of Criminology
Smuggling & Trafficking in Human Beings site, includes documents, reports and legislation regarding the Institute's assistance to the U.N.'s Global Programme Against Trafficking in Human Beings.
http://www.aic.gov.au/research/traffick/

CIA Center for the Study of Intelligence
International Trafficking in Women to the US-A Contemporary Manifestation of Slavery and Organized Crime – This eighty-page monograph, written by U.S. State Dept. analyst Amy O'Neill Richard in 1999, reports on the trafficking of foreign women into the U.S.
http://www.cia.gov/csi/monograph/women/trafficking.pdf

CAST – Coalition to Abolish Slavery and Trafficking
"CAST is an alliance of nonprofit service providers, grassroots advocacy groups and activists dedicated to providing human services and human rights advocacy to victims of modern-day slavery. The mission is to assist persons trafficked for the purpose of forced labor and slavery-like practices and to work toward ending all instances of such human rights violations." Site includes fact sheet, goals, media, students & academics page, links & resources and donor information.
http://www.trafficked-women.org/main.html

Criminal Justice Resources – Human Trafficking
Michigan State University site, which contains a very long list of links to articles, documents and sites relevant to human trafficking issues.
http://www.lib.msu.edu/harris23/crimjust/human.htm

Global March Against Child Labor
Comprehensive site with all kinds of information relating to child labor, trafficking and general rights issues. Also includes newsletter.
http://globalmarch.org/index.html

Global Survival Network
This Washington-based group focuses on environmental and human rights issues. Included on the site is a report, which summarizes a two-year investigation into the trafficking of Russian women for prostitution.
http://www.globalsurvival.net/femaletrade/index.htm

Human Rights Watch
The website of this well-known international organization includes information on women's and children's rights.

http://www.hrw.org/
La Strada Ukraine A Ukrainian NGO dedicated to the prevention of traffic in women program in Central and Eastern Europe. Site includes new & conferences, cases, links and hotlines. http://www.brama.com/lastrada/index.html
Organs Watch Based at UC Berkeley. Organs Watch brings together a team of anthropologists, human rights activists, physicians, and social medicine specialists to conduct a multi-year project on "Medicine, Markets, and Bodies." Site includes policy info, international hot spots of organ trafficking, research, reports and contact info. http://sunsite.berkeley.edu/biotech/organswatch/
Perm Center Against Violence and Human Trafficking While not an extensive site, this Russian-based organization lists its mandate, history, projects, and partners, as well as contact information. The Center is a member of the Global Alliance Against Traffic in Women and the Association of Crisis Centers of Russia. http://www.civilsoc.org/nisorgs/russwest/pcenter.htm
SaveASlave.com "The mission of SaveASlave.com is to inform the world about the issues surrounding modern involuntary servitude -- slavery. We also wish to encourage former slaves by providing linkage to resources for training, financial and spiritual support." Site includes adoption tools, links on slavery, online news, resources and Sudan Watch pages. http://www.saveaslave.com/
UNDCP Trafficking In Human Beings Official UN site, includes general trafficking info, anti-trafficking protocol, protocol to prevent, suppress and punish trafficking in persons, technical cooperation projects and awareness raising campaigns. http://www.undcp.org/trafficking_human_beings.html
U.S. Dept. of State – Global Issues: Human Trafficking Site includes official policy, fact sheets, reports & documents, resources, "subject in depth" section, international initiatives and links to other sites on the topic. http://usinfo.state.gov/topical/global/traffic/
University of Toronto Women's Human Rights Resources Extensive site, includes documents, articles, books and links on slavery and trafficking of women and girls. http://eir.library.utoronto.ca/whrr/display_annotation.cfm?ID=24&sister=utl

219

Starvation & Deprivation

Disaster Relief The Disaster Relief website aims to help disaster victims and the disaster relief community worldwide by facilitating the exchange of information on the Internet. Site includes details of natural and manmade disasters, as well as ways in which to assist. http://www.disasterrelief.org/
Disaster Relief Agencies From Disaster Center, this excellent site includes a lengthy list of links to disaster relief agencies. http://www.disastercenter.com/agency.htm
Food & Agriculture Organization of the UN Vast site, includes much information on international food and agriculture- related issues, as well as disease, trade and other topics. http://www.fao.org/default.htm
HungerWeb, at Brown University, attempts to help prevent and eradicate hunger by facilitating the free exchange of ideas and information regarding the causes of, and solutions to, hunger. The HungerWeb has been organized along four categories, responding to four types of publics interested in hunger: research, field work, advocacy and planning & education & training. http://www.brown.edu/Departments/World_Hunger_Program/
ICROSS International Committee for the Relief of Starvation and Suffering – ICROSS is a small grassroots NGO active in Kenya and Tanzania. It was founded in 1981 and now has 18-years experience of effectively implementing a wide-range of community-based health care. The mission is to reduce disease, suffering and poverty among the most deprived communities through development projects run by the people themselves, using their language and their belief and value systems. Site includes research & project info, future programs, organizational chart, photogallery, and friends and links. http://www.kenyaweb.com/icross/
National Association for the Prevention of Starvation A U.S.-based Christian organization, "NAPS builds schools and shelter for the most disadvantaged in the United States and abroad. NAPS uses its college volunteers to motivate other students at small colleges both in the United States and abroad. NAPS has successfully undertaken many humanitarian endeavors both in the United States and foreign countries." Site includes info on missions, testimonies, news letters and donation info. http://www.napsoc.org/
Oxfam International The official website of this well-known organization includes the latest news on poverty and starvation issues, links to other sites and "get involved" info. http://www.oxfam.org/

PovertyNet
World Bank site displays resources and support to alleviate poverty. Topics include understanding and responding to poverty, poverty reduction strategies, social capital, poverty newsletter and a number of other areas.
http://www.worldbank.org/poverty/index.htm

U.S. AID Food for Peace Program
Headlines, emergency program references, non-emergency program references, and related links are represented on this site.
http://www.usaid.gov/hum_response/ffp/

World Food Program
Set-up in 1963, WFP is the United Nations frontline agency in the fight against global hunger. Included on the site are newsroom, appeals, policies, how to help, and contact info.
http://www.wfp.org/index2.html

World Hunger Program
Sponsored by Brown University, the program combines research, education, and recognition to address long-term problems of hunger. General information, research, hunger-related courses taught at Brown, hunger research & briefings are included online.
http://www.brown.edu/Departments/World_Hunger_Program/hungerweb/WHP/overvie
w.html

Terrorism

Centre for the Study of Terrorism & Political Violence –
University of St. Andrews
The centre is the only independent academic research institute in the United Kingdom dedicated to the study of terrorism and related forms of political violence. Its major aims are to: investigate the roots of political violence; develop a body of theory spanning its various and disparate elements; and recommend policy and organisational initiatives that the government and private sectors might adopt to better predict, detect, and respond to the threats and challenges of the post-cold war era; to create an academic forum for debate of these issues.
http://www.st-and.ac.uk/academic/intrel/research/cstpv/

FAS Intelligence Resource Program – Terrorism
Extensive site includes documents on and links to 9/11 and the aftermath, general terrorism info, Middle East terror, CBW, patterns of global terrorism and significant incidents of political violence against Americans.
http://www.fas.org/irp/threat/terror.htm

International Association for Counterterrorism & Security Professionals
"The International Association For Counterterrorism & Security Professionals was founded in 1992 to meet security challenges facing the world as it enters an era of

globalization into the 21st century. We believe that all elements of the world's societies must become better educated about the threats of terrorism as a first step toward developing innovative and effective countermeasures to combat these ongoing threats."
http://www.iacsp.com/

International Policy Institute for Counterterrorism
The International Policy Institute for Counter-Terrorism (ICT) was established in 1996 at the academic Interdisciplinary Center, Herzliya (IDC) in Israel. ICT is unique in that it focuses solely on the subject of counter-terrorism. All of its efforts and resources are dedicated to approaching the issue of terrorism globally - that is, as a strategic problem that faces not only Israel but other countries as well.
 http://www.ict.org.il/

Open Directory Project – Terrorist Organizations
Excellent site with links to information on over forty terrorist organizations.
http://dmoz.org/Society/Issues/Terrorism/Terrorist_Organizations/

Political Terrorism Database
This web database was created as a resource on political terrorism and violence. The database is divided up into geographic areas containing an index to each region's terrorist groups, as well as a detailed international terrorism incident database.
http://polisci.home.mindspring.com/ptd/

South Asia Terrorism Portal
"The South Asia Terrorism Portal is an indispensable resource for all individuals and institutions the world over that seek information, data, commentary, research, critical assessment and analysis on terrorism, low intensity warfare and sectarian strife in South Asia. The South Asia Terrorism Portal website is a project created and executed by the Institute for Conflict Management." Based in India.
http://www.icm-satp.com/

Terrorism Research Center
The Terrorism Research Center is dedicated to informing the public of the phenomena of terrorism and information warfare. This site features essays and thought pieces on current issues, as well as links to other terrorism documents, research and resources.
http://www.terrorism.com/index.shtml

U.S. Air Force Air War College Counter Proliferation Center – War on Terrorism
Site looks at current war on terrorism, includes maps, reflections, info on Bin Laden. Also contains a number of useful links, as well as info on response, state and local, agro-terrorism, technology, terrorism research, psychology of terrorism, making a terrorist, and other general terrorism information.
http://www.au.af.mil/au/awc/awcgate/cps-terr.htm

U.S. Dept. of State Counterterrorism Website
Contains up-to-date information on international terrorism and counterterrorism issues. Includes list of groups designated by the State Dept. as foreign terrorist organizations.
http://www.state.gov/s/ct/

Transnational Crime

Amnesty International The official website of the world's leading human rights organization. http://www.amnesty.org/
Cybercrime The U.S. Dept. of Justice site for computer crime, cyber crime and IPR violations. http://www.cybercrime.gov/
Drug Enforcement Administration The official DEA website is chock full of information regarding the illicit drug business. http://www.dea.gov
Drugwar Facts: International Fact & Trends Included in Common Sense for Drug Policy site – contains drug policies of various nations and the U.S. http://www.drugwarfacts.org/internat.htm
Federal Bureau of Investigation Official website. Pages include info about the Bureau, press room, library and reference materials, most wanted (the "top ten," as well as terrorists), and a kid section. http://www.fbi.gov
International Court of Justice Official website. Features news, docket, decisions, general information, basic documents, publications and searches. http://www.icj-cij.org/
International Money Laundering Information Network IMoLIN is an Internet-based network assisting governments, organizations and individuals in the fight against money laundering. Included in the site is a database on legislation and regulation throughout the world. Also included are current events, country pages, and links to other sites. https://www.imolin.org/
International Terrorism and Crime: Trends & Linkages A paper written by James Madison University Professor James Anderson. http://www.jmu.edu/orgs/wrni/it.htm
International Trends in Crime: East Meets West Proceedings from the Australian Institute of Criminology's 1990 conference. http://www.aic.gov.au/publications/proceedings/12/
Interpol The official site of Interpol. Includes wanted, terrorism, children & human trafficking, works for art, financial crime, corruption, forensics, vehicle crime, regional activities, IT crime, weapons/explosive, and criminal intelligence analysis pages. http://www.interpol.int/
National Crime Prevention Council The U.S. national focal point for crime prevention. Site provides information on education, neighborhood crime prevention strategies, and the "McGruff" campaign.

223

http://www.ncpc.org/
Transparency International Transparency International is a non-governmental organisation dedicated to increasing government accountability and curbing both international and national corruption. http://www.transparency.org/
U.S. Dept of State – Global Issues Site includes several articles on a variety of international crimes and the U.S. role in combating those crimes. http://usinfo.state.gov/journals/itgic/0801/ijge/ijge0801.htm
U.S. Dept. of Justice Bureau of Justice Statistics: International Justice Statistics – Primarily links to a variety of international statistics sites. http://www.ojp.usdoj.gov/bjs/ijs.htm
United Nations Crime & Justice Information Network Statistics & Research Sources – More links to crime statistics sites http://www.uncjin.org/Statistics/statistics.html
United Nations Interregional Crime and Justice Research Institute World Organised Crime Report – published biennially, providing qualitative and quantitative information on trends in organized crime activities and the structure of groups operating at the international level; types and distribution patterns of illicit markets; major initiatives taken internationally against organized crime by both governmental and non-governmental organizations, and developments in national legislation against organized crime. http://www.unicri.it/html/world_organised_crime_report.htm
United Nations Office for Drug Control and Crime Prevention Features news and publications, drug abuse and demand reduction, drug supply reduction, crime prevention and criminal justice, treaty and legal affairs, analysis and statistics pages. http://www.odccp.org/about.html

Annotated Bibliography on National Security Issues

A third of this volume is devoted to this annotated bibliography for two simple reasons: first, this book is intended to be a portal, encouraging further exploration; and second, the annotations allow the author to summarize these excellent works in a manner that cannot be done in the body of the book, while also making observations in the context of signal contributions from others, leaving the very substantive works of others in the forefront.

The absence of a number of popular books, for instance, those on terrorism, stems from their being less important than those listed here when considered from a strategic perspective—while also being beyond the author's reach in terms of time available to read. Please note that individual authors as well as title elements are included in the Index to this book. The greatest deficiency of this bibliography is its lack of coverage of foreign language materials—the absence of a national strategy for acquiring, translating, and promulgating essential perspectives in foreign languages is *the* greatest threat to our security—Washington is literally operating on 2% of the relevant information. I believe that citizens working together can master the vast domains of open information, can develop common sense policy, and can instruct their elected officials such that we begin acting as the Smart Nation that we are capable of becoming....if you read, think, and vote.

America in the Eyes of Others

Barber, Benjamin R, *Jihad vs. McWorld: How Globalism and Tribalism are Reshaping the World* (Ballantine, 1996)

The heart of this book, in my opinion, is on page 210 where the author carefully distinguishes between the Jihad's opposition to McWorld consumerism and development patterns, as opposed to democracy or other political notions.

All groups have their extremists and lunatics, and all groups have their bureaucracies and overly-rigid institutionalizations of past preferences. The one needs to be stamped out, and the other radically reformed--no matter what beliefs you aspire to.

Where I see the vitality and promise of this generation is in the possible energizing of the publics of many nations, including the nations of Islam, and public engagement of the core question of our time: what changes must we make in our corporate and consumerist behavior in order to, at once, establish both a sustainable model for the quality of life and choice we aspire to, while simultaneously establishing new forms of regional political and cultural accommodations that respect very strongly held beliefs?

There are two books that bracket this one in interesting ways. The first, readily identified from top-notch reviews such as appear in the Los Angeles Times, is Chalmers Johnson book, *BLOWBACK: The Costs and Consequences of American Empire*. The second, less readily perceived, is Howard Bloom's *GLOBAL BRAIN: The Evolution of Mass Mind from the Big Bang to the 21st Century*. Among the core ideas in Bloom's book are two: that we as a species, never mind our inter-tribal conflicts, are losing the survival war against ever-more powerful bacteria and the epidemics that carry them forward; and that language in combination with culture kills half our brain cells as our brains "conform" into the accepted social constructions of reality that our sponsoring society imposes on us.

In a nut-shell, then, we are engaged in three world wars right now: one between cultures that cannot talk to one another because the necessary portions of the brain have been literally killed in the course of intra-cultural development; one between the political and economic manifestation of our respective cultures, between a politics subservient to corporations on the one side and a politics terrified of the religious zealot individuals on the other side; and a third war, the most important, the war that has not really started yet, between individuals and corporations over campaign finance reform and the consequent outcomes that can be managed with respect to political economy and political education.

Chomsky, Noam, Ramsey Clark, and Edward W. Said, *Acts of Aggression: Policing Rogue States* (Seven Stories Press, 1999)

This small 65-page paperback is part of The Open Media Pamphlet Series. In three separate articles by internationally-recognized humanists, it makes three important points:

- first, that U.S. policies toward "rogue states" comprised largely of embargoes that result in infant mortality, local epidemics, starvation, infertility, and so on, are a direct violation of the Universal Declaration of Human Rights;

- second, that the U.S. appears to have been both an active practitioner of bio-chemical warfare resulting in the deaths and deformation of hundreds of thousands of South Vietnamese civilians (Agent Orange) as well as a passive practitioner in biological warfare qua disease promulgation through embargo and non-intervention; and

- third, that the U.S. has consistently refused to abide by international arbitration and other means for settling disputes, but instead generally utilized force as its preferred vehicle for getting its own way, regardless of international agreements to which it has been a signatory.

Too few write credibly in this vein, and this pamphlet is therefore a helpful off-set to the more conventional wisdom that comes from the military-industrial complex and the politicians this complex supports.

McNamara, Robert S. and James G. Blight, *Wilson's Ghost: Reducing the Risk of Conflict, Killing, and Catastrophe in the 21st Century* (Public Affairs, 2001).

Of all the books I have read or reviewed in the past two years, this is the only one that comes close to addressing the bitter truth about the fundamental disconnect between our perception of ourselves as "the beacon of truth", and the rest of the world's perception of us as "interventionist, exploitative, unilateralist, hegemonic, and hypocritical." Those that would seek to understand just how long our Dark Ages will last would do well to start with this book while also buying a copy of the map of *World Conflict and Human Rights Map 2000* available from the PIOOM Project at Leiden University. Beyond that,

227

selected portions of the Shultz et al book on *Security Studies for the 21st Century*, where detailed comments are made about both knowledge gaps among our policymakers and non-traditional threats, are recommended.

There is no question but that the Attack on America of 11 September 2001 has awakened and even frightened the American public. It has elicited conventional assurances from other nation states. What most Americans do not understand, what this book makes brilliantly clear, is that two thirds of the rest of the world is glad it happened. I quote from page 52: "...at least two-thirds of the world's people--Chinese, Russians, Indians, Arabs, Muslims, and Africans--see the United States as the single greatest threat to their societies. They do not regard America as a military threat but as a menace to their integrity, autonomy, prosperity and freedom of action."

Whether one agrees with their depiction of two-thirds or not (or whether they see the Attack as a well-deserved bloody nose or an atrocity beyond the pale), the fact is that the authors paint--together with the PIOOM map—a compelling picture of billions—not millions but billions—of impoverished dispossessed people suffering from failed states, crime, slavery, starvation, water shortages—and an abundance of media as well as propaganda showing the US fat and happy and living the consumer society dream on the backs of these billions.

The deep insights that I find throughout this book—a partnership between McNamara with the global reality and power game insights and James Blight with the scholarly underpinnings—are extraordinarily applicable to the challenges that we face in the aftermath of the 11 September 2001 Attack on America. In particular, their dissection of the United Nations-what works and what does not—and their recommendations for future initiatives that are multilateralist and focused on the prevention and amelioration of the root conditions that are spawning our terrorist challenges, are vital reading for policymakers, diplomats, warriors, and financial magnates. We should read this book before we through money at the problem in counterproductive ways.

Biology, Evolution & World Brain

Bloom, Howard, *Global Brain: The Evolution of Mass Mind from the Big Bang to the 21st Century* (John Wiley, 2000)

Very very few books actually need to be read word for word, beginning with the bibliography and ending with the footnotes. This is one of those books. While there are some giant leaps of faith and unexplained challenges to the author's central premises (e.g. after an entire chapter on why Athenian diversity was superior to Spartan selection, the catastrophic loss of Athens to Sparta in 404 BC receives one sentence), this is a deep book whose detail requires careful absorption.

I like this book and recommend it to everyone concerned with day to day thinking and information operations. I like it because it off-sets the current fascination with the world-wide web and electronic connectivity, and provides a historical and biologically based foundation for thinking about what Kevin Kelly and Stuart Brand set forth in the 1970's through the 1990's: the rise of neo-biological civilization and the concepts of co-evolution.

There are a number of vital observations that are relevant to how we organize ourselves and how we treat diversity. Among these:

1) The five major elements of global inter-species and inter-group network intelligence are the conformity enforcers; the diversity generators; the inner-judges; resource shifters; and inter-group tournaments. You have to read the book to appreciate the breadth and value of how these work within all species from bacteria to homo sapiens.

2) Bacteria have extraordinary strategies for rapid-fire external information collection and exchange, quick-paced inventiveness, and global data sharing. Species higher up on the evolutionary scale do not always retain these capabilities--they internalize capabilities while losing organic connectivity to others.

3) Imitative learning, while beneficial in general, can be extremely hazardous to inventiveness and adaptation. This ties in with his wonderful discussion of reality as a shared hallucination--fully one half of a person's brain cells are killed off by culturally-driven framing.

4) Non-conformists--diversity generators--are absolutely vital to the survival of any species because they are "option generators"--but too often those in power (e.g. a corporate presidency that thinks it knows all it needs to know) will shut out and even ruin the very non-conformists it most needs to adapt to external challenges it does not understand.

5) Labor theories of productivity that exclude calculation of the time and energy spent on information exchange are out-moded and counter-productive. In this the author is greatly reinforced by Paul Strassmann's many books on Knowledge Capital (TM) and information productivity--we have the wrong metrics for evaluating individual information productivity, something Alan Greenspan saw early, but we also have the wrong metrics for evaluating *group* information productivity,

something most have not figured out yet: it is called the "virtual intelligence community" or the "world brain", and that is the next information revolution.

6) World War III is here now, and it is an inter-species group tournament in which we are losing because we are not collecting and exchanging vital information fast enough. The rampant continent-wide diseases (not just AIDS but the square of AIDS, malaria-anemia, tuberculosis, and hepatitis, best described by Robert D. Kaplan's works as well as Laurie Garrett) and the antibiotic-resistant (and freezer resistant) strains of toxic disease and disease carriers will kill most of us much sooner than a gun in the hands of a fellow man....unless we figure out that early warning, global coverage, and rapid response non-military surge intervention is vital to our survival.

7) Language as well as culture are killers of thought. The author is compelling and fascinating as he discusses this in detail, comparing different language-cultural "toolkits" for concepts like the environment, alternative food sources, discipline options, and so on.

8) The author, who clearly has suffered some himself from being excluded or not taken seriously, is careful to discuss both the positive and the negative aspects of the "conformity police"--the conclusion I draw from his overall discussion is that we are seriously at risk, as humans in general but as Anglo-Saxons in particular, because the conformity police control all the resources (including National Science Foundation grants) and the iconoclasts are being shunned and starved.

9) The chapters on the kidnapping of the mass mind and how reality is a shared group hallucination draw ably on earlier works such as *The Social Construction of Reality*. The author excels at discussing how a very small number of people--25,000 in the case of Hitler's takeover of Germany--can combine cultural conformity traits with a little terror and corruption to dominate much larger groups of otherwise intelligent beings.

10) Internal processing matters more than external collection. I found this fascinating. Kevin Kelly and Stuart Brand and others have led the way in earlier decades, but the author does a great job of pointing out how an effective learning machine has far more internal connections than external windows, and that in a "hive mind" what you do with what you know individually--in terms of sharing with others--is vastly more important than how much you as a single individual might know.

I am not as upbeat as other reviewers about how this book suggests endless possibilities for a return to the perfect earth and inter-galactic migration. If anything, I am fairly concerned that the bacteria will win this war and that it will be another human species,

230

billions of years from today, that may finally get it right. While we know everything we need to know to radically alter the manner in which we collect, process, and share information, our political conformity police and our economic robber barons are intent on keeping us stupid as a people in this generation. Nothing stands between us and Howard Bloom's vision for bio-diverse salvation but our own inherent timidity, rigidity, and inertness--we are chained by old ideas and loath to explore new ones. We prefer death by habit to life by choice. This is very scary stuff--this is a *great* book.

Harman, Willis, *GlobalMindChange: The Promise of the 21st Century* (Berrett-Koehler, 1998)

This is a wonderful indictment of the Western scientific tradition, less comprehensive than Voltaire's Bastards but more readable and more focused as a result. The author shows a clear connection between existing global problems (ethnic violence, water scarcity, pollution, poverty, criminalization of society) and the earlier Western decisions to adopt scientific objectivity (with all of its inherent bias and ignorance) as well as the primacy of economic institutions such as have given rise to the consumerist society, regardless of the external diseconomies, the concentrations of ill-gotten wealth, and the cost to the earth resource commons. The author is especially strong on the need to restore spirituality, consciousness, and values to the decision-making and information-sharing architecture of the world--only in this way could community be achieved across national and ethnic and class lines, and only in this way could environmental sustainability and justice (economic, social, and cultural) be made possible. This is not a "tree hugger" book as much as it is a "master's class" for those who would be master's of the universe. It is a very fine portal into the growing body of people who wish to be cultural creatives, and easily one of the guideposts toward the next major paradigm shift, away from scientific materialism and toward a new communitas in which people really matter.

Wells, H. G., *World Brain* (Ayer, 1999)

First published in 1938, a modern edition is vastly improved by the addition of a critical introduction by Alan Mayne. Very much focused on how a world-brain might alter national policy-making, how Public Opinion or an "Open Conspiracy" might restore common sense and popular control to arenas previously reserved for an elite.

The information functionality of the World Brain easily anticipated the world wide web as it might evolve over the next 20-30 years: comprehensive, up to date, distributed, classification scheme, dynamic, indexes, summaries and surveys, freely available and easily accessible. We have a long way to go, but the framework is there.

The communication functions of the world brain would include a highly effective information retrieval system, selective dissemination of information, efficient communication facilities, effective presentation, popular education, public and individual awareness for all issues, and facilitate social networking between organizations, groups, and individuals.

The world brain is the "virtual intelligence community" qua noosphere. This is one of the fundamental references for anyone thinking about the future of politics, economics, or social systems.

Bureaucratic & Western Reasoning Pathologies

Gordon, Andrew, *The Rules of the Game: Jutland and British Naval Command* (Naval Institute Press, 2000)

I really like and recommend this book to anyone remotely connected to national security decision-making. There are four major points in this book that neither the publicity prose nor the earlier reviewers emphasize, and I focus on these because they are the heart of the book and the core of its value:

1) Peacetime breeds officers, systems, and doctrine that are unlikely to stand the empirical test of war. As the author notes, every incompetent in war has previously been promoted to his or her high rank in peacetime. Systems are adopted without serious battle testing or interoperability (and intelligence) supportability being assured, and doctrine takes a back seat to protocol and keeping up appearances.

2) Technologists are especially pernicious and dangerous to future warfighting capability when they are allowed to promulgate new technology under ideal peacetime conditions, and not forced to stand the test of battle-like degradation and the friction of real-world conditions.

3) Doctrine based on the lessons of history rather than the pomp of peacetime is the ultimate insurance policy.

4) Robust--even intrusive and pervasive--communications (signaling) in peacetime is almost certain to denigrate healthy doctrinal development, has multiple pernicious effects on the initiative and development of individual commanders, and can have

232

catastrophic consequences when it is severely degraded in wartime and the necessary doctrinal foundation and command initiative are lacking.

This is a very long book at 708 pages, and I would hasten to note that the book is worth purchasing even if only to read Chapter 25, pages 562-601, in which the author brilliantly sets forth 28 distinct "propositions". The balance of the book is extraordinary in its detail and a pleasure to scan over, but its primary role is to absolutely guarantee the credibility and industry of the author.

Each of the 28 propositions, one sentence in length with varying explanatory summaries, is compelling, relevant, and most critical to how we train both flag officers and field grade officers of all the services. Were the author so inclined, I would encourage him to develop the final chapter as a stand-alone primer for military leaders seeking to learn from history and avoid the dangerous juxtaposition of too much technology and too little thought. While the author draws his propositions from an excruciatingly detailed study of the Battle of Jutland and the British naval cultures in conflict before and after Jutland, this book is not, at root, about a specific battle, but rather about the constantly forgotten "first principles" of training, equipping, and organizing forces for combat. Hard to do in peacetime with the best of leaders, a tragedy in waiting with the more common peacetime pogues in charge. "Ratcatchers", the author's phrase for those who do well in war, are crushed by the peacetime protocols, and this is perhaps the greatest lesson of all: we must nurture our ratcatchers, even place them on independent duty to travel distant lands, but somehow, someway,

keep them in play against the day when we need them.

Kuhn, Thomas, *The Structure of Scientific Revolutions* (University of Chicago, 1996)

Two points are worthy of emphasis:

1) the paradigm shift is always forced and

2) until the paradigm shift occurs, always suddenly, the incumbents can comfortably explain everything with their existing paradigm.

There will be many from the current *laissez faire* academics without accountability environment who would be critical of this book, but the fact is that it's fundamentals are on target; as the sociology of knowledge has shown time and time again, "thinkers" are nepotistic, incestuous, and generally lazy, as well as mono-lingual and culturally-

233

constrained, and it takes a major shock-wave to push any given intellectual domain up to the next plateau.

Lessig, Lawrence, *the future of ideas: the fate of the commons in a connected world* (Random, 2001)

I struggled with this book, in part because I really dislike the manner in which the law has been complicated to the point of unreason—beyond the ken of normal people. Having concluded the book, however, I have to say this is really worth the effort. The author is laying bare the raw threats to the future of the electronic commons. He discusses in detail how very specific government policies to sell and control bandwidth, and very specific corporate legal claims being backed by ignorant lawyers within government, are essentially "fencing" the Internet commons and severely constraining both the rights of the people and the prospects for the future of ideas and innovation.

I am not a lawyer and I cannot speak to the points of law, but I am a voter and I can speak to that; what is happening to the Internet through legal machinations that are largely invisible to the people is a travesty, a crime, treason against the Nation, and grounds for a public uprising demanding the recall of any official that permits and perpetuates the theft of the commons by corporations and their lawyers.

In the aftermath of 9-11, when our secret national intelligence and counterintelligence capabilities failed us, there is a need for a restoration of the people's intelligence in the aggregate as our first line of defense against enemies both foreign and domestic. I regard this book as a very serious, thoughtful, and well-intentioned "public intelligence estimate" and warning, of the harm to our security and prosperity that will ensue from a legal system that is now "out of control" and not being audited by the common sense of the people.

I would go so far as to say (shudder), that along with Internet standards we now need a public advocacy group (our own lawyers), funded by the people, to fight these government and corporate lawyers at every turn.

Moynihan, Daniel Patrick, *Secrecy: The American Experience* (Yale, 1999)

Senator Moynihan applies his intellect and his strong academic and historical bent to examine the U.S. experience with secrecy, beginning with its early distrust of ethnic minorities. He applies his social science frames of reference to discuss secrecy as a form of regulation and secrecy as a form of ritual, both ultimately resulting in a

234

deepening of the inherent tendency of bureaucracy to create and keep secrets-secrecy as the cultural norm. His historical overview, current right up to 1998, is replete with documented examples of how secrecy may have facilitated selected national security decisions in the short-run, but in the long run these decisions were not only found to have been wrong for lack of accurate open information that was dismissed for being open, but also harmful to the democratic fabric, in that they tended to lead to conspiracy theories and other forms of public distancing from the federal government. He concludes: "The central fact is that we live today in an Information Age. Open sources give us the vast majority of what we need to know in order to make intelligent decisions. Decisions made by people at ease with disagreement and ambiguity and tentativeness. Decisions made by those who understand how to exploit the wealth and diversity of publicly available information, who no longer simply assume that clandestine collection-that is, 'stealing secrets'-equals greater intelligence. Analysis, far more than secrecy, is the key to security....Secrecy is for losers."

Postrel, Virginia, *The Future and Its Enemies: The Growing Conflict Over Creativity, Enterprise, and Progress* (Free Press, 1998)

This is a quick read, in part because it is a series of essays that are loosely connected. It is a reasoned attack on both government regulation and imposed technical standards. To the extent that it seems to deny the value of any standards, any oversight, any structure, it is unreasonable.

Indeed, while I whole-heartedly agreed that government regulation has gotten completely out of control, I am much more concerned about corporate corruption (Enron simply being the latest case), and so I would say this book is valuable and worth reading but it is missing the bridge chapter to "what next?"

However, I like the book and I recommend it. Its value was driven home to me by an unrelated anecdote, the tales from South Korea of my data recovery expert. Bottom line: they are so far ahead of the United States, with 92% wireless penetration in urban areas, and free-flowing video and television on every hand-held communications-computing device, in part because they have not screwed up the bandwidth allocations and reservations as badly as we have. I was especially inspired by the thought that we should no longer reserve entire swaths of bandwidth for the exclusive use of the military or other government functions--let them learn how to operate in the real world rather than their artificial construct of reserved preference.

The book is well footnoted but the index is marginal—largely an index of names rather than ideas.

Saul, John Ralston, *Voltaire's Bastards: the Dictatorship of Reason in the West* (Vintage, 1993)

There is much in this book, depending on one's particular interests, which can be skimmed or skipped. With patience, however, the book in its entirety is a rewarding experience for it calls into question much about how we organize ourselves politically, economically, and socially.

The bottom line, and very consistently with other great books such as *The Manufacture of Evil* on the low end and *Consilience* on the high end, is that Western thinking has been corrupted to the point that the West has become, as the inside flap says, "a vast, incomprehensible directionless machine, run by process-minded experts....whose cult of scientific management is bereft of both sense and morality."

As my own interests run toward public intelligence and public effectiveness in guiding the polity, I found his several chapters related to secrecy, immorality, and the "hijacking of capitalism" to be especially worthwhile.

He concludes that secrecy is pathological, undermining both public confidence and the public dialog. Intelligence in his view is about disseminated knowledge, not secrets.

Throughout the book the author discusses the contest between those who feel that the people cannot be trusted--the elites who strive to remain in power by making power appear an arcane skill with rites and formulas beyond the ken of the people--and those who feels that the people--and especially the larger consciousness of the people--are more in touch with nature and reality and the needs of the people than these elites.

This is a difficult book to absorb and enjoy, but I recommend because it sets the broad outlines for the real power struggle in the 21st Century--not between terrorism and capitalism, but rather between the government-corporate elites with their own agenda, and the larger body of people now possibly ready to turn every organization into an employee-owned and managed activity.

Strahan, Jerry E., *Andrew Jackson Higgins and the Boats that Won World War II* (Louisiana State University Press, 1994)

I wish every doctoral dissertation were this useful. Under the guidance of Stephen E. Ambrose, well known for his books on the citizen-soldiers of World War II, the author has produced a very readable and moving book about one brilliant caustic citizen's forgotten contributions to World War II.

Two aspects of this book jump out at the reader: the first is that Americans are capable of anything when motivated. Andrew Jackson Higgins and his employees, most trained overnight for jobs they never thought to have, was able to create an assembly line producing one ship a day. He was able to design, build and test gun boats and landing craft on an overnight basis. He is remembered by Marines, and especially General Victor Krulak, for having given America the one missing ingredient necessary for successful amphibious landings-in this way, he may well have changed the course of the war and the history of our Nation.

The second aspect that jumps out at the reader is that of bureaucratic pettiness to the point of selfishly undermining the war effort within the Department of the Navy and the Bureau of Boats. In careful and measured detail, the author lays out the history of competition between trained naval architects with closed minds, and the relatively under-trained Higgins team with new ideas, and shows how the bureaucracy often conspired to block and demean Higgins at the expense of the Marines and the sailors on the front line. There is less of that sort of thing these days, but it is still with us, as we contemplate the need for a 450-ship Navy that is fully capable for Operations Other Than War (OOTW).

This book should be included on the Commandant of the Marine Corps and the Chief of Naval Operations lists of recommended professional readings, and it should be studied by anyone contemplating the hidden dangers of bureaucratic interests that often override the public interest and undermine our national security.

Citizenship, the Polity, and Power of the People

Aleinikoff, T. Alexander and Douglas Klusmeyer (eds.), *Citizenship Today: Global Perspectives and Practices* (Carnegie Endowment for International Peace, 2001)

I have mixed feelings about this book. On the most positive side, it is the only, and therefore the best, treatment of the issues of citizenship that I could identify, and that is why I bought it. The range of authoritative essays that have been brought together is very worthy, and anyone contemplating this topic must take this work into account.

On the other hand, as I went through chapter after chapter, what I tended to see was an awful lot of academic whining about how the world is getting too complex and too multi-cultural to be able to pin someone down to just one citizenship, let them have many. Reality check needed here. Governments exist to preserve and protect very

237

specific moral, ideological, and cultural values, and governments are the means by which a Republic finances what are called external diseconomies--those things that are needed for the common good but not profitable for the private sector to do.

There are glimmers here and there of how one might better integrate new immigrants and otherwise promote good citizenship, but overall what this book is missing is a major commitment to thinking about how one draws the line between nationalized citizens truly loyal to their newly chosen nation-state, and those who choose to retain another primary citizenship and simply enjoy the bounty of the land they have chosen to VISIT....

Of all the contributions, the one that stood out for me was by Adrian Favell, on "Integration Policy and Integration Research in Europe: A Review and Critique." Despite the title, the heart of this chapter concerns the information "sources and methods" that underlie conclusions about citizenship and the policies on citizenship. There is a great deal of meat in this chapter, and it could useful guide the next book in what I hope will become a series.

I like this book. It forced me to think and it certainly opened my eyes to how we are letting a whole bunch of people debate the nature of citizenship without ever really being committed to the idea that an oath of loyalty is fundamental--as universal service should be fundamental, not to flesh out the military, but rather to provide a common foundation for knowing one another intimately, for respecting one another from that common ground. How one defines citizenship is fundamental to the future of every nation--this book both enlightens and frightens.

Carter, Barry C., *Infinite Wealth: A New World of Collaboration and Abundance in the Knowledge Era* (Butterworth Heineman, 1991)

First off, this book made the cut above another ten or so options on the fringes (the amazon reviews helped). It was a good choice. The author captures the essence of many other books as well as real-world experience with two fundamental points that every manager and every employee--including fast-food employees and others in "drone" jobs--needs to absorb:

- first, that the existing bureaucratization of the economy at every level is costing so much as to place those companies in jeopardy during the forthcoming economic shake-out, and

- second, that the sooner every individual begins the process of inventorying their personal capabilities and creating the networks for offering their personal services and knowledge via the Internet to all comers, the sooner they will be able to share in the profits associated with their direct individual contributions to the new economy.

The Department of Defense acquisition and contracting examples are especially shocking because they show, so credibly and in detail, how we have institutionalized multi-billion dollar waste.

This is a special book. It is by a practical man who has drawn very personal and transformative lessons from the school of hard knocks, and whose recounting of those lessons have value for anyone who expects to work for a living today and in the future. This is not a "get rich quick" book as much as it is a "get rich together or get left behind" book.

Dalai Lama, *Ethics for the New Millenium* (Riverhead, 1999)

Every single person, and especially those with the power to harm others through their corporate or government roles, should read this book.

The Dalai Lama begins by recognizing that religion is no longer providing an ethical compass for the majority of us, and ends by recommending a world parliament of religions (just as some believe a world parliament of cultures is also needed to represents nations without states).

At it's most fundamental, this easy to read and very practical book is about obeying the Golden Rule--or a variation of the physician's rule, "first do no harm."

This is not a book for mantra lovers. At its most strategic level, the book focuses on the fact that the problems facing nation-states and entire societies cannot be solved in the absence of ethical restraint. Technology and law enforcement can address deviants in the minority, but not a majority that chooses deviance as a routine lifestyle.

This is the first book I have encountered in my religious reading that actively respects all other religions as well as personal ethical systems apart from religion. In essence, the Dalai Lama calls for each person to restore their spiritual base, either by honoring their chosen religion, or by adopting a personal ethical philosophy that is consistent with the generic teachings of various religions.

At a very personal level, as I read this book I saw clearly how my competitive and confrontational instincts, honed over a half century by a "dog eat dog" culture, have in fact hurt me and hurt others. I was reminded by this book that a Nobel Prize has been

239

awarded to those showing that trust lowers the costs of business transactions--Fukiyama managed to get an entire book out of that one word. Reflecting on this book, and its measured discussion of how each of us simply seeks happiness and avoidance of suffering, caused me to reflect on how often each of us reduces the happiness of others and impose suffering through rudeness, harm by omission (not sharing useful information) and in other more aggressive ways.

On a global scale, and very consistent with other social science works on the complexity and inter-connectedness of the world, the book clearly addresses the urgent need for major world powers to understand that our existing life style and its damage to world resources is both unaffordable and suicidal. This book on ethics applies to Nations and to organizations, not just to individuals. It is a very elegant "dummy's guide to survival in the 21st Century."

Gladwell, Malcolm, *The Tipping Point: How Little Things Can Make a Big Difference* (Little, Brown & Company, 2000)

For those aspiring to revolutionary change in any aspect of life (e.g. the Cultural Creatives), this book is a subtle revolutionary manifesto--at a more mundane level it is a sales guide. I like this book because as we all deal with the information explosion, it provides some important clues regarding what messages will "get through", and what we need to do to increase the chances that our own important messages reach out to others.

This book is in some ways a modern version of Kuhn's *The Structure of Scientific Revolutions*. While more of a story than a thesis, there is a great deal here that tracks with some of the more advanced information theory dissertations, and the book could reasonably be subtitled "The Precipitants of Social Revolutions."

The most subtle message in this book is that substance is not vital--perception is. The contagiousness of the idea, the life-altering potential of the smallest ideas, and the fact that revolutionary change is always cataclysmic rather than evolutionary, will frustrate those who think that years of intellectual exploration will be rewarded with acceptance.
However, despite the revolutionary nature of the final "tipping point", there is actually a clear path taking up to 25 years, from the Innovators to the Early Adopters, to the Early Majority, to the Late Majority. My sense is that America today, with its 50 million Cultural Creatives, is about to cross over from the Early Adopters to the Early Majority stage, and will do so during the forthcoming Congressional elections when we see a rise in Independents and more attention to energy and other alternative sustainable lifestyle issues--hence, this book is relevant to anyone who either wants to promote a shift in America or elsewhere away from consumerism (or who wants to go on selling

240

consumerism), or who wants to seriously revisit what many would call the failed strategies of the early environmentalist, human rights, and corporate accountability advocates.

The book ends on an irresistibly upbeat note--change is possible, people can radically transform their beliefs for the common good in the face of the right kind of impetus. Each of us has a role to play, whether as a Connector, a Maven, a Salesman, or a Buyer, and our role will not be defined in rational terms, but rather in social terms. In many ways, this book is about the restoration of community and the importance of relationships, and it is assuredly relevant to anyone who thinks about "the common good."

Stein, Herbert, *Governing the $5 Trillion Economy* (Oxford, 1989)

This absolute gem from 1989 should be updated and republished. I have resurrected it in relation to my reading on federal budgeting and the dangers of the deficit spending now in vogue in Washington (2002).

This is the best book I have read on the strategic aspects of the federal budget--needed reforms, key issues in allocation policy, using the budget to stabilize the economy.

Where the book excels is in its analysis of how the federal budget should be used to steer private sector outlays—as Osborne and Gaebler suggested, we must steer rather than row—guide the private sector rather than use taxpayer dollars for direct products and services.

In his discussion of priorities, the author focuses heavily on the lack of investment in education and the resurrection of education both public and private. As we enter the 21st Century largely ignorant as a Nation (of external realities, not at individuals), I cannot help but think that the time has come for the public to take charge of "political economy," and begin actively setting forth its priorities. Just this week, in The *Washington Post* of 27 February 2002, David Ignatius suggests that Washington has turned its back on the Nation. It seems to me that's pretty dangerous, but if the Nation allows itself to be ignored by Washington, then we have the government—and the federal spending priorities—we deserve.

Halsted, Ted, and Michael Lind, *The Radical Center: The Future of American Politics* (Doubleday, 2001)

Those who have bought *The Cultural Creatives* by Paul Ray and Sherry Ruth Anderson, or *IMAGINE: What America Could be in the 21st Century*, will not only be thrilled by this book, they will understand that the "citizen-centered" system of governance is finally achievable and imminent--we should all try to buy, read, discuss and relate this book to the Congressional elections in 2002 and the Presidential election in 2004.

This book is *loaded* with common sense. It is absolutely not a political spin manual, a manifesto for revolution, or a ponderous think tank "blue sky" prescription for curing all the ills of the world. This book has three simple focal points and they are powerful:

1) More Americans identify themselves as Independents than as either Republicans or Democrats, and the way is open for a new "radical centrist" choice of leadership;

2) The original social contract that placed highly educated experts in charge of everything (government, corporations, even non-profits), taking care of the largely ignorant masses, is *history*. The people are smart, the people are connected, and the people want *choices* rather than ideologically-contrived menus.

3) Young adults are the key to the future and will decide the next few major elections, but only (a huge caveat) if leaders of vision and charisma can come forth with truthful options grounded in reality--the authors are carefully critical of political "triangulation" that seeks to manufacture false representations of common interest, only to betray those the moment after election.

The bottom line in this book is that the artificial trade-offs imposed on the people by menu- and elite-driven party politics are no longer acceptable nor enforceable, and the opportunity now presents itself for the voting public to remake the government from the outside in.

They focus on the core segments and core values that make America great: the market with its liberty; the state with its equality of opportunity; and the community (including religions) with its solidarity and nurturing of civic virtues.

Among the core negatives they identify where citizens could and should be free to choose rather than accept imposed combinations, are:

242

1) Elections tied to rigid political parties that have veto rights over candidates, and selections that allow minority winners where more than two candidates split the majority vote.

2) Pension and health care programs tied to organizations rather than individuals-- trapping individuals and constraining innovation.

3) Educational systems tied to mass conformity rather than individual customization-- with gross inequalities across counties and states because property taxes fund education, rather than a national normalized program with equal investments for every child.

4) Tax systems tied to loopholes, patronage, and earnings, rather than to consumption and savings (tax breaks for savings).

5) Immigration policies tied to old needs for low-skilled labor instead of new needs for high-skilled labor and the protection of the nation from dilution, disease, and excess demands on our tax-payer funded safety nets.

There are many other gems in this well-written and self-effacing book. The authors come across as very sensible, very devoted to America and its values, and very much ahead of the curve.

They conclude that major renovations of our society usually result from a combination of three factors: an external shock to the system; the emergence of new political alliances, and the availability of compelling new ideas for social reform.

They specifically note that an obstacle to innovation is the lack of a well-formed political worldview among both the new generation of young voters, and the new elites (most of whom have eschewed politics).

While they say that realignments are not excepted in the next presidential or congressional cycle, but rather over the next ten to twenty five years, I believe they underestimate the power of the Internet and self-organizing groups such as represented by the Cultural Creatives.

I hope the authors consider launching a *Journal of Citizen Governance* and a web-site where citizens' can self-organize, because unlike the cultural creatives and the imaginative individuals who focus in niche areas, these two authors have finally "cracked the code" in a common sense manner that anyone can understand and anyone can act upon.

This is a unique and seminal work that could influence the future of national, state, and local politics, and hence the future of the Nation. This is *very* well done.

Howe, Neil and William Strauss, *Millennials Rising: The Next Great Generation* (Vintage Books, 2000)

I was very impressed by the author's earlier book, *Generations*, and when this one came along I grabbed it, for I have three children in the 1982-1998 birth date range that demarcates the Millennial Generation.

As we come away from the 11 September attack on America, the horrors of genocide from Kosovo to Burundi to East Timor, the stock market crash and the threat of recession, this book is nothing if not uplifting.

I strongly recommend this book for anyone who has children, deals with children or young employees, or who likes to speculate on where the future will take us.

According to the authors, and their earlier book provides a very fine and well-research foundation for their prognostications, the Millennial Generation is the next "great generation" and it will be fully capable of rising to the many challenges that face us all. Especially encouraging is their view that much of the malaise felt by our teenagers in the post Cold-War years is being rapidly eliminated--our young people appear, at least in the most developed portions of the world, to be moving decisively toward a kinder and gentler demeanor, including a restoration of family values.

The structure of the book is useful (see the table of contents) but there is one very serious deficiency for a book of this caliber: there is no index. When I went to see all the references to "culture wars", the one somber note in this otherwise very positive assessment of the future, the lack of an index prevented me from using the book as a reference work.

This gives rise to my one concern about this generation (I have three children in the Millennials), and that is their lack of international studies and comparative religion training. It is my impression that even the best of our schools are failing to teach foreign affairs and global conditions, and failing to show how what happens beyond our water's edge has a direct bearing on our future peace and prosperity--the author's would have done well to spend more time on the differences between our US-born millennials and foreign millennials (whom they characterize as several years behind but on the same track), and to address the gaps in our education of this otherwise stellar generation.

244

Every parent and teacher, and every politician who wants to be elected in the next 20 years, needs to read this book. If Hollywood and other purveyors of products to the 10-25 year old marketplace were to read this book, we might get to a kinder and gentler broadcast, print media, literature, and family entertainment culture even more quickly than the book predicts.

Lewis, Michael, *LOSERS: The Road to Everyplace but the White House* (Vintage, 1999)

The older version, *Trail Fever*, is available at stores that sell everything for a dollar or less, this book is a hard-copy bargain. Even for those who have read other campaign trail books, this book offers a combination of unvarnished sad truths (Presidential candidates speaking to empty rooms, waving to empty runways, all to create the "virtual reality" of having something to say and someone to listen to it) together with a sense of lost opportunities.

As campaign reform looms on the horizon, I found this book especially appealing for its detailed look at "the people's candidate," Morry Taylor, the "Grizz"--a person I never heard of during the actual campaign. The book really drives home how flawed our existing electoral system is today, as well as all the campaign contributions, "rented strangers," and other anomalies that make good Presidents an accident rather than a choice.

I read the book shortly after reading Ted Halstead and Michael Lind, *The Radical Center*, on citizen-centered politics of choice, and there could be no better book for appreciating just how radical Halstead and Michael are, than this book.

Ray, Paul H. and Sherry Ruth Anderson, *The Cultural Creatives: How 50 Million People Are Changing the World* (Harmony, 2000)

This book should be read together with *IMAGINE*, edited by Marianne Williamson. Taken together, the two books are inspirational while still being practical.

Cultural Creatives as a book, and some of the other reviews, tend to over-sell the success of the emergence of an alternative lifestyle to Traditionalists (stereotyped as somewhat red neckish and religious rightists) and Moderns (stereotyped as ravish the earth anything-goes corporate carpetbaggers). The reality is that there are as many "cultural creatives" as there are people with disabilities in the United States--50 million. Not one quarter of the population, as one reviewer claims.

245

Having said that, by way of somber stage-setting, I cannot say enough good things about this book. It should be required reading for every citizen, every student, and every public official. In a very real sense, this book strikes me as a truly seminal work that could help millions of individuals reframe their personal connection to one another, to their Republic, and to the earth.

This is neither a tree-hugger book nor a mantras R us book. This book provides a thoughtful review of how different movements--first the environmental movement, then the human rights movement, and finally the consciousness movement--have come together to define an alternative lifestyle and alternative paradigm for political and economic and social relationships in the larger context of a sustainable "whole" earth.

I found this book motivational and meaningful at both a personal level and a larger national level.

At the personal level, its detailed and well-organized description of fifteen very distinct aspects of a "cultural creative" lifestyle helped me understand--as it has helped many others--that there is actually a category of people who have come to grips with and found solutions that enrich their lives--and this explains my great disappointment that the book does not offer a "resources" section at the end. I would have been very glad to discover, for example, a "Cultural Creative" journal or magazine that combined a strong book review section, art and culture, a consumer reports section tailored to the higher standards of the "CCs", new innovations in home restoration and remodeling, vacation options known to be attractive to CCs, etcetera.

At the higher political level, I found the book constructive and just this side of a tipping point. An increasing number of people, all of them generally outside of Washington and not associated with Wall Street, clearly have some strong positive values and a real commitment to achieving reform through "many small actions".

What this group has lacked is a means of communicating and orchestrating itself on a scale sufficient to demand respect from politicians and corporation. The Internet now provides such a vehicle--and as the Internet explodes from 3.5M people worldwide to 3.5B people worldwide, in the next ten years, I am convinced that Cultural Creatives may finally come into their own as a new form of global political party. Cultural Creatives would sign the Kyoto Treaty (and know what it is); Cultural Creatives would demand a 100% increase--from a half-penny a dollar to a full penny a dollar--in America's foreign diplomatic and humanitarian assistance budget--and Cultural Creatives could conceivably give the Republican Party a real beating in the next Congressional elections if President Bush persists in breaking his campaign vow on reducing carbon emissions. A peaceful revolution in our national agenda may truly be a near-term reality.

This is not a book where a summary can do it justice. It needs to be experienced at an individual level and ideally also at a community level, where it could be understood and accepted as a common point of reference for individual choosing to live "in relation" to one another and to the world, at a level much higher and more satisfying than our current arrangements. When this book makes it to the best-seller list, America will have matured and there will be hope for our children's future quality of life.

Williamson, Marianne (ed.), *IMAGINE: What America Could Be in the 21st Century* (Rodale, 2000)

I almost did not buy this book, and I say that because an awful lot of really smart folks might be inclined to turn away on the basis of the title and the possibility that this is a fairy tale wishful-thinking la la land kind of book. It is not. It is practical (and political), it is enriching, and it is over-all a very high quality endeavor that has been well executed.

Four "great truths" are articulated many times over across the various readings, and they merit listing here:

1) Campaign finance reform is the absolute non-negotiable first step that must precede every other reform. Until the people can reassert their great common sense for the common good, and restore the true democratic tradition, nothing else will happen.

2) Neighborhoods are the bedrock of both democracy and sustainable development, and we have spent fifty years building in the wrong direction. New legal and economic incentives must be found to redirect both urban and suburban real estate management back in the direction of self-contained neighborhoods.

3) Local production of everything, from electricity to food to major goods like automobiles) appears to be a pre-requisite for deconflicting high quality of life needs from limited resource availability. The book includes several very intelligent discussions of how this might come about.

4) Networking makes everything else possible, and by this the book means electronic networking. I was especially fascinated by some of the examples of near-real-time sharing that electronic networking makes possible--everything from a neighborhood car to scheduled hand-me-downs of winter coats from one family to another. We have not progressed one mile down the road of what the Internet

247

makes possible at a personal and neighborhood level, and I would recommend this book for that perspective alone.

The creative editorial role must be applauded. From the identification and recruitment of the contributors, to the selection of the photographs that each tell their own story, to the quality of the paper used to create the book, all testify to the competence and knowledge of the editor.

Lastly, it merits comment that the book serves as a very fine calling card from something called The Global Renaissance Alliance.

Wishard, William Van Dusen, *Between Two Ages: The 21st Century and Meaning* (Xlibris, 2000)

I've been in and out of this book over the past couple of months and I would sum up my reactions in three ways: 1) I will never be able to sum this book up or feel I have gotten all I could out of it--it would be on my list of books to take to a desert island and read over and over again; 2) it is, together with Will and Ariel Durant's *The Lessons of History*, a remarkable short-hand survey of the past two centuries; and 3) at the end it cuts to the chase and agrees with Zbigniew Brzezinski—the big global challenge today is about moral, ethical, cross-cultural, philosophical *grounding*.

I don't see the author's vision happening in any sort of structured officially-sanctioned way. And I don't see this book impacting on people the way *IMAGINE* or *Cultural Creatives* can impact—but if you have the time and the intellectual curiosity to go deep, this is a very engaging book that will take a long time to fully appreciate.

Conflict in Every Clime and Place

Arquilla, John and David F. Ronfeldt, *Networks and Netwars: The Future of Terror, Crime, and Militancy* **(RAND, 2001)**

Although their references lean toward "the usual suspects" among the beltway bubbas, and none of the authors demonstrate real access to the various hacker groups that I have gotten to know over the past decade, this is without question one of the best sets of articles, put together by two people I view as being the most capable in this area of inquiry, and therefore I recommend it very strongly as a starting point.

As with most publications by RAND it lacks an index, for which I deduct one star. The value of an index does not appear to be appreciated by those who publish these taxpayer-funded collections, and I continually lament the myopia that prevents the publishers from making such a useful collection even more valuable by taking the time to create an aggregate index.

I hope this is the last of the theoretical volumes. While it has some operationally-oriented contributions, one of the best being by Phil Williams on Transnational Criminal Networks, it is too theoretical overall, and much too US-centric. There are French, Nordic, and Singaporean, and Australian authorities, to mention just a few, that the editors must now make an effort to bring into a larger dialog. At the same time, it is now vital that we get on with much deeper study and discussion of the actual networks and specific practices--we must do much more in documenting the "order of battle" for netwar. One article, for example, lists a sample of Arabic web sites but goes no further--I would have liked to see some discussion of the 396 terrorist, insurgent, and opposition web sites, including the "Muslim Hackers" who asked for a clerical ruling on whether the Koran encouraged hacking as a means of war (it does, according to the same people that support bin Laden's views), and I would like to see much more integration with the investigative efforts of both law enforcement authorities and private sector security and fraud authorities. I am especially disappointed that all of these authorities appear to be largely oblivious to or at least not making substantive reference to the ten-year-long track record compiled by Winn Schwartau and his InfoWarCon speakers and web site, an event that is arguably the only serious international venue for addressing these issues in a serious manner, with a commensurately valuable web site.

There is one other major gap in this book's approach to networks and netwars. With the exception of Paul de Armond's article on netwar against the World Trade Organization, there are no references to intelligence failures and intelligence requirements *vis a vis* this threat domain. I am reminded of Congressional testimony by General Alfred Grey, then Commandant of the Marine Corps. Explaining why his was the only service to have one general in charge of both communications and computers on the one hand, and intelligence on the other, he stated with force: "Communications and computing without intelligence is just noise; and intelligence without communications and computing is irrelevant." The editors and authors need to establish intelligence concepts and doctrine for this threat.

This book represents the very best that DoD money can fund in isolation, and therein lies the problem. What few taxpayer funds are spent by DoD in addressing such important matters and not being spent wisely because there is no serious commitment to creating a data warehouse of all studies related to networks and netwar; there is no commitment to accessing and understanding the considerable lessons learned outside the somewhat nepotistic DoD network of standard experts; and there seems to be no commitment to creating a center of excellence that can nurture *public* understanding and new *public* standards for protecting both our critical infrastructure and the vital data that circulates on that infrastructure.

The editors and the authors are of the very highest caliber. They are also operating in a vacuum. I for one would like to see them get serious funding, to include the establishment of a public international center of excellence on netwar, with branch offices in London and Singapore.

We are losing the Third World War, between governments and gangs, in part because the military-industrial-congressional complex continues to define security in terms of very expensive mobility and weapons systems--communications, computing, and intelligence are an afterthought, and the authors are quite correct in the aggregate when they suggest that we are our own worst enemy in failing to redirect substantial funds toward cyber-war and cyber-peace. The editors and authors could be very helpful if they address in their next volume, both an intelligence order of battle against which capabilities might be created; and specific proposals for establishing international, national, and state & local capabilities. What should they be, what will it cost, who should manage them? "It ain't real until it's the budget." The authors are gracious to a fault, but it is clear from their work in the aggregate that they share a concern with our lack of preparedness for a 9-11 level of effort against our financial, transportation, power, and communications networks. They merit the greatest of respect and a full hearing from the public.

250

Chomsky, Noam, *9-11* (Seven Stories, 2001)

Chomsky is somewhat predictable and irritating in his repetitive condemnation of all past and present U.S. interventions around the world, and he harps heavily on the U.S. being the only country in the world actually condemned for terrorism (against Nicaragua) by the World Court but one has to give him credit--his is one of the few credible voices seeking to enlighten the American people with respect to two major global realities: first, that America is violating others with impunity and regularity; and second, that we have no idea just how hated we are for these actions.

There were a couple of tid-bits in this book that made me especially glad to have obtained it for reading and retention. His evaluation of the Sudan situation, and his detailed review of the impact on Sudanese reliant on the low-cost medicines from the factory bombed into oblivion on the now-disputed suggestion of the CIA, provides a perspective that needs more respect.

His lengthy discussion of the contradictory record of the United States on human rights--in favor when it does not interfere with business, actively obstructionist when it takes place in Saudi Arabia or Indonesia where financial equities (generally mining and energy company equities) are great, is disturbingly sensible.

I will always read Chomsky, for he provides a leavening of forthright candor and intellectual honesty that is too often absent from mainstream discussions. Indeed, as I was reading the bit on Sudan, it occurred to me that we are long over-due for the next revolution in learned discourse--the digitization of all such books so that a reader can, to take Sudan as an example, see on their screen a "map" of Sudanese issues, and then select from across a range of competing viewpoints on any issue. One has to seek out Chomsky now--in the future it may be salutary to find him automatically served up as a side dish whenever the pundits wax too pontifical.

Clark, Wesley K., *Waging Modern War: Bosnia, Kosovo, and the Future of Combat* (Public Affairs, 2001)

Every citizen should read this book so they can instruct their elected representatives and vote for military reform. As things now stand, we will lose the war on terrorism over time because of the perennial flaws in our system that this book identifies.

1) Don't Bother Us Now. The U.S. political system is not structured to pay attention to "early warning". Kosovo (as well as Croatia and Serbia beforehand and later Macedonia) were well known looming problems, but in the aftermath of the Gulf War, both Congress and the Administration in power at the time said to the U.S. Intelligence

Community, essentially: "don't bother us anymore with this, this is inconvenient warning, we'll get to it when it explodes." We allowed over a hundred thousand to be murdered in genocide, because our political system was "tired."

2) "Modern war" is an overwhelming combination of micro-management from across the varied nations belonging to the North Atlantic Treaty Organization; a reliance on very high-tech weapons with precision effect that are useless in the absence of precision intelligence (and the lawyers insist the intelligence be near-real-time, a virtual impossibility for years to come); and an obsession with avoiding casualties that hand-cuffs our friendly commanders and gives great encouragement to our enemies.

3) Services versus Commanders. The military services that under Title 10 are responsible for training, equipping, and organizing the forces--but not for fighting them, something the regional commanders-in-chief must do--have become--and I say this advisedly--the biggest impediment to the successful prosecution of operations. The detailed story of the Army staff resistance to the use of the Apache helicopters is the best case study I have ever seen of how senior staff generals with political access can prevent operational generals with field responsibilities from being fully effective. In combination with the insistence of the services that forces be held back for Korean and Persian Gulf threats that might not be realized, instead of supporting a real war that existed in Europe, simply stated, makes it clear that there is a "seam" between our force-creating generals and our force-fighting generals that has gotten *out of control*. The fog of war is thickest in Washington, and the greatest friction--the obstacles to success in war--are largely of our own making.

4) Lawyers, Fear, and Micro-Management. Just as we recently witnessed a lawyer overruling the general to avoid killing the commander of the Taliban, General Clark's war was dominated by lawyers, a fear of casualties, and micro-management, from Washington, of his use of every weapons system normally left to the discretion of the field commander. This has gotten completely out of hand. Within NATO it is compounded by multi-national forces whose commanders can refuse orders inconsistent with their own national view of things, but reading this book, one is left with the clear understanding that General Clark was fighting a three-front war at all times: with the real enemy, with the media, and with Washington--his NATO commanders were the least of his problems.

5) Technology Loses to Weather and Lacks Intelligence. Throughout the book there are statements that make it clear that the U.S. military is not yet an all-weather military, and has a very long way to go before it ever will be. Aligned with this incapacity is a high-technology culture that suffers from very weak maintenance and an almost complete lack of intelligence at the level of precision and with the timeliness that is needed for our very expensive weapons to be effective. Nothing has changed since

MajGen Bob Scales wrote his excellent *Firepower in Limited War*, pointing out that artillery still cannot be adequately supported by the intelligence capabilities we have now.

6) Strategic Mobility Shortfalls, Tactical Aviation Constraints. Although General Clark judges the air war to have been a success, and an essential factor in facilitating "coercive diplomacy", he also communicates two realities about U.S. military aviation: 1) we do not have the strategic aviation lift to get anywhere in less than 90-180 days, and his request for a 75 day mobilization was not possible as a result; and 2) our tactical aviation assets are so specialized, and require so much advance preparation in terms of munitions, route planning, and so on, that they cannot be readily redirected in less than a full day. A full day. This is simply outlandish.

7) We Don't Do Mountains. No statement in the book hurt me more than one by an Army general telling General Clark that his plans for the ground campaign could not be supported by the U.S. Army because "we don't do mountains" This, in combination with the loser's attitude (no casualties) and the general reluctance of the services to put their high-tech capabilities like the Apache at risk in a real war, sum up the decrepitude of the U.S. military leadership and the Revolution in Military Affairs-Andrew Gordon in *Rules of the Game* has it exactly right-the post Viet-Nam and post Cold War era has left us with a bunch of high-tech chickens in control of military resources, and we need to find ourselves some rat-catchers able to redirect our military toward a lust for man to man combat in every clime and place-and the low-tech sustainable tools to do the job.

8) General Clark's concluding words, on page 459: "In Kosovo my commanders and I found that we lacked the detailed prompt information to campaign effectively against the Serb ground forces. Most of the technologies we had been promoting since the Gulf War were still immature, unable to deal with the vagaries of weather, vegetation, and urban areas, or the limitations of bandwidth and airspace. The discrete service programs didn't always fit together technically. And (sic) the officers who operated the programs were not qualified to work across service lines and did not understand the full range of national capabilities. I worried about the nature of Joint skills even among senior officers." Are we ready? No.

Godson, Larry P., *Afghanistan's Endless War: State Failure, Regional Politics, and the Rise of the Taliban* (Washington, 2001)

This is a very impressive book, perhaps one of the best all-around books on Afghanistan, yet when I finished it I had the strongest feeling that it had been a rather antiseptic review. Eurudite, one of the best outlines I have ever seen for examining a truly chaotic situation, everything falling into place from chapter to chapter--yet at the end of it I simply did not have the guts of the matter in my hands.

I found the answer in other materials, including a special project to map all of the existing tribes, sub-tribes, and individual leaders where they could be identified. The project required monitoring of local radio stations in various languages, some of which did not have print media. At the end of it all what came across was massive--massive-- chaos in a medieval environment where everyone, without exception, regards every foreign power--and especially the superpowers--as an intruder, and every other Afghan as someone to be killed, exploited, or followed, depending on the situation.

This is a very fine book, but when one examines the list of organizations (14) and key individuals (16), what comes across is antiseptic simplicity. This is not a criticism of the author, the research (virtually every English-language reference of note), or the conclusions--all fit well within a very thoughtful approach to describing this failed state called Afghanistan. What jumps out at me is the fact that we do not have the access to the same story as told in Russian, Chinese, Dari, Farsi, Pashto, Urdu, Hindi, and we have done nothing to actually get below the state level--what I call "two levels down"-- to the sub-tribe level.

As the world gets more complex, as "wild cards" such as Omar bin Laden cause massive dislocations within major developed countries, not just in isolated failed states, it seems to me that we do not have the sources and tools in hand to get a truly comprehensive coherent view of any particular situation. I would go so far as to say that each book such as this can only be considered a calling card--an audition--and that a real understanding of the Afghan situation could only emerge from a multi-national effort that brings together such talented authors, across cultural and national lines, and gives them the kind of collection, processing, modeling, and operational intelligence support that are normally reserved for just a few great nations. In brief, what we understand about Afghanistan is now too important to be left to a single author or a single perspective--and certainly too important to be left to a single failed intelligence community that thinks only in English.

Heidenrich, John G., *How to Prevent Genocide: A Guide for Policymakers, Scholars, and the Concerned Citizen* (Praeger, 2001)

The author of this book not only completed graduate work with a direct focus on genocide, but spent over a year supporting the Office of War Crimes at the Department of State, each day creating an open source intelligence report on genocide-at the time he was engaged in this activity, there were eighteen (18) such active genocidal movements going on around the world.

This is a brilliant and compelling book that is also practical and essential for anyone who desires to understand the complete inadequacy of the diplomats, the policymakers, the media, and the intelligence communities. It is unnerving in its calm and reasoned detailing of how genocide can take place, its survey of the millions upon millions of post-WWII holocausts taking place today--as the media and policymakers ignore these realities.

Citizen-voters, in my view, will benefit considerably from this book because it will help them understand that there are three worlds out there, and we as a nation are not dealing well with two of the three--the most dangerous two. There is the world of well-fed diplomats and businessman, traveling and negotiating in their warm safe buffer zones. There is the real world as experienced by normal people, many of whom are oppressed and poor and feel helpless in the face of dictatorial regimes and local warlords who may do as they wish absent the rule of law. And then there is the world of genocide, an underworld of such horrific pervasive violence and inhuman brutality that one can only wonder if we are all guilty of mass insanity for turning our backs on this murder of millions.

The author is a world-class scholar and ardent champion for informing the public and achieving informed policy in this vital area, and I can only hope that serious people put some money behind his thinking.

Kaplan, Robert D., *The Coming Anarchy: Shattering the Dreams of the Post-Cold War* (Random House, 2000)

This is *not* a capstone work. It is a set of simple samples from the author's much deeper and more complex writing and reporting. If you have time for only one book by this author, this is the one.

He is strongest on historical continuity and ground truth reality. He is weakest on intelligence issues but asks the right question: how do we reduce risk around the world when traditional military forces are unsuited to the task?

Writing as he does for the prestigious and eclectic *The Atlantic Monthly*, where he is the primary (some would say the only) voice on foreign policy matters, one can only hope that he will focus in the coming year on the fundamentals of information sharing across national, cultural, and organizational boundaries--this book, and all the other books by this author, are highly recommended because they open a window on the real world that has not been opened by our very expensive government intelligence and diplomatic capabilities, and is not available from our inexpensive but all too mundane media. I

255

would go so far as to suggest that this kind of personal travel and reflection--that the author represents so ably--is precisely the kind of future alternative intelligence capability (in the open legal ethical sense) that we must have more of, and so the question we should all be asking when we finish this book by Robert D. Kaplan is: how do we clone this guy so we have 1000 more like him, and all their reporting is easily accessible to citizens?

Kaplan, Robert D., *Eastward to Tartary: Travels in the Balkans, the Middle East, and the Caucasus* (Random, 2000)

This will not be a long review. There is a similarity to Robert Kaplan's books, and my reviews of his other books will suffice for additional detail.

Having said that, I will also say that this book continues an excellent pattern of combining prior reading of history, a solid understanding of geography, and a gift for drawing out from an astonishing diversity of individuals, those little details that may bore in the aggregate but are priceless when endured and absorbed.

He seems to have missed the genocide against the Tatars, but perhaps that was hidden from him.

There is one huge gem, at least for me, in this book, and that is his assessment of the potential for a new schism between Western and Eastern Christianity, and how that must be avoided at all costs. This one sentence and the surrounding text is alone worth the price of the book.

Kaplan, Robert D., *The Ends of the Earth: A Journey to the Frontiers of Anarchy* (Random House, 1996)

If you ever wondered why the U.S. Intelligence Community tries so desperately to keep its annual budget secret from Congress and the citizens, this book might provide a clue: one man, very well-grounded in historical and contextual reading, is capable of reporting extremely valuable insights that neither a $30 billion a year spy world nor a $3 billion a year diplomatic community seem capable of either comprehending or communicating to the public.

Robert D. Kaplan gets three big things right: he studies history before visiting; he is firmly grounded in a geographical or geophysical appreciation of every situation; and he travels on foot and at the lowest common level. The world he sees and reports on is not the world that the pampered and sheltered diplomats, businessmen, and journalists see or understand.

Reading Kaplan is a treat for anyone who takes the rest of the world and America's naiveté with some seriousness. He is correct when he posits a new World War, "a protracted struggle between ourselves and the demons of crime, population pressure, environmental degradation, disease, and culture conflict."

He is at his best when mixing his historical reading with his personal intellect and observations, to arrive at conclusions that contradict conventional wisdom--for instance, his appreciation of Iran as a structured and stable society, and of Turkey as the next mega-power and the keeper of the Islamic flame. His extremely sharp observations about Saudi Arabia as the hidden enemy of the United States of America are very very provocative, especially when one realizes that we are providing them with an extremely generous military and economic program at U.S. taxpayer expense. Saudi funding of terrorism, including Bin Laden, is increasingly documented in the public domain, and U.S. taxpayers need to begin questioning U.S. policy in this specific area.

This personal travel narrative is invaluable as a means of contemplating the realities of nations that exist (e.g. the Kurds) alongside states that continue to persecute and deny these nations a right to live. Although another hundred pages follow, the real end of the book is on page 336 where he discusses a living map of the future world, one that is constantly changing and that reflects several realities--a reality of overlapping group identities such as those of language and economic class; a reality of legal boundaries and overlapping and sometimes conflicting cultural boundaries; a reality of power distributed and often shared openly between police, criminals, terrorists, white-collar thieves, and politicians; and a reality of population growth, disease, refugee migrations and genocide; as well as soil and water scarcity.

His bibliography is quite worthwhile, and helps make his personal reporting even more valuable. I have but one disappointment, and that is that this prolific author and policy commentator, a major force (indeed, the only continuous voice on foreign policy matters for *The Atlantic Monthly*), has failed to provide a concluding section that pulls it all together in an executive briefing suitable for policy consideration. There are many valuable lessons and observations in this book, I recommend it highly, but I fear that the policy-makers who most desperately need to be educated will never, ever actually read the book.

Klare, Michael T., *Resource Wars: The New Landscape of Global Conflict* (Metropolitan, 2001)

This is a very thoughtful and well-documented book that has been 20 years in the making—the author is on record as having discussed water wars in 1980, and should be credited with anticipating the relationship between natural resources, ethnic conflict, and great power discomfort well before the pack.

He covers oil in particular, energy, and in more general terms, water, minerals, and timber. His footnotes are quite satisfactory and strike a very fine balance--unusually good--between policy, military, and academic or industry sources. Sadly, I believe that this book, as with Laurie Garrett's book on the collapse of public health, will be ignored by the Administration, which appears to have decided that real war is only between states, that energy is something to be increased, not moderated in use, and that real men do not concern themselves with ethnic conflict, small wars, or the Third World.

As I reflect on this book, and its deep discussion of the details of existing and potential resources wars (it includes a very fine illustrative appendix of oil and natural gas conflicts, all current), I contemplate both my disappointment that the author and publisher did not choose to do more with geospatial visualization--a fold out map of the world with all the points plotted in color would have been an extraordinary value--and the immediate potential value of adding the knowledge represented by this book on resources and the Garrett book on public health threats—to the *World Conflict & Human Rights Map 2000* published by PIOOM at Leiden University in The Netherlands.

What I really like about this book is its relevance, its authority, its utility. What I find frustrating about this book is that it is, like all books, an isolated fragment of knowledge that cannot easily be integrated and visualized. How helpful it would be, if US voters could see a geographic depiction of the world showing all that the author of this excellent work is trying to communicate, and on the same geographic depiction, see the military dollars versus the economic assistance dollars that the U.S. is or is not investing. The results would be shocking and could lead to political action as the community level, for what is clear to me from this book is that there is a huge disconnect between the real threat, our national security policies, and how we actually spend our foreign affairs, defense, and trade dollars from the taxpayers' pockets.

A trillion dollar tax cut, or a trillion dollar investment in deterrence through investments in natural resource stabilization and extension? Which would be of more lasting value to the seventh generation of our children? The author does not comment--one is left to read between the lines.

Marshall, Monty, *Third World War: System, Process, and Conflict Dynamics* (Rowman & Littlefield, 1999)

This book is deeply important to our future, for it is the first over-all comprehensive look at the global reality of failed states, spreading non-state violence, and the emergence of complex emergencies where 90% of the casualties are civilian.

Drawing on a wide-variety of databases and field studies around the globe, the author focuses the societal groups and their migration toward protracted violence in the context of failed states. He puts forward a theory on the diffusion of insecurity, how this leads to arrested development, and why, for very practical reasons, the more developed nations must devise new means of structured and focused intervention leading to the creation of peace.

The author does not advocate intervention willy-nilly--if anything, he joins Jessica Matthews, William Shawcross, and others in pointing out that incompetent interventions actually make matters worse--external actors and external resources have a way of prolonging internal conflicts rather than resolving them. Military forces, the ones most often used, are also the least effective--new combinations and new capabilities are needed.

He is especially effective at criticizing, in a very gracious but pointed manner, the institutionalist and realist schools that have never moved beyond sovereign states, political boundaries, conventional militaries, and a Euro-centric perspective.

He is much better than Fukiyama at dealing with reality, and the equal of Huntington in considering cultural clashes rooted in social identities and real-world resource difficulties.

I found two major observations in this work that merit broad repetition:

First, and the author gives due credit to the path-finding work of Ted Gurr and the Minorities at Risk project, there is an established pattern, world-wide, in which violent political action is always preceded by a period of nonviolent activity that was either ignored or repressed.

Second, once violence has been inculcated into a social group as the normative condition, there is a distinct loss of capacity to engage in meaningful exchanges, negotiation, etcetera. Outcomes become irrelevant, and as Ralph Peters has pointed out so often, war and conflict become the raison d'être rather than any kind of rational means to a political end.

Throughout the book, and worthy of a focused chapter or future article, there are comments on data, information, and analysis that are extremely valuable when embraced and integrated. Apart from numerous observations on the difficulty of obtaining reliable data on sub-state violence when the state is the normal analytical unit and also the repressor of information; the author has insights into how models drive what data is visible, collected, or accepted; and how the social units in conflict themselves become filters, channels, or barriers to communication.

The concluding recommendations for systemic policy call for a global arms moratorium; a migration from regional collective security arrangements to global normative security arrangements including an international stand-alone range of capabilities for monitoring, facilitating, and imposing non-violent conflict resolution; a general proscription of force by any nation or social group; regional associations or what he called a "complex federalism"; a decentralization of systemic authority, which really means a reduction of U.S. impositions in favor of localized influences with greater legitimacy; and a criminalization of individual acts of violence within war--the ending of war (or state sovereign direction) as an excuse for individual acts of violence and depravity.

If I had one criticism of the book--and in no way does this undermine the brilliance and utility of the work itself--it is that it does not include, either as a preface or as an appendix, a summary of the actual "state of the world" such as the author has helped create in the World Conflict and Human Rights Map project out of Leiden University (PIOOM). A description and enumeration of the 29 complex emergencies, 67 countries with hundreds of thousands of refugees, 59 countries with plagues and epidemics, 27 countries with massive famine--as well as the torture, child soldiers, and other distinct manifestations of the sub-state instability the author studies so well--would have helped the non-academic and policy readers to better grasp the urgent vitality of this seminal work.

The author and his insights deserve the very highest levels of attention, for all that he has done here is call into question the out-dated political science concepts and the policies--including the defense acquisition and force structure policies--of every so-called modern nation. The globe is burning, every President and Prime Minister is fiddling, and the author documents very clearly that this fire is headed straight for our homeland.

Ngemi , Yaa-Lengi M., *Genocide in the Congo, Zaire: In the Name of Bill Clinton, and of the Paris Club, and of the Mining Conglomerates, So It Is* (iUniverse.com, 2000)

This book is a perfect complement to the more scholarly and policy-oriented book by John Heidenrich on *How to Prevent Genocide: A Guide for Policymakers, Scholars, and the Concerned Citizen* (reviewed in this section). I strongly recommend that both books be bought and read at the same time.

This book is a cry from the heart of a Congolese, it has explicit photographs, and you can get through it in half an hour--what you see and feel will be with you for the rest of your life.

It is a good thing when a book of this utility and importance can make its way from the lower depths of Africa and--with the help of amazon--into the mainstream world where anyone can learn of its availability. This is not a book that will be found in libraries or used in classrooms--it is a book that is at once so inexpensive and so horrifying, that any adult who in any way cares about the future of the international community, should buy it....at the same time that they get the Heidenrich book. Two men, world's apart, with one mind and the same broken heart.

Pelton, Robert Young, *The World's Most Dangerous Places* (Harper, 2000)

Robert Young Pelton is thoughtful and provocative. He has written an extraordinary book that ordinary people will take to be a sensationalist travel guide, while real experts scrutinize every page for the hard truths about the real world that neither the CIA nor the media report.

Unlike clandestine case officers and normal foreign service officers, all of them confined to capital cities and/or relying on third party reporting, Robert Young Pelton actually goes to the scene of the fighting, the scene of the butchery, the scene of the grand thefts, and unlike all these so-called authoritative sources, he actually has had eyeballs on the targets and boots in the mud.

I have learned two important lessons from this book, and from its author Robert Young Pelton:

First, trust no source that has not actually been there. He is not the first to point out that most journalists are "hotel warriors", but his veracity, courage, and insights provide compelling evidence of what journalism could be if it were done properly. Government sources are even worse--it was not until I heard him speak candidly about certain situations that I realized that most of our Embassy reporting--both secret and open--is largely worthless because it is third hand, not direct.

Second, I have learned from this book and the author that sometimes the most important reason for visiting a war zone is to learn about what is NOT happening. His accounts of Chechnya, and his personal first-hand testimony that the Russians were terrorizing their Muslims in the *absence* of any uprising or provocation, are very disturbing. His books offers other accounts of internal terrorism that are being officially ignored by the U.S. Government, and I am most impressed by the value of his work as an alternative source of "national intelligence" and "ground truth".

There are a number of very important works now available to the public on the major threats to any country's national security, and most of them are as unconventional as this one--Laurie Garrett on public health, Marq de Villiers on Water, Joe Thornton on chlorine-based industry and the environment--and some, like Robert D. Kaplan's books on his personal travels, are moving and inspiring reflections on reality as few in the Western world could understand it--but Robert Young Pelton is in my own mind the most structured, the most competent, the most truthful, and hence the most valuable reporter of fact on the world's most dangerous places.

What most readers may not realize until they read this book is that one does not have to travel to these places to be threatened by them--what is happening there today, and what the U.S. government does or does not do about developments in these places, today, will haunt this generation and many generations to follow. I strongly recommend this book to anyone who cares to contemplate the real world right now.

Petterson, Donald, *Inside Sudan: Political Islam, Conflict, and Catastrophe* (Westview, 1999)

When compared to the other book on Sudan that I read at the same time, *White Nile, Black Blood: War, Leadership, and Ethnicity from Khartoum to Kampala,* this book, while worth reviewing, is extremely disappointing. If this is the best our Department of State can do--if this bland account of endless repetitive meetings and meaningless demarches is the best that America can do in addressing the deep challenges of Sudan-- then we need a whole new State Department.

It struck me immediately, as I worked through the book, that it is the diary of someone who means well, but lacks historical and cultural contextual knowledge. Not only are there no references to learned studies, but the short-sighted thesis of the author is

262

summed up on page 136: "The cumulative combination of factors putting Sudan in such a bad light (with the U.S. Government) began with the military takeover in July 1989." When one contrasts this statement--this shallow perception--with the rich 200-year survey provided by *White Nile, Black Blood*, one can only feel a deep sadness for the isolation of our foreign service from the larger reality of the real world.

Early on in the book the author-ambassador confesses to not knowing Arabic and to having had six months training in Arabic before reporting. This demonstrates two things clearly: first, that the Department of State is incompetent in Arabic affairs if it does not have legions of qualified officers fluent in Arabic from whom it can select an Ambassador and second, that obviously the language is not considered critical to the job if six months will suffice--just enough to get to the toilet, not enough to accept directions across town.

This book is a travel diary. I have annotated page 148 with the note: "substitutes travel for thinking." There is no analysis in this book, no grasp of history, no real grip on the regional realities (other than a passing reference to the fact that water is going to be a cause of war in the future--something well covered in Marq de Villiers *WATER: The Fate of Our Most Precious Resource.* Neither de Villiers nor Michael Klare's *RESOURCE WARS: The New Landscape of Global Conflict* are cited by this book.)

At the very end there was a tiny glimmer of hope as the author began a chapter on working with the United Nations, and made it clear that the UN practice of allowing each of its agencies to appoint independent ambassadors to the same country, rather than subordinating all UN agencies to a single UN ambassador, was a big part of their problem. After three paragraphs, it became clear there was nothing else to be had from this chapter. I have the note "This is not a serious book."

At one point in the book the author observes that neither Congress nor the U.S. public would allow the Administration to be more pro-active in Sudan. It immediately occurred to me that if this is true, *ergo* Department of State has failed miserably, ignominiously, at informing the U.S. public of the true situation in Sudan, for any informed citizen would be sure to support extremely aggressive action against the (northern) Sudan despots and supporters of terrorism and genocide.

Shawcross, William, *Deliver Us From Evil: Peacekeepers, Warlords, and a World of Endless Conflict* (Simon & Schuster, 2000)

This book is serious, scholarly yet down to earth, compassionate, insightful, terribly relevant and most useful to any citizen, overseas practitioner, or policymaker. By the books own rendering, "good will without strength can make things worse." Most compellingly, the author demonstrates both the nuances and the complexities of "peace operations", and the fact that they require at least as much forethought, commitment, and sustainment as combat operations. Food scarcity and dangerous public health are the root symptoms, not the core issues.

The most dangerous element is not the competing sides, but the criminal gangs that emerge to "stoke the fires of nationalism and ethnicity in order to create an environment of fear and vulnerability" (and great profit). At the same time, humanitarianism has become a big part of the problem-we have not yet learned how to distinguish between those conflicts where intervention is warranted (e.g. massive genocide campaigns) and those where internal conflicts need to be settled internally. In feeding the competing parties, we are both prolonging the conflict, and giving rise to criminal organizations that learn to leverage both the on-going conflict and the incoming relief supplies. Perhaps more troubling, there appears to be a clear double-standard-whether deliberate or circumstantial-between attempts to bring order to the white western or Arab fringe countries and what appears to be callous indifference to black African and distant Asian turmoil that includes hundreds of thousands victim to genocide and tens of thousands victim to living amputation, mutilation, and rape.

When all is said and done, and these are my conclusions from reading this excellent work,

1) there is no international intelligence system in place suitable to providing both the global coverage and public education needed to mobilize and sustain multi-national peacekeeping coalitions;

2) the United Nations is not structured, funded, nor capable of carrying out disciplined effective peacekeeping operations, and the contributing nations are unreliable in how and when they will provide incremental assistance;

3) we still have a long way to go in devising new concepts, doctrines, and technologies and programs for effectively integrating and applying preventive diplomacy, transformed defense, transnational law enforcement, and public services (water, food, health and education) in a manner that furthers regionally-based peace and prosperity instead of feeding the fires of local unrest.

Schwartau, Winn, *CYBERSHOCK: Surviving Hackers, Phreakers, Identity Thieves, Internet Terrorists and Weapons of Mass Disruption* (Thunder's Mouth Press, 2000)

There will be those quick to trash this book as sensationalist, and they are partly right. What most people, including the critics, do not realize is that Winn Schwartau went out on a limb in the late 1980's and early 1990's and is *the* primary reason Congress got concerned enough about these issues to demand a Critical Infrastructure Protection program funded at over $1B--it was Winn, not others quick to claim the line, that testified to Congress about an "electronic Pearl Harbor" on 24 June 1991. This book is unabashedly populist and seeks to make this very complex threat entertaining and understandable, and for that reason alone it is worth the time to consider. There are many other serious books for engineers, this is the one for anyone at all from housewife to student to executive. Great airplane book, won't save the world, but will certainly increase your consciousness across the board.

Equally good are two earlier books by the same author, *Terminal Compromise* and *INFORMATION WARFARE: Chaos on the Electronic Superhighway*. The first is a novel of how terrorists might attack America using only electronic means, while the second is the original book on information warfare that finally got Washington to treat this topic seriously.

Schwartau, Winn, *Pearl Harbor Dot Com* (Interpact, 2002)

This book is a based on a *non-fiction* manuscript about U.S. vulnerabilities to electronic that was so hot that the author's lawyers insisted he turn it into a novel to avoid liability.

It is absolutely superb and written by one of the most authoritative persons around. Unlike most academic and industry security specialists, the author has from the very beginning understood, respected, and been in touch with the elite hackers who worked very hard in the 1980's to expose the outrageously vulnerable electronic systems used by our financial, transportation, power, and communications industries.

In my view, books like this as well as the non-fiction books such as *Information Warfare: Chaos on the Electronic Superhighway* have been vital elements in educating consumers, stockholders, and voters. If you want to know just how vulnerable your bank account is, read this book.

I won't reveal the surprise ending, but will say that it is absolutely a shocker, and totally credible.

Spaulding, Jay and Stephanie Beswick (eds.), *White Nile, Black Blood: War, Leadership, and Ethnicity from Khartoum to Kampala* (Red Sea, 1999)

I read this book at the same time that I read the quasi-official story on Sudan (Donald Petterson's *Inside Sudan: Political Islam, Conflict, and Catastrophe,* reviewed in this section) and I have to say, not only is this collection of edited articles--and the editorial summary--quite pleasing in its professional grasp of history, its depth, its coverage of the core issues in a comprehensive and actionable way--but it also causes me grave anguish when I compare it to what can only be described as a self-centered mediocre State Department memoir.

This is good solid stuff. It is especially helpful in setting aside the superficial views that ethnic conflict or European-drawn borders are the root of Sudan's internal conflict issues, and it cuts to chase: "it's about wealth, simpleton!".

The history of Sudan is well-drawn out, with the bottom line being that the southerners and their especially rich territory have been constantly besieged and ravished by the northern elite. The only time of peace in the 200-year-war has been when the British imposed that peace, and there is a suggestive air about that finding.

The varied discussions of genocide and "cultural cleansing", including the forced rape of the women in the groups being eradicated, and the use of famine to kill two million, are dismaying in the extreme.

"Ecology and economics provide controlling metaphors." This is an excellent summary of the book.

Also helpful is the book's coverage of the relations between Egypt and Sudan (both historical and current), the explicit (northern) Sudanese sponsorship of terrorism and hosting of many Islamic and other terrorist groups within its territory, and the general references to the varying influences of the Turks, the British, and the missionaries.

This is a serious book, by serious people, and it does the Sudan issues full justice. One puts the book down feeling somewhat aghast at the ignorance of the U.S. government, the incapacity of the United Nations, and the blatant malevolence of the northern Sudanese predators. This book is strongly recommended for any person who wonders about their government's competence and compassion. Sudan is a cancer, not just within Africa, but within the larger world, and the continued acceptance of the genocide and slavery and related plagues that characterize this place call into question the legitimacy, the ethics, the accountability, of all Western governments.

Corporate Corruption & Irresponsibility

Czech, Brian, *Shoveling Fuel for a Runaway Train: Errant Economists, Shameful Spenders, and a Plan to Stop Them All* (University of California, 2000)

There are some very harsh truths in this book, in which a very thoughtful Conservation Biologist takes on the very hard challenge of defining a political and economic model that is survivable.

From his early doctrine of "competitive exclusion" (one species can benefit only at the expense of others) to his methodical and progressive dismantling of economic growth as an unquestioned political goal, of the prevailing economic theories as being totally insane (efficiency does not prevent the depletion of natural capital from a limited earth), to his sensible and moral and provocative outlining of the ecological economics (or the economics of environmental survival), this is a book that teaches and this is a man I would trust to counsel a future President....

This book will appeal to anyone who considers himself or herself a Cultural Creative, and I hope it appeals to the "silent majority" that could yet make a difference in "political economy." Whether we save the Earth for future generations boils down to this: are the citizens of the various nations, the employees of the various corporations, prepared to think for themselves? Are they prepared to join the global grid of free thinkers and cyber-advocates that are finding that the Internet is the lever that will move the world and empower the people once again? The author argues, in a compelling, academically sound and morally encouraging way, that America above all nations finds itself in a new civil war, a war between the "liquidating class" and the "steady state" class.

Besides citizens, this book will provoke and enlighten venture fund managers, political action campaign managers, and leaders of any organization. Others have certainly been down this road, the Club of Rome being especially noteworthy as an early attempt to establish trade-off values, but I believe this gentle, capable professional (with the U.S. Fish and Wildlife Service, Division of Refuges) has written a timely book that is in its own way the "Silent Spring" of this generation. Perhaps more to the point, he makes it clear that all environmental issues, all economic issues, are inherently political, and we the voters have a choice in every election: between the candidate indebted to corporate carpetbaggers, and the candidate beholden to the people.

267

Eichenwald, Kurt, *The Informant: A True Story* (Broadway, 2000)

The level of detail in this book is extraordinary, as is the meticulous documentation of sources. Even the index is surprising in both its presence and its quality.

A few little gems jump out at me from all the detail:

1) Corporate corruption appears to not only be routine, but massive among more industries and companies than we might believe.

2) The government does actually try to regulate and prosecute, but this is both very expensive, and appears to result in the public *not* becoming conscious of the mis-deeds--no massive boycott, for example, seems to result.

3) The executives that conspire to cheat the public are remarkably ignorant. I was stunned to read how one of the principals in this story fell victim to what I thought was a really well-known Nigerian scam for defrauding numerous Americans of tens of thousands of dollars each, claiming that it will "release" millions in hijacked funds from the national bank.

4) The government often mistreats its own people. I was especially troubled, having seen employee abuse at other national agencies, when the book related how a senior FBI agent was not allowed to transfer--and save his mental health--because of his boss's selfish interests.

5) Lastly, I was left with the impression that there is an elaborate dance that goes on between the very expensive top law firms that protect corporate criminals, and the government. While the government seems to have worked hard on this one, the general impression that is left is that the normal drill when the public has been defrauded of hundreds of millions of dollars, is for the culprits to plead "no contest" and agree not to do it again--in return for token fines and guaranteed immunity.

At the end of the book I was left feeling dismayed at the depth and breadth of corporate corruption, at the general inadequacy of government in keeping the private sector economy honest, and at the lack of alternative public advocacy devices for truly focusing public spotlights such that fair pricing and fair practices are widely understood and enforced by customers, not just under-funded over-worked oversight bodies.

Although the book is very very long at 629 pages, I would have liked to see an author's epilogue titled "What Is To Be Done?" The author of this book can rightly claim to be among a select few intimately familiar with this problem in a manner no book by itself could communicate, and so a public policy analysis, some sort of prescription, would have been a valuable postscript to this excellent, really superior, investigative report.

Mitchell, Lawrence E., *Corporate Irresponsibility: America's Newest Export* (Yale, 2001)

I just realized this is the third book by a lawyer I have absorbed in this month's reading, and that is somehow a scary thought. If lawyers are starting to write popular reformist tracts against unfettered capitalism and the export of the flawed U.S. approach to capitalism, something very interesting must be happening in the dark recesses of our national mind.

This is not an easy book to read but on balance it is a very important book and one that would appear to be essential to any discussion of how we might reform the relationship between the federal government with its 1950's concepts and regulations, corporations with their secularist and short-term profit and liquidation notions, and the people who ultimately are both the foundation and the beneficiaries (or losers) within the political economy of the nation and the world.

The author lays out, from a business law perspective, all the legal and financial reasons why our corporate practices today sacrifice the long-term perspective and the creation of aggregate value, in favor of short-term profit-taking. He makes a number of suggestions for improvement.

Toward the end of the book, citing Lipsett but adding his own observations, he digs deep and summarizes our corporate culture as one that threatens traditional forms of community and morality (Lipsett), while increasingly dominating—undermining—foreign governments and cultures. Elsewhere in the book the stunning failure of our form of capitalism is selected countries is explored.

Although there are adequate notes, there is no bibliography and the index is extraordinarily mediocre—not containing, for example, the references in the book to oversight, political, or regulation. One star is deducted for this failure by the publisher to treat the book's content seriously.

Soros, George, *The Crisis of Global Capitalism: Open Society Endangered* (Public Affairs, 1998)

I think George Soros and Robert Kaplan, as well as others that are starting to realize that the opposite of virtue is not vice but rather virtue carried to an extreme (Jim Fox said it first, at least in this era), are on to something.

Although economists of great traditional standing (Robert Samuelson comes to mind) have been very quick to denigrate, even trash, the ideas of George Soros, my personal reaction, and my own reading of 225 or so books that I have reviewed for Amazon, suggests that he is right on target. Unfettered capitalism and corporate consumerism is killing us, and is part of the problem between Western secularism and Islamic fundamentalism--we don't have a model for sustainable faith-based prosperity they can buy into (I am mindful of Bernard Lewis's What Went Wrong thesis).

Most recently, in The Washington Post of 24 February 2002, George Soros is quoted as saying, "We can't be successful in fighting terrorism unless we fight that other axis of evil--poverty, disease and ignorance." Right on. Both The Future of Life and The Future of Ideas (see my reviews of those titles), and many other books now coming together in a critical mass, support basic propositions about the failure of politics, the erosion of moral contexts, and the dangers of capitalism upon public health, the environment, and the social fabric.

I would normally have rated this book with 4 stars for its lack of reference to others, but in light of the importance of the argument that George Soros makes, and the value of his own unique experiences bridging the worlds of poverty and wealth, American and Eastern European challenges and biases, I have to give this a 5--and wait to see our academic economists do better.

Environment & Public Health

Cook, Robin, *TOXIN* (Penguin, 1999)

If you're the type of person that does not have the time to read Laurie Garrett's *BETRAYAL OF TRUST: The Collapse of Global Public Health* (Hyperion, 2000), at 754 pages a real challenge, then this book, and the other books in the series, are a very worthwhile means of exploring real truths in an engrossing manner. The fact of the matter is that we are creating an increasingly dangerous environment for ourselves, with cross-contamination, increasingly resistant strains of difficult to diagnose diseases, and so on. The naive will lambaste the book for scare-mongering, and they will be wrong--if this book gets you through an airline flight, or an afternoon, and causes you to think just a tiny bit about the reality that we can no longer trust our government to protect the food supply and preparation process, and to think just a tiny bit about how you might protect your children from inadequate "due diligence" by the food service industry, then you will be richly rewarded. The author himself recommends the non-fiction book by Nicols Fox, *SPOILED: What is Happening to Our Food Supply and Why We Are Increasingly at Risk* (Basic Books, 1997 or Penguin, 1998). The bottom line is that this novel is for serious people, and chillingly worthwhile for those who like to learn while being entertained.

De Villiers, Marq, *WATER: The Fate of Our Most Precious Resource* (Houghton Mifflin, 2000)

I rank this book as being among the top ten I have read in the decade, for the combined reason that its topic concerns our survival, and its author has done a superior job of integrating both scholarly research (with full credit to those upon whose work he builds) and what must be a unique background of actually having traveled to the specific desolate areas that comprise the heart of this book—from the Aral Sea

> *"the exposed seabed, now over 28,000 square kilometers, became a stew of salt, pesticide residues, and toxic chemicals; the strong winds in the region pick up more than 40 million tons of these poisonous sediments each year, and the contaminated dust storms that follow have caused the incidence of respiratory illnesses and cancers to explode."*

to the heart of China

> *"According to China's own figures, between 1983 and 1990 the number of cities short of water tripled to three hundred, almost half the cities in the country; those whose problem was described as 'serious' rose from forty to one hundred."*

The author provides a thoughtful and well-structured look at every corner of the world, with special emphasis on the Middle East, the Tigris-Euphrates System, the Nile, the Americas, and China; and at the main human factors destroying our global water system:

- pollution,

271

- dams (that silt up and prevent nutrients from going downstream or flooding from rejuvenating the lower lands),

- irrigation (leading to salination such that hundreds of thousands of acres are now infertile and being taken out of production),

- over-engineering, and

- excessive water mining from aquifers, which are in serious danger of drying up in key areas in the US as well as overseas within the next twenty years.

The author provides a balanced and well-documented view overall. His final chapter on solutions explores conservation, technical, and political options.

Two statements leapt off the page:

- first, that it is the average person, unaware of the fragility of our water system, that is doing the most damage, not the corporations or mega-farms; and

- second, that for the price of one military ship or equipped unit ($100 million), one can desalinate 100 million cubic meters of water.

The bottom line is clear: we are close to a tipping point toward catastrophe but solution are still within our grasp, and they require, not world government, but a virtual world system that permits the integrated management of all aspects of water demand as well supply. This book should be required reading for every college student and every executive and every government employee at local, state, and federal levels; and every citizen.

Fagan, Brian M., *Floods, Famines, and Emperors: El Nino and the Fate of Civilizations* (HarperCollins, 2000)

This book is an excellent complement to David Key's book on *Catastrophe* (reviewed in this section), and I found it a worthwhile fast read.

It has one really big core idea that ties environmental, political, economic, and cultural readings together--it explores the inter-relationship between sustainability of any given society within the constraints of the time and the legitimacy of the government or other form of political organization.

Two things appear to help: long-term vision on the part of the leader, and whatever it takes to maintain the people's faith in their leadership.

The author concludes with an overview of where we stand today, and draws attention to the especially dangerous combination of overpopulation, global warming, and rapid climate changes occurring all at once.

For me, this book combined an overview of how seriously we must take ocean currents and related climate changes; and how important it is that our leaders understand these issues and take long-term views that add stability and sustainability in the face of varying challenges to our well-being.

Garrett, Laurie, *BETRAYAL OF TRUST: The Collapse of Global Public Health* (Hyperion, 2000)

It took me over a month to do justice to this book, and I have taken into account the thoughts of other reviewers. A book of this importance would indeed have benefited from an international advisory board of public health, medical, insurance, and policy experts; it would certainly have benefited from greater structure, firmer editing, and a foreword by someone like a former Surgeon General of the United States.

As it is, it appears to have overcome these deficiencies with hyped-up marketing and sweetheart reviews, and this in some ways counterproductive because this book could have, should have, become a mainstream topic in the Presidential campaign. It failed to do so for several reasons, not least of which is the propensity of both candidates and their advisors to avoid serious thinking, but also because the book is not helpful to a popular understanding of the very real global and domestic threats to the health of our children today and in future generations.

Having said all this, I commend the book for its content. It is worth the effort! There are some very important points that the book brings out, and I will itemize these in order of importance:

1) Public health is about detection and prevention, medicine is about remediation. In the long run, investments in public health are vastly cheaper and more effective than after-the-fact medical intervention;

2) The insurance industry in the developing world has failed to support public health investments, and in a remarkable collusion with the pharmaceutical, hospital and managed health care industries, has created a very expensive and increasingly

273

ineffective system focused on drugs (to which diseases are increasingly resistant) and hospitals;

3) Hospitals are no longer reliable in terms of protecting patients from both error and secondary infection from other patients. People are coming out of hospitals, in many cases, with more diseases than when they went in;

4) The health of our nation depends on the health of all other nations-not only does a collapse of public health in Africa lead to failed states and forced migrations, but it also is but an airline flight away from infecting Kansas;

5) Clean drinking water, uninfected food, and good environmental and occupational health conditions are at risk in many parts of the United States and Europe, not only in Russia and the rest of the world;

6) The United Nations, and the World Health Organization in particular, are in disarray and ineffective-in large part because of a lack of support from member nations-at dealing with the public health commons. There is no question but that the author has hit a "home run" in terms of describing the harsh reality of epidemics in India and Africa, the collapse of public health in Russia, the rapid migration of many diseases from Russia through Germany to the rest of Europe and the U.S., and the severe costs in the U.S. of a retreat from the collective good with respect to public health.

Unfortunately, it is a home run hit in isolation, not a game-winning home run, because it fails to drive home, to the only audience that matters-the U.S. voter-exactly what political and economic initiatives are required to achieve three simple objectives:

1) re-establish the public health infrastructure in the U.S.;

2) redirect the entire health care industry toward preventive measures-including water and food quality controls-instead of remedial prescriptions; and

3) provide compelling incentives to the rest of the world for cleaning their own house (this presumes that we are able to clean our own first, a very questionable assumption at this point in time).

This is a valuable book, a five in terms of content, a three in terms of execution, and I am glad that I took the time to read it. It provides a wonderful foundation for enjoying, at an intellectual and policy level, the medical and public health novels by Robin Cook.

Helvarg, David, *Blue Frontier: Saving America's Living Seas* (W. H. Freeman, 2001)

This is the worst of several environmental books I have reviewed, largely because its style is too chatty, the type and presentation formats chosen by the editor are terrible and make it difficult to read and enjoy, and there is isn't a single map or chart or table or figure in the entire book. This is a *super book* that got screwed up by the publisher and a lack of decent editorial guidance. It should be fixed in the second edition, and I hope it gets to a second edition. Given the author's clearly superior access to and understanding of the individual personalities and organizational players across America, I am really stunned and disappointed that there is not an appendix to the book listing all of these, with contact information and URLs.

There is so much solid, worthwhile information in this book, including valuable insights in why Western political interests are undermining proper representation of our national oceans, coasts, and Exclusive Economic Zone (EEZ) in Congress, that I would urge those interested in the oceans (hugely more important to our future than the Amazon or global forestry, just to make the point), to buy this book, suffer its limitations, and ultimately benefit from the wisdom and experience of the author, for whom my respect is unqualified and whole-hearted. In passing, it would probably be helpful if the first thing we all demanded was that EEZ stand for Exclusive Environmental Zone, rather than treating the oceans as a for-profit target area.

There is one other information-related observation I would make that emerged from reading this book: both the United Nations and the National Oceanic and Atmospheric Administration (NOAA) are clearly doing heroic and deeply important work vital to the future of the oceans--and they are doing a terrible job of communicating the basic information about the oceans and their work to the larger world of voters and concerned citizens. What really came home to me as I reflected on what to emphasize in this review is that there is a very wide, almost impenetrable, barrier between what the UN and NOAA know, and what is being communicated to the citizens who have the right to know (they paid for that information with their tax dollars) and the need to know and the desire to know. From this I would say that the next big step for those who would seek to save the oceans, is to demand that all UN and US Government information paid for by the taxpayer be put online henceforth, available at no further cost to the public. It is this information, the bullets and beans of the information war between corporate and citizen interests, that will decide the future of the oceans.

Keys, David, *Catastrophe: An Investigation into the Origins of Modern Civilization* (Ballantine, 2000)

The ending is meant to be a surprise, so care must be taken, but this book is really extremely worthwhile to anyone who wants to have their thinking stretched.

It starts with an examination of the Dark Ages (literally) and how the loss of sunlight and all the related catastrophes, from drought and famine followed by flooding and plagues and epidemics, impacted on each continent in turn--including the Islam and Turkish and Jewish dimensions.

This is humbling book, for its grasp of time and the movement of history--in stretches of hundreds of thousands of years--does tend to call into question any human anxiety over current events.

Yet, at the same time, and in keeping with other books reviewed in this series pertaining to the decline of the state (nation) and the environmental situation, the author takes great care to make this sweeping work relevant to today's concerns.

Without revealing the details, I will just say that the way in which this books links cause and effect and new cause and new effect, across many continents, over decades and then centuries and then tens of centuries, provides an excellent foundation for putting everything else in perspective.

Two aspects stand out: the degree to which natural causes of catastrophe lurk within the Earth and are predictable yet taken with enormous complacence because they seem so remote until they actually occur; and the degree to which an established well-organized state (nation) can dramatically reduce the effects of drought, famine, or other disasters if it has planned ahead.

When a recurring catastrophe is known to occur every 600,000 to 700,000 years, and the last occurrence was well into the middle of this period (i.e. we are at 650,000 years), one can ignore it, or ponder our readiness for an imminent recurrence.

Lomborg, Bjorg, *The Skeptical Environmentalist: Measuring the Real State of the World* (Cambridge, 2001)

I rate this book a 5 for effort, a 3 for half-truths, and a 4 over-all. It is a *tour de force* for Lomborg and his students (the latter appear to have done most of the tedious data gathering and basic analysis)---at its best, it provides a severe spanking for environmentalists who get careless with their data and their assertions. At its worst, it provides a semblance of cover for corporate carpet-baggers intent on liquidating what any child can understand is a closed system with limits.

At root, Lomborg is a disciple and blind follower of the paradigm best articulated by Julian Simon, who has himself been discredited here and there by well-educated environmentalists. Lomborg's professionalism and devotion to data are not questioned here--one either shares his paradigm or one does not. It merits comment that there are now several web sites, one of them in Denmark founded by his own colleagues, dedicated to exposing the flawed assumptions and analysis that went into this corporately attractive politically-biased treatise.

This is indeed a brilliant and powerful book, just as a nuclear explosion is brilliant and powerful—and very destructive. However well-intentioned—and I do not question, even applaud, the author's intentions, what we have here is a rather scary combination of fragmentary analysis in depth, combined with a strong belief system that accepts as a starting point the concept that the earth is infinitely renewable and no matter what happens, that is a "natural" turn of events.

I found Brian Czech's *Shoveling Fuel for a Runaway Train* (reviewed in section on Corporate Consumerism & Irresponsibility) much more persuasive and much more useful to the average citizen whose common sense is always under-estimated by the politicians and the corporate patricians who support them. Czech's effort, including a complete chapter refuting Julian Simon's assertions, actually provides a theoretical foundation for resolving the conflict between economic growth and environmental protection.

Just as 9-11 was necessary before a paradigm shift in national security concepts could be achieved (now we know that individuals without weapons can turn our own civilian instruments against us in really damaging ways), I fear that a major environmental--perhaps even a terrorist-environmental event, such as exploding train cars full of chlorine, will be required before citizens as a whole experience the paradigm shift and understand that a) we live in the closed system and b) the burden of proof must be precautionary rather than exploitative.

We are soiling our seed corn and the earth it grows in. Lomborg would have us believe that what we grow within such a paradigm is natural and good--no doubt he has an explanation for the dramatic drops in sperm counts around the world, the troubling increases in asthma across Canada and the East Coast and other nations reeling from antiquated coal-fueled power plants (most of them in the mid-West), and other documented demographic costs to uncontrolled liquidation of the earth.

277

I will end with one very significant concession to Lomborg and his adherents: this book, compelling in isolation, makes it clear that nothing less than the full application of the distributed intelligence of the citizenry on a 24/7 basis, will be sufficient to monitor, evaluate, and comprehend the breadth and depth of our attacks on the earth. It is now clear to me that until we have a global web-based community of citizen observers able to enter data at the neighborhood level, using peer-to-peer computing power to analyze distributed data, that the citizens will continue to be at the mercy of corporate computers and political manipulation.

I strongly recommend this book, and Czech's book, as companion volumes framing a much higher level of data and debate that is now beginning.

Novacek, Michael J. (contributing editor), *The Biodiversity Crisis: Losing What Counts* (New Press, 2001)

This is very much an edited work, with most of the entries being but two or three pages in length. All of the authors are world-class proven naturalists and related professionals, and the photography that accompanies each work is top of the line. Of all the bio-diversity books available, this one appears to be both the easiest to digest and the most pleasing to the eye.

Biodiversity is an option-generator. More diversity, more options for the future. See also Howard Bloom, *Global Brain*.

Hyperdisease happens more often than we might think, and is very relevant to concerns today about the collapse of public health. See also Laurie Garrett, *Betrayal of Trust*.

Biological elements are being inserted into commercial off the shelf products with unanticipated effects, some of which are damaging to humans. One noteworthy example: Corning added an ingredient to its tubes to make them less brittle, and scientists were finding their experiments infected and contaminated. Corning would not reveal what had changed, claiming it was a trade secret. Independent investigation finally determined that there was a synthetic chemical mimicking estrogen and having the effect of an estrogen injection on the cells exposed to the Corning tubes. Buyers beware--there would appear to be some disclosure standards required!

Mass catastrophes have occurred many times over history, eliminating up to 75% of all living things, with varied outcomes in the millions of years thereafter. See also David Keys, *Catastrophe*, on the most recent, the Dark Ages, circa 535 A.D.

Naturalists and natural science--the study of nature in its own environment, are endangered. Most universities are failing to support this vital area of study, with a result that our understanding of nature stems largely from lab work and computer models that are far removed from reality. See also John Paul Ralston, *Voltaire's Bastards*.

I highly recommend this book. It is both discouraging (so much yet to be done to stabilize the world) and encouraging (many good things being done by many small groups).

Raffensperger, Carolyn and Joel Tickner, *Protecting Public Health & The Environment: Implementing the Precautionary Principle* (Island Press, 1999)

This is the second best of several books on environmental policy I have reviewed, and it merits careful scrutiny in part because it brings together a number of expert authors and there is in essence "something for everyone" in this edited work. What is lacks, though, is a good summary chapter that lists how the "precautionary principle" should be applied across each of the top ten environmental areas of concern--something that could circulate more easily than the book, and perhaps have a beneficial policy impact at the local, state, and national levels--and I suggest this because the meat of the book is good, it needs an executive summary.

As I was reading through the book, I suddenly realized that many of its contributions could be better understood if one adopted the paradigm from *Seven Habits of Highly Effective People*[1] to see that what they are talking about is the *important* but seemingly non-urgent—when plotted on an XY matrix with gravity on the X and time lapse to irrecoverable disaster on the Y, both public health and the environment are way up and out, while senior issues, crime, and day to day politics are near the double zero—and everything else, including education, taxes, government debt and immigration, is in the loose middle.

The chapter that was most meaningful to me, the one that I think needs to be migrated into business education, international affairs education, science & technology policy education, is by Gordon K. Durnil, Chapter 16, and it deals with "How Much Information Do We Need Before Exercising Precaution." This is a brilliant piece of work that dissects our current environmental policy information collection, processing, and analysis system, and finds it very deceptive, disingenuous, and consequently seriously flawed.

---

[1] Stephen R. Covey, *Seven Habits of Highly Effective People* (Running Press, 2001).

For the best on the environment, read *Pandora's Poison*. For the best on public health, read *Betrayal of Trust*. For a very fine cross-over book that has good chapters from various good people, this is the book to buy and enjoy.

Thornton, Joe, *Pandora's Poison: Chlorine, Health, and a New Environmental Strategy* (MIT, 2000)

This is the best of the several environmentally-oriented books I have reviewed recently, and it offers a double value: not only does it lay out a persuasive social, economic, and political case for abandoning the Risk Paradigm of permissive pollution in favor of an Environmental Paradigm of zero pollution; but it also provides a very fine—really excellent—case for why the current government and industry approaches to information about the environment and threats to the environment are severely flawed. In a nutshell, the current approach divorces "good science" (code for permitting what you can't prove will kill the planet today) from social consciousness and good policy; and the current approach insists on studying risk one contaminant at a time, rather than as a whole.

This book is persuasive; I believe the author has the right stuff and should be consulted on major policy issues. I believe the underlying moral values and intellectual arguments that this book makes, about both science and social policy, should be adopted by the Cultural Creatives and the independent voters of America, and that the recommendations of this book are so serious as to warrant country by country translations and promulgation.

This book is exceptional in that is combines a readable policy essay for the non-technical citizen, with deeply documented technical appendices and notes that support a middle ground series of chapters relating scientific findings to long-term policy issues.

From many small actions come revolutionary change--this book is a necessary brick in the road to environmental reform. The bottom line is clear: every year more and more toxins are building up in our blood streams, and this is going to have an overwhelmingly negative impact on the humanity, capability, and survivability of our great grandchildren three generations down--we have not have grandchildren seven generations down if the insights from this book fail to reach the people, and through the people, the policy makers and legislators.

Wilson, Edward O., *The Future of Life* (Knoph, 2002)

Whereas the author's last really big book, *Consilience*, addressed the integral relationship between the knowledge offered by the humanities and that of the sciences (too often isolated and out of context), this book brings together political economy and nature.

It is more easily readable than his more heavily foot-noted and astonishingly deep earlier work, but all the more valuable for its smooth overview of why life on the rest of the planet matters to the American heartland; why we must deal with the limits of food production and control population (both in terms of numbers and in terms of consumption per capita).

The heart of the book, for me, can be found in three profound numbers—numbers that we must all appreciate:

Value of the Ecosystem/Cost to Replace: $33 trillion per year in increased Gross National Product (GNP)--and presumably everything would be artificially recreated.

One-Time Cost of Fund for Preserving Nature: $24-72 billion one-time funding. His numbers vary from $24 billion (one -time) to preserve 800,000 square kilometers already under protection, to $28 billion to preserve a (different?) representative sample. The bottom line: for a one-time $100 billion investment, 25% of what the US spends on its military *every* year, we could, at our own expense, save the world.

Subsidies for Unsound Acts Against Nature: $2 trillion per year and rising ($2000 per American alone--this refers to energy, water, deforestation, and agricultural subsidies that encourage and perpetuate unsound acts against nature as well as unneeded exploitation--one example: $20 billion a year in subsidies for fishing--this is the difference between the actual value of $100 billion and the lower subsidized revenues of $80 billion a year).

Wilson's book, in combination with those by Brian Czech and L. O. Stromborg, is in my view a capstone endeavor that moves the environment to the forefront of any intelligent person's agenda. As he concludes, we have entered the century of the environment--we must save it or lose it.

Foreign Affairs and International Security Policy

Boren, David L. and Edward J. Perkins, *Preparing America's Foreign Policy for the 21st Century* (University of Oklahoma, 1999)

I know of no finer collection of relevant views on our current and prospective foreign policy challenges. In the foreword to the book, William Crowe, former Chairman of the Joint Chiefs of Staff and then Ambassador to the Court of Saint James, observes that "A reappreciation of government is also in order." He clearly articulates both the range of challenges facing us (most of them non-military in nature), and the disconnect between how we organize our government and how we need to successfully engage. His bottom line is clear: we are not spending enough on the varied elements of national security, with special emphasis on a severely under-funded and under-manned diplomatic service.

From Gaddis Smith and Walter Mondale to Sam Nunn and Robert Oakley, from David Gergen to David Abshire to David Boren, from Kissinger to Brzezinski to Kirkpatrick, in combination with a whole host of lesser known but equally talented practitioners, capped off by comments from five Directors of Central Intelligence, this books sets a standard for organized high quality reflection on the future of U.S. foreign policy.

Most interestingly, there is general consensus with David Abshire's view that we are in a strategic interregnum, and still lacking for a policy paradigm within which to orchestrate our varied efforts to define and further our vital interests.

David Gergen clearly articulates the shortfalls in our national educational, media, and political patterns that leave the vast majority of Americans ignorant of our foreign interests and unsupportive of the need for proactive engagement abroad. Reading this book, I could not help but feel that our national educational system is in crisis, and we need both a wake-up call and a consequent national investment program such as occurred after the first Sputnik launch.

David Boren is clearly a decade or more ahead of most current commentators in his call for a new paradigm, for a new analytical framework, for the internationalization of American education across the board. I am reminded of the quotation from early America: "A Nation's best defense is an educated citizenry." Interestingly, he cites Daniel Boorstein's caution that we must not confuse information with knowledge, and in the next sentence notes: "I watched during my term as chairman of the Senate

282

Intelligence Committee while the CIA greatly increased its information, its raw data, but became overwhelmed and unable to separate the important from the unimportant."

I would itemize just a few of the many, many useful insights that this book offers:

1) Diplomacy is the sum total of familiarity with the role, knowledge of the component parts of the overall national security policy, and the ability to design and implement comprehensive policies that achieve the national objectives;

2) Politicians and policy-makers are losing the ability to think objectively and act with conviction...they are too dependent on short-term domestic polling and opinion;

3) (Quoting Donald Kegan): Power without the willingness to use it does not contribute to world peace;

4) We must strengthen the domestic roots of national power if we are to have a sound strategy;

5) Future of U.S. education and strength of U.S. family unit will quite simply determine whether U.S. can meet the economic challenges of the 21st Century;

6) Our domestic insecurity and domestic violence-and resulting foreign perceptions and disrespect for our competence at home-reduce our effectiveness overseas;

7) U.S. is its own worst enemy, with declining attention to foreign policy matters;

8) Weapons of mass destruction are our only substantive vital interest today;

9) Hunger, pestilence, and refugees within Africa will affect all nations;

10) Corruption has replaced guerrilla movements as the principal threat to democratic governance;

11) Commerce rather than conflict will be the primary concern of 21st century foreign policy;

12) The environment joins trade and commerce as an essential objective for foreign policy;

13) Long-term non-military challenges, and especially global financial markets, require refocusing of our security perspectives;

283

14) Asia will edge out Europe as our primary trading partner;

15) China in Asia and Turkey in the West are linch-pin nations;

16) NATO will survive but we must take care not to threaten Russia;

17) The UN is not very effective at peacekeeping operations-it is best confined to idea exchanges;

18) Our military is over-extended and under-funded but still the best in the world;

19) For the cost of one battalion or one expensive piece of military equipment, one thousand new Foreign Service officers could be added toward preventive diplomacy;

20) Lessons from the Roman empire: its decline results in part from a loss of contact with its own heartlands, a progressive distancing of the elite from the populace, the elevation of the military machine to the summit of the power hierarchy, and blindness in perceiving the emergence of societies motivated by nationalism or new religious ideologies; and

21) We may need a new National Security Act.

If I had one small critical comment on the book is would be one of concern—concern that these great statesmen and scholars appear—even while noting that defense is under-capitalized—to take U.S. military competence at face value. I perceive a really surprising assumption across a number of otherwise brilliant contributions to the effect that we do indeed have all that we need in the way of information dominance, precision firepower, and global mobility (strategic lift plus forward presence) —we just need to use it with greater discretion. I do not believe this to be the case. I believe-and the Aspin-Brown Commission so stated-that we lack effective access to the vast range of global multi-lingual open sources; that our commitment to precision munitions is both unaffordable and ineffective (we ran out in 8 days in the Gulf, in 3 days in Kosovo); and that we fail terribly with respect to mobility-naval forces are generally 4-6 days from anywhere, rather than the necessary 24-48 hours. This book is a very fine starting point for the national dialogue that must take place in 2001 regarding our new national security strategy.

Creveld, Martin van, *The Rise and Decline of the State* (Cambridge, 1999)

Anything Martin van Creveld writes is a five, and this book is as good as history can get. His notes are world-class, including a highly relevant note in the final chapter, to wit, that according to Soviet General Lebed's 1997 public statement that, "out of 100 suitcase-sized nuclear bombs manufactured for the Soviet Union's special forces, two-thirds could no longer be accounted for."

To begin with, van Creveld damns the state for its consistent increase of taxes and its decrease in public services. The state has become, in a word, incompetent and archaic--its grossly over-funded militaries are increasingly helpless in the face of covert and guerrilla violence, at the same time that states are spending more and more on police forces and less and less on a rapidly growing politically deprived disenfranchised underclass.

He ends, as a historical purist, without making recommendations for change. Indeed, he quotes Mao Tse Tung, "The sun will keep rising, trees with keep growing, and women will keep having children."

In many ways van Creveld's book serves as a capstone to the fifty or so books I have reviewed in the past year, most of them about strategy, threat, intelligence, and the so-called revolution in military affairs, for what I take from this work is that the state does have an extremely important role to play in assuring the common security and prosperity of the people, and we abandon the state at our own peril.

Every nation, but especially the most prosperous nations that have allowed virtually out of control immigration and set no real standards for citizenship, must very carefully examine its policies and premises, both with regard to what constitutes citizenship and loyalty, and what services it must offer to preserve and protect the commonwealth.

I am told that the FBI was prevented from searching the homes of several of the suspects in the weeks prior to the 11 September attacks, because we have granted to our visitors--illegal as well as legal--all those rights that might better be reserved for proven citizens. Van Creveld's work is not, as some might take it, the death knell for the state, but rather the bath of cold water for the statesmen--and for those citizens who care to instruct their politicians on our demand for renewed focus on resurrecting the connection between citizenship, taxation, representation, and security.

Hoge, James F. Jr. and Fareed Zakaria, *The American Encounter: The United States and the Making of the Modern World* (Basic Books, 1997)

This compilation of the "best of the best" articles from the journal Foreign Affairs is a real gem that is especially relevant today as America continues to neglect its international responsibilities and certain Senators and Congressman have the ignorant temerity to brag that they don't own nor need an American passport. The conclusion of the July 1932 article by Edwin F. Gay, "The Great Depression", is instructive: "The world war affirmed the international political responsibilities of the United States; the world depression demonstrates the economic interdependence of the United States with other states. It cannot be a hermit nation."

With four seminal articles from each decade (1920's forward), including just about every great name in the international discussions of the century, this book is a fundamental reference point for those who would dare to craft a vibrant foreign policy for the United States in the 21st Century. The book ends with several thoughtful pieces including, most fittingly, an interview with Lee Kuan Yew of Singapore on culture as destiny, an article whose subtitle might have been "How extended families and the collective good still matter."

Kissinger, Henry, *Does America Need a Foreign Policy?* (Simon & Schuster, 2001)

The book begins with a lamentation that foreign policy has been neglected in the last three Presidential campaigns; that the American public is terribly apathetic about foreign affairs; and that Congress is overly interventionist--he refrains from adding the obvious caveat regarding most Members lack of knowledge of the world. In brief, we have a long way to go as a Nation before we can devise and sustain a credible foreign policy.

The core point in this entire work is that both economics and technologies, including Internet and communications technologies, have so out-paced politics that the world is at risk. Globalization, terrorism, and other threats cannot be addressed with our existing international, regional, and national political constructs, and new means must be found--new political solutions must be found--if we are to foster security and prosperity in the age of complexity, discontinuity, and fragmentation.

There are some useful sub-themes:

1) Each region must be understood in its full complexity, with special attention to both emerging powers and to the subtleties of relations between regional actors-- we should not confine ourselves to simply addressing each actor's relationship to the United States.

2) We must take great care to never interpose ourselves or allow ourselves to become a substitute for a regional power, e.g. in the dialog between North and South Korea, or India and Pakistan.

3) We must strive at all times to ensure that the historic context is clearly appreciated and underlying every policy formulation, at the same time that we must recognize and define the vast cultural differences between US approaches to foreign policy, and the approaches of others, such as China.

4) Military compromise, whether in the Gulf War, Bosnia, or Kosovo, leaves a strategic vacuum that will inevitably require attention.

5) Africa is the true test for whether a world community can be devised and new solutions found for addressing the severe conditions in Africa that ultimately threaten the well-being of the rest of the world.

6) Our foreign service officers and the political leaders they serve must have history and philosophy restored to their diets, or they will fail to devise long-range concepts, global strategies, and sustainable policies.

Dr. Kissinger ends with what some might overlook and what I found to be absolutely core: no economic system can be sustained without a political basis. However much major multinational corporations may care to buy their comforts and their arrangements of convenience, at root, they prosper only because some set of political arrangements among great nations is providing a safety net, including the financial system with one major node in New York.

The books ends with an appeal for American humility and discretion as it makes it way forward--we must act as if we are one of many co-equal nation-states, while recognizing that our pre-eminence demands more of us than might be expected from others.

There is one major gap in this book, and I suspect it was deliberate: there is no discussion at all of the means by which American foreign policy is to be devised. As America moves into the early months of the "war on terrorism", it would have been helpful to have a really well-qualified rant on how it is impossible for this great Nation to have a foreign policy when we have gutted almost into extinction what passes for a

Department of State today. Our Foreign Service, our Embassies, our foreign assistance programs, our Peace Corps, our external research, our sponsorship of international conferences on topics of vital importance to the US, have all faded into decrepitude. If ever there was a time when Kissinger, Brzezinski, and Powell should come together and champion a major restoration--at least a $10 billion a year increase--in Program 150 (our soft power), this is that time. That they have all failed to do so troubles me-- that Senator Biden was castigated publicly for speaking the plain truth about how the world perceives us--troubles me. The attacks of 11 September represent, primarily, a failure of our ability to monitor and understand the world. That failure must lie heavily- -and equally--on the shoulders of the foreign service (State), the clandestine service (CIA), and the counterintelligence service (FBI).

Shultz, Richard H. Jr., Roy Godson, George H. Quester, *Security Studies for the 21st Century* (Brassey's, 1997)

This book is actually a guide for professors, with chapters presenting specific courses in security studies complete with fifteen-week outlines and all recommended readings. It is in my view a very fine structured reading program for the adult policy maker who is well beyond the need for going back to school, but much in need a fast means of coming to grips with the dramatic changes that have occurred in our international security environment.

Early on the book addresses the competing approaches to security studies—from the traditionalist national, international, and regional security approaches to the emerging transstate (non-state actors acknowledged as major sources of conflict and instability) to the global (to include human rights, environmental protection, economic prosperity, and social development as fundamental security issues).

The book's cataloguing of the weaknesses of 20th century security studies reads like a list of current biases inherent in those prescribing defense reform today: overemphasis on theory (or worst-case scenarios); insufficient attention to non-combat missions for military forces in peacetime; excessive focus on the US, Europe, and Russia to the exclusion of the rest of the world; too little attention to culture and the relationship of culture to conflict deterrence and resolution; insufficient attention to history prior to World War II; and finally, a neglect of non-military instruments of power and their interaction with the military.

Intelligence in particular is singled out as being a relatively recent open topic for discussion, meriting more study. The chapters on Transstate Security by Roy Godson (on non-state actors and the growing prevalence of "global ungovernability") and on

288

Nontraditional Uses of Military Force by George H. Quester, as well as the introduction and conclusion by Richard H. Schultz, Jr., are each, alone, worth the price of the book.

Each chapter, with its course outline, discussion, and recommended references, is worthy of careful examination by any serving or aspiring policymaker. However distinguished one's pedigree, we are all students today, and Graham E. Fuller is correct when he notes on page 124 that "most policymakers do not even fully realize the dynamics of the new world we live in."

Intelligence (Fiction)

Bearden, Milt, *The Black Tulip* (Random House, 1998)

I was fascinated to read this book by one of America's greatest espionage warriors—not only did he run the Afghan war from the field, he was also Chief of the Soviet Division and Chief of Station in Germany, the equivalent of an Olympic "clean sweep." I read this book critically. It is simply super, and full of nuances that get better with a second reading. The most important of these is the thoughtful manner in which the fall of the Soviet military in Afghanistan is related to the subsequent weakening of the Soviet hold over Eastern Europe, a hold that eventually broke and led to the unification of Germany and chaos in those portions of Eastern Europe where neither Europe nor the US was ready to help convert communists to capitalists. This is an inspiring book that shows in great detail how covert action--behind the lines action--can serve a great nation. This book will cleanse the palate of all those who soured on covert action as done so badly (and occasionally in violation of the law) in Central America.

Harris, Robert, *ENIGMA* (Ivy Books, 1996)

For captivating true life signals intelligence there are several books one can go to, including those by James Bamford on the American system (*Puzzle Palace, Body of Secrets*) but for really getting into the enormity of the challenges and the thrill of the individual code-breakers when they succeeded, this is the book I recommend.

It completely ignores the enormous contributions made by the Poles (who gave the English two Enigma machines at the beginning of the war) as well as the heroic deeds of Tommy Brown (youngest George Medal winner at 16, survived with code materials taken from a sinking German ship), but I have found no better novel to communicate the absolute goose-bump emotional roller-coaster ride that the Bletchley Park gang experienced.

289

If anything, this novel convey a human side to code-breaking that offsets the modern-day obsession with massive computers.

Silva, Daniel, *The Unlikely Spy* (Fawcett Crest, 1996)

Together with *Enigma* and *The Black Tulip*, and of course the George Smiley series by John Le Carre, this is one of my few really recommended fictional accounts related to espionage.

The art of lying to one's own people, at multiple levels of duplicity, some venal, much of it unnecessary, has helped to mystify, confuse, and sometimes glorify the intelligence profession.

As an intelligence professional myself, I will simply say that this is one of my top six and that it would not be called fiction if it did not depart for the pure realities as much as it does. This book captures the "essence" of duplicity within government in a time of war, and I find the whole book absolutely captivating and worthwhile.

Intelligence & Information Studies (Non-Fiction)

NOTE: I do not repeat reviews for those books on intelligence and the information and management environments around intelligence—over 150 titles in fifty-one pages—that appear in the first book, *ON INTELLIGENCE: Spies and Secrecy in an Open World.* There are some exceptions: several books by Berkowitz and Goodman, Moynihan, Turner, and by Zegart are fundamental to the case this book makes; and the books by Johnson and Treverton that were reviewed in more depth after their formal publication; and new original reviews are provided here.

Allen, George, *NONE SO BLIND: A Personal Account of the Intelligence Failure in Vietnam* (Ivan R. Dee, 2001)

This book is destined to be a classic. There is no other person who spent over 17 years focused on intelligence about Viet-Nam, and very rare is the person who can say they have spent over 50 years in continuous intelligence appointments, 20 of them after retirement. It is a personal story that I consider to be balanced, deep, and trustworthy.

290

While it has gaps, these are easily addressed by reading, at least on the intelligence side, such books at Bruce Jones' *War Without Windows*, Orrin DeForest's *SLOW BURN*, Douglas Valentine's *The Phoenix Program*, Jim Wirtz's *The Tet Offensive: Intelligence Failure in War*, Tom Mangold & John Penycate's *The Tunnels of Chu Chi* and the Viet-Nam portions of Jim Bamford's *Body of Secrets*.

I mention these books in part to emphasize that George Allen has produced a book that will stand the test of time and should be regarded as an exceptional historical, policy, intelligence, and public administration case study. It is truly humbling and sobering to read such a calm, complete, and broad treatment of the history of both American intelligence in relation to Viet-Nam, and the consistent manner in which policy-makers refused to listen to accurate intelligence estimates, while their Generals and Ambassadors steadfastly "cooked the books." The manipulation of truth from the Saigon end, and the refusal to listen to truth on the Washington end, resulted in the deaths of hundreds of thousands of people, Vietnamese, Laotian, Cambodian, and American, as well as allied nationalities.

This book is gripping. I could not put it down. It is one of the most serious personal accounts I have ever read where the vivid realities of intelligence, ignorance, and policy come together. The author excels at painting the details in context, and his many specific portraits of key individuals and situations are superior.

This book is relevant to today's war on terrorism. Many of the same issues prevail--rather than enumerate them, I will give this book my very highest mark, and simply say that you cannot understand intelligence, or the intelligence-policy relationship, without having absorbed all this author has to say.

He's hit it out of the park. Every voter who wonders what it will take to hold politicians accountable for "due diligence" in decision-making, needs to read this book.

Arnold, Stephen E., *New Trajectories of the Internet: Umbrellas, Traction, Lift and Other Phenomena* (infornautics UK, 2001)

You won't find this book on amazon.com. It is one of two examples (the book by Ben Gilad in this section being the other) of extremely good stuff that never gets into the mainstream. Although readily available if you know how to get hold of the publisher (send email to hcollier@infonortics.com) this is a "niche" book that reaches the top information professionals who follow niche publishers, but it does not reach the normal academic, industry specialist, or government specialist.

Baer, Robert, *SEE NO EVIL: A True Story of a Ground Soldier in CIA's War on Terrorism* (Crown, 2002)

As a former clandestine case officer, leaving the Agency in 1988 after unsuccessfully chasing terrorists for a few years, I knew we were in bad shape but I did not realize just how bad until I read this book. The author, working mostly in the Near East (NE) Division of the Directorate of Operations, and then in the Counter-Terrorism Center when it was just starting out, has an extremely important story to tell and every American needs to pay attention. Why? Because his account of how we have no assets useful against terrorism is in contradiction to what the Director of Central Intelligence (DCI) told the President and his top advisors at Camp David on Saturday 15 September. According to the Washington Post of 31 January 2002, page A13, on the 15th the DCI laid out an ambitious "Worldwide Attack Matrix" and told the President that the United States had a "large asset base" from its years of working the terrorism target. One of these two men one is closer to the truth than the other. In my judgment, I believe Baer has three-quarters of the weight on his side. This discrepancy warrants investigation, for no President can be successful if he does not have accurate information about our actual capabilities. [NOTE: It is of course possible that the DCI himself has been lied to and deceived by the people he has in charge of clandestine operations, in which case one would expect an investigation to lead to a change in management at lower levels.]

There are four other stories within this excellent book, all dealing with infirm bureaucracies. At one level, the author's accounting of how the Directorate of Operations has declined under the last three leaders (as the author describes them: a recalled retiree, an analyst, and a "political" (pal)) is both clearly based on ground truth, and extremely troubling. The extraordinary detail on the decline and fall of the clandestine service is one that every voter should be thinking about, because it was the failure of the clandestine service, as well as the counterintelligence service (the Federal Bureau of Investigation) that allowed 9-11 to happen...at the same time, we must note that it was a policy failure to not have investigated similar incompetencies when a military barracks in Saudi Arabia, two Embassies, and a naval destroyer were attacked, and it was clearly known in open sources that bin Laden had declared war on America and had within America numerous Islamic clerics calling for the murder of Americans-- all as documented in an excellent Public Broadcast Service documentary.

At a technical level, the author provides some really excellent real-world, real-war anecdotes about situations where clandestine reporting from trusted operations officers has not been accepted by their own superiors in the absence of technical confirmation (imagery or signals). As he says, in the middle of a major artillery battle and break-out of insurgent elements, screaming over the secure phone, "its the middle of night here". We've all known since at least the 1970's that the technical intelligence side of things

292

has been crushing human sensibility, both operational and analytical, but this book really brings the problems into the public eye in a compelling and useful manner.

At another level, the author uses his own investigation for murder (he was completely cleared, it was a set-up) by the Federal Bureau of Investigation, and at one point by the Secret Service, to shed new light on the complete break-down of internal security processes within the CIA. At its lowest point, he is pressured by DO management with a psychological evaluation to determine his fitness for duty--shades of Stalinism! I know this technique, of declaring officers unfit for duty based on psychological hatchet jobs, to be a common practice over the past two decades, and when Britt Snider was appointed Inspector General at CIA, I told him this was a "smoking gun" in the 7th floor closet. That it remains a practice today is grounds for evaluating the entire management culture at CIA.

There is a fourth story in the book, a truly interesting account of how big energy companies, their "ambassadors" serving as Presidential appointees within the National Security Council, and corrupt foreign elements, all come together. In this the spies are not central, so I leave it as a sidenote.

In my capacity as a reviewer of most intelligence-related books within these offerings, I want to make it clear to potential buyers of this book that the author is not alone. His is the best, most detailed, and most current accounting of the decrepit dysfunctionality of the clandestine service (as I put it in my own book's second edition), but I would refer the reader to two other books in particular: David Corn's *Blond Ghost: Ted Shackley and the CIA's Crusades*--its most memorable quote, on covert action in Laos, being "We spent a lot of money and got a lot of people killed, and we didn't get much for it."--and Evan Thomas' *The Very Best Men--Four Who Dared: The Early Years of the CIA*--its best quote: "Patriotic, decent, well-meaning, they were also uniquely unsuited to the grubby, necessarily devious world of intelligence." There are many other books, including twelve (12!) focused on reform and recommended by the Council on Intelligence.

The author is a brave man--he was brave on the fields of war and clandestinity, and he is braver still for having brought this story to the public. We owe him a hearing.

Bamford, James, *Body of Secrets: Anatomy of the Ultra-Secret National Security Agency—From the Cold War Through the Dawn of a New Century* (Doubleday, 2001)

I like this book because it is a deeply researched investigation of the National Security Agency, a part of the U.S. government that is always "in harms way", and because it offers up over 15 genuine journalistic investigative "scoops", shows how much can be learned about secret matters through persistent and professional exploitation of open sources, and paints a compelling dramatic picture of the honorable and courageous NSA employees, the less capable senior officers in the Joint Chiefs of Staff who risk their lives and do not provide them with emergency plans and air cover, and the man in the middle, LtGen Mike Hayden, whom the book portrays as a truly competent person who "gets it." This is the stuff of history and a very well-told tale.

Among the "scoops" that I as a professional intelligence officer will list for the sake of showing how wide and deep the book goes, are:

1) Extremely big scoop. Israel attacked U.S. military personnel aboard the USS Liberty with the intent of simulating an Egyptian attack on US forces that would permit a joint US and Israeli retaliation. Even after the ship was destroyed, with very clear evidence from NSA tapes that the Israeli's deliberately attacked a US ship while the ship was flying US colors, President Johnson is reported to have betrayed his military and his Nation by covering this up, intimidating all survivors, and saying he would "not embarrass our allies." In consultation with my naval colleagues, I am satisfied that the author has it right.

2) US SIGINT failed as North Korea invaded South Korea. Our lack of preparedness, in both systems and linguists, was dereliction of duty at the highest levels. Fast forward to Sudan, East Timor, Burundi, Yugoslavia, Somalia, and Haiti.

3) US "Operations Security" (OPSEC) is terrible! Bad in World War II, bad in Korea, bad in Viet-Nam, bad in Somalia and bad today. This book is a stark and compelling indictment of the incompetence of U.S. military and political leaders who refuse to recognize that the rest of the world is smart enough to collect our signals and predict our intentions with sufficient effectiveness to neutralize our otherwise substantial power.

4) Eisenhower, as President, controlled the U-2 operations over Russia and lied to the world and the people about his individual responsibility for those missions.

5) US SIGINT failed in Arabia and against Israel. "The agency had few Arabic or Hebrew linguists and it was not equipped to eavesdrop on British, French, or Israeli military communications." We are often unable to sort out the truth in conflicts between Arabs and Israel, and this allows Israel to deceive and manipulate American policy makers.

6) In the early years of the Cold War, the US was the aggressor, and ran incredibly prevocational full bombing runs into northern Russia, simply to test for defenses

and to see if it could be done. Young American military personnel were sent as expendable cannon fodder, with the ultimate result that Russia spent billions more on its defenses than it might have if America have been a "good neighbor."

7) The Joint Chiefs of Staff was "out of control" during our confrontations with Cuba, and proposed to the President of the United States that U.S. military capabilities be used to murder Americans in order to provide a false cover for declaring war on Cuba.

8) The most senior military officers serving under Kennedy did not have the moral courage to tell him that the Bay of Pigs was a doomed operation. They allowed hundreds to die and be captured rather than "speak truth to power." NSA provided ample SIGINT.

9) Imagery intelligence beat signals intelligence in answering the ultimate question about the presence of Soviet missiles in Cuba. Those who practice "OPSEC" can defeat our SIGINT capabilities.

10) US telecommunications companies have for years been giving NSA copies of all telegrams sent by foreign embassies and corporations, compromising their private sector integrity.

11) US military power is hollow. For both the USS Liberty and the USS Pueblo, a combination of screw-ups put military personnel in harms' way and a combination of incapacities helped get them killed and captured. In all of Korea only six U.S. aircraft were available to help protect the USS Pueblo, and they required several hours to get ready. The South Koreans, ready to launch defense forces instantly, were forbidden to do so, US leaders being more concerned about avoiding provocation of the North Koreans than about protecting U.S. military personnel.

12) US successes against the Russians and other targets were completely offset by the combination of the John Walker betrayal (turning over the key lists, this has been known) and the Soviet receipt from the Vietnamese (this has not been known) of a complete warehouse of NSA code machines left behind in Saigon. The Soviets have been reading our mail since 1975, and NSA did not want the President or Congress or the people to know this fact.

13) The North Vietnamese beat us on SIGINT, with 5000 trained SIGINT personnel and a system that stretched from Guam (where the B-52's were launched and the ground crew radios were in the clear) to the day-to-day operational orders going out to helicopters and fighters "in the clear". The book paints an extraordinarily

295

stark contrast between North Vietnamese competence and US incompetence across all areas of SIGINT and OPSEC.

14) There are others, but the final scoop is summed up in the author's concluding chapter on NSA's race to build the largest fastest computer at a time when relevant signals are growing exponentially: "Eventually NSA may secretly achieve the ultimate in quickness, compatibility, and efficiency-a computer with petaflop and higher speeds shrunk into a container about a liter in size, and powered by only about ten watts of power: the human brain."

Beesley, Patrick, *Very Special Intelligence: The Story of the Admiralty's Operational Intelligence Centre 1939-1945* Stackpole, 2000)

This is a brilliant piece of work, and extremely relevant today. Had America had an Operational Intelligence (OpIntel) Plot (24/7 operationally-oriented put it all together all the time watch center), I daresay the terrorist attacks on America would have been prevented in good time. This work provides valuable insights on how best to manage an operationally-oriented watch center that does "all-source fusion" against a constantly changing real-time real-world threat. The Operational Intelligence Center (OIC) whose story is told here worked with no fewer than seventeen distinct sources streams, each with its own idiosyncrasies, its own fits and starts--and it worked directly with its operational clients, fully appraised of friendly plans and intentions and able to provide workmanlike inputs at every turn.

There are a number of vital lessons to be learned from this book, which I recommend in the strongest terms as one of my "top ten" relevant *today*. Among them:

1) **Sharing Secrets Matters.** It was the Russians who helped the British get started in 1914 with a gift of a German Naval Signal book, and it was the Poles who saved the day early on in World War II with a gift of two working Enigma machines.

2) **Ops Must Sleep With Intel.** Operators ignore intelligence because they do not understand it-there are too many breakdowns in communication along the way, and if the operators have not really gotten to know their intelligence counterparts, the two cultures do not come together effectively in times of crisis.

3) **Ops Cannot Do Raw Sources.** The corollary of the above is that Ops simply cannot keep up with nuances and is not able to evaluate sources in context to good effect.

4) **Intel Must Sleep With Ops.** The intelligence propensity to compartment everything to the point of meaningless, and the "green door" mentality that is especially characteristic of the crypto-analysis community, amounts to a death wish. Some secret sources must be "ultra" secret, but some form of bridge is needed-the OpIntel Center appears to be a vital and relevant solution.

5) **Plots Must Be Co-Located and Ideally Integrated.** Early separation and distance between the intelligence plot, the commercial shipping plot and the operational plot leads to waste and death. Ultimately an integrated plot, or at least a blue-green plot next door to the red plot, is vital to effective prosecution of real-time war.

6) **Lose the Old Guys.** The first thing that needs doing when preparing for a long war is to lose the old guys. No disrespect intended, but as has been documented time and again, those that get promoted in peacetime bureaucracies tend to be too conformist and too subservient to peacetime protocols to adapt well to unconventional and very fast-moving wartime conditions.

7) **Hire the Retired.** This is not a contradiction. Old guys with big egos and high ranks have to go—but bringing in the best of the retired, generally at the field grade level, can have an extraordinary positive impact in the rapid maturation and stabilization of the full-speed-ahead wartime watch.

8) **Doctrinal Disputes Kill.** Unless there is a homeland defense doctrine that fully integrates and exercises the capabilities and internal cultures of the Air Force, Navy, Coast Guard, and civilian agencies there will be a year or two of major and almost catastrophic losses until it gets sorted out the hard way.

9) **Home Arrogance Kills (UK Version).** The persistent unwillingness of home side personnel to admit that their own security measures can be broken by clever enemies, and the general sloppiness of all hands with respect to Operations Security (OPSEC) will take a heavy toll.

10) **Home Arrogance Kills (US Version).** There is a theme with regard to the Americans. While their money and their manpower are gratefully accepted, their arrogance knows no bounds. They entered the war believing that there was nothing the British could teach them-further on into the war, the Americans risked Ultra by acting too aggressively on its information.

11) **Red Cell Oversight Needed.** One thing that jumped out at me from this book was the urgent need for having a very senior person-a retired Chairman of the Joint Chiefs of Staff, for example, managing a Red Cell to provide oversight over operational decisions to exploit the most sensitive sources. [By this I mean, a

297

senior authority who can overrule and forbid operations whose success might endanger the special source.]

12) **Negative Reports Matter.** I was really struck by the circumstances surrounding a German break-out up the Channel, in which a number of normally reliable and overlapping intelligence collection endeavors all were forced back by weather, broken down or what-not. From this I took the lesson that negative reports matter. By failing to report to the OIC on their non-status, they failed to focus the OIC on all the possibilities. Thinking the flank covered, the OIC left the flank open.

13) **Tommy Brown Matters.** The book ends on a marvelous note, pointing out that without the heroism of Tommy Brown, a 16-year-old cabin boy and youngest recipient of the George Medal as well as two other adults who died in the process of grabbing vital enemy signals materials off a sinking vessel, the allies would have been deaf for much of 1943. At the end of the day the best technical intelligence comes down to a brave human who risks all to make it possible.

Bowden, Mark, *Killing Pablo: The Hunt for the World's Greatest Outlaw* (Atlantic Monthly, 2001)

This book provides an excellent overview of sensitive sources and methods used by the U.S. military to intercept and locate electronic transmissions. It specifically "blows" a cover company, two specific kinds of aircraft, and several U.S. Special Operations Forces standard operating procedures. I suspect that NSA and the CIA Centers dealing with terrorism and with crime and narcotics are having the same difficulties recovering from this book that NSA had when President Reagan inadvertently revealed in public that he was receiving transcripts of Politburo cell phone conversations made while in transit, from their car phones.

Having said that, I find that the author has performed very responsibly as an investigative journalist, and that his story is superior in every respect. I even find that he has withheld some key information out of respect for his sources, and that there are many lessons to be learned from this book about how we might improve our transnational campaign against non-state forces that have vastly more money, ruthlessness, and sheer people power than we do.

I like and recommend this book--it is a real-world story, well-researched and well-told.

Cronin, Blaise and Helen Barsky Atkins, *The Web of Knowledge: A Festschrift in Honor of Eugene Garfield* (Information Today, 2000)

This was not the book I was looking for, but it is still worthy of buying if you have any interest at all in charting knowledge terrain and "knowing who knows". In honor of Eugene Garfield, arguably the most influential man in the sociology of knowledge in this century or any other, the book provides a wonderful collection of *methodological* articles about the bibliometrics and indicators associated with charting who quotes whom and what does it mean in terms of influence within and among nations, organizations, schools of thought, and individual cabals.

I was intrigued to find that the book, perhaps because it is so original and represents the first book-length collection of its kind, did not include an article on a topic near and dear to my heart, that is, developing algorithms to identify anomalies in citation such that one can weed out those who are citing one another simply to "beat the game." As citation analysis becomes a more mainstream means of measuring intellectual contributions (it is still not mainstream--too many otherwise talented intelligence community managers of analysts have no clue it exists), some form of citation validation and policing will be needed.

There are three other areas where I would say that this book is a vital and valuable foundation, and desperately in need of three distinct sequel publications:

First, we need to migrate the value of citation analysis to the Internet, not only to electronic journals but to citations of self-published papers on web sites as well as to informed observations in expert forums. Neither the classification schema nor the industry standards for making this possible exist today. I would go so far as to suggest that a new Internet standards committee dedicated to this specific issue should be created, immediately.

Second, an analogous situation exists with those experts who are not permitted to publish in the open literature, but who are very well known by virtue of their title, organizational affiliation, participation in conferences, or classified work revealed to a very few. As the core competency of government becomes the nurturing of national knowledge--not only in science and technology but also in all international as well as domestic matters--some form of citation analysis process must be developed that makes these experts (or if not expert, then influentials by virtue of their position at the international, national, state/provincial, or local levels) and their counterparts in non-governmental organizations (e.g. Red Cross, World Bank, elements of the United Nations) readily identifiable. The Internet, and the public availability of email communication pattern analysis information that does not intrude on the substantive privacy of electronic communications, may possible be helpful here.

Third, and finally, we come to the area of interest that originally led to my purchasing this book, which is that of actually identifying centers of excellence and "portals" into the entire range of published and unpublished knowledge on any given topic. Such a sequel publication must not only document, in an evolutionary or "living" way, who the top 100 people are across every social science and science topic, but also the top 25 institutions with deliberate distinctions between Asian, Americas, European, and African centers of excellence. The Institute of Scientific Information (ISI) has been unwilling to do this as an internal investment, and has not heard from enough governments and corporations to warrant its moving aggressively to create what I would regard as an extraordinarily valuable and relevant guide for all manner of investments and improvements in international, national, and state-based research and education. I would go so far as to say that such a guide, such a service of common concern, would go a very long way toward making possible extraordinary new means of leveraging distributed intellectual resources, lowering the cost of seminal research, and introducing new forms of transnational collaborative work.

Garfield, and citation analysis and all those who have built on Garfield's work, together represent the first mile in a hundred mile journey toward creating the *World Brain* that H.G. Wells, among a select few, has envisioned. There is much yet to be done.

Davenport, Thomas H. and John C. Beck, *The Attention Economy: Understanding the New Currency of Business* (Harvard, 2001)

I rank this book as easily one of the top 25 books on information fundamentals, and quite possibly in the top 10. The book is well-presented and what some might see as showmanship I consider to be good editing and publishing. The book starts strong, focusing on "attention deficit" in both individuals and organizations, and the consequences of failing to pay attention to the right things at the right time--corporate CEOs and their business intelligence professionals, as well as government leaders and their national intelligence professionals, can learn a great deal from this book.

Especially useful to me, and a major reason why I rank this book so highly, was its distinction between the need to first, constantly scan the world ("global coverage") for AWARENESS; second, be able to surge resources to accomplish local focus for ATTENTION; and finally, third, to be conscious of domestic (or internal corporate) political considerations before taking ACTION.

At a national level, I found myself thinking that this book could be the first step in an evaluation of how we spend our time--and how we compensate ourselves for spending our time. Of course others have observed that we spend too much time in front of the television or eating fast food or whatever, but I found this book extremely helpful in thinking about the economics of personal and organizational information management. Applying this book's lessons, for example, might cause any manager to forbid Internet access because of the very high negative return on investment--searches should be done by specialists who can be relied to avoid personal browsing on company time. The author's specifically note that the Western culture is less well equipped to manage "attention" than other cultures. The book also focuses on the fact that client attention and teamwork *compete* with innovation, and that some form of time management guidance is needed that permits employees to focus on just one of these primary duties.

The author's identification of relevance, community, engagement, and convenience as the four key factors in attracting and holding attention from individuals--and the lengthy discussion in the book on each of these--is very worthwhile. So also is their specification of four "attention tracks" that each individual must manage: focusing one's own attention; attracting the right kind of attention to oneself; directing the attention of those under one's oversight; and maintaining the attention of one's customers and clients (and one could add, one's family). It goes well beyond the current state of the art and outlines new ideas that could and should have a fundamental impact on how we spend our time, what information services we buy, and how we use information technology.

Dertouzos, Michael L., *The Unfinished Revolution: Human-Centered Computers and What They Can Do For Us* (Harperbusiness, 2001)

In some ways this is the gold-collared knowledge worker counterpart book to Ted Halstead and Michael Lind's *The Radical Center: The Future of American Politics* (citizen-centered). Those who liked The *Cultural Creatives* or *IMAGINE: What America Could be in the 21st Century*, can adopt this book as their user's guide for demanding change in information technology.

I recommend it because it is full of common sense, is the first really helpful "requirements document" for a clean sheet new approach to software and hardware and ergonomics ($3000 word for user friendly). The bad news is that nobody is listening. We are ten years away from this being a reality because the legacy providers (big hardware, one certain software company) are not about to retool their empires for the sake of delivering better value.

301

It is more than a little amusing to me to have this book endorsed by the CEO of the one company that prides itself on producing software with mutated migrated Application Program Interfaces that are used to extort tribute from third party software developers, where no sane consumer will invest in his products until they've had three years to "mature" in the marketplace.

The opening listings of the "standard faults" in today's "consumer electronics" is alone worth the price of the book--unintegrated systems fault; manual labor fault; human servitude fault; crash fault; excessive learning fault; feature overload fault; fake intelligence fault; waiting fault; ratchet fault...

The book ends on a low note and high note. The low note is a description of Oxygen, a $50M project seeded by DARPA and including several major company partners such as HP and Nokia. This project has some excellent ideas, including a new focus on an architecture for nomadic computing with three aspects: a Handy 21 (hand-held), Enviro 21 (intermediate personal computers at home, office, and in car), and N21 Network (Intentional Naming System, every computer and peripheral everywhere is in the public domain and broadcasting its location and status, use on the fly). Good stuff. What he doesn't mention is that the U.S. Government is spending over half a billion dollars on completely uncoordinated desktop analysis toolkits, and there is probably 2-3X that much being spent in the private sector. He does note that we will never get our act together if we continue to develop hardware and software in a very fragmented and hardware-based manner.

On the high note, the author has clearly thought about the consequences of having an information revolution here in the USA, creating information royalty, while leaving the rest of the world dispossessed, in poverty, and unconnected. He has a very practical appreciation for the fact that the USA must fund two distinct foreign assistance programs--a Digital Marshall Plan (my phrase) to jack in the entire world; and a commensurate literacy, birth control, disease control, and famine control program to stabilize populations to the point where they can be productive within the global grid.

I read this book on the airplane coming back from the Consumer Electronics Show in Las Vegas (Federal Emerging Technologies Conference sub-set), and I was really struck by the contradiction between the vast fragmentation spread out over Las Vegas (the man who has everything also has to carry it) and the elegant simplicity of this book's vision--one hand-held able to be any of 100+ devices. "It's the software, simpleton...."

What saddens me, especially when considering the billions of dollars being given away by our richest software developer, someone who seems to favor gestures on the margin instead of quality control and open source at the core, is that we knew all this in the

302

mid-1980's. The eighteen distinct functionalities needed for a desktop analysts' workstation were identified by CIA in 1986--everything from data ingestion and conversion softwares to modeling and simulation and pattern detection and of course desktop publishing. The year after the CIA prototypes were working so successfully on UNIX (Sun), CIA decided that the PS2 would be the standard "dumb" terminal, and all UNIX efforts were ordered to shut-down. The big organizations, the ones with the power to make the revolution, chose control and dumb terminals over freedom and smart software. I am very skeptical that the vision in this book will come to fruition...

Drucker, Peter, *Innovation and Entrepreneurship: Practice and Principles* (Harperbusiness, 1993)

Drucker has a remarkable ability to deflate any self-styled entrepreneur and "innovator." His book discusses the sources of innovation, concluding rather significantly that knowledge-based innovation is rarely successful—that innovation generally works best when all the factors are known and put into new combinations that work exceedingly well—and that successful innovations start small, focus on the simplest element that can be understood by any half-wit, don't cost a lot, and are never grandiose.

Drucker, Peter, *Post-Capitalist Society* (Harperbusiness, 1994)

Drucker and Toffler agree on one important idea: fiscal and monetary policy is no longer the real driver for national prosperity. At best it is a place-holder, a means of keeping the economy stable. There is a strong element of accountability throughout the book, first with respect to the managers of governments and corporations, and finally with the managers of schools that must ultimately be held accountable for producing students who are competent at both learning and sharing knowledge. For Drucker, the organization of the post-capitalist society must commit itself to being a destabilizer able to change constantly. "It must be organized for systematic abandonment of the established, the customary, the familiar, the comfortable-whether products, services, processes, human and social relationships, skills, or organizations themselves. It is the very nature of knowledge that it changes fast and that today's certainties will be tomorrow's absurdities." So speaketh Drucker of the U.S. Intelligence Community....

Gilad, Benjamin, *Business Blindspots: replacing myths, beliefs and assumptions with market realities* (infonortics UK, 1996)

This is a "gray literature" gem. Although published by a very reputable organization in the United Kingdom, amazon.com does not accept books for listing from international publishers that do not have a U.S. warehouse or representative. This is an extraordinary book, perhaps the finest book on real-world intelligence using legal sources and methods, ever written. It is especially valuable to the chief executive officer willing to entertain the possibility that they just might *not* know how to properly follow external developments in the most methodical manner possible. This excellent work is especially strong because of its deep knowledge and consequently its deep credibility, in presenting anecdotes that make it clear that the largest corporations and banks are not immune to the ignorance and myopia that prevail among spies and others who think that their secrets are all that matter. Order via email to hcollier@infonortics.com.

Herman, Michael, *Intelligence Power in Peace and War* (Cambridge, 1999)

This is the textbook for the best and the brightest of both the academic world and the policy world. It is not an easy read, between the British language form and the deep thinking, but it is, as Christopher Andrew says, "the best overview" and "surely destined to become a standard work". I especially liked its attention to components and boundaries, effects, accuracy, and evaluation. Perhaps most usefully within the book is the distinction between long-term intelligence endeavors that rely primarily on open sources and serve to improve state understanding and state behavior, and short-term espionage that tends to be intrusive and heighten the target state's feelings of vulnerability and hostility. No intelligence library is complete without this book--it provides a rock-solid foundation for serious thinking about the intelligence in the 21st Century.

Herman, Michael, *Intelligence Services in the Information Age: Theory and Practice* (Cass, 2002)

Intelligence Power in Peace and War remains the author's greatest work but this collection of well-focused essays, most never before available to the general public, provides a very easy-going (that is to say, easy to read) advanced reader that touches of some vital issues for the future including the restoration of ethics to the practice of intelligence, and the need to internationalize intelligence in the war between governments and gangs or other threats of common concern.

Every essay has its gems, from the first that explores the contradicting views of the essence of intelligence (one view from Kent has it as a particular kind of knowledge, another view has it as defined solely by its secrecy). The author excels at drawing out the relativism of intelligence as well as the changes--more concerned today with the security of others than of one's own state; and more committed (in the best of the services) to forecasting the future rather than manipulating the present.

The essay on intelligence and diplomacy is absolutely vital, beginning with the observation that we are now spending more on intelligence than diplomacy (in the US, 10 times more on secret intelligence than on normal diplomacy). The author concludes, without belaboring the paucity of diplomatic resources, that the UK model of intelligence--the allied model in some respects--has done well in not abusing its special knowledge to influence policy.

Discussing intelligence and the Revolution in Military Affairs, there are several trenchant observations, among the most helpful being that the current RMA is too obsessed with technology applicable to "things" (both as tools and as targets) while completely over-looking a revolution in technology applicable to text and to thinking. This is down-right brilliant and a long over-due issue for policy consideration. Interestingly, the National Imagery and Mapping Commission Report concluded in December 2000 that the USA has spent billions on collection technology during the Cold War, without a commensurate expenditure in what the Americans call TPED: tasking, processing, exploitation, and dissemination. If the Americans are to make a worthy contribution to allied intelligence in the 21st Century, one might hope they heed the author's observation and invest in global multi-lingual open source data ingestion, and multi-media analytic tools for "making sense" of the vast flows of readily available information--most of it not yet digital.

The middle section of the book covers many critical issues including the continued separation of security and foreign intelligence, a separation that allowed 9-11 to occur in the USA. Among the really brilliant gems in this section: "The best test of an intelligence system is the all-source memory it builds up..." The reader can judge for themselves whether any intelligence organization can pass this rather plain-spoken test. The author is in the vanguard in terms of tapping into external expertise, shifting priorities from collection to analysis, and substantially improving inter-departmental coordination of assessments at the action officer level. Two reviews of Norwegian and New Zealand contributions and issues offer a helpful appreciation of where further gains might be made. Over the course of several chapters the author addresses the lessons of history and answers the question "did intelligence make a difference?" All of this material is quite stimulating, coming as it does from a man who was at the very heart of joint intelligence assessments, and his findings, some negative, must bear on how we adjust to the future.

Good as the first parts are, the best is held for last. Part IV, titled "Intelligence and a Better World", contains two chapters--one on intelligence and international ethics, the other an afterword on the attacks of 9-11. These two are my most heavily marked sections, and in my own mind represent some of the author's freshest and most valuable thinking. The author is fully aware of the importance of shifting attention to the sub-

305

state and non-state actors, and also of the need to begin sharing all-source intelligence in a multi-lateral fashion, in effect (citing two former US intelligence leaders) treating intelligence as an international good. He carefully explores the ethical and opportunity cost dimensions of covert intelligence activities against other sovereign state (certainly excluding rogue states), concluding that on balance open sources and good analysis are a better bet when combined with the increased trust that could result from eschewing intrusive covert penetrations that are not really necessary in relation to government secrets (terrorists of course being fair game for all available covert methods).

Addressing 9-11, the author has many helpful things to say, among them the observation that "The problems of counter-terrorist intelligence cannot be solved just by throwing money at them." He ends with the compelling observation that the United States of America is incapable of protecting itself from international threats, even with its vast resources, unless it first devises new means of sharing intelligence and cooperating more closely with all other governments. I agree with him. Both "hard targets" and "global coverage" are beyond the ken of any single nation, and the "new craft of intelligence" that I and others are devising seeks to harness the full distributed intelligence of the Whole Earth--not just the intelligence of governments, but of legal non-state actors and citizens--the intelligence "minutemen" of the future. There are perhaps twelve really high-caliber commentators on intelligence in the English-speaking language, but this author, Michael Herman, continues to be the soft-spoken master of the domain--offering the best combination of erudition, experience, and ethical grounding--and we are lucky to have this book from him to help us all as we seek to revitalize intelligence in the aftermath of 9-11.

This book is especially recommended as a reader for university classes, and one hopes that gradually it will be understood within academia and business that intelligence is not some arcane secret priesthood, but rather the essence of governance in the age of information. The author, and this book, are most helpful contributors to the "Great Conversation".

Holden-Rhodes, James, *Sharing the Secrets* (Praeger, 2002)

It is always a shame when a really great book is badly marketed and consequently does not reach as many professionals and citizens as it should. This is such a book.

What the blurbs don't tell you, such as they are, is that the author was one of the true pioneers in the world of open source intelligence (creating useful actionable intelligence using only legal and ethical sources and methods). His brilliant efforts in the early 1990's were easily a decade ahead of where the Foreign Broadcast Information Service (FBIS) is today--using a wide variety of Latin American newspapers and lots of brainpower, he was able to create tactical intelligence that contributed significantly to the success of operational missions by the U.S. Southern Command and the Drug Enforcement Administration, leading the destruction of cocaine laboratories, the interdiction of aircraft, and the arrest of key people in the transnational criminal structure.

This book is an essential reference for any agency or command library concerned with asymmetric warfare, unconventional threats, and non-traditional methods of providing intelligence support to those responsible for dealing with anything other than traditional war. The sources and methods that the author discusses are especially pertinent to the study of terrorism, proliferation, transnational crime, cross-national toxic dumping, and other sub-state and non-state threats.

Johnson, Loch, *Bombs, Bugs, Drugs, and Thugs: Intelligence and America's Quest for Security* (New York University Press, 2000)

The opening quotation from Harry Howe Ransom says it all-"Certainly nothing is more rational and logical than the idea that national security policies be based upon the fullest and most accurate information available; but the cold war spawned an intelligence Frankenstein monster that now needs to be dissected, remodeled, rationalized and made fully accountable to responsible representatives of the people."

Professor Johnson is one of only two people (the other being Britt Snider) to have served on both the Church Commission in the 1970's and the Aspin-Brown Commission in the 1990's, and is in my view one of the most competent observers and commentators on the so-called U.S. Intelligence Community. The book is a *tour d'horizon* on both the deficiencies of today's highly fragmented and bureaucratized archipelago of independent fiefdoms, as well as the "new intelligence agenda" that places public health and the environment near the top of the list of topics to be covered by spies and satellites.

Highlights of this excellent work, a new standard in terms of currency and breadth, include his informed judgment that most of what is in the "base" budget of the community should be resurrected for reexamination, and that at least 20% of the budget (roughly $6 billion per year) could be done away with--and one speculates that this would be good news to an Administration actively seeking trade-offs permitting its promised tax cut program. His overviews of the various cultures within the Central Intelligence Agency, of the myths of intelligence, and of the possibilities for burden sharing all merit close review.

He does, however, go a bridge too far while simultaneously rendering a great service to the incoming Administration. He properly identifies the dramatic shortfalls in the open source information gathering and processing capabilities of the various Departments of the Federal government-notably the Department of State as well as the Department of Commerce and the various agencies associated with public health--but then he goes on to suggest that these very incapacities should give rise to an extension of the U.S. Intelligence Community's mission and mandate--that it is the U.S. Intelligence Community, including clandestine case officers in the field and even FBI special agents, who should be tasked with collecting open sources of information and with reporting on everything from disease to pollution. This will never work, but it does highlight the fact that all is not well with *both* the U.S. Intelligence Community *and* the rest of the government that is purportedly responsible for collecting and understanding open sources of information.

On balance I found this book to be a very competent, insightful, and well-documented survey of the current stresses and strains facing the U.S. national intelligence community. The conclusion that I drew from the book, one that might not be shared by the author, was that the U.S. Government as a whole has completely missed the dawn of the Information Age. From the National Security Agency, where too many people on payroll keep that organization mired in the technologies of the 1970's, to the U.S. State Department, which has lost control of its Embassies and no longer collects significant amounts of open source information, to the White House, where no one has time to read-we have completely blown it-we simply have not adapted the cheap and responsive tools of the Internet to our needs, nor have we employed the Internet to share the financial as well as the intellectual and time burdens of achieving "Global Coverage." More profoundly, what this book does in a way I have not been able to do myself, is very pointedly call into question the entire structure of government, a government attempting to channel small streams of fragmented electronic information through a physical infrastructure of buildings and people that share no electronic connectivity what-so-ever, while abdicating its responsibility to absorb and appreciate the vast volumes of relevant information from around the globe that is not online, not in English, and not free.

It was not until I had absorbed the book's grand juxtaposition of the complementary incompetencies of both the producers of intelligence and the consumers of intelligence that I realized he has touched on what must be the core competency of government in the Information Age: how precisely do we go about collecting, analyzing, and disseminating information, and creating tailored intelligence, when we are all inter-dependent across national, legal bureaucratic, and cultural boundaries? This is not about secrecy versus openness, but rather about whether Government Operations as a whole are taking place with the sources, methods, and tools of this century, or the last. To bombs, bugs, drugs, and thugs one must add the perennial Pogo: "We have met the enemy, and he is us."

Matthias, Willard G., *America's Strategic Blunders: Intelligence Analysis and National Security Policy, 1936-1991* (Pennsylvania State University Press, 2001)

I like and recommend this book because it is an important personal account from a very talented senior intelligence estimates professional. It documents in great detail a number of extremely serious mistakes on the part of U.S. policy makers from World War II through to Reagan years, while also recounting the history of how the Pentagon helped destroy CIA's independent assessments capability.

Time and time again throughout this book one sees references to "state of mind" and "mindset", and this is important. The author has a very fine grasp of how debilitating ingrained mindsets can be--the military mindset that focuses on buying more and more high technology even though it is demonstrably irrelevant to our most urgent strategic needs; the policy mindset that emphasizes the need for a tangible "main enemy" even as we destroy the environment and ignore catastrophic diseases and failed states; and the intelligence mindset that values secrecy and blind loyalty over public disclosure and public service.

I am especially impressed by the author's past responsibility for preparing the "Estimate of the World Situation", and how compellingly he distinguishes between the great days when such estimates were both produced and consumed, and today's state of affairs, where only "hard targets" are the object of our obsession, and "rest of the world" is poorly addressed.

The integrity of intelligence is a theme than runs throughout the book, and for that reason alone I recommend it for every policy and intelligence professionals' library. There are also compelling insights and thoughtful quotes.

The author's itemization of seven structural anomalies and states of mind that were present in World War II and can be seen today is worth abstracting here:

1) Absolute commitment to unconditional surrender eliminated possibilities for undermining Hitler from within;

2) Allied command structure was not unified in fact;

309

3) There were no functioning lines of communication between tactical military and tactical (field) intelligence units;

4) Military leaders had a tactical intelligence state of mind, not a strategic intelligence state of mind, and were overly dependent on signals intelligence;

5) Military leaders were absolutely committed to established plans and unwilling to deviate or consider alternatives even in the face of compelling intelligence;

6) Moral self-righteousness and political naiveté blinded Allied political and military leaders to the efforts of moderating forces in Germany ready to start an internal war;

7) Concept of war shifted away from the Clausewitzian "trinity" toward a "total war" emphasizing societal destruction and victory at any cost.

As his book goes on to document, these problems have been with us through the entire Cold War period, and have resulted in great waste of the taxpayer dollar as well as extraordinary risk of nuclear war with the Soviets during the 1980's when we played a very confrontational game with very limited policy level appreciation of just how desperate the Soviets might be.

This is not a book that offers solutions or suggestions for improving the vitality of intelligence or the attention span of policy makers, but it is an excellent contribution to what one can only hope will eventually be a truly public debate about the need for restoring America's strategic intelligence analysis capabilities, and making both intelligence producers and intelligence consumers accountable for "informed policy."

Persico, Joseph E., *Roosevelt's Secret War: FDR and World War II Espionage* (Random House, 2001)

Intelligence professionals will be very disappointed by this book, citizens interested in Presidential approaches to intelligence, somewhat less so. The author's brilliant biography of William Casey, OSS Veteran and Director of Central Intelligence under President Ronald Reagan, was a much more satisfying book. What we have here is by and large a mish-mash of the works of others, together with an original composition on FDR's involvement in intelligence that is uneven--partly because the subject did not put much in writing, and partly because the author chose to rely primarily on secondary published sources.

310

From the perspective of one interested in "Presidential intelligence," that is, how does a President manage various means of keeping informed, the book is a must read but also a shallow read. We learn that FDR was a master of deception and of running many parallel efforts, balancing them against one another. We learn that FDR was remarkably tolerant of amateurism and incompetence, while good at finding the gems these same loose but prolific intelligence endeavors could offer.

Perhaps most importantly, we gain some insights into how Presidents, even when properly informed by intelligence (e.g. of Pearl Harbor in advance, or of the lack of threat from domestic Americans of Japanese descent) must yet "go along" and provide either inaction pending the public's "getting it", or unnecessary action (the internments) to assuage public concern.

There are enough tid-bits to warrant a full reading of the book, but only for those who have not read widely in the literature of intelligence and/or presidential history. The British lied to the President and grossly exaggerated their intelligence capabilities, in one instance presenting a man "just back from behind the lines" when in fact he was simply on staff and lying for effect. We learn that the Department of State was twice offered, and twice declined, the lead on a global structure for collecting and processing intelligence. We learn that FDR himself concluded that Croatia and Serbia would never ever get along and should be separate countries.

On the NATO side, we learn that Eisenhower went with bad weather and the invasion succeeded in part because of a successful deception and in part because of Ike's courage in going forward in the face of bad weather--fast forward to how weather incapacitates our high-technology today. Most interestingly, we learn that FDR finally approved Eisenhower as leader of Overload, in lieu of his favorite, General Marshall, in part because he recognized that the allied joint environment required a general and a politician in one man.

This book is a hybrid, attempting to mesh presidential history with intelligence history, and perhaps this should gain the author some margin of tolerance. Unfortunately, in focusing on the relationships among the various intelligence principals and the president, he seriously passes over the enormous contributions of military as well as civilian and allied intelligence to the larger undertaking, and one is left with the narrow impression that American intelligence consisted largely of a number of self-serving clowns vying for Presidential favor.

The flaws inherent in a Federal Bureau of Investigation dominated by J. Edgar Hoover, and the lack of cooperation between the FBI and other major intelligence activities that continues today, are noted throughout the book.

Bottom line: worth buying and reading to gain insight into the challenges facing a President who can become isolated from reality by a corporate staff, but nowhere near the quality of Christopher Andrew's *For the President's Eyes Only*, or any of many good histories of espionage in World War II.

Rudgers, David F., *Creating the Secret State: The Origins of the Central Intelligence Agency, 1943-1947* (University Press of Kansas, 2000)

This is an admirable and unusual work, of doctoral-level quality in its sources and methods, while also reflecting the professional intelligence career status of the author. It complements Amy Zegart's broader book, *Flawed By Design*, in an excellent manner. This book, focusing as it does on the CIA alone, and on internal sources not readily available to Zegart, fills a major gap in our understanding of the CIA's origins.

The author excels at demonstrating both the actual as opposed to the mythical origins of the agency, and pays particular heed to the role of the Bureau of the Budget and that Bureau's biases and intentions. At the end of it all, the author notes that the agency was moving in controversial directions within four years of its birth, quickly disturbing Harry Truman, who is quoted as saying, twenty-years after the fact (in 1963), "For some time I have been distributed by the way CIA has been diverted from its original assignment. It has become an operational arm and at times a policy-making arm of Government....I never had any thought when I set up the CIA that it would be injected into peacetime cloak-and-dagger operations."

The author himself goes on to conclude that "the nature of the new threats and the revolution in information acquisition and dissemination have thrown traditional ways of intelligence organization, collection, evaluation, and distribution into question. ... CIA has entered the second half-century of its existence striving to avoid the fate of its OSS parent. In the process, it is groping for new missions and purposes while blighted by the legacy of its past derelictions, and while operating amid a rapidly changing global environment and technological revolution that are rendering its sources, methods, organizations, and mystique obsolete."

I would hasten to add, as my own book documents, that we will always have hidden evil in the world and will always needs spies and secret methods to some extent, but this book, combining academic rigor with insider access, must surely give the most intelligent of our policy, legislative, and intelligence managers pause, for it very carefully documents the possibility that 75% of what we are doing today with secret sources and methods need not and should not be done. This book has much to offer those who would learn from history.

Tapscott, Don, *The Digital Economy: Promise and Peril in the Age of Networked Intelligence* (McGraw Hill, 1996)

After demolishing Business Process Reengineering (BPR) as a necessary element of but insufficient substitute for corporate strategy, organizational learning, or reinvention, the author goes on to address twelve themes central to success in an economic environment characterized by networked intelligence: knowledge, digitization, virtualization, molecularization, integration/internetworking, disintermediation, convergence (a big one), innovation, prosumption, immediacy, globalization, and discordance (another big one). He stressed the need for "busting loose from the technology legacy", the need to dramatically transform both the information management and human resource management concepts and also a turning on its head of how government works-from centralized after the fact "leveling" and gross national security to decentralized, proactive nurturing of individual opportunity before the fact, providing individual security through individual opportunity and prosperity within the network.

Treverton, Gregory F., *Reshaping National Intelligence for an Age of Information* (Cambridge, 2001)

There are other books on intelligence reform--the best being those by Bruce Berkowitz and Allan Goodman and by Loch Johnson--but this book is very special because it is written by an insider who has come to grips with the imperative for change and who is able to articulate the case for change in a way that others have not. This is arguably the single best and most elegant presentation for why our $30 billion a year intelligence industry must be turned upside down and shift resources away from secret satellite technology and toward analysis, analytic tools, and access to open sources of information.

The author very correctly focuses on the fact that intelligence is about getting useful tailored information to the policy consumer, not about secrets per se. He is perhaps the best spokesperson for the view that the old paradigm--collecting secrets at great expense about a single enemy--must be replaced by the new paradigm--making sense of vast quantities of information that is not secret and covers a diversity of constantly changing targets. He correctly focuses on the selection and intelligent analysis of information rather than the collection of isolated secrets--on making the most of open information.

The book is rich with anecdotal examples and makes a compelling case for dismantling the current intelligence stovepipes while simultaneously dismantling the culture of secrecy that prevents the sharing of useful information, not just within the Nation (e.g. with state and local law enforcement) but with coalition government and non-government allies of the moment.

The author, a past Vice Chairman of the National Intelligence Council and a learned man with deep ties to Harvard, the Council on Foreign Relations, and RAND, concludes on a bitter-sweet note that demands Congressional and Presidential reflection. He firmly believes that both the intelligence community budget and as much intelligence analysis as possible should be made public and be in the public service. This book is highly recommended, and could-together with the other intelligence reform books published in the past two years--reasonably be used as the starting point for a complete make-over of the U.S. Intelligence Community.

Turner, Stansfield, *Secrecy and Democracy: The CIA in Transition* (Harper & Row, 1985)

Stansfield Turner was a Rhodes scholar and naval officer who rose to command of a carrier task group, a fleet, NATO's southern flank, and the Navy's most prestigious intellectual institution, the Naval War College. He served from 1977-1981 as Director of Central Intelligence under President Jimmy Carter, and his book in my mind was the first serious contribution-perhaps even a catalyst-to the growing debate over whether and how much reform is required if the U.S. Intelligence Community is to be effective in the 21st Century. His eleven-point agenda for reform is of lasting value, as are his ideas for intelligence support to those responsible for natural disaster relief and other non-military challenges:

1) Convince the IC that good oversight is essential to effective intelligence.
2) Improve analysis.
3) Broaden the analytic efforts beyond current events and Soviet military strength.
   a) What makes the Soviet Union tick?
   b) Secondary country analysis
   c) Economic analysis
   d) International threats
4) Separate the role of the DCI from that of the head of the CIA.
5) Merge the espionage and analytic branches of the CIA.
6) Strengthen the DCI's authority over the National Security Agency.
7) Help the Defense Intelligence Agency improve its analysis.
8) Take more effective precautions against leaks of intelligence information.
9) Enact a charter for the Intelligence Community.
10) Reduce the emphasis on covert action.
11) Depoliticize the role of the DCI.

Wheaton, Kristan J., *The Warning Solution: Intelligent Analysis in the Age of Information Overload* (AFCEA International Press, 2001)

I first heard Kris Wheaton lecture in Europe, and was just blown away by the deep understanding that he demonstrated of why commanders and CEOs are constantly missing the warnings their subordinates and forward scouts are sending back--the huge cost! Kosovo, for example, could have been a $1 billion a year problem if acted upon wisely and early, instead it became a $5 billion a year problem. I like this book very much because it makes his deep insights available to everybody in a very readable, well-illustrated, and concise book.

I strongly recommend this book because it offers the only thoughtful explanation I have ever seen on the conflict between the senior decision-maker's attention span (can only think about $50 billion problems) and the early warning that *is* available but cannot break through to the always over-burdened, sometimes arrogant, and rarely strategic top boss. In this regard, his book is a fine complement to the more historical work by Willard Matthias on *America's Strategic Blunders*.

This book also offers solutions. It is a book that should be required reading for all field grade officers in all military services, as well as state and local governors and majors, university and hospital and other non-profit heads, and of course the captains of industry who spend billions, often unwisely, because they have not established a scouting system that can be heard at the highest levels *in time*. America, among many other nations and organizations, has a habit of ignoring its iconoclasts and mavericks-- in an increasingly complex world where catastrophic combinations of failure are going to be more common, such ignorance will eventually become unaffordable and threatening to the national security as well as the national prosperity of those who persist in thinking about old problems in old ways.

There is one other aspect of this book that merits strong emphasis: it focuses on human understanding and human engagement with the world, and makes it clear that technology has almost nothing to do with how well we cope with the external environment that defines our future. There aren't five people in the US government, to take one example, that adequately understand the rich intellectual history of Islam nor the core difference between the Islamic emphasis on knowledge integration as the core value and the Christian emphasis on love as the core value. The author of this book is one of America's foremost authorities on the Balkan conflict and the deep importance of historical and cultural understanding as part of current political and operational competency--we need 1000 more intelligence professionals just like him. This book will inspire and provoke and is a great value for anyone who deals with the world at large.

Woodward, Bob, *MAESTRO: Greenspan's Fed and the American Boom* (Simon & Schuster, 2000)

I am quite taken with this book, which at 234 pages is "just right" and well crafted and edited to tell an important story. This is a story about applied intelligence in the finest sense of the word. It is a story about a man well-versed in traditional economic research, traditional models, traditional assumptions about the marketplace, who was put into the most important position in the global financial system at just the right time. His intuition allowed him to detect unexplained changes in productivity and to direct new lines of research that helped persuade more conventional authorities to follow his strategy.

This is also a story about a uniquely successful partnership between a Republican central banker and a Democratic President-the very heart of the story centers around Greenspan's ability to persuade a very smart President that deficit reduction was the critical ingredient for a long-term restoration of American prosperity. Aided by an equally smart Secretary of the Treasury, Rubin, it was the President's initiative to reduce the deficit by over $140 billion dollars that allowed all else to follow. There is a clear message here for those who would reduce taxes before finishing the job of eliminating the deficit.

As a professional intelligence officer, I am very very impressed by the author's recounting of how Greenspan actually "does" the job of intelligence collection and analysis at his level-the Central Intelligence Agency could learn a great deal from this man. The integration of constant (every fifteen minutes) monitoring of key indicators, the preparation of detailed research and statistics reports, and-by far the most important element-the continuous cycle of direct telephone calls and personal meetings across all sectors of the economy and around the globe, define what must be the most efficient and effective and valuable directed intelligence operation in the world-and one that does not steal the information it needs!

There are a number of observations throughout the book that are helpful at a strategic level:

1) deficit reduction is the single best thing any President can do-that enables the Fed to be effective;

316

2) we forget so quickly how desperate the American economy was in the late 1980's-in a volatile world it would be all too easy to enter a recession or have a major financial panic;

3) structured decision-making is extremely dependent on the models and the data-Greenspan's place in history is assured because he had the intellect and the patience and the gut instincts to realize that the data was incomplete or too aggregated and the modeling assumptions were dated and no longer sufficient to plot the course of the new economy;

4) the psychology of the marketplace is at least as important as the reality, and is likely to be hurt by loose-cannon White House elements with good intentions but out of bounds;

5) even the so-called best and brightest in any Presidential administration will categorize new ideas they do not understand as "incoherent if not idiotic", as Greenspan's emerging new ideas were labeled by the top Treasury economists;

6) the concept of wealth redistribution fails to understand that even if $1 trillion from the 225 richest people in the world were redistributed to the poorest of the earth, this would only give them $1 a day for a year-Greenspan's focus is on underlying structural changes and the advancement of capitalism such that wealth can be created for the poor on a sustained basis; and

7) there will always be wild cards, such as the Savings & Loan crisis, the LTCM (Long Term Capital Management) crisis, and the Mexico crisis, that require a financial management or central banking network able to capitalize on personal relationships and deep knowledge to find impromptu solutions. On the latter note, it makes one realize that in an increasingly volatile marketplace, there should probably be much stricter limits on "leveraged" actions, where the majority of the money for gambling on the stock market or in the bond market-as much as 95% of the money-is borrowed and therefore likely to be defaulted if the wrong bet is placed.

There is nothing in the book regarding any steps that Greenspan has taken or is considering in order to bring added stability to the marketplace. If I have one criticism of this otherwise superb book, a book that sheds light on many aspects of the Fed and its Chairman, it is that there is no hint here of what Greenspan has learned that might lead him to suggest legislative or regulatory changes intended to improve public transparency of key economic transactions, limitations on risk intended to prevent one rogue elephant (e.g. LTCM) from bringing down the market, and so on.

317

I would have liked to see a summation, even a two-page appendix, on the "before" and "after" economic models that Greenspan helped to change, and also some sense in the conclusion of what needs to be changed to keep future market crises within the bounds that can be managed by the Fed--Greenspan clearly has broad shoulders and a broad mind, but he can't carry the load forever and this book fails to focus on what changes are needed to institutionalize the Greenspan wisdom.

Zegart, Amy, *Flawed by Design: The Evolution of the CIA, JCS, and NSC* (Stanford, 2000)

This is a very worthy and thoughtful book. It breaks new ground in understanding the bureaucratic and political realities that surrounded the emergence of the National Security Council, the Joint Chiefs of Staff, and the Central Intelligence Agency. The CIA was weak by design, strongly opposed by the military services from the beginning. Its covert activities emerged as a Presidential prerogative, unopposed by others in part because it kept CIA from being effective at coordinated analysis, for which it had neither the power nor the talent.

Most usefully, the book presents a new institutionalist theory of bureaucracy that gives full weight to the original design, the political players including the bureaucrats themselves, and external events. Unlike domestic agencies that have strong interest groups, open information, legislative domain, and unconnected bureaucracies, the author finds that national security agencies, being characterized by weak interest groups, secrecy, executive domain, and connected bureaucracies, evolve differently from other bureaucracies, and are much harder to reform.

On balance, the author finds that intelligence per se, in contrast to defense or domestic issues, is simply not worth the time and Presidential political capital needed to fix but that if reform is in the air, the President should either pound on the table and put the full weight of their office behind a substantive reform proposal, or walk away from any reform at all-the middle road will not successful.

Reference

The Economist Pocket World in Figures 1999 (Wiley, 1998)

This is the best value for having global figures handy, and is one tenth the cost of the other great reference work, the *Fitzroy Dearborn Book of World Rankings*. Perhaps

318

even more to the point, this book has something the other one does not: country by country data (although one could always go to the *CIA World Factbook* online for similar data as well as biographic listings). Having said that, it does not have the full range of detail that is offered by the other, such as domestic water shortages and energy consumption. This book has Internet and music charts--but none of the charts are comprehensive, generally listing top and bottom countries, not all countries. Bottom line: this is the best value for a portable book about global figures relevant to political economy.

Fitzroy Dearborn Book of World Rankings (Fitzroy Dearborn, 1998)

Although this book does not have country by country, and it has not been "modernized" with a special section on the Internet, I could not do without it. While I recommend The *Economist Pocket World in Figures* as the best value (one-tenth the cost), I find that this...book is essential to any serious personal library. However, for what the book costs, I would like to see a web-based password-access database offered that would allow data extraction and chart creation. This book is superior to The Economist version in that it lists all countries for which data is available (generally 135-185), and it is a more diverse and well-presented collection of data.

Gessaman, Don, with Michael O'Bannon and Joseph Hezir, *Understanding the Budget of the United States Government* (The EOP Foundation, fifth edition, March 2001) ISBN 0-96582-1-9

This amazing little book is not listed on Amazon, which is a real shame, because it is one of the best guides, be it for citizens or officials, to the ins and outs of the U.S. federal budget process. In nineteen chapters, totaling 201 pages, the book methodically and elegantly covers budget concepts, revenue, taxes, spending, the rules, key players, the inter-play between the Administration and Congress on the three budgets in progress at any one time, and the basics of budget execution, the government performance and results act as well as the government-wide performance plan. The book concludes with chapters on the politics of the budget, governance, the regulatory process, the information collection budget and information technology management, opportunities, challenges, and terms (glossary).

It is my understanding that this book is used by Cabinet officers as a reference. It can be ordered by writing to the EOP Foundation at 819 7th Street, N.W., Washington, D.C. 20001, or by calling (202) 833-8940.

Keegan, John and Andrew Wheatcroft, *Zones of Conflict: An Atlas of Future War* (Simon & Schuster, 1986)

Zones of Conflict has not yet been surpassed by other published works, mostly because others focus on specific regions. This is still a valuable work, largely because of the process and the framework it provides for thinking about geographically and culturally based sources of conflict. Published in 1986, it missed some big ones: Somalia, Rwandi-Burundi, the Congo, the break-up of Yugoslavia with the Kosovo aftermath. We'll give them credit for the Gulf flashpoint. What's the point? No one can predict with any certainty where major humanitarian conflicts will emerge, but if one combines Keegan and Wheatcroft's approach with environmental and economic and social overlays (such as are offered by several other *State of the World* endeavors), then a useful starting point is available for asking two important questions: what kinds of conflicts will we be dealing with, under what kinds of terrain and cultural conditions; and second, given those realities, what kinds of forces and capabilities should we be developing? Against this model, the U.S. Joint 2020 vision falls woefully short, and the NATO alliance appears equally unprepared for a future that will be characterized by "dirty little wars" well out of NATO's area but highly relevant to the well-being of the NATO population. One might also make the somewhat puckish point that it does not take a $30 billion dollar a year spy community to create a common-sense strategic document such as this—it $20 (now out of print, 16 used copies are available at Amazon for between $5 and $7.50).

Pack, Thomas, *10 Minute Guide to Business Research on the Net* (Que McMillan, 1997)

The bottom line on this little book is that it merits buying and throwing in your suitcase if you are the kind of person that needs to do your own research from the road. In a nutshell, it is: 1) valuable because it brings together in one place a very easy to read and use guide to a wide range of Internet-based resources; 2) dangerous because it may tempt business managers to do their own research from a hotel room rather than rely on real information professionals; 3) incomplete in many ways--two obvious ones are its neglect of the meta-search engines such as Copernic and its oversights of the *Burwell Worldwide Directory of Information Brokers*; and 4) worth buying as a light-weight (double entendre intended) reference. I like it, it is worth the price and still relevant today.

320

Smith, Dan, *The State of the World Atlas* (Penguin, 1999)

This book, together with *The State of War and Peace*, is a desktop classic that would make an outstanding gift for any student of any age, and for any adult concerned about the state of the world we are leaving to our children. This is much more than a book of graphic generalizations; as a researcher myself I especially appreciate the specific identification of the sources that were consulted, and the summaries of each of the major political-legal, socio-economic, techno-demographic, ideo-cultural, and natural-geographic conditions threatening the stability of the "Whole Earth". I dare to think this book should be required reading for our elected representatives as well as our military commanders charged with "shaping" their regional environments.

The past editions Michael Kidron and Ronald Segal, both published by Simon & Schuster in 1981 and 1991, are still worth collecting as the specifics have changed over time and some useful differences remain.

Smith, Dan, *The State of War and Peace Atlas* (Penguin, 1997)

Together with the *State of the World Atlas*, this book ranks as one of the very best and most useful compilations of what I call "strategic generalizations", but with the very great added value of being presented in a graphical form that is easy to understand. As the international media becomes less and less useful as a means of appreciating how global conditions threaten our own internal security and prosperity, guide books like this one become all the more valuable to citizens and their elected representatives. This is an essential desk reference for every student striving to learn how to think, not just memorize, and for every adult who cares to understand just how unstable and diminishing is the world we are leaving to our children. The book is *not* out-of-date in 2000, but we would all benefit from a new edition coming out that might expand on the core value of the 1997 edition.

Strategy

Aaron, Henry J. and Robert D. Reischauer (eds.), *Setting National Priorities: The 2000 Election and Beyond* (Brookings, 1999)

The public policy overviews by Brookings are always among the best, and they are even more valuable this year when several think tanks appear to have defaulted on their traditional role in offering up reviews for consideration by the transition team. Across the various issue areas, including international, social, domestic, and governance policy domains, they present thoughtful recommendations.

Unfortunately, despite their deep understanding of the dilemmas facing the next President, the book does not provide the two things I would most like to have seen:

- one or two page "decision-papers" that set out the choices to be made within each issue area, and the specific budget costs and timelines for those choices; and

- a larger over-all budget choice document in no more than 2 pages that outlines what changes might be made in both the budget construction already underway in CY 2001 that the new President can influence, and the budget to be prepared from scratch in CY 2002 that should reflect the vital trade-offs as well as the vital plus-ups that need to be made in defense, intelligence, public health, and education, to name just my top four.

In defense and intelligence, my specific area of interest, I would have liked to see some specific recommendations, and their costs, for restoring the 450 ship Navy, creating the contingency and peacekeeping force as well as the humanitarian assistance and disaster relief forces, and some specifics on considerably reinforcing diplomatic, peace corps, and economic assistance operations including a Digital Marshall Plan. This is not to quarrel with findings and views of the authors, all of whom merit very serious consideration, but rather to note that the book does not go far enough, either in specific programmatic terms, or in politically useful presentation terms.

This is an excellent book, but it is also a classic example of unfettered brilliance-without the concise decision papers and the over-all budget numbers, this book will only be read by staffers, not by principals, and that is a shame, because on balance I think there is a great deal to be learned from each of the authors contributing to this work.

Abshire, David, *Preventing World War III: A Realistic Grand Strategy* (Harper & Row, 1988)

This book, apart from being the world's longest job description (for a Counselor to the President for Grand Strategy), remains a vibrant and provocative discussion relevant to guiding the Nation into the 21st Century. Part I discusses the "world theater" and Part II discusses in turn a grand strategy and then political, public, deterrence, negotiating, resources, technology, Third World, and economic strategies. The book ends with thoughts on organizing for strategy that should, because of who wrote them and how good they are, be required reading, in their twelve-page entirety, for the President and his entire Cabinet team.

Brzezinski, Zbigniew, *The Grand Chessboard: American Primacy and Its Geostrategic Imperatives* (Basic Books, 1997)

Anyone concerned with America's national security should be reading this book. The fact that it is four years old (older if one considers the intellectual gestation period), simply adds historical proof that its author is, as the Chinese have noted publicly, America's greatest strategist.

This book is written in plain English. That alone sets it apart from the next level down. This is a carefully presented essay that makes eminent sense. It deals with the most important region in the world: the troubled Eurasian land mass. Rich in resources, rife with ethnic conflict and water scarcity issues, it is surrounded by major powers with global ambitions: France and Germany to the West, Russia to the North, China to East, and Iran and Turkey to the South. A number of clearly presented maps add considerable value to the book.

With a level of calm and reason that is rare in books of this sort, Brzezinski provides an understandable yet sophisticated articulation of a real-world "grand strategy" essential to the future of America in this new century. His strategic vision honors both France and Germany as co-equal and vital elements of a new European community; shows how the larger Europe (ultimately co-equal to America) is essential to the salvation of Russia; makes the case for an American-Chinese strategic accommodation as the anchor for America's involvement in Eurasia; carefully integrates America's direct and special relations with Japan, Korea, and India as the bowl beneath China and Eurasia, and then concludes with decisive evaluations of the future importance of drawing Turkey into the European community while encouraging Iranian-Turkish collaboration and Iranian commercial and commodities channels from Eurasia out to the world. In passing, the author validates Australia's new strategy of working closely with Indonesia to resolve the latter's many ethnic issues while establishing a southern line against excessive Chinese influence in the region.

There are numerous subtle and deep insights throughout the book, from the observation that war may now be a luxury only the poorest of nations can afford, to why China should consider America its natural ally and why Russia is at risk of becoming genetically Asian instead of European within a generation or two. The author proposes a new Trans-Eurasian Security System (TESS) that engages Russia, China, Japan and America-one would assume that at some point Turkey, Iran, and the new Europe would be included. The author gores a number a sacred oxen, including those associated with the demonization of Iran (this should end) and the exaggeration of China as a global threat (it will at best be a regional super-power at the high end of Third World per capita earnings). While other poor Nations have defeated America decisively (Viet-Nam, for example), the author deliberately itemizes China's 3 million men under arms, it's 9,400 tanks and 5,224 fighters, as well as its 57 surface ships and 53 submarines, and offers his final judgment that China and America have too many common interests to permit a demonization of China to become a self-fulfilling prophecy, as it might if China were confronted across the board and denied its reasonable historical claim to having influence over the region that hosts the "Middle Kingdom."

A special note is in order about the importance of this book as an antidote to two viral infections now afflicting many otherwise excellent thinkers. This book is a marvelous, deeply grounded treatment of the historical constancy of strategy qua "enduring interests" and grand players-as much as one may wish to speculate about the globalization and localization of international politics, Brzezinski puts it all in a grand strategic context that is compelling in its logic as well as its understanding of the deep cultural threads that we must weave together if we are to survive one another's less enlightened machinations. Another strength of the book is its avoidance of the technophilia that has corrupted strategic thinking at the highest levels. The Revolution in Military Affairs and the "systems of systems", while well-intentioned, are both devoid of serious strategic reasoning-as Colin Gray among others have pointed out, technology is not strategy, nor does it follow that strong technology will defeat an enemy with weak technology but a stronger strategic culture and the ability to wage war by means other than force on force.

This book, together with Colin Gray's *Modern Strategy*, Robert Young Pelton's *World's Most Dangerous Places*, the two books by Robert Kaplan on his travels in the Eurasian region, and both Michael Klare's book on *Resource Wars* as well as Marq de Villier's book on *Water: The Fate of Our Most Precious Resource*, will make any intelligent person as conversant as they need to be with the most pressing geopolitical issues of our time. If one adds Joe Thornton's book on *Pandora's Poison*, David Helvarg's book on *Blue Frontier: Saving America's Living Seas*, Laurie Garrett's *book Betrayal of Trust: The Collapse of Global Public Health,* and William Shawcross *on Deliver Us From Evil: Peacekeepers, Warlords, and a World of Endless Conflict,* the lesser but still vital long-term issues of the environment, public health, and ethnic conflict will be fully appreciated.

I mention all these books deliberately, to make the point that it is Brzezinski's book that is both the foundation and the capstone for integrating the analysis from these other diverse renditions into a grand strategy. No one else has done it. He is America's foremost strategist and likely to remain so for some time to come.

Carter, Ashton B. and William J. Perry, *Preventive Defense: A New Security Strategy for America* (Brookings, 1999)

The authors provide a coherent discussion of fully half of the security challenges facing us in the 21st century. They wisely avoid the debate swirling around the so-called Revolution in Military Affairs (RMA)-but deserve credit for their predecessor "offset strategy"-and simply note that the absence of "A List" threats gives us an opportunity to strengthen and maintain our traditional nuclear and conventional capabilities against the day when a Russia or China may rise in hostility against us. The book as a whole focuses on the "B List" threats, including Russia in chaos, a hostile China acting aggressively within its region, proliferation of weapons of mass destruction, and catastrophic terrorism. They note, correctly, that most of the spending and effort today is focused on responding to the crisis *de jure*, some but not enough resources are applied to preparing for the future, and virtually nothing is being done against the latest concept, that of "shaping" the environment through "forward engagement." Perhaps most importantly, they introduce the term "defense by other means" and comment on the obstacles, both within the Administration and on the Hill, to getting support and funding for non-military activities with profound security benefits.

Although others may focus on their discussion of Russia and NATO as the core of the book, what I found most helpful and worthwhile was the straight-forward and thoughtful discussion of the need for a new national strategy, a new paradigm, for dealing with potentially catastrophic terrorism. Their understanding of what defense resources can be applied, and of the impediments to success that exist today between state & local law enforcement, federal capabilities such as the Federal Bureau of Investigation (FBI) and the Federal Emergency Management Agency (FEMA) and defense as well as overseas diplomatic and intelligence capabilities, inspire them to propose several innovative approaches to this challenge. The legal and budgetary implications of their proposals are daunting but essential-their proposals for dealing with this one challenge would be helpful in restructuring the entire U.S. government to better integrate political-diplomatic-military-law enforcement operations with judicial and congressional oversight as well as truly all-source intelligence support.

Interesting side notes include 1) the early discovery in US-Russian military discussions that technology interoperability and future collaboration required the surmounting of many obstacles associated with decades of isolated (and often secret) development; 2) the absence of intelligence from the entire book-by this account, US defense leaders spend virtually all of their time in direct operational discussions with their most important counterparts, and there is very little day to day attention to strategic analysis, estimative intelligence, or coordination with diplomatic, economic, and law enforcement counterparts at home; 3) the difficulty of finding a carrier to send to Taiwan at a time when we had 12 carriers-only four appear to have been "real" for defense purposes; and 4) the notable absence of Australia from the discussion of security in Asia.

The concept of Preventive Defense is holistic (requiring the simultaneous uses of other aspects of national power including diplomacy and economic assistance) but places the Department of Defense in a central role as the provider of realigned resources, military-to-military contacts, and logistics support to actual implementation. Unfortunately the concept of Preventive Defense has been narrowly focused (its greatest success has been the dismantling of former Soviet nuclear weapons in the Commonwealth of Independent States), and neither the joint staff nor the services are willing to give up funds for weapons and manpower in order to make a strategy of Preventive Defense possible.

This resistance bodes ill for the other half of the 21st Century security challenge, what the author's call the "C List"-the Rwandas, Somalias, Haitis and Indonesias. They themselves are unwilling to acknowledge C List threats as being vital to U.S. security in the long-term (as AIDS is now recognized). I would, however, agree with them on one important point: the current budget for defense should be repurposed toward readiness, preparing for the future, and their concept of preventive defense, and it should not be frittered away on "C List" contingencies-new funds must be found to create and sustain America's Preventive Diplomacy and its Operations Other Than War (OOTW) capabilities.

It will fall to someone else to integrate their concept of Preventive Defense with the emerging concepts of Preventive Diplomacy, International Tribunals, and a 21st Century Marshall Plan for the festering zones of conflict in Africa, Arabia, Asia, and the Americas—zones where ethnic fault lines, criminal gangs, border disputes, and shortages of water, food, energy, and medicine all come together to create a breeding ground for modern plagues that will surely come across our water's edge in the future.

On balance, through, this book makes the top grade for serious bi-partisan dialogue, and they deserve a lot of credit for defining solutions for the first half of our security challenges in the 21st Century.

Cimbala, Stephen J., *Clausewitz and Chaos: Friction in War and Military Policy* (Praeger, 2001)

The author, and this book, may well be among the strongest elements of what I perceive to be a growing backlash against the prevalent technophelia characteristic of the military-industrial complex that President and General Eisenhower warned us against--a technophelia that advocates a "system of systems" with no provision for strategy, doctrine, or intelligence; and a Revolution in Military Affairs (RMA) that looks to micro-UAVs (unmanned aerial vehicles) and robotic ants as the primary means for defeating any enemy. We will simply assume every enemy will conveniently expose themselves to the narrow range of capabilities that we have devised at great expense!

The author provides as good a review of "friction" in war and in policy as one could hope for. Although sometimes tedious and not always easy to follow, this book is a must for any serious scholar of future conflicts between states, nations, and organizations. Above all, this book is a giant compressed Castor Oil pill for the techno-meisters so eager to believe they can shape a world where our money and our technology can overcome every obstacle and every opponent.

A few highlights intended to recommend the purchase of this book and its digestion:

1) Friction is not receiving the attention it merits from modern social scientists, including all those on the Department of Defense payroll. We still conceptualize our capabilities along techno-rational lines instead of human-normal chaos lines.

2) It is the combination of thoughtful doctrine, individual and unit discipline, initiative at all levels, and good intelligence (individual, organic, and external) that leads to victory through the reduction of friction--what General Alfred M. Gray, former Commandant of the Marine Corps institutionalized with his concept of "commander's intent" on top of training for war with the assumption that communications and computing *will* collapse in the heat of battle.

3) Although very brief in his coverage of intelligence per se, the author is helpful in reviewing Clausewitz's top eight sources of friction, the first three of which deal with information: insufficient knowledge of the enemy; unreliable information from patrols and spies; and uncertain knowledge of our own capabilities and dispositions. The author administers the *coup de grace* to technophiles with some elegant quotes from these worthies claiming that the new world of satellite intelligence is taking us to a non-Clauswitzian world where friction can be overcome by "information superiority"--these are the same folks that cannot find Bin Laden and had to invade Panama in order to capture Noriega--the same folks that let a warlord in Somalia run amok and let a small crowd chase away a U.S. Navy ship of war from docking in Haiti...the same folks that ignore 18 distinct genocide campaigns on-going today, with all that implies in terms of forced migration and epidemic disease and failed states and rampant destabilizing crime.

4) The author's review of groupthink (Janis) and how this leads to policy fiascos is very worthwhile, not only because it is acutely relevant to how we are making decisions today in defense, energy, health, and fiscal policy, but because it highlights so clearly the dangers that come from a leadership that thinks it is invulnerable, morally superior, self-censored, sharing illusions of unanimity, subject to stereotyped visions of the world, and--worst of all--protected from reality by self appointed "mind guards" who put direct pressure on "deviant" naysayers (or dump them from the team).

6) The author is one of the few to focus on the impact of friction on what Clausewitz calls the ultimate disconnect, that between ends and means in war. As America prepares to rethink its military force structure, it is especially appropriate to note that we are planning to downsize the conventional forces while investing heavily in electronic capabilities, at the same time that the most advanced thinkers have moved beyond asymmetric war to non-traditional soft power including major emphasis on disease control, water preservation, transnational law enforcement, and major diplomatic and economic assistance options. Looking at today's situation through the author's eyes and this book, one can see that we do not have a strategy; we don't even try to understand what everyone else's strategy might be; and we are completely ignoring the need to fully integrate home front and overseas defense, foreign affairs, and trade strategy and capabilities management.

Over the course of 7 chapters, the author reviews friction both at the policy/acquisition level and the operational level of command, in relation to irrelevant and inflexible war plans; nuclear crisis management; within Desert Storm; in small wars, "faux wars" and peace operations; in modern deterrence; and in relation to mass destruction and information warfare paradigms. In the latter instance, he is acutely sensitive to the teachings of Dr. Steve Blank, that one man's information "warning" attack is another man's signal for "total war"--witness Russian doctrine that considers a C4I attack to be fundamental and requiring an immediate "dead hand" retaliatory attack.

The author concludes the book with a review of simple, compound, and complex friction in policy and operations, with examples, and for this section alone the book merits inclusion in any serious library concerned with international security.

Gray, Colin S., *Modern Strategy* (Oxford, 1999)

First published in 1999, this is an original *tour d' horizon* that is essential to any discussion of the theory and practice of conflict in the 21st Century, to include all those discussions of the alleged Revolution in Military Affairs (RMA), the need for "defense transformation", and the changing nature of civil-military relations.

328

I am much impressed by this book and the decades of thinking that have gone into it, and will outline below a few of its many signal contributions to the rather important questions of how one must devise and manage national power in an increasingly complex world.

First, the author is quite clear on the point that technology does not a revolution make-nor can technology dominate a national strategy. If anything-and he cites Luttwak, among others, with great regard-an excessive emphasis on technology will be very expensive, susceptible to asymmetric attack, and subversive of other elements of the national strategy that must be managed in harmony. People matter most.

Second, and this is the point that hit me hardest, it is clear that security strategy requires a holistic approach and the rather renaissance capability of managing a multiplicity of capabilities-diplomatic, economic, cultural, military, psychological, information-in a balanced manner and under the over-arching umbrella of a strategy.

Third, and consistent with the second, "war proper" is not exclusively about force of arms, but rather about achieving the national political objective by imposing one's will on another. Those that would skew their net assessments and force structure capabilities toward "real war" writ in their conventional terms are demeaning Clausewitz rather than honoring him.

Fourth, as I contemplate in this and other readings how best to achieve lasting peace and prosperity, I see implicit in all that the author puts forward, but especially in a quote from Donald Kegan, the raw fact that it is not enough for America to have a preponderance of the traditional military and economic power in the world-we must also accept the burden and responsibility of preserving the peace and responding to the complex emergencies around the globe that must inevitably undermine our stability and prosperity at home.

Fifth, it is noteworthy that of all the dimensions of strategy that are brought forward, one—time--is unique for being unimprovable. Use it or lose it. Time is a strategic dimension too little understood and consequently too little valued by Americans in particular and the Western alliance in general.

Sixth, it merits comment that the author, perhaps the greatest authority on Clausewitz in this era, clarifies the fact that the "trinity" is less about people, government, and an army, than about primordial violence, hatred, and enmity (the people); chance and probability on the battlefield, most akin to a game of cards (the army); and instrumental rationality (the government)-and that these are not fixed isolated elements, but interpenetrate one another and interact in changing ways over time and space.

329

Seventh, the author devotes an entire chapter to "Strategic Culture as Context" and this is most helpful, particularly in so far as it brings forward the weakness of the American strategic culture, notably a pre-disposition to isolationism and to technical solutions in the abstract. Perhaps more importantly, a good strategic culture with inferior weapons can defeat a weak strategic culture with an abundance of technology and economic power.

Eighth, and finally, the author courageously takes on the issue of small wars and other savage violence, seeking to demonstrate that grand strategy applies equally well to the savage criminal and warlord parasites that Ralph Peters has noted are not susceptible to our traditional legal and military conventions. While he does not succeed (and notes in passing that Clausewitz's own largest weakness was a failure to catalogue the enemy and the dialog with the enemy as a major factor in strategic success and failure), the coverage is acceptable in making three key points:

1) small wars and sub-national conflicts are generally not resolved decisively at the irregular level-conventional forces are required at some point;

2) special operations forces have a role to play but lack a strategic context (that is to say, current political and military leaders have no appreciation for the strategic value of special operations forces); and

3) small wars and non-traditional threats-asymmetrical threats-must be taken seriously and co-equally with symmetrical regular conflicts.

At the end of the day, this erudite scholar finds common cause with gutter warrior Ralph Peters and gang-warfare iconoclast Martin Van Creveld by concluding his book with a quote from Alexander Solzhenitsyn: "In the Computer Age we will live by the law of the Stone Age: the man with the bigger club is right. But we pretend this isn't so. We don't notice or even suspect it-why surely our morality progresses together with our civilization."

Howard, Michael, *The Invention of Peace* (Yale, 2000)

This is an essay with deep insights, but it is not a portal to other knowledge as it lacks any notes or bibliography. The author is one of our top strategists, historians, and teachers of war and peace.

The settlement of disputes among groups whose grievances are so great they are willing to die rather than accept impositions from others, are a fact of life. As 11 September has shown us, we are vulnerable to unconventional attacks against civilians, within our own borders--this book is relevant and readable.

The core idea is that only organized nation-states that can command the loyalty and obedience of their citizens, are capable of preventing war and championing peace. The concepts of corporate peace and non-governmental peace are explicitly disavowed.

Legitimization and brutality are recurring themes in history--peace among nations occurs when mutual respect or fear legitimize the status quo, and incredible brutalities, including routine massacres of "infidel" civilians, occur when states fail to control themselves or their populations.

A major disruptive factor in today's world is the combination of educated but unemployed masses within the Arabian and Islamic nations, and the globalization of communications--but it is a one-way globalization, firehosing the Muslims with corporate consumerist visions and impositions, while a Muslim Press Service has yet to form. Individual states--one could suggest that the United States is among them-- failing to nurture a clear definition of citizenship, and the requisite loyalties--are destined to suffer internal fragmentation and external attack.

Strong militaries are needed to win wars, but overt military intervention is not the route to a sustainable peace in today's complex environment--only diplomacy, cultural outreach, and mutually agreed consensus can create and sustain peace....this is the simple yet brutal message of this book, one our leaders have yet to grasp.

Kagan, Donald and Frederick W. Kagan, *While America Sleeps: Self-Delusion, Military Weakness, and the Threat to Peace Today* (St. Martin's Press, 2000)

Two proven historians, a father-son team, draw stark comparisons between the post World War I period in which Britain took a gigantic "peace dividend" and allows its national defenses to crumble, and the post Cold War period in which America has done the same. Those who trust the Kagan's analysis-as does the distinguished Colin Gray, master of strategic thinking-may skip the first half of the book and go directly to the second half focusing on the American experience.

This is not, as some might claim, an ideological treatise. It is firmly grounded in history and the authors strive to present a balanced reasonable theme. I believe they succeed. Even for those steeped in the literature of the American military, there are new lessons in this book. Perhaps the three most important lessons are these: 1) regional threats can become global threats without sufficient warning such as is necessary to reconstitute

331

global defenses; 2) successful diplomacy is best founded on the immediate availability of armed force that can be projected to any point on the globe with great credibility; 3) national security, unlike domestic policies, is not something to be achieved by consensus-this is where the President earns their keep, by guiding and forging a consensus in the absence of domestic constituencies for spending on external affairs and external security.

Especially gripping for anyone who anticipates a future in which Dick Cheney and Colin Powell have something to say about our national security, is the authors' analysis of their strategic decisions following the Cold War. Both Cheney and Powell get very high marks for understanding that global strength is a pre-requisite for stability and security. The Powell vision for a Base Force with Atlantic, Pacific, Strategic, and Contingency force elements is categorized as brilliant. Powell does, however, get very low marks for being consistently unwilling to use force to impose order in the absence of clear objectives-the authors are very clear in calling the Weinberger Doctrine (setting conditions under which force may be used) completely out of date and at odds with today's needs. Both President Bush and Chairman Powell are severely castigated for having ended the Gulf War too soon and without a decisive result-the author's compare this to the similarly indecisive outcome of World War I, an outcome that left the aggressors strong enough to come back and fight another day.

The authors then go on to systematically review a series of major foreign policy and defense failures in the Clinton administration, an Administration characterized by a consistent failure to understand and address the mismatch between wandering and vacillating foreign policies and attendant commitments, and the real-world capabilities of a declining military force. Especially dangerous, in the authors' view, was the Bottom Up Review approach that abandoned the Cheney-Powell appreciation for maintaining sufficient force to deter two regional surprise attacks (Russia and Iraq on one side, China and North Korea on the other), and instead adopted the premise that 6 months warning would be available, that reconstitution of both the force and its industrial base was possible, and that forces could be justified only in terms of existing threats, most of them from non-state actors. Bosnia, Somalia, Haiti, Iraq inspections, North Korea inspections, these are all reviewed and all are found to have left America with a legacy of half measures. "By trying to ignore the problem, to leave it to others, whether the UN or NATO, by declaring it to be of no vital interest to the United States, by refusing to use any force once involved and then to use adequate force once committed, they [Bush Sr. and Clinton] found themselves making the very mistakes that brought defeat and disaster in Vietnam, the fear of which had played so great a role, first in their failure to act and then in their inadequate response."

In their conclusion, the authors find that the next Administration will assume responsibility at a time when the rest of the world has learned, from the past eight years, that America is not willing to summon the forces to defeat aggression; that developing weapons of mass destruction is the fastest means to elicit billion dollar bribes from America; that ethnic cleansing and politically driven mass starvation will not inspire intervention by America. "The most likely American response will be neglect, at first, followed by some attempt at negotiation. If, at last, driven to action, the Americans attack, it will be from the air, employing limited rules of engagement, and it will not destroy the aggressor. Ground forces will almost certainly not be used until the aggressor himself invites them in as part of a negotiation that gives him [the aggressor] most of what he wants. Above all, he should be sure to develop weapons of mass destruction. Even the hint of such a program in a threatening country will bring high-level American officials on top-secret missions to bribe its leaders to abandon the program. They will probably be able to keep the bribe and to pursue the programs they like, as well. These are the lessons America has given the world in the past eight years..."

The book closes by concluding that the strategic pause is gone and it is almost too late. Forces have declined severely (one can only lament the ill-considered Navy program for decommissioning destroyers and frigates that, once decommissioned, are almost impossible to resurrect), coalitions and alliances are in disarray, and non-state actors have learned how to play on the naiveté of the U.S. Government. America's responsibilities for global stability and security are "inescapable", and the next President must make the necessary commitments and be materially and morally ready to meet them.

Kagan, Robert and William Kristol (eds.), *Present Dangers: Crisis and Opportunity in American Foreign and Defense Policy* (Encounter, 2000)

This is a very worthy book, and should be much much higher in the popular sales ranking. I bought this book at the same time that I bought the more historically grounded *While America Sleeps*, and could not have asked for a better companion volume. Finally, I understand the forces that are tearing George W. Bush in two-on the one side, the conservative isolationists, who believe that we must reject internationalism in all forms, and eschew intervention or "911 missions" at all costs-and on the other side, the conservative internationalists, who by this excellent account have both a pragmatic and realistic grasp of the lessons of history, of the shrinking globe that we find in the present, and of the speed with which "regional" threats can become global challenges.

The two introductory contributions, one on the national interest and global responsibility, the other on the differences between conservative isolationists and conservative internationalists and all others, are extraordinarily essential readings for anyone who hopes to understand the early days-and contradictory signals-of the next Administration. Individual chapters by very well-qualified experts cover the conservative internationalist view of China, Russia, Iraq, Iran, North Korea, Europe and NATO, Asian Allies, and Israel. More general chapters address the decline of America's armed forces and the strategic case for dealing with weapons proliferation. The book concludes with three truly essential readings for any citizen, student, businessman, bureaucrat, or policymaker: on morality and foreign policy by William Bennett, on statesmanship in the new century by Paul Wolfowitz, and on strength and will in historical perspective by Donald Kagan.

Well-footnoted and indexed, this is a very serious professional contribution to the rather lackluster national discussion about where our national security and foreign policy should be going. As one who previously advocated a change from 2+ major regional conflicts (MRC) to 1 MRC and three separate forces for dealing with crime, environmental and cultural movements, and electronic and economic warfare (1+iii), I am now fully persuaded, mostly by the Kagan's book *While America Sleeps* but also by this book, that we should go toward a 2+iii national security strategy.

My one concern about this book is that it completely ignores what is quaintly called Program 150--all that State Department, Peace Corps, Agency for International Development stuff. It also mentions intelligence and counterintelligence only in passing. Conservative internationalists clearly have the brain power and the strategic vision and the historical understanding to be vital protectors of America's interests, but they must expand their vision to go beyond guns and consider the potential contributions of both diplomatic and economic butter, and applied intelligence. There is in fact a need to have a very strong Presidential program that fully advances, in an integrated fashion, American investments in diplomacy, defense, transnational crime fighting, economic assistance including a Digital Marshall Plan, and cultural exchanges worthy of a great Nation. This book lacks an appreciation for all the "soft" stuff, but it covers three of the four bases very nicely. A "strong buy."

Kupchan, Charles A., *The Vulnerability of Empire* (Cornell, 1994)

This book is extremely relevant to the forthcoming 2001 debate over alternative national security strategies. The author studies a number of cases of "adjustment failure" where great powers, at the height of their strength, engaged in self-defeating behavior—either overly cooperative behavior that resulted in strategic exposure, or overly competitive behavior that resulted in self-encirclement or over-extension.

334

The author pays special attention to the inter-relationship between economic versus military resources (means) and international commitments (ends). Strategic culture is defined and discussed in an integrative fashion, in relation to the three levels of analysis (system, state, and individual), and is found to be the critical factor that constrains elites by trapping them in a strategic paradigm of their own making-one used to justify major expenditures that are now counterproductive, but whose abandonment would exact too high a domestic political price if reversed (such as a Revolution in Military Affairs?)

The author finds that strategic culture, unlike individual strategic beliefs, is resistant to incoming information and to change. States that are in decline and states that are rising tend to fall prey to "adjustment failure" and consequently to present other states with instability issues. In both cases elites tend to utilize national propaganda and education to inculcate a mass understanding that may support their intermediate objectives but ultimately frustrates strategic adjustment when they realize that what they are doing is only increasing their vulnerability.

Most interestingly for the United States of America, the author finds that it is only when a state is truly in a position of strength, that it can best recognize and adapt to radical changes in the external environment—in other words, now is the time to dump the 2+ Major Theater War strategy and adopt a competing strategy that more properly integrates economic and military means to achieve our national security ends. The author concludes with several specific prescriptions that are clearly pertinent to forthcoming Presidential and Congressional decisions at the dawn of the 21st Century and that must be appreciated if we are to have an effective national security policy in the next decade or two.

- First, the author is at one with Donald Kegan and Colin Gray in noting that the dissolution of the Soviet Union does not mean the end of U.S. strategic responsibilities in Europe;

- second, that at a time when there are many rising states emerging from the dissolution of the Soviet Union (as well as the fragmentation of larger states elsewhere) it is vital that these states be buffered against economic shock so as to avoid the instability conducive to the rise of aggressor governments;

- third, that there must be deliberate international programs in place to suppress or eliminate domestic pathologies that lead to aggressive behavior, and these must be progressively strong, beginning with economic assistance to eliminate the root causes of the instability; to sanctions and information operations as well as military preparations; and finally to outright military intervention with overwhelming force.

The author explicitly notes that the international community must exercise great care to identify and decisively stop emerging aggressors before they can become full-blown aggressor states--history as documented in the case studies contained in the book suggests that when confronted by a full-blown aggressor state, members of the international community will tend toward strategic accommodations policies and tolerance of aggression rather than the decisive interventionist action easiest to adopt at an earlier stage.

Finally, the author offers a prescription for avoiding surprise and confrontation, recommending that some form of international body be used to monitor and sanction any use of nationalist propaganda (such as generally precedes genocidal campaigns), and that this monitoring range from normal public sources down to educational materials used in the schools as well as government archives. By intention, the book focuses only on Europe and only on relations between states—there is much that could be done to broaden these useful insights to inform our strategy toward Asia, the Third World, specific failed states and "states of concern", and non-state groups.

Trade-Offs (Instruments of National Power)

Friedman, George and Meridith, *The Future of War: Power, Technology, and American World Dominance in the 21st Century* (St. Martin's, 1998)

The authors begin by noting that there is "a deep chasm between the advent of technology and its full implementation in doctrine and strategy." In their history of failure they note how conventional wisdom always seems to appreciate the systems that won the past wars, and observes that in the U.S. military there is a long history of transferring power from the political and military leadership to the technical and acquisition managers, all of whom have no real understanding of the current and future needs of the men who will actually fight.

They address America's vulnerability in both U.S.-based logistics and in overseas transport means.

> *"Destroying even a portion of American supply vessels could so disrupt the tempo of a logistical build-up as to delay offensive operations indefinitely."*

They have a marvelous section on the weaknesses of U.S. data gathering tools, noting for example that satellites provide only a static picture of one very small portion of the battlefield, rather that the wide-area and dynamic "situational awareness" that everyone agrees is necessary.

They go on to gore other sacred oxen, including the Navy's giant ships such as the carrier (and implicitly the new Landing Platform Helicopters (LPH) for Marines as well as the ill-conceived arsenal ship) and the largest of the aircraft proposed by the Air Force.

They ultimately conclude that the future of war demands manned space stations that are able to integrate total views of the world with control of intercontinental precision systems, combined with a complete restructuring of the ground forces (most of which will be employed at the squad level) and a substantial restructuring of our naval force to provide for many small fast platforms able to swarm into coastal areas.

Goure, Daniel and Jeffrey M. Ranney, *Averting the Defense Train Wreck in the New Millenium* (CSIS, 1999)

The authors provide compelling evidence of a forthcoming "train wreck" in U.S. defensive capabilities, and make an excellent case for increasing the defense budget by $60-100B a year for a mixture of preserving readiness; acquiring mid-term capabilities needed to replace a 20-30 year old mobility, weapons, and communications base force; and implementing the Revolution in Military Affairs (RMA).

This is a well-documented and heavily fact-laden book-the authors as individuals and the case they make in general terms-must be heeded by the next President and the next Congress.

Where the book does not go, and a companion book by the same authors would be of great value, is into the detail of WHAT threat, WHAT force structure. They accept, for example, the Navy's 304-ship Navy that keeps adding gigantic carriers and does nothing for littoral warfare or putting Marines within 24 hours of any country instead of 6 days. Similarly, they accept Air Force emphasis on fewer and fewer bigger and more sophisticated platforms of dubious utility in a 21st Century environment that requires long loiter, ranges of several hundred nautical miles without refueling, full lift in hot humid weather, and survivability in the face of electromagnetic weapons in the hands of thugs.

This book demonstrates a clear mastery of defense economics, and it is an important contribution to the bottom line: our national defense is desperately underfunded, and this must be in the "top three" issues facing the 43rd President and the 107th Congress. What we buy, and why, has not yet been answered to my satisfaction.

Know, MacGregor and Williamson Murray, *The Dynamics of Military Revolution: 1300-2050* (Cambridge, 2001)

This is the only serious book I have been able to find that addresses revolutions in military affairs with useful case studies, a specific focus on whether asymmetric advantages do or do not result, and a very satisfactory executive conclusion. This book is strongly recommended for both military professionals, and the executive and congressional authorities who persist in sharing the fiction that technology is of itself an asymmetric advantage.

It merits emphasis that the author's first conclusion, spanning a diversity of case studies, is that technology may be a catalyst but it rarely drives a revolution in military affairs-- concepts are revolutionary, it is ideas that break-out of the box.

Their second conclusion is both counter-intuitive (but based on case studies) and in perfect alignment with Peter Drucker's conclusions on successful entrepreneurship: the best revolutions are incremental (evolutionary) and based on solutions to actual opponents and actual conditions, rather than hypothetical and delusional scenarios of what we think the future will bring us. In this the authors mesh well with Andrew Gordon's masterpiece on the rules of the game and Jutland: we may be best drawing down on our investments in peacetime, emphasizing the education of our future warfighters, and then be prepared for massive rapid agile investments in scaling up experimental initiatives as they prove successful in actual battle.

The book is noteworthy for its assault on fictional scenarios and its emphasis on realism in planning--especially valuable is the authors' staunch insistence that only honesty, open discussion among all ranks, and the wide dissemination of lessons learned, will lead to improvements.

Finally, the authors are in whole-hearted agreement with Colin Gray, author of *Modern Strategy*, in stating out-right that revolutions in military affairs are not a substitute for strategy as so often assumed by utopian planners, but merely an operational or tactical means.

This is a brilliant, carefully documented work that should scare the daylights out of every taxpayer--it is nothing short of an indictment of our entire current approach to military spending and organization. As the author's quaintly note in their understated way, in the last paragraph of the book, "the present trend is far from promising, as the

American government and armed forces procure enormous arsenals only distantly related to specific strategic needs and operational and tactical employment concepts, while continu[ing], in the immortal words of Kiffin Rockwell, a pilot in the legendary First World War Lafayette Escadrille, to 'fly along, blissfully ignorant, hoping for the best.'"

Lest the above be greeted with some skepticism, let us note the 26 October 2001 award of $200 billion to Lockheed for the new Joint Strike Fighter calls into serious question whether the leadership in the Pentagon understands the real world--the real world conflicts of today--all 282 of them (counting 178 internal conflicts) will require the Joint Strike Fighter only 10% of the time--the other 90% of our challenges demand capabilities and insights the Pentagon is not only not capable of fielding, it simply refuses to consider them to be "real war." Omar Bin Laden beat the Pentagon on 11 September 2001, and he (and others who follow in his footsteps) will continue to do so until we find a military leadership that can lead a real-world revolution in military affairs.... rather than a continuing fantasy in which the military-industrial complex lives on regardless of how many homeland attacks we suffer.

Oakley, Robert B., Michael J. Dziedzic and Eliot M. Goldberg (eds.), *Policing the New World Disorder: Peace Operations and Public Security* (National Defense University Press, 1998

In considerable detail, with substantial commonality between a number of case studies, this book examines the traditional public security (police, internal order) function in relation to failed states and external interventions. This is not a book about the larger issue of when and how to intervene in the internal affairs of states beset by internal conflict and it is not a book about the actual conditions around the world that require some form of imposed or reinforced public order. Rather, it is the most detailed book one could hope for on the need for an international law enforcement reserve that is capable of rapidly filling the gap in local public police services that occurs when the indigenous capability collapses and traditional military forces arrive unprepared to meet this need.

All of the case studies are world-class, with primary source detail unlike any normally seen in the literature. All agree that this is a "force structure" issue that no government and certainly not the United Nations, has mastered, but most give due credit to UN civilian police operations for being the best available model upon which to build a future capability.

The summary of conclusions by Ambassador Oakley and Colonel Professor Dziedzic are alone worth the price of the book. If the Cold War era might be said to have revolved around early perceptions of a "missile gap", the 21st Century with its Operations Other Than War (OOTW) could reasonably be said to have two issues: first, the natural conditions such as depleted water resources, which is not the book's focus, and the "globo-cop gap", which is.

The book documents in a very compelling manner the fact that there is a major capabilities (and intelligence) chasm between preventive diplomacy on the one side, and armed military forces on the other, and that closure of this gap is essential if we are to improve our prospects for rescuing and maintaining public order around the world.

The capabilities of U.S. military police and civil affairs specialists are touched on by several pieces, but I for one would have liked to see more emphasis on what changes in their force structure is required-my understanding is that we have not increased their numbers in the aftermath of the Cold War despite the fact that these units are being used up all over the world, without relief.

The conclusion highlights the need for constabulary forces, and helpfully identifies the following specific national capabilities as being relevant (in this reader's interpretation) to a future standing international gendarmerie: U.S. Military Police and Special Forces, French gendarmerie, Spanish Guardia Civil, Chilean carabineros, Argentine gendarmes, Italian carabinieri, Dutch Royal Mariechaussee). I would add the Belgian Gendarme, the first national force to establish an open source intelligence network across all police precincts in the entire country.

It is clear from both the conclusion and the case studies that this constabulary-police capabilities requirement needs agreed-upon international concepts, doctrine, training, earmarked resources including surge capabilities and transport, and so on. We do not appear to have learned any lasting lessons from the various interventions, in that civil affairs and military police continue to be "last in line" for embarkation into areas where military forces are being introduced, and there is no U.S. program within Program 150 where we can demonstrate a real commitment to "law and order" as part of our contribution to peace in the 21st Century.

The book lacks an index, a typical shortcoming of think tank and defense educational institutions, and this is a major flaw that should be corrected in the next printing. This book is "Ref A" for every foreign service, military, and law enforcement officer interested in doing a better job of integrating diplomatic, gendarmerie, and military capabilities in every clime and place.

O'Hanlon, Michael, *Defense Policy Choices for the Bush Administration 2001-2005* (Brookings, 2001)

Every citizen needs to read and think about the future of national defense. This book is one of the core readings.

Among the recommendations in this book that make it essential reading for anyone concerned with streamlining and revitalizing national security, I consider the following to be sensible:

1) cost savings should not be achieved through the wholesale abandonment of overseas commitments (13);
2) achieve additional cost savings as well as increased operational utility by sharply limiting spending on the most advanced weapons and mobility systems, applying the savings to maintaining readiness and buying larger numbers of "good enough" weaponry (83);
3) citing Stephen Rosen-he could also have cited Colin Gray-he urges a slowdown in the so-called Revolution in Military Affairs (RMA) while emphasizing that true RMA's are less about technology and more about the very best mix of people, time, and information to produce innovation (88);
4) in this vein, he noted the continued excessive focus on mobility platforms rather than C4I or joint service experimentation (90);
5) homeland defense needs several billion more dollars per year (129), a recapitalization of the U.S. Coast Guard by with at least a $750 million a year increase (135), and a sharply increased focus on setting C4I security standards for unclassified communications and computing networks across the nation, with roughly $100 million a year additional;
6) politely put, National Missile Defense is best conceptualized as theater missile defense (TMD, 143); and
7) Taiwan would be a nightmare for all sides.

Among the assertions in this book that give me pause are

1) defense down-sizing in the past ten years has been successful, trimming a third of the budget and manpower while retaining quality and cohesion (p. 1);
2) that 3% of the Gross Domestic Product is adequate for defense spending and we do not need to go to the less-than-traditional 4% (3-4);
3) that the Marine Corps should be employed to relieve Army troops in the Balkans (57) or Korea (80);
4) that North Korean armored forces would have great difficulty breaking through Allied lines to Seoul (71);

5) that rogue nations like North Korea would attempt to provide their infantry with chemical protective gear when using chemical weapons (73);

6) that US airpower is both a rapid-response solution for distant threats as well as an overwhelming response for sustained threats (76, passim);

7) that arsenal ships are survivable in off-shore loiter mode (111); and

8) that an overseas deployment rate of 8% of the total force is too high (227).

The author, easily one of the top three citizen-reviewers of the national security spending program, ultimately recommends less expensive weaponry, a different two-war capability ("1+A+i"), selective reductions in overseas deployments, more defense and less nuclear offense, selective increases in homeland defense including the U.S. Coast Guard and joint experimentation, and a modest increase (roughly $25 billion) of the defense budget that would combine with his recommended savings to yield the $60 billion or so transformation delta that others have recommended.

I like and recommend this book. Out of context, however, it is a dangerous book, for it will lead an inexperienced President and a Cold War team to the conclusion that only a transformation of the traditional military (Program 50) is necessary. O'Hanlon has done it again—he has provided the baseline from within which a reasonable public debate about defense transformation might ensue. The military issues he addresses comprise both the foundation and one of the four corners of our future national security-my concern about this book is that it is completely isolated and makes no mention of the other three corners without which we cannot maintain a proper roof over our heads: intelligence (threat understanding), strategy, and Program 150 soft power-power that today is both silent and emaciated.

O'Hanlon, Michael, *Technological Change and the Future of Warfare* (Brookings, 2000)

Graciously, and with wicked clarity, the author knocks the so-called Revolution in Military Affairs flat on its back, and then helps it to one knee. His introductory review of the RMA schools of thought (system of systems, dominant battlespace knowledge, global reach, and vulnerability or anti-access or asymmetric), with appropriate notes, is helpful to any adult student.

The heart of his book can be distilled down to one chart showing the expected rates of advance in the various technical domains relevant to military operations. Of 29 distinct technical groups across sensors, computers and communications; projectiles, propulsion, and platforms; and other weapons, he finds only two technology areas-computer hardware and computer software-capable of revolutionary change in the foreseeable future. Eight others-chemical sensors, biological sensors, radio

342

communications, laser communications, radio-frequency weapons, non-lethal weapons, and biological weapons-are judged capable of high but not revolutionary advances.

All other technical areas, namely those associated with mobility platforms and weaponry itself, are unlikely to develop at anything above a moderate pace. In the course of his discussion of each of these he brings forth the basics of physics and real-world constraints and points out that even the best of our sensors are frustrated by heavy rain and other man-made countermeasures.

He correctly evaluates the inability of our existing and planned Intelligence, Surveillance, and Reconnaissance (ISR) to keep up with targeting needs, particularly in urban and heavy canopy terrain. He also notes in passing that human intelligence may well prove to be the sustaining element in finding individual people, and that there has been no significant change since World War II in the numbers of troops needed per 1,000 inhabitants-infantry is still the core force.

He systematically dismisses a variety of RMA claims, among the most dangerous being that we can afford to stand down many of our forward bases, by pointing out that combat aircraft continue to have short ranges, ground forces continue to require heavy logistics sustainment, ships remain slow to cross oceans, and it continues to be extremely difficult to seize ports and other fixed infrastructure.

He concludes the book with a number of budgeting recommendations, both for the USA and for its allies.

For the USA he would emphasize communications and computing, the one area truly open to an RMA in the near term. Other areas meriting immediate investments include strategic sea and air lift, the rapid development of a lighter tank and a mine-resistant infantry vehicle, and improvements in naval mine warfare. He supports the National Missile Defense and would sustain more robust RDT&E experimentation.

For a major US ally, with a fraction of our funding, he recommends a $15 billion total investment over several years to acquire a thoughtful mix of advanced C4I enhancements including ground stations, a fleet of Unmanned Aerial Vehicles (UAV), 1000 cruise missiles, 5000 short-range munitions, 500 advanced air to air missiles, a squadron of stealth aircraft, and several batteries of theater missile defense radars and missiles.

A very nice listing of major Pentagon acquisition programs supports his recommendation that we economize on major weapons platforms and pursue a high-low mixed strategy, limiting, for example, our procurement of the F-22 and joint strike fighters so as to afford more F-15s and F-16s.

343

Overall this book fulfills its mission of reviewing technologies in relation to the future of warfare, and it provides the reader with a very strong stepping stone for venturing into the literature of defense transformation. Those who would criticize this work for failing to consider the competition or the metrics of evaluation have a point, but only a point-the book does what it set out to do. It evaluates specific technologies in relation to the inflated and often delusional claims of the proponents of the RMA. One book cannot solve all our problems, but it can, as this book does, blow away some of the foggy thinking emanating from the Pentagon and other places where a number of flag officers and their staffs have lost sight of ground truth.

O'Hanlon, Michael and Carol Graham, *A Half Penny on the Federal Dollar: The Future of Development Aid* (Brookings, 1997)

This is a hard-hearted practical look at development aid, and so it should be. The "official development assistance" (ODA) element of Program 150, the international affairs budget commonly recognized as the "preventive diplomacy" budget that runs alongside Program 50 (the traditional military budget), is evaluated by the authors in terms of amounts (are we doing enough), allocations (are we giving to the right countries), and directions (are we doing the right things). It is a small amount of money that is being discussed--$9 billion a year in 1997 for ODA alone-said to represent a half penny of each dollar spent by the U.S. government.

This works out to about $15 per year for the members of the targeted populations. Larger more populous states receive less aid per capita than smaller states. India, Pakistan, Bangladesh, and China are especially disadvantaged. In contrast to today's $15 per person investment, the Marshall Plan provided in excess of $100 to $200 per person in Europe (but for only several years, working out to an equivalent amount when compared to sustained aid flows today).

Several thoughtful observations jump out from the book:

1) Foreign aid is not preventing conflicts from emerging (if anything, and this is not implied by O'Hanlon but is explicit in William Shawcross' book *DELIVER US FROM EVIL: Peacekeepers, Warlords and a World of Endless Conflict* (Simon & Schuster, 2000), foreign aid contributes to instability by giving rise to warlords and black markets);
2) Foreign aid is of limited use in reconstructing societies ravaged by conflict, especially those with limited infrastructures that cannot absorb resources as well as European nations;

344

3) Foreign aid's best return on investment appears to be the education of women-even a few years of education has a considerable impact on birth control, health, and other areas of interest;
4) Foreign aid shapes both our own philosophy of foreign affairs, and the perceptions others have of our foreign role-it also shapes our domestic constituencies perception of why we should have a foreign policy arm;
5) Foreign aid does not play a significant role in most countries where there is access to open markets and stability does not frighten away investors-indeed the emerging expert consensus appears to lean toward debt forgiveness combined with private capital investment as the best approach to economic reform;
6) Foreign aid is least effective in those countries that are either unstable or have a range of harmful economic policies including trade barriers, large budget deficits, oversized public sectors, and overvalued exchange rates. Roughly half the countries receiving aid today have poor economic policies in place;
7) The U.S. is the least generous of the Office of Economic Cooperation and Development (OECD) members, providing just over one third as much of its Gross Domestic Product (GDP) as the other OECD countries-0.10 percent instead of 0.27 percent.

Having said all this, the author's document their views that our ODA investments need to rise from $9 billion to at least $12 billion a year, with other countries increasing their combined contributions from $51 billion to $68 billion per year. The authors favor increased foreign aid investments in poor countries with good economic policies, for the purpose of building transportation infrastructure, enhancing local health and education programs, and accelerating the expansion of utilities and communications services.

They also recommend a broader distribution of foreign aid for countries in conflict throughout Africa, and suggest that Public Law 480 food aid should be focused only on responding to disaster relief rather than indiscriminate distribution that benefits U.S. farmers but undermines foreign agricultural programs.

They conclude with the somewhat veiled suggestion that all of this could be paid for by a reduction of foreign military assistance to Egypt and Israel. One is left, at the end of the book, with two strong feelings:

•   first, that U.S. foreign aid is on "automatic pilot" and rather mindlessly muddling along; and

•   second, that this is a very small but very important part of the total U.S. national security budget, one that merits its own ombudsman within the National Security

345

Council, and one that is worthy of no less than a penny on the dollar as we plan our future Federal investments.

What is left unsaid by the authors is whether the other $60-80 billion in foreign aid by various actors including the United Nations agencies, is well managed--one is left with the impression that the U.S. really faces two challenges: an internal challenge of improving its performance with respect to foreign aid, and an external challenge in demanding a more rational and coordinated approach to various forms of aid being sponsored by others.

Ould-Abdallah, Ahmedon, *Burundi on the Brink, 1993-95: A UN Special Envoy Reflects on Preventive Diplomacy* (US Institute of Peace, 2000)

This book is depressing. One sees both the heroism and the futility of United Nations activities. Sadly, whereas the Texas Rangers might have gotten away with sending one great man to handle a major crisis, the United Nations, sending one great man and an assistant, is decades behind the times in terms of understanding what it is about and how to obtain results in today's world.

The lessons from Burundi summarized by the author at the end of the book are an excellent conclusion:

Problem Area #1: Shortcomings in UN Machinery and Culture, including no intelligence gathering and analysis; weak institutional memory; lack of accountability; and luxury and inefficiency.

Problem Area #2: Overreliance on Military Intervention

Problem Area #3: Unintended Consequences of Humanitarian Assistance

This book left me with a profound respect for the people that work for the United Nations, and with a continuing profound distrust and disrespect for the United Nations as an entity. It is not working. It needs a complete make-over, and one wonders if the time has not come for a new international gathering of governments and non-governmental organizations, to conceptualize a completely fresh start that harnesses distributed resources spanning the full range from civil economic assistance to police protection and training, to violent military intervention.

Let me say this again: this is a very good book, it is only for the best and the brightest, and it calls into question the entire United Nations structure and management. Instead

346

of paying our dues to the United Nations, instead of Ten Turner giving them a billion dollar tax avoidance contribution, we should probably create a new international Fund for Peace that uses the Internet and the network effect to nurture "many small acts" instead of one large industrial-age monstrosity called the United Nations.

Owens, Bill, *Lifting the Fog of War* (Farrar Straus Giroux, 2000)

This is a well-intentioned book and the best available manifesto for the "system of systems" that can integrate intelligence, precision strike, and communications technologies by exploiting the Revolution in Military Affairs (RMA).

On balance it provides several important contributions, but its core assumption that technology can be a substitute for people is flawed, as is its completely insupportable assumption that our allies might be willing to follow us down this very expensive and dubious interoperability trail.

Perhaps even more troubling, the school of thought represented by this book suffers from the severe delusion that everything that needs to be seen can be seen by national technical means, and processed in time to be relevant to the commander. Nothing could be further from the truth—fully 90% of what is needed to succeed in today's environment is not in digital form, not in English, and not collectible by technical means.

The most important point made in the whole book, and here I give the author high marks, is its compelling description of why military reform cannot be achieved from within: because there is no decision process by which a "joint" leadership can determine force structure and weapons acquisition without fear of service politics. His approach to reform, shifting from a focus on system stovepipes to joint mission areas, is valuable and could be helpful in defense transformation if it were cleansed of its unhealthy obsession with expensive technology and forced to face the fact that three-quarters of our challenges in this new century are Operations Other Than War (OOTW) that call into question virtually every dollar being spent under existing RMA auspices.

The book is also helpful in pointing out the redundancy between the four services, the 12:1 support ratio in personnel, and the need to embed information handling capabilities in all future mobility and weapons systems.

Perhaps most disappointingly, this book by a distinguished Admiral and apparent out-of-the-box thinker fails to outline a force structure, including a 450-ship Navy, capable of dealing effectively with all four levels of war in every clime and place.

347

Treason & Traitors

Herrington, Stuart A., *Traitors Among Us: Inside the Spy-Catcher's World* (Harvest, 2000)

This book, highly recommended by the Association of Former Intelligence Officers (AFIO), grabbed me from the beginning. Stuart, whom I know as one of the most thoughtful and self-effacing Colonels in military intelligence, wisely chooses to focus on the two most important cases in recent U.S. military history. For a catalog of all the others, see *Merchants of Treason* by Tom Allen and Norman Polmar.

A few things about this valuable book bear emphasis here:

1) early on, the FBI tried to shut the CIA out of the first case, and Col Herrington very wisely insisted on including them--leading to critical CIA contributions without which the case would not have been solved;

2) counterintelligence is incredible tedious, boring, *hard* work, and it takes a special kind of commander to maintain morale under such circumstances;

3) both Defense and Justice lawyers screwed up big-time by not being aware that military intelligence activities in Austria were illegal in Austria and therefore warranted early involvement of the Austrian government--this ignorance cost us heavily;

4) allowing soldiers to "homestead" in sensitive intelligence positions anywhere is very dangerous; and finally--bringing to bear some personal knowledge here

5) success is temporary, failure is forever...I'll wager the Army's Foreign Counterintelligence Activity has gone downhill since this book was written, and that the old "go along easy" habits of those that have been homesteading too long at FCA are again rearing their ugly heads.

Counterintelligence is still a backwater, and any commander, however exceptional, is going to need strong Service-level support if they are to keep their senior civil servant (bureaucratic) elements in line. This book is an excellent touchstone for Congressional members and staff, Service and DoD chiefs who care little for counterintelligence but need to do more, and for citizens who need to know that counterintelligence is on the "front lines" every day, in every clime and place.

348

Abbreviations

9-11	11 September 2001
24/7	24 hours a day, 7 days a week
ADCI	Associate Deputy Director of Central Intelligence
AFB	Air Force Base
AFCEA	Armed Forces Communications and Electronics Association
AID	Agency for International Development
AIIP	Association of Independent Information Professionals
AIJ	*American Intelligence Journal*
AKUF	Working Group on the Causes of War
AO	Area of Operations
API	Application Program Interface(s)
AWACS	Aerial Warning and Command System
BBC	British Broadcasting Corporation
C4I	Command, Control, Communications, Computing, and Intelligence
CA	Covert Action
CAC	Community Analysis Center (state and city levels)
CI	Counterintelligence
CIA	Central Intelligence Agency
CINC	Commander-in-Chief (for a joint theater or type command)
CIO	Chief Information Officer
CMS	Community Management Staff
CNN	Cable News Network
COSPO	Community Open Source Program Office (COSPO)
CRES	Community Requirements and Evaluation Staff
CRS	Congressional Research Service
CSA	Clandestine Service Agency (proposed)
CVN	Carrier Nuclear (Ship)
D&D	Denial & Deception
DARO	Defense Advanced Reconnaissance Office (defunct)
DARPA	Defense Advanced Research Projects Agency
DCI	Director of Central Intelligence

DDCI	Deputy Director of Central Intelligence
DDCI/CIA	DDCI for the Central Intelligence Agency
DDCI/CMS	DDCI for Community Management
DDNI	Deputy Director of National Intelligence (proposed)
DGNI	Director General for National Intelligence (proposed)
DIA	Defense Intelligence Agency
DMA	Defense Mapping Agency (now NIMA)
DNI	Director of National Intelligence (proposed)
DO	Directorate of Operations (CIA)
DoD	Department of Defense
DPCR	Department of Peace and Conflict Research
ECON	Economic Espionage, Theft, and Vandalism
EEI	Essential Elements of Information
EOP	Executive Office of the President
FAA	Federal Aviation Administration
FAO	Foreign Area Officer
FBI	Federal Bureau of Investigation
FBIS	Foreign Broadcast Information Service (CIA)
FEMA	Federal Emergency Management Agency
FICE	Future Intelligence Collaborative Environment
G-2	Intelligence Staff for a Major Command
G-3	Operations Staff for a Major Command
GDIP	General Defense Intelligence Program
HDAC	Homeland Defense Analysis Center (national level)
HIC	High Intensity Conflict
HIIK	Heidelberg Institute for International Conflict Research
HOPE	Hackers on Planet Earth
HPSCI	House Permanent Select Committee on Intelligence
HQS	Headquarters
HUMINT	Human Intelligence
IC21	*Intelligence Community in the 21st Century* (HPSCI Report)
ICRC	International Committee of the Red Cross
ICSA	International Computer Security Association
IIMCR	Institute for International Mediation and Conflict Resolution
IJIC	International Journal of Intelligence and Counterintelligence
IMINT	Imagery Intelligence
INR	Bureau of Intelligence and Research (Department of State)
IO	Information Operations
ISI	Institute of Scientific Information

JCS	Joint Chiefs of Staff
JFCOM	Joint Forces Command
JMIP	Joint Military Intelligence Program
LCC	Landing Command and Control (Ship)
LEA	Law Enforcement Agencies
LHA	Landing Helicopter Amphibious (Ship)
LIC	Low Intensity Conflict
LLP	Limited Liability Partnership
MA	Master of Arts
MASINT	Measurements and Signatures Intelligence
MBA	Master of Business Administration
MCE-2	Joint Military Intelligence College (DIA)
MIC	Methyl Isocyanate
MPS	Maritime Propositioning Supply
MRC	Major Regional Conflict
NATO	North Atlantic Treaty Organization
NDA	Non-Disclosure Agreement
NFIP	National Foreign Intelligence Program
NGO	Non-Governmental Organizations
NHC	Naval Historical Center
NIC	National Intelligence Council
NIO	National Intelligence Officer
NIMA	National Imagery and Mapping Agency
NPA	National Processing Agency (proposed)
NPIC	National Photographic Interpretation Center (now NIMA)
NRF	Naval Reserve Force
NRO	National Reconnaissance Office
NSA	National Security Agency
NSC	National Security Council
OOB	Order of Battle
OODA	Orient-Observe-Decide-Act (Colonel John Boyd)
OOTW	Operations Other Than War
OPG	Operational Planning Group
OpIntel	Operational Intelligence (near-real-time plotting on map)
OPSEC	Operations Security
OSD	Open Source Data
OSIF	Open Source Information
OSINT	Open Source Intelligence
OSINT-V	Open Source Intelligence-Validated

OSO	Open Source Officer
PA	Pennsylvania
PAO	Public Affairs Officer
PCR	Protracted Conflict Region
PfP	Partners for Peace (with NATO)
PIOOM	Interdisciplinary Research Program on Root Causes of Human Rights Violations
POLAD	Political Advisor (generally from State to CINC)
PRC	People's Republic of China
PSYOP	Psychological Operations
RFI	Request for Information
RMA	Revolution in Military Affairs
ROW	Rest of World
SACLANT	Supreme Allied Commander, Atlantic
SASC	Senate Armed Services Committee
SCI	*Science Citation Index*
SCI	Sensitive Compartmented Information
SI/TK	Sensitive Information/Codeword Information
SIGINT	Signals Intelligence
SIO	State Intelligence Officer
SME	Subject-Matter Expert
SOG	Special Operations Group (CIA)
SOLIC	Special Operations and Low Intensity Conflict
SSCI	Senate Select Committee on Intelligence
SSCI	*Social Science Citation Index*
STATE	Department of State
STN	Scientific & Technical Network
TIARA	Tactical Intelligence and Related Activities
TPED	Tasking, Processing, Exploitation, and Dissemination
USG	United States Government
USGS	U.S. Geological Service
USIA	U.S. Information Agency (now part of STATE)
VLS	Vertical Launch System
VPN	Virtual Private Network
VSTOL	Vertical Short Take-Off and Landing
WAN	Wide Area Network
WHO	World Health Organization
WTC	World Trade Center
WTO	World Trade Organization

About the Author

Robert David Steele (Vivas) was born in New York in 1952. The son of a petroleum engineer, he spent most of his life in Latin America and Asia, including four years in Viet-Nam (1964-1967). Married to Kathy Lynette Steele, he is the father of Patrick James, Matthew Brian, and Sean Joseph. The family lives and votes in Virginia.

Steele and his company are featured in *The Year in Computers* (2000), he has twice named to the *Microtimes* 100: Industry leaders and unsung heroes...who created the future, and he and his vision are profiled in the chapter on the "The Future of the Spy" in Alvin and Heidi Toffler's book, *War and Anti-War: Survival at the Dawn of the 21ˢᵗ Century*, among other publications.

Steele has been a Marine Corps infantry officer serving in a variety of command & staff positions, a military intelligence officer with responsibility for the tactical exploitation of national capabilities, and the senior civilian responsible for creating and managing the USMC Intelligence Center, our Nation's newest intelligence production facility. He has also been a spy, serving three-back-to-back tours as a clandestine case officer, one of them in a combat environment. Unusually for a case officer, he has served in three of the four Directorates of the Central Intelligence Agency, with Washington-based roles in determining future intelligence collection requirements and capabilities; the application of advanced information technology to global operations; and global counterintelligence operations against a denied area country.

Steele holds graduate degrees in international relations (Lehigh University, thesis on predicting revolution) as well as public administration (University of Oklahoma, thesis on strategic and tactical information management for national security), and certificates in intelligence policy (Harvard University) and defense studies (Naval War College). He has received the Meritorious Honor Award (Group) from the Department of State, Certificates of Exceptional Accomplishment and Special Achievement from the Central Intelligence Agency, and the Certificate of Achievement from the Department of Defense, the latter for his role as the architect and first civilian leader of the Marine Corps Intelligence Center (now Command). He speaks fluent Spanish and elementary French.

353

About the First Book
ON INTELLIGENCE

This is a 495-page book with a 50-page annotated bibliography, a 62-page index, and 30 pages of proposed legislation for the U.S. Senate. It has been cleared for publication by the CIA Publications Review Board, and was published by the AFCEA International Press in 2000, by OSS in 2001. It ranked 908 on amazon.com the week it came out, and ranked 374 the week after the 9-11 attacks. The first edition sold out two months thereafter. The book is available from www.amazon.com only; it is not sold in bookstores.

The foreword is by Senator David L. Boren (D-OK), former Chairman of the Senate Select Committee on Intelligence, now President of the University of Oklahoma. Other endorsements: Alvin & Heidi Toffler, Bruce Sterling, a former Deputy Director of Central Intelligence, a former Deputy Director of the Soviet KGB, a German Admiral, an English Commodore, & an Ambassador.

The book contains fifteen chapters in three parts:

- Part I, from Secrecy to Openness, is an extremely detailed critique of US (Western) intelligence at the strategic, operational, tactical, and technical levels of operation.

- Part II, from War to Peace, is a review of the asymmetric and emerging threat environment as well as open source intelligence capabilities and relevant information needs that can be applied on behalf of both the diplomat and the warfighter. The author is the original conceptualizer of the two related concepts of the "virtual intelligence community" and "information peacekeeping."

- Part III is an explicit program for renewal comprised of a detailed financial program for U.S. intelligence; detailed recommendations for the next President of the United States; and detailed legislation for consideration by Congress.

Practical Highlights:

This is the only book ever published (or likely to be published) that contains detailed proposals for $11.6 billion dollars a year in *cuts* against the U.S. intelligence community budget, and $1.6 billion dollars a year in *offsetting increases*. The author does not believe that the cuts should be made, but uses this device to demonstrate the depth and breadth of existing redundancies and inefficiencies whose elimination would free up funds for needed new initiatives.

Chapter 13, written as if for a President, is an executive-level overview of what has changed in our world, and what corresponding changes must be made in how America manages it global intelligence capability. This chapter is available free as an electronic document from the home page of www.oss.net.

Chapter 14, written as if for a Member of Congress, provides both a review of the National Security Act of 1992 as proposed by the Senate and the House of Representatives, followed by a detailed *pro forma* of a National Security Act such as might implement the various reforms the author recommends.

The index is perhaps the most detailed, cross-referenced index every provided for any book about the craft of intelligence. In combination with the depth of substance in the book, the index ensures the value of the book as an on-going reference for any intelligence professional, whether in private or public service.

Reader Reviews (Excepts):

"This book is a goldmine of ideas, suggestions, possibilities. I bought it for information purposes, only now I realise that I have purchased a book for life. …it is the genuinely GLOBAL piece of writing of the highest probe."

"On Intelligence is written from the 'bottom up' with a 'top down' brain and shows a passion for, and knowledge of, a subject which few can aspire to."

"The author of this book has produced one of the very best and most interesting books to date on intelligence reform and transformation."

… Steele's thinking is always provocative and his work thrills with its insights and ideas."

About OSS.NET

OSS.NET was started on a shoestring in 1994, back before the web existed as a consumer environment. The domain name is one of those in the exclusive 2% of the Internet active in 1994 or earlier. Back then it was a Gopher site, with numerous documents arranged in simple table format.

In 1996 it was converted into a web site, and in 1997, with help from Autometric (now Boeing Autometric), the site was restructured to be both a source of free information, and—behind a firewall and other security measures—a private information banking facility for OSS clients.

Today the site, www.oss.net, provides the following free resources:

1) Open Archive of close to 5,000 pages from over 500 international authorities who have spoken at one of the fifteen international conferences sponsored by the author, and including numerous White Papers as well as press releases (many in the aftermath of 9-11), multi-media presentations, and all past issues of *OSS NOTICES*.
2) Open Source Marketplace of various vendors offering open sources of information, software, and open source information services. This is an entirely voluntary collection with a free "Add-A-Link" feature at the bottom of the page that allows anyone to list their offering at no cost.
3) Convenience Center of useful Internet links for citizens, military and law enforcement personnel, and international travelers.

Hidden from sight, but available to clients, are private archives of reports done on a weekly basis and following various areas of concern to OSS clients, including unconventional or asymmetric warfare, proliferation of weapons of mass destruction, information warfare and information operations, and terrorism. Among OSS successes in recent years has been the identification and evaluation of 396 terrorist, insurgent, and opposition web sites in twenty-nine languages. Prospective clients are encouraged to email the author at bear@oss.net.

357

About the
Council on Intelligence

The Council on Intelligence is a web-based self-organizing international network intended to encourage, educate, inform, and empower individual citizens interested in using public intelligence to enhance public policy decisions at every level of governance. Within the United States, the Council is for the interim funded by OSS Inc. as a not-for-profit element.

The Council offers the following elementary services at no cost:

1) List of recommended books on intelligence reform, with direct linkages to each book's page at www.amazon.com.
2) List of recommended papers on intelligence reform, with direct linkages to their location at www.oss.net and other web sites.
3) Several discussion groups, including one for intelligence community seniors discussing the current efforts to develop legislation and another for the general public on the future of intelligence.

At this time the Council is largely an idea seeking a body of citizens interested enough in the concept of a Smart Nation, to engage in a sustained dialog and form their own neighborhood, county, and state networks and discussion groups.

The founding members of the Council on Intelligence are varied and international, and include Mats Bjore, CEO of Infosphere in Sweden; James Buie, a cyber-advocate based in Maryland; Ran Hock, founder of Online Strategies; Berto Jongman, producer of the *World Conflict & Human Rights Map*; Robert Young Pelton, author of *The World's Most Dangerous Places*; Winn Schwartau, author of *CYBERSHOCK* and other publications on safety in cyberspace; and the author.

Index

365

392

393

394

402

417

419

427

429

434